全国高等学校建筑美术教程　名校名师系列

香港大學·贾倍思

型和现代主义

THE SERIES OF TEACHING MANIFESTOS IN ART OF ARCHITECTURE
THE GOOD TEACHERS FROM THE PRESTIGIOUS DESIGN SCHOOLS IN CHINA

ARCHITECTONICS OF MODERNISM

JIA BEISI
THE UNIVERSITY OF HONG KONG

贾倍思 著

陕西新华出版传媒集团　陕西人民美術出版社

再版前言

最近读到英国人杰弗里·斯科特（Geffrey Scott）的《人文主义建筑》一书。这是他在意大利工作旅行中撰写，于1914年出版的。我看的是1999年的再版。从初版到再版，经历了现代主义建筑运动对世界城市造成天翻地覆的变化。通过对意大利文艺复兴建筑的考察和相关的意大利文献的研究，他批判了19世纪后期的建筑观点，即伟大的建筑不是来自宗教、科学、材料、建造方式、社会运动，或大的业主（当时的教皇），虽然这些都和建筑相关。他认为伟大建筑的决定因素是人性的美。至于什么是美，可以留给好事者继续争论。但不可否认，美至少是和艺术相通的，在这个层面上，建筑不再孤独，不必世俗。

文艺复兴时期的建筑，包括那个时候大量传统建筑、城市结构和公共空间以及文艺复兴的绘画、雕塑一起完整地保留了下来，变成了全人类的文化遗产。虽然当时的功能、使用方式、业主和居民早已淹没于历史长河，但这些建筑和城市空间依然服务于今天的社会。今天外国旅游者徜徉于这里的大街小巷、宫殿教堂，而不用去关心建造技术、材料或构造，或早已逝去的那个社会。吸引他们的是美。

看来美比现代主义建筑强调的功能或建造更加永恒。我长期以来一直从事建筑的灵活性、开放性、被动式节能，和“可持续建筑”的研究和实践，我越来越相信，真正的可持续建筑是美的建筑，而且是和艺术紧密结合的。

现代主义建筑有美的和艺术的一面，却常被它的实用性、技术性、社会性和功能性所遮掩，13年前出版的《型和现代主义》试图平衡一下扭曲的建筑学术观点。每每遇到颇有成就的青年建筑师说上学的时候读过这本书，我都觉得有点尴尬——这本书是否真的对他们有一点影响？和13年前相比，今天的中国已是“轻舟已过万重山”！但中国的建筑从“量的增加”到“质的提高”的转型可能才刚刚开始，这本书的再版也许还有意义。但囿于个人能力和时代所限，书中谬误尚待读者不吝赐教。除了修改了几处明显的文字错误、重新排版和少量更换练习图片外，全书基本和初版一致，保持原貌。以期读者以时代的距离感来看这本书。

2016年春于香港大学

Foreword to the Second Edition

My latest reading found The Humanism of Architecture, written by British writer Geffrey Scott. It was published in 1914 for the first time, following his trip and working in Italy. The edition I read was published in 1999, after a tremendous change of urbanization in the world accompanied by modernism ideology in Architecture. Based on the studies of documents and observations of Italian Architecture of Renaissance, he criticize a few Architectural fallacies prevailing in the late 19th century. He found the great buildings were not outcomes of religious, science, material, construction, social movements, or big clients, such as Pops, no matter how influential of these factors. The determinate factor of the great buildings is humanism esthetic. What esthetic is, remains for debating of different interests. Nevertheless, esthetic paves the ground shared with art—Architecture is never alone or has to be pragmatic.

The buildings of Italian Renaissance, including large amount of conventional buildings, urban structure and open spaces, are largely preserved as human heritage together with the paintings and sculptures of the time. The original purposes and functions of the buildings have changed many times. The clients, occupants, residents faded in the history. However, these buildings and urban spaces continue serve the needs of current society. Lingering around the streets, palaces and churches building built in this period, the tourists from all over the world are attracted by the beauty of Architecture, without much understanding of the technology, materials and construction belong to that society which is long forgotten.

Apparently, the esthetic can last longer than any function or construction technology, the dogma of Modernism in Architecture. I have been engaging in research and design of technical flexibility, Open Building, passive low energy buildings and sustainable development. I tend to believe the truly sustainable buildings are the beautiful buildings bonding within art.

The esthetic component of the Modern Movement in Architecture is hidden in the shadow of pragmatism, technocratic, social ideology and Functionalism. The publication of Architectonics of Modernism 13 years ago, was a critic to the ill minded Architecture critics prevailing at the time. However I was still hesitated to ask if the book was really useful, whenever a young established architect told me he read the book when he was a student. China has changed a lot in last 13 years. However the transition from quantity orientated design in Architecture to quality orientate design may have just started. Therefore this second edition of the book may still have its significance. Confined by the personal capability and the day, there might be some hidden bias in this book to be corrected by the audience. However, this edition is largely the same as the first edition, except a new layout, correction obvious typo, and the adjustment of a few illustrations in student exercises. I hope the massage of the book can still be detected in a distance of time.

Jia Beisi
Spring 2016 at the University of Hong Kong

前　言

望着墙上的斑渍，炉边的煤堆，天上的白云或者流水不一定是愚蠢的。当一个画家仔细观察这些东西的时候，会有惊人的发现，通过充分发挥想象力和智慧，他可以勾画出人兽争战、群魔乱舞等奇幻壮丽的图卷。

（列奥纳多·达·芬奇　1452—1519）

照相机是白痴的工具，他以机器代替眼睛来看东西。而绘画是用线条组织形体和机理。这是一个从看到观察最后到发现的过程。随之而来的是启发和灵感。发明和创作都归因于一个观察行动，行动改变了事物。其他人视而不见——而你却看到了！

（勒·柯布西耶：我的作品，1960）

应黎锦超教授邀请，我于1996年到香港大学执教，我跟他说我要教“型的构造”，当时他是主席教授和建筑系主任。他看了我的报告后想了一会儿，同意了，而且放手让我自己独立组织全部的教学计划和内容。这门课后来吸引了许多学生，也引起不少校内外朋友的兴趣。黎教授在我到来一年后不再当系主任，三年后也不再当主席教授，并退休离开了学校。这门课也就此终止。

我和学生们度过了一段快乐的时光，我觉得有话要说，决定写一本有关这门课的书。这件事拖了很久，但我一直想写完之后让黎先生看一下，也许他还会写一篇序，但就在我刚把初稿写完，交到出版社，开始考虑写这个“前言”的时候，黎先生却突然去世了。这本书是献给他的，我想我的学生也会有同感。这样想并不能帮我从巨大的悲痛和深深的内疚中解脱出来，相反也许还将伴我度过余生。

教学程序和由此产生的创造性思维的关系是本书的中心所在。它也是在对理论和教学实践两方面深入研究的一个成果。这个研究建立了一个试验的基本框架，并通过“型的构造”设计组的学生合作而完成。建筑设计实践和建筑教育实践是两个不同事情。这种二分法已经存在了超过200年了。在工作中我越来越相信，前者属于过去，而后者面向未来。

当前建筑教育的问题之一是羞于或不敢提倡建筑教育的学术性。许多学校囿于现状，或者在过时的思想库里翻箱倒柜，或者重复过去培养专业人才的做法。这种状况应该改变。学校实际上提供了一个一般实践领域无法提供的对建筑学本身执着探求的环境，学校应领导建筑学，而且责无旁贷。

建筑与艺术密不可分，房子也许可以。并且，这种建筑实在太普遍了！艺术之于建筑之重要，并不在于造一个什么样的形体，而在于它是否能给建筑一个灵魂。对敏锐的观察者来说，这种审美质量是可以感知的，至少能看到，有时感觉非常强烈。这种质量非常难以捉摸。建筑中的艺术教育非常困难，除非将其视为既是建筑又非建筑的东西。这个问题类似于为了寻找鼓声来源而将鼓皮撕破一样，只能失望地发现鼓里面什么都没有——更糟糕的是，鼓也被损毁了！从这个神秘的意义上来说，鼓声既不属于鼓的蒙皮也不属于鼓腔。或者说，建筑中的艺术既不是建筑也不是纯艺术，我称之为型的构造，当然这个词在不同的环境中有不同的含义。

这本书由三部分组成：理论、练习和构成原理，它们互相关联。理论是课程和练习的基石，其部分内容也是课程中运用的资料。理论部分又分为两个小部分：一是建筑教育史中的艺术训练，二是当前建筑趋势中的艺术思考。理论部分展示教育的许多观点和方法已在过去讨论和运用过了，而21世纪带来的新的问题却被忽视了，而且历史对这些新问题无法回答。未来还在黑暗中，需要创造性的心灵去探索和发现。练习部分包括课题内容、要求和方法，也包括部分学生作业插图，没有这些插图，书中的教育内容无法理解。这些练习是按由浅入深的顺序排列的。构成原理是一些在其他设计和艺术形式中常用的方法，在书中无非用形体构造的方法表现出来。

我首先感谢参与这门课的学生，特别是那些为本书插图贡献作品的学生。在本书的写作过程中，也得到建筑系几位出色的研究助理的协助，他们是艾米·薛、何文青和保罗·陈。研究生贺珺妍、弗朗西斯·弗里克和贾云艳将我的草稿加工成可发表的文章。我对他们的协助深表感谢。我也特别感谢王微琼女士的无私帮助，在我超时工作、夜夜晚归时所表现出的宽容态度，对此我受之有愧。

香港大学建筑系

2003年10月16日

Introduction

It is not to be despised if, after gazing at a spot on the wall, at the coals in the grate, at the clouds, or at a flowing stream … If the painter looks at them carefully, he will discover some admirable inventions of which his intelligence may take full advantage to compose battles of animals and men, of landscapes or monsters, of devils and other fantasic thing that bring him honor and fortune.

Leonardo da Vinci,1452—1519

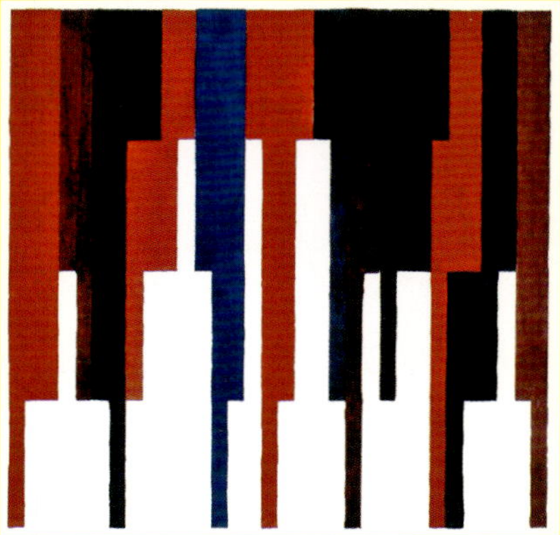

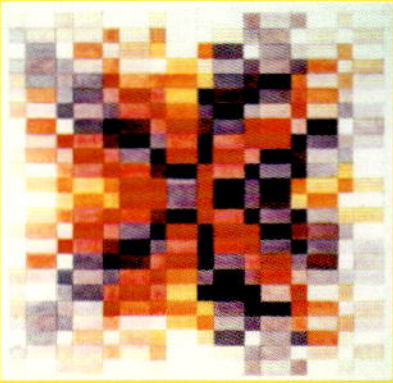

The camera is a tool for idlers, who use a machine to do their seeing for them.To draw oneself, to trace the lines handle the volumes, organize the surface…all this means first to look, and then to observe and finally perhaps to discover...and it is then that inspiration may come. Inventing, creating, one's whole being is drawn into action, and it's the action which counts.Others stood indifferent—but you saw!

Le Corbusier:My Work,1960

When I was invited by Prof.Eric K-C Lye to come to the University of Hong Kong in early 1996 to teach, I told him that I want teach Architectonics. As the Chair Professor and Head of the Department of Architecture,he considered my proposal for a while.Then he agreed and granted me a completely free hand in its arrangement and content.This course later aroused tremendous interest from students and many friends both inside and outside the Department. Eric then retired from the Head position a year later, followed by his subsequent retirement from his parallel Chair position three years after. It was no surprise that this course was cancelled in his absence.

I had a wonderful time with my students. After the experience I felt I had something to say, so I decided to write a book about it. It took longer than I expected. However it has been always in my plan that Eric could enjoy a preview and write a preface if possible.But my timing was perversely unlucky. Just after I finished the book and started to write this introduction, he passed away. So I feel this book is best dedicated to him. I believe my students, whose works are illustrated here,feel the same way. Of course this can not release me from the deep sorrow—and gratitude—I feel towards him,which will probably accompany with me for the rest of my life.

In my teaching work,the relation between discursive procedures—language—based activities—and nonverbal creative thinking gradually evolved and finally become central to this book. Research was done both within the domain of theory as well as in reference to educational practice. These two research undertakings established the basic framework of an experiment completed in collaboration with the students in my Architectonics studio. Those unfamiliar to architectural training will be surprised to learn that architectural practice and architectural education are two very different things. Yet this dichotomy has existed for more than 200 years. A belief behind all my work here is that the former—professional practice and it accepted norms and expectations—belong to the past, and the latter-architectural education, in its deepest(and misunderstood) aspects—belongs to the future.

Architectural pedagogue and instructors have become shy or afraid of concerned about being perceived or labeled as"academics"who allegedly lose touch with the day-to-day realties of professional architectural practice. At the same time, it is also true to say that many schools are merely lazy: they are content to stand still, recycle their thoughts and repeat the same actions that have produced competent professionals in the past. This situation should be changed. Academia provides a situation that potentially allows the discipline of architecture to be pursued with a thoroughness that is impossible to achieve in conventional professional practice.The schools bear the heaviest responsibility to advance pure architectural thought.

True architecture cannot be separated from art; or more aptly, from hyped dimensional art. Of course, mere functional buildings can be totally artless. And such buildings are all too common! The relationship of art to architecture is important, but not simply because it might give a building its "shape". Art injects into an otherwise lifeless building a creative soul. To the sensitive observer, this aesthetic quality is felt at least as much as it is seen, and sometimes most strongly felt. This quality is highly elusive. Identifying or locating "artistic"elements in pure architectural terms is impossible, unless we could artificially separate these from the physical building, yet somehow preserve the original coherent whole which we call Architecture. The problem here is similar to that of tearing off the skin of a musical drum in hope of finding from where the sound comes, only to be disappointed finding that "nothing" is inside the drum—and worse, now the even drum itself has been destroyed! In this mysterious sense, just as the drum sound belongs neither to the drum skin nor to the drum cavity, art in architecture belongs to neither "building" nor "fine art". I call this elusive aesthetic effect architectonics, although the term has different meanings

in different contexts.

This book consists of three parts: *Theory, Exercise and Composition Principles.* They are interrelated. *Theory* lays a foundation for the course and exercises.Part of it was delivered to students in my lecture series.*Theory* is also divided into two sessions:art training in history of architectural education,and art thinking in current architectural movement.This work reveals,with evidence,that many educational issues have been studied and/or implemented a long time ago.It also points out that new challenges imposed by our own 21st century—to which architectural history fails to give appropriate answers—has been neglected in current architectural education.The future lies in the darkness waiting for creative minds to explore and discover.Documented exercises,issue in this book.The practice section includes topic coverage, requirement, method and student work illustrations. The educational content of the book can't be understand without these illustrations.Organization of these exercises aims to help students progress into increasingly complex and deep modes of thought and work.Although the same composition principles are frequently used through out the world of design and art,here they are represented in *architectonic* ways.

I remain grateful to all the students who participated in the course,especially those who contributed illustrations to the book. In working through the book,I received generous support from several remarkable research assistants in the Department of Architecture.To Amy Oi Wah Sit,Man Ching Ho and Paul Chan,I owe a special debt of gratitude.My thanks also go to Jessica Junyan He,Francis Frick,and Yunyan Jia who converted my scrawl into a polished manuscript.I wish to thank to Joanne Weiqiong Wang for her selfless support.She offered far more patience and forbearance than I deserved during my overtime work in the office.

Jia Beisi
Department of Architecture
The University of HongKong
16th October, 2003

目录

理论

1.建筑教育中的造型训练

练习

原理

理论

练习

原理

理 论

练 习

原 理

Contents

Theories

2. Creative Formation and Information

Exercises

Principles

Theories

Exercises

Principles

三维构成训练简介

三维构成的定义是对空间要素，如形体、形状、大小、质感、色彩、体积、容积、光影等在三维空间中的组织和关系的研究。空间的形是三维的状态。三维构成训练旨在掌握空间设计中的基本形态规律。

一个设计得很好的形，往往在形体和空间构成原理的运用上富有创造性，而且表达清晰。对一个初学者来说，这些原理往往难以辨认，因为建筑是一个集历史、文化、功能、技术为一身的复杂的综合体。而且在职业化的建筑教育体制下，建筑设计要求适应不同的需要，形态的原理变得无足轻重。这个三维构成训练课程正是针对以上问题而设置的，它的目的是将学生的注意力集中在纯粹美学和抽象的形体构成原理和技巧方面。

在课程练习中，我们的工具包括剪刀、刻刀、钉锤、胶水和任何可用的东西。当然常用的材料是模型木，如木条、木板，还有瓦楞纸、铁皮、玻璃与各种织体布料等。我们要求学生“做”，而不仅仅是画。

我们通过一系列练习来开发和提高学生对三维形体的感知力。我们鼓励观察形体和空间、光和影、尺寸和尺度。我们鼓励用接触和感觉来理解空间和材料。我们对手工制作要求很高，因为它是自由和诗意化表现的基础。

我们强调工作的速度，要求手的速度快过脑的速度，避免让评价和权衡打断和干扰创造性工作过程。探索未知，无论成功或失败都其乐无穷。当我们挣脱自我束缚，才可以开始领略三维构成课程的益处。

Architectonics: COURSE INTRODUCTION

Architectonics is defined as the basic study of the composition of, and the relationship between, various properties of forms, shape, size, texture, color, mass, volume, light and shadow in three dimensions. An architectural form is a three-dimensional entity. Architectonics deal with the fundamentals of spatial design.

When we say that a form is well designed, it also means that principles of composition in form and space have been creatively applied and clearly expressed. For a beginner in architecture, however, these principles are difficult to discern because other aspects of architecture such as history, culture, function and technology come into play, adding complexity to the building form. Furthermore, since compromises often have to be made and requirements are often revised—especially in professional practice—design principles become ever more obscure. In this Architectonics course, we will concentrate on the basic principles and skills of form composition in purely aesthetic and abstract ways.

For this course, we will use scissors, cutters, hammers, glues and found objects as tools for the various exercises. We will also use wood rods, wood veneers, corrugated paper, metals, glass, all kinds of fabrics as a few of several possible materials. We “make” things in this course—not simply draw them.

We are encouraged to expose and develop our sensitivity to architectural form through a series of design exercises. We are encouraged to see forms and space, light and shadow, dimension and scale. We are encouraged to understand space and materials by touching and feeling. Equally important is the appreciation of the qualities of handwork and handcraft, which embody a free and poetic expressiveness.

We are encouraged to work quickly; in fact more quickly than we can think. By suspending judgement and saving evaluation for later, we can more easily maintain a creative flow. Trying something new—having fun—is the most important attitude in this extended study. When we place fewer critical demands upon ourselves, we begin to enjoy the process of Architectonics.

练习一　黑与白

目的：

我们能看见东西，是因为有光。不同的亮度和对比让被看的东西千变万化。我们能在黑中看到白，白中看到黑，看到在黑白之间的不同色调。这个练习的目的是训练我们眼睛区分不同色调的能力，训练我们的手敏锐地表达这些不同。

Exercise 1. BlACK-AND-WHITE

Objective:

The sun gives the world light. With light we see things. We see things differently with different degrees of brightness and contrasts of light. We can distinguish white from black, black from white, and many intermediate tones between white and black. This first exercise trains our eye to distinguish different tones and our hands to produce them.

方法：

1. 用铅笔画一个外框为24厘米×24厘米的网格，中间分九格或十二格，由学生自己决定。

2. 用不同深浅的水墨将格子填满，观察其视觉效果。

3. 几个格子可以合并成一个大格子，研究大小格子对比。

4. 应注意的是，白色格子是在白纸上留出来的。白纸本是图底，而由于灰色和黑色格子的作用，白格子成了图案。这种图底转换的视觉原理还将在以下其他练习中探讨。

注意事项：

1. 练习虽然简单，但最简单的图像也能形成视觉上的愉悦和厌恶之分。练习要求努力寻找令人愉悦的形象。

2. 我们用网格来做图，设计活动体现在两个不同层面：网格和色韵。

3. 我们注意到，当网格改变了，图形也随着改变；我们也注意到，在同一网格中，有无限多的图形变化。

4. 我们也体会到设计需要时间、耐心和注意力。在不同的图案中找到最美的一个并不容易。

工具和材料：

1. 中国墨；
2. 水；
3. 毛笔；
4. 水彩纸（A3）；
5. 几只茶碟和杯子；
6. 一只盛水洗笔的水瓶（1.5升）。

成果：

一幅在A3纸上的黑白构成图案。

Exercise:

1.With pencil, draw a grid with 9 squares, or a grid with 12 squares, depending on individual choice. The outline of the grid is 24 cm × 24 cm.

2.Fill the squares with different plain tones of ink, and study the visual effects.

3.We can combine two or more small squares into a large square, and study the contrast between large and small.

4.The white square is actually not painted white. It is a part of the white paper, which is surrounded by gray or black squares. It is a negative figure. But now, try instead to study the visual impact of the white square as a positive figure seen against a ground of gray and black. This is the figure and ground principle, which we will study further in the lateral exercise.

Notes:

1.This is the simplest of exercises. We know that even the simplest thing makes a crucial difference between pleasant and unpleasant visual results. We need to make a conscious design effort to achieve pleasant results.

2.We notice that we use a grid to control our painting. The painting is composed with two levels of design: the grid and the tones.

3.We notice that the design changes if the grid changes. We also notice that there are endless varieties of tones and arrangement of pattern within the same grid.

4.We also notice that design needs time, patience, and attention. Finding the most beautiful patterns from so many possible varieties is not easy.

Tools and materials:

1.Chinese ink;
2.Water;
3.Chinese brush for calligraphy ;
4.Water color paper (A3-size);
5.Several small dishes or tea saucers;
6.One bottle as a water container for washing brushes (about 1.5 litres).

Presentation:

A black-and-white composition assembled on an A3-size sheet of paper.

Lin Wai Tung
Lo Kit Sum, Stephanie
Li Kwok Chi, Daphone

高级练习：

用水墨刻画阴影。

实用原理：

1. 受光面、暗面和影子

在同一本色的物体上，影子比暗面深，暗面比受光面深。

受光面离视点越近越亮，暗面离视点越近越黑。换句话说，离观察者越近，物体表面的明暗对比越强；离观察者越远，这种对比也越弱。

2. 明暗对比

离视点越近，明暗对比越强；离视点越远，明暗对比越弱。

3. 反光和退晕效果

任何物体表面在光线中都呈现由浅到深的退晕效果。如光自左上角，受光面上部比下部亮，左边比右边亮。而阴影面，反光来自周围物体和环境，反光有时很强，暗面不是永远漆黑一片。

4. 空气感

有时自上而下，画面的整体光亮度有退晕变化，有时画面中部的明暗对比比四周要强。

5. 无一相同色韵

图上物体的任何一个色块明暗都不相同。

Advanced exercise:

Using ink to render a shadow cast upon an object

Useful principles:

1. Light, shade and shadow

On the same element, a cast shadow is always darker than a surface in shade, and any part in shade is always darker than a lighted part.

For lighted parts, the closer it is, the brighter it appears.For shaded parts, the closer it is, the darker it appears.

In other words, the closer any part is to the observer, the stronger the contrast between its lighted and shaded surfaces. The further away any part is from the observer, the weaker the contrast between its lighted and shaded surfaces.

2. Contrast between lightness and darkness

The closer the element is, the stronger the contrast is.

3. Effect of light reflection

Every part or element has a variable, graduated gray tone which varies with the angle of the light source. If the light source comes from the upper-left, then the reflected tone on an object surface is lighter at the top than at the bottom, and at left than at the right. On every shaded part or shadow, backwards reflection of light onto the shaded surface from the surrounding environment really does occur. It is very effective. Shaded surfaces are never pure black.

4. Airy atmosphere

From top to bottom, the tone of the whole painting changes from dark to light. Around the center of the painting, a focus point should be highlighted with stronger contrast between light and dark.

5. No tone is the same

Every part or element has a unique tone.

Law Wai Ming,Vivian

Yuen Chui Yin,Tommy

练习二　色彩基础

目的:

渲染是建筑表现的传统方法，而其中水彩是基本工具。通过实验我们可以理解这种传统工具和水彩画的特性。同时我们也学到色彩构成的基本原理:

1. 原色对比：以一组原色不规则组合而形成生动的效果。

2. 明暗对比："退晕"和"饱和度"的变化在同一色彩中可以形成明暗对比。

3. 冷暖对比：趋向于蓝和绿的色彩显得"冷"，而趋向于橙和红的色彩显得"暖"。

4. 补色对比：在色彩环中相对的色彩关系是补色关系。将其并置，各自的色性强化，鲜明；将其混合，产生没有色彩趋向的灰黑色。

5. 同时性对比：人对任何一种原色在心理上都有寻找其补色的倾向。如果图面上没有这种补色，人的眼睛会在原色周围制造它的补色。

6. 彩度对比：这是在同一色彩的鲜明和灰暗度之间的对比。

7. 色彩的数量对比：不同大小的色块对比（伊藤，1963）。

方法:

1. 在24厘米×24厘米的图框内，用铅笔画出九宫格，作为基本的色块框架。

2. 用三原色（红、蓝和黄）填入方格，并用叠加法，用三原色形成其他彩色，如绿色、棕色、灰色、紫色等。

3. 用留空法形成白色。

4. 将九宫格细分，形成更多样的色彩组合。

注意事项:

1. 色彩和情感关系密切，通过确定某一种情感，如快乐、恐惧、愤怒、安定、冷酷等，来选择色彩基调。

2. 在绘画过程中体会工具的特性，如纸张、毛笔和水。要一直提醒自己"这些工具能做到什么效果"。

3. 色彩原理是理论课中的重要部分，课上将分析世界名画。绘画过程是寓发现、体验和理解于乐的过程。结果是否完美并不重要，重要的是享受过程中的乐趣。

工具和材料:

1. 红、黄、蓝三种水彩颜料;

2. 水彩笔或者毛笔;

3. 2张A2水彩纸;

4. 小茶杯;

5. 茶碟;

6. 洗笔水罐（1.5升）。

Exercise 2. COLOR FUNDAMENTALS

Objective:

Rendering is among the most common architectural presentations. And watercolor is one of the basic tools of architectural rendering. By testing and experimenting, we understand the characteristics of drawing materials, and the nature of the watercolor painting. We will also learn some color composition principles:

1.The pure color contrast: The vivid effect of random combination of pure colors

2.The light-dark contrast: "Tone" and "value" scales can be made with colors when different brightness of colors are used.

3.The cold-warm contrast: Colors appear to "feel" cold in the blue-green direction and appear to "feel" warm in the orange-red direction.

4.The complementary contrast: In the color circle the complementary colors occupy opposite positions. When they are adjacent, complementary colors mutually intensify their luminosity; when mixed, they produce gray-black.

5.The simultaneous contrast: Each pure color physiologically demands its opposite color—its complement. (If this color is absent, the eye will perceive it simultaneously.)

6.The contrast of quality: This is the contrast between luminous and dull colors.

7.The contrast of quantity: the size difference of colored areas (Itten, 1963).

Exercise:

1.With pencils, divide a 24cm × 24cm square into a grid of nine equally-sized small squares. This will be the basic framework for the watercolor painting.

2.Fill in the small squares with the three elementary colors: red, blue and yellow in between and create other colors, such as green, brown, gray, violet, etc., by over lapping the three elementary colors.

3.Create white color by leaving the background white.

4.The grid can be subdivided into smaller pieces to give variety to the painting.

Notes:

1.Color strongly relates to emotion. Choose a color tone for a painting by defining an emotion, such as joy, fear, anger, warmth, coldness, etc..

2.Paint the painting by exploring the potentials of painting tools, such as paper, brushes and water. We may encourage ourselves by asking "What can these instruments do?"

3.Lectures are given on color principles. The works of master painters are analyzed in class. With the drawing process, we work with the pleasure of discovery, experience and understanding. It does not matter if the outcome is not a finished piece. It is important to enjoy and have fun with the process.

Tools and materials:

1.Red, blue, and yellow water color tubes;

2.Watercolor brushes or Chinese painting brushes;

3.At least 2 sheets of A2-size watercolor paper;

4.Baby tea cups or Chinese wine cups;

5.Several small dishes or tea saucers;

6.One bottle as a water container for washing brushes (about 1.5 litres).

成果:

A3尺寸水彩构成图案。

Presentation:

A3-size water color painting.

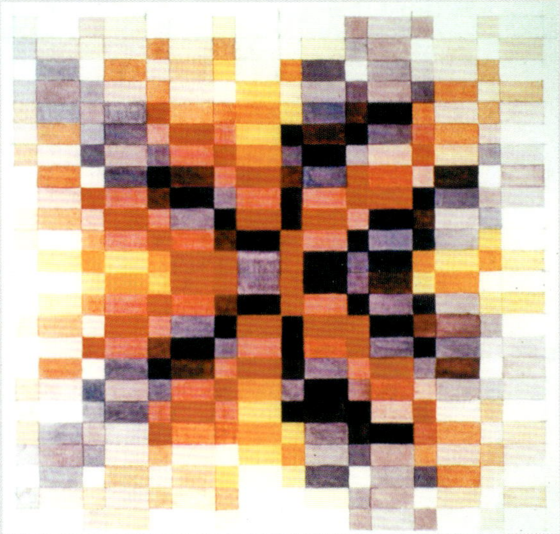

Lo Kit Sum, Stephanie
Li Pak Yee, Tuesday
Lam Chi Wan, Joanne

高级练习：

1. 水彩技法探索
2. 水彩时装人体及组合
3. 水彩建筑速写

Advanced exercises:

1.Watercolor technique exploration
2.Human figure drawing and composition with water color
3.Architectural sketches with water color

Lo Kit Sum, Stephanie
Lam Chi Wan, Joanne
Li Yan, Linda
Law wai ming, vivian

练习三　规律性和多样性

目的：

规则和模度是形体空间组合中创造规律性和秩序的手段之一。在这个练习中，我们在一个方形框架中剪贴图案。设计过程强调用模度创造视觉效果。

方法：

设计过程分为4个步骤：

1. 在给定方框内用水平和垂直线条分成网格。
2. 研究网格产生不同图案效果的潜力。
3. 取一种图案发展为一幅图。所需研究的形体和色彩构成原理有均衡、图底转换、重复、放射、镜面反转和旋转等。
4. 仔细研究报纸的材料特性，特别是有图像和照片的部分。在选材和剪贴的过程中要体现灵感和创造性。

注意事项：

1. 在第二个步骤中需要用足够的时间研究各种可能出现的图案。
2. 挖掘出的图案类型越多越好，选择2至3个发展为最后成果。
3. 这个练习也让我们认识"废物"的作用，如废报纸，可以通过艺术创造重新获得价值。在艺术中没有"废物"的概念。
4. 我们知道一张废报纸本身已经完成了自己作为信息载体的任务、目的和必要性。这个练习让我们发现它的新的潜力：过去的变成未来的素材，成为新的任务、目的和必要性的载体。设计没有尽头。

工具和材料：

1. 废报纸；
2. 切割刀、剪刀、胶水；
3. A3白纸。

成果：

一幅由报纸剪贴而成的32厘米×32厘米的色彩图案。

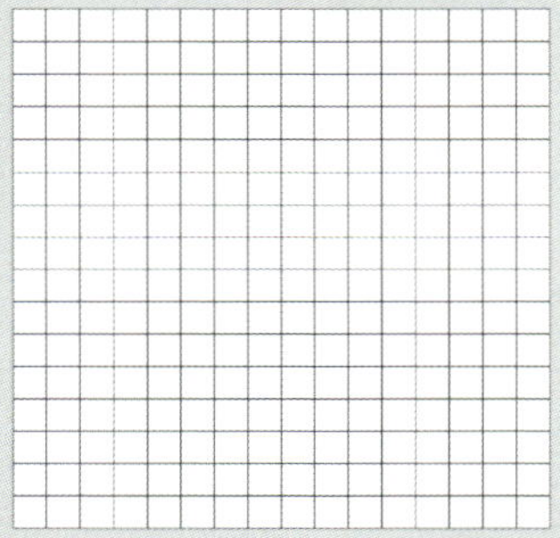

Exercise 3.　REGULARITY AND DIVERSITY: A PAPER-CUT GRAPHIC

Objective:

Rules and modules create regularity and order in the composition of form and space. In this exercise, we design a graphic within a square, and present the graphic with a newspaper-cut. Emphasis is placed upon the design process, in which we study the use of modules to create visual quality.

Methods:

The design process includes four steps:

1.Divide a square into different grids, each with orthogonal and diagonal lines.

2.Explore the potential of the grids to generate the graphic patterns.

3.Choose one of the graphic patterns and make a graphic. The principles of balance, figure and ground, repetition, dilatation, mirror reflection, and rotation, both in form and colors, should be studied and used.

4.Carefully study the material property of newspaper, especially those parts with photos and graphics. Creatively select and cut the newspaper to present the design.

Notes:

1.Stay long enough in the second step to explore the possible graphic patterns before moving to the third.

2.Test as many variations as possible, and choose two or three favorite designs for final presentation.

3.We learn that a so-called "waste" material, such as newspaper, can obtain high value in the hands of an artist. So there is no such thing as "waste".

4.We also learn that a piece of newspaper completes or fulfills a message which conveys duty, purpose or imperative. We then discover a new potential: the former work acts as raw material for the next one, which carries within it another duty, purpose, and imperative. Design is an infinite process.

Tools and materials:

1.Waste newspaper;

2.Knife, scissors, glue;

3.White paper (A3-size).

Presentation:

One sheet showing color graphics (32cm × 32cm) with newspaper cuts.

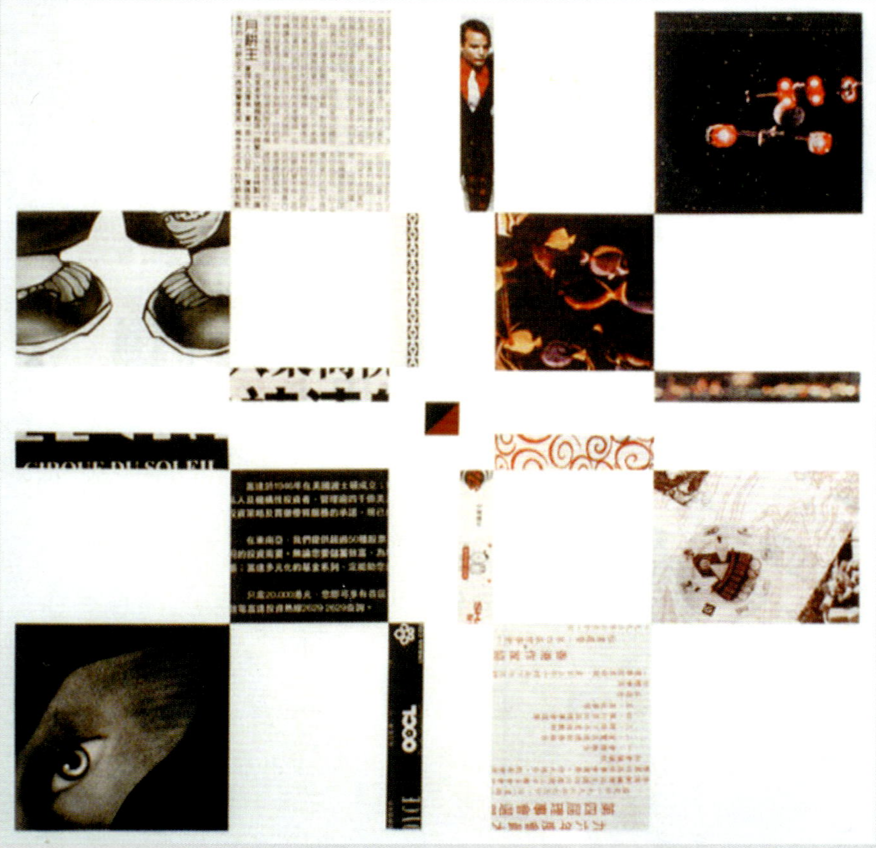

Lau Pui Chuen
Chung Ho Wai
Ng Pik Kei
Yeung Mei Nai
(Sketch Book)
Wong Ming Tak
Law Sin Hang
Yu Ka Wah

鄧氏宗祠
孝

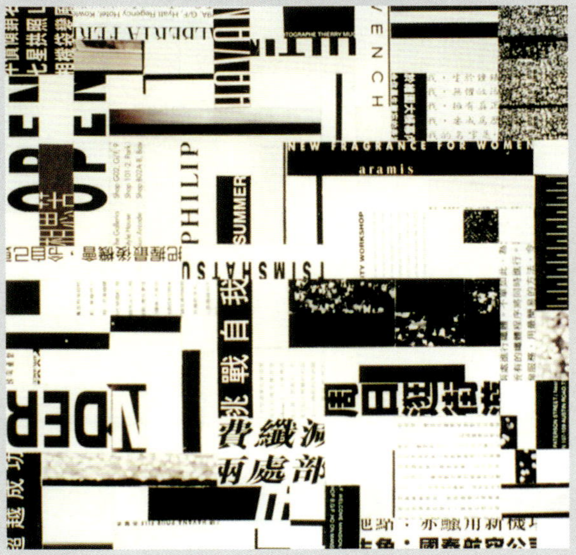
NEW FRAGRANCE FOR WOMEN
aramis
PHILIP
SUMMER

MasterCard
Baby-G
oney

图1-1-1 阿尔伯蒂设计的圣·安德里亚教堂，蒙都瓦，约1470年

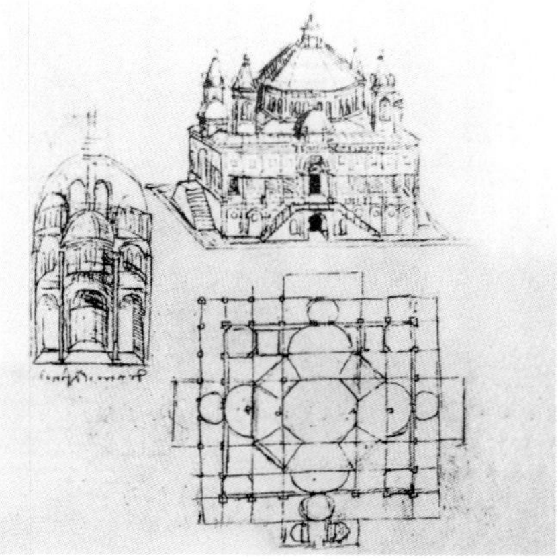

图1-1-2 达·芬奇（1452—1519）设计草图体现了网格、平面、空间和造型的一体化设计思维

1. 建筑教育中的造型训练

1.1 “巴艺”

在15世纪以前，没有正规的建筑专业院校，建筑知识基本上以师徒传艺的方式在工匠、承造商和手艺人中代代相传。最早的有据可查的建筑学校可能要算文艺复兴时期建筑大师阿尔伯蒂在15世纪70年代中期于佛罗伦萨创立的柏拉图学院。雕塑家乔瓦尼任校长。当时已有一些古典学院教文学和艺术。开办建筑学院的目的是与中世纪遗留下来的建筑行会和其流毒对抗，阿尔伯蒂认识到推广建筑理论的重要性，认为必须在学术环境中传授（图1-1-1）。[1] 尽管当时的教学计划流传下来的不多，但可以肯定的是，学院培养了大批著名艺术家，如1475年入学的达·芬奇，1490年入学的米开朗琪罗，还有小桑加罗等（图1-1-2，图1-1-3）。建筑教育史学家认为，这座建筑学院的意义在于它证明学院式教育在培养建筑师、画家和雕塑家方面，具有传统师徒传授所无法替代的作用，它也证明建筑教育和艺术教育原本一体（图1-1-4）。

意大利文艺复兴的传统延续到17世纪的法国。当时巴黎集中了舞蹈、芭蕾、文学、历史及考古、科学和音乐等多个专业学院。1671年路易十四开办了皇家建筑学院，“……布朗代尔任院长，他每星期举办两次公共讲座。开设的讲座有数学、几何、机械、军事建筑、防卫工程、透视和砖石技术。1717年始改为2至3年的课程。”学院在早期只有讲座而没有给学生提供设计室，学生只能在他们老师（师傅）的工作室里练习绘画、设计。学生在“房师”私人事务所内学绘图和设计。与阿尔伯蒂一样，学院的目的是反击当时法国的建筑行会，将建筑师从工匠提高到哲学家的思想水平。1819年学院正式改名为国立高等艺术学院（下称“巴艺”），开设有建筑理论、建筑史、建造学、透视和数学课程。建筑教育中演讲课与设计课的分离也源于此，这种传统延续至今，尽管现在学生数量增加，“房师”由现代的设计教师和教授代替。

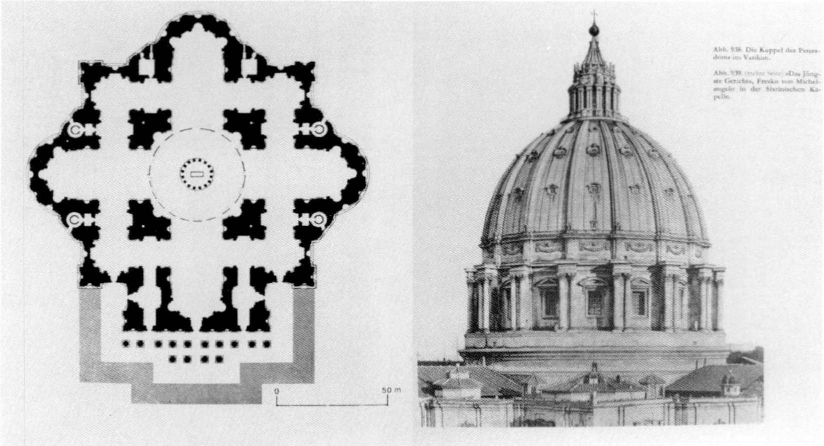

图1-1-3 米开朗琪罗设计的圣·彼得教堂平面和穹顶，罗马，16世纪

1721年，奥地利史学家费希尔写的《世界建筑史》出版，成为当时最有影响的建筑史书。[2] 此书的目的是详尽记录世界各类建筑（图1-1-5）。自此之后，教育和实践都受到折中主义的影响，即认为建筑只有风格之异同，而无好坏之分。并寻找可能的建议和什么时候采用什么样风格的“规则”。但与此同时，教学中第一次出现了国际主义，即古典法式，“巴艺”的教学目标之一是将这种“最好”的建筑推向世界各地。

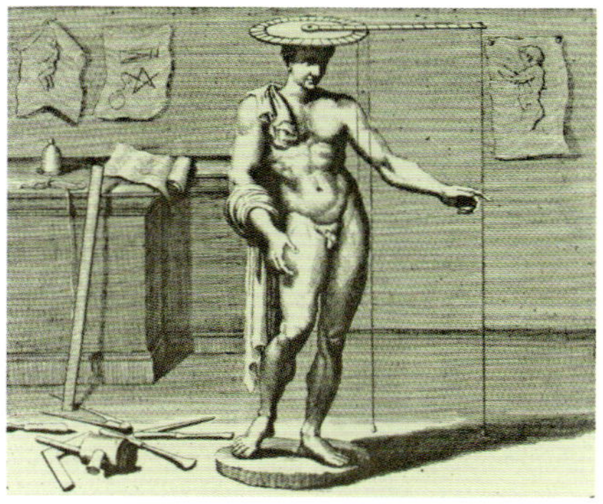

图1-1-4 《阿尔伯蒂建筑十书》中的插图，1651年版本

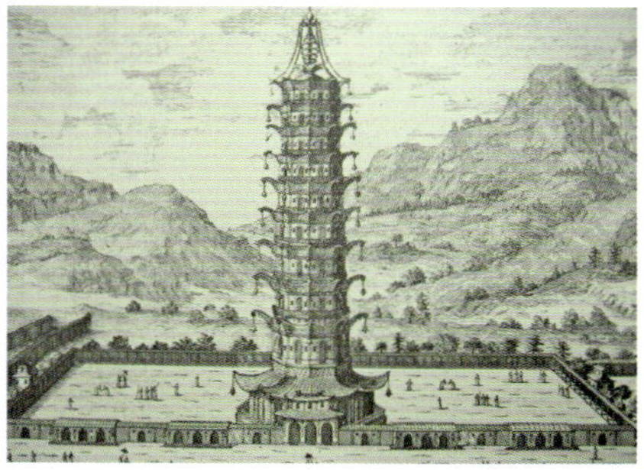

图1-1-5 费希尔《世界建筑史》插图：南京大报恩寺塔

1. Art Taught in Architectural School

1.1 A Confusion of Beaux Art

Architecture had always belonged to laymen, builders and craftsmen. It had never been taught in an academic way before the 15th century. Evidently the first formal "architecture school" was probably the Academia Platonic, founded by Renaissance master architect Alberti in Florence in the mid-1470s. At that time there were academies teaching literature and other arts, all based on Classical models. The objective was to counter the baleful influence of the craft guilds which still survived from the Middles Ages . Alberti understood the importance of theory in the promotion of architecture and convinced many that it must be taught in an academic setting (Pic.1-1-1).[1] Bertoldo di Giovanni, a sculptor, was appointed as the school director. Although there are no records on the teaching program, the graduates of the Academia almost definitely included famous historical figures, such as Leonardo da Vinci, who entered in 1475; Michelangelo, there from 1480; and Antonio da Sangallo the younger, as well as and many sculptors (Pic.1-1-2,Pic.1-1-3). Broadbent regarded the founding of the architectural school—the Academy—significant, because it proved a more than viable alternative to simply working on the job with a master by which architects, painters and sculptors had been taught until then. It also proved that art and architecture, as taught subjects, could be tightly integrated in such an environment (Pic.1-1-4).

The Italian Renaissance and post-Renaissance tradition has never died since. It inspired the French in the 17th century, when a number of institutions for "Dance, Belles, Literature, History and Archaeology, Science, and Music" were founded in Paris. In 1671 Louis XIV founded the Academie Royale d'Architecture, "… with Francois Blondel as Director who gave public lectures twice a week. There were lectures also on arithmetic, geometry, mechanics, military architecture, fortifications, perspective drawing and stone cutting. By 1717 these had become a two- or three-year course". At this early time the Academy offered only lectures; there were no formal design studies. Students learned drawing and design in the studios of their masters. The objectives of school, similar to Alberti, were political: to attack the trade guilds, and to raise architects from the status of craftsman to that of philosopher. The lectures included architectural theory, architectural history, construction, perspective drawing and mathematics since 1819 when indeed the school was formally named as the Ecole Royale des Beaux Arts by King Louis XVIII. The separation of lecture courses and design studios taught by "the masters" remained since then. This tradition can still be perceived today although student numbers have increased and the status of "masters" has changed to tutors, teachers or professors.

In 1721, Fischer von Erlach, the great Baroque architect of Vienna, published a most influential architectural history book. [2] *Illustrated History of Architecture* was meant to be survey of all architecture. Since Fischer(Pic.1-1-5), there have been many reactions and counter-reactions in academic and professional circles: eclecticism in which any style is as good as any other; and a search for "rules" which might suggest which style to use, and when. One of its goals was to teach the students the Classical orders—the first "International Style"—was based on a "one best way" that ought to be built everywhere.

图1-1-6 19世纪“巴艺”的水墨渲染图

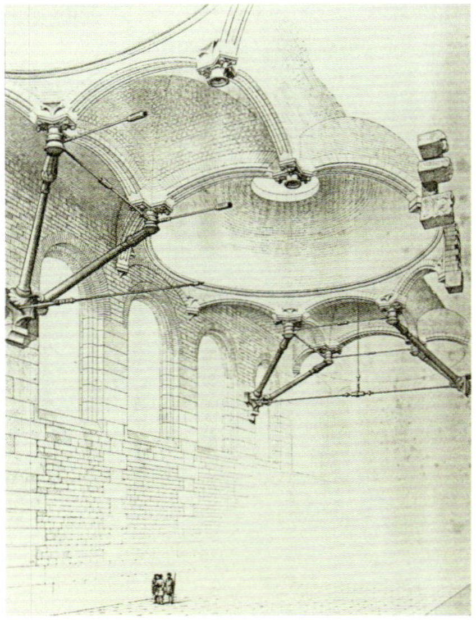

图1-1-7 19世纪末沃莱的透视图表现替代传统的新结构和新材料

图1-1-8 宾夕法尼亚大学前建筑系馆（现为艺术学院图书馆）

虽然“巴艺”本身有绘画和雕刻专业，艺术不是一个独立的或主要的建筑学专业课程，但是巴艺建筑学将设计图视为艺术作品，并极尽其精艺巧绘之能力。建筑图之所以非常重要是因为每年举行的学生作品竞赛，一张好的表现图无疑能吸引评委的注意。但自20世纪初期开始，“巴艺”的画术却因为其忽视空间和构造等现代主义建筑所强调的内容而备受批评。这类批评至今仍不绝于耳。

但实际上这些批评缺少理论依据，有些更囿于主观臆断。虽说一张立面渲染图是为了表现而不是为了建造，但实际上所有最后表现图都是平面的、二维的，尺寸、尺度和比例极其精确。平面和立面的黑墨渲染强调的是进深、光、影和质感（图1-1-6）。虽然几乎所有的平面都呈轴线秩序，体现装饰性的艺术质量，但据有些史学家考证，在竞赛过程中，起主要作用的正是平面而非我们今天所误认为的透视图。竞赛评委也特别重视“平、立、剖（指平面图、立面图、剖面图）”和人的流线的完美组合。鲍威尔和利兹巴罗在他们的《建筑绘画中的大师作品》一书中，甚至指出：20世纪现代主义直接源自“巴艺”的传统。[3] 柯布西耶的名言“平面为重”正是“巴艺”的传统，尽管他将其转译为另一种视觉语言。而特别令人震惊的是，建造学一直是“巴艺”的主课之一，而且也通过竞赛来考核（图1-1-7），这种竞赛到19世纪末时变得极其重要。竞赛图要有详细构造内容和尺寸计算。[4] 建造竞赛在今日之建筑院校中几乎绝迹，是落后于“巴艺”对构造艺术重视度的实证之一。实际上，在褪去新古典主义的外衣后，“巴艺”的教育精神，如视建筑为艺术、为哲学，专注比例、秩序、光和影等，在今日仍然有借鉴意义。现代建筑大师，美国“巴艺”教育代表——宾夕法尼亚大学（图1-1-8）毕业生路易斯•康，对现代建筑的贡献举世公认。他对光和影的执着追求，厚重的材料，轴线构图和具有震撼力的纪念形象的塑造，实际上都反映了其“巴艺”教育的背景（图1-1-9）。

“巴艺”之重要，不仅在于它20世纪20年代以前对教育思想的长期主导地位，而且在于它坚持将建筑学带出建筑行会、商业性建筑师和建筑职业团体（现代中世纪行会）的控制，并将建筑学变成精神追求。这也是为什么“巴艺”将建筑图作为艺术品，如其他艺术品一样，而不在乎是否能实现。因为建与不建是行会或者是承造商的事情，“巴艺”不愿与其同流合污。

A–1 统一

统一是构图美的首要特征，是指和谐的整体，或者一种完整的感觉。统一可以通过多种构图原理（均衡、对比、和谐、重点、比例、简洁、重复、统治、对称、尺度、节奏等）的结合运用来获得。

Unity

First aesthetic quality of compositions is defined as a harmonious whole, or a feeling of completeness, that is referred to as “unity”. Unity can be achieved by associations with other organisation principles: equilibrium/balance, contrast, harmony, emphasis, proportion, simplicity, repetition, dominance, symmetry, scale, rhythm.

图1-1-9 a.1928年发表的路易斯·康的学生作业“雕塑喷泉”

图1-1-9 b.路易斯·康设计的加利福尼亚萨克学院，1959—1965年

It seems that art was not an independent course, although it was neither addressed in the curriculum nor taught by artists. However, Beaux Arts has a unique way to produce architectural drawings as artworks of their own right. Artistically refined presentations were driven and motivated by the annual student competition, an early practice of grading and evaluating student projects, which is commonly applied in many schools today. A well-presented scheme was certainly necessary to catch the jury's eye. However, since the time of early 20th century Modernism, Beaux-Arts draughtsmanship has been criticized for ignoring three-dimensional spatial design and construction. Criticisms are still heard today, but some lack evidence; others are based on misconceptions.

It is true that the typical rendered facade was suited less for the construction of real buildings than for display at an exhibition. However, all the finished drawings, rendered in ink, used orthographic projections to give very precise dimensions, scales and proportions. In order to give a real feeling of depth, light and texture, all the shadows were carefully cast in elevation, even on the plan (Pic.1-1-6). Although the plans universally reflected a consistent doctrine of axial planning, and paid particular attention to the artistic quality of the plan as a piece of graphic design, according to Powell & Leatherbarrow,[3] it was the plan which won or lost a competition; everything else, including perspectives, was subsidiary to it. The close relations between plan, sections, elevations, and movement of people were also addressed in these competitions. They argued that “the moral quality attributed to planning in the twentieth century is the direct outcome of the tradition of the Beaux Arts…” Le Corbusier's phrase “the plan is the generator” is only a repetition of the traditional method of the Ècole, although he translated it into different visual terms. Most strikingly, construction was an important subject of study, and was tested in separate competitions (Pic.1-1-7). Construction competitions were greatly elaborated towards the end of the 19th century when drawings were required for the construction of a building with all the necessary details and calculations.[4] The construction design competition is almost never heard of in architectural schools today. It suggests that today's education is not advanced as Beaux-Art. Actually, stripped of the Neo-Classical motifs, the spirit of Beaux-Art education, such as promoting architecture as art and philosophy through consistent study of proportion, order, light and shadow, is still relevant today. There should be no question about the remarkable achievement in the works of Louis Kahn, a modern architect and graduate of an American architecture school in the Beaux-Art tradition, University of Pennsylvania (Pic.1-1-8). His consistent curiosity in light and shadow, massive materials, axial planning, powerful and monumental images can be seen as a direct outcome of a Beaux-Art training (Pic.1-1-9).

The Beaux-Art spirit is significant for me in composing this book, not only because it dominated architecture until the 1920s when the Bauhaus presented a different scheme, but also for its attempt to liberate architecture from the narrow constraints of the construction business, business-oriented practitioners, and the professional institutions (a modern equivalent to Middle-Age guilds). Architectural design became spiritual pursuing. That is why the drawings of Beaux-Art became art work as paintings, independent from construction. For them construction was the responsibility of contractors, whom Beaux-Art wanted to be distinguished from.

A-2　和谐

和谐是指按照某种视觉秩序安排相似或相关的构图元素，使整个构图由于一致性而赏心悦目。

Harmony

Harmony usually refers to a pleasing consistency among the different parts of a composition that brings visual order to sets of similar or unrelated elements.

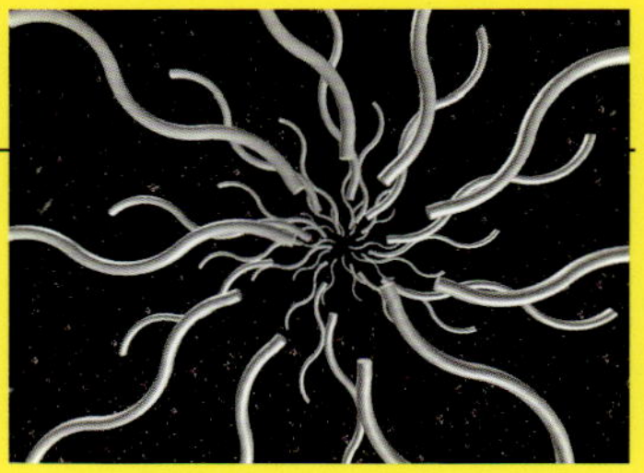

图1-2-1　画家多奈笔下的伦敦平民区，1872年

图1-2-2　奥比利奇设计的达姆施塔特艺术宫，1907年

1.2　现代主义时代

包豪斯的背景和发展动力可以追溯到19世纪的英格兰和德国的工业革命，大规模的产业化，动摇了手工业者和工人阶级的生存环境。快速工业化的发展生产着大量廉价产品，但也加速了社会重组。同时，现代科学的发展、新材料、新技术以及理性思维，激励着人们对未来的信心。

社会重组不可避免地引发了严重的社会问题，穷人首当其冲。与建筑相关的问题首推工人住区水深火热的条件。这些住宅的夯土地面阴冷潮湿，外部道路泥泞，建筑密集，室内常常没有日照和通风（图1-2-1）。在这种居住环境中，工人极易染病，有些长期卧床，甚至死亡。瘟疫不时席卷整个住区，甚至整个城市。1917年英国的一项研究显示，恶劣的居住环境所造成的损失远远超过了原先的估计：恶劣的居住环境使得大量青年因健康原因无法应征入伍；2/3的儿童有生理缺陷；工人不断罢工和暴动，从而影响了经济发展。

德国在第一次世界大战后，经济和社会结构遭到的重创仅次于俄国。传统的金字塔形的权力结构崩溃，虽然一些银行家和军官等右翼势力维持着政权的延续，但经济不断遭受罢工、暴动影响，货币贬值，社会革命一触即发。另一方面，工业化的科学和技术在动荡时期的作用像是一针强心剂。无论怎样，这是一次不可逆转的革命，一个新时代的开始。

19世纪欧洲工业国首推英国。自70年代始，欧洲各国积极效仿英国工业生产的成功经验。1896年德国普鲁士政权派穆特休斯去英国学习，一去就是6年。他是一位建筑师，也是后来德意志制造联盟的创办人之一。他回国后建议所有的手工艺学校都要设立车间工作室，聘请现代艺术家为师，开办小型私人车间生产日用品、家具和铁器。不久德国超过英国成为先进工业国，直到1914年第一次世界大战爆发。

然而，德国转向机械化生产也不是一帆风顺的。德国的青年风格派（图1-2-2）与英国的手工艺运动、法国的新艺术运动（图1-2-3）有不少相似性，如主张摒弃或改造艺术、建筑和设计中的学院派标准，探索文学和音乐的发展对新建筑的影响，提倡乡土传统、新的空间和新的装饰手法。他们认为艺术和设计应紧密结合，主张反映社会和美学方面的“个人价值”。[5]

A–3　简洁

越简单的形式，人在感知时所需的能量越小，因此格式塔理论认为，最简单的结构最“好”。“简洁”的属性包括易于识别，便于记忆、熟悉，等等。

Simplicity

As using Gestalt research, “good” constitutes the simplest structure, hence, the resulting units of form in the perceptual field are simple and require a minimum amount of energy for the viewer to perceive them. Some of the qualities for describing “simplicity” are easy recognition, easy to remember, familiarity, and etc..

图1-2-3 霍塔设计的塔塞尔旅馆，1893年

1.2 Time for Modernism

The background to and impetus for the Bauhaus can be traced to 19th century England and Germany. Increased industrialization meant increasingly cheap goods production, but also led to accelerated social restructuring. At the same time, the development of modern science, new materials and technology, and rationalist thinking inspired confidence in the future.

Social restructuring caused tremendous problems especially for the poor. Those directly related to architecture involved the workers' settlements. Workers toiled under very severe conditions. In many houses the ground floor was only stamped or moulded earth which was often cold and moist. In the streets the mud accumulated. The houses were built so closely together that no sunshine could neither penetrate them nor wind ventilate them(Pic.1-2-1). Conditions were so bad that many became ill, crippled or died at a very young age. Epidemics repeatedly spread though the workers' quarters, sometimes even over whole towns. The probable dimensions of this crisis became clear in 1917 England, when accumulating evidence began to indicate that the external costs of inadequate housing were far more costly than expected:

—Large number of military recruits was rejected on medical grounds.

—Two-thirds of the children surveyed were physically defective.

—Industrial unrest was common and widespread.

Germany, next to Russia, was the country whose economy and social structure was most drastically altered by the First World War. In both cases the traditional pyramid of power collapsed, and although in Germany the adroit action of certain bankers and militarists maintained the semblance of continuous central government, in practice, deep-seated problems festered and compounded upon each other: industrial and civil unrest, currency crises, the loss of a major industrial area (the Ruhr). Social problems maintained a potentially revolutionary situation. However, there also seems to have been a decided optimism with industrialization, science and technology in the uncertainty of the time. This was, after all, a veritable revolution, the beginning of a new age.

England rose to become Europe's leading industrial nation in the 19th century. Since the 1870s, other European countries attempted to copy England's success in the field of industrial production. As an architectural indicator of the widespread desire to emulate things English, the Prussian government in 1896 sent Hermann Muthesius, an architect and one of the founding members of Deutscher Werkbund, to study in England for six years. Upon his return, he recommended workshops to be introduced at all Prussian handicraft schools, modern artists to be appointed as teachers and small private workshops to be established in making household goods, furniture and metal utensils. On a much larger scale, Germany quickly overtook England as the leading European industrial nation and maintained this position until the outbreak of the First World War in 1914.

However, the switching to machine production in Germany was not without struggle. The Yugendstil movement (Pic.1-2-2) in Germany shared many of the impulses of Arts and Crafts in England and Art Nouveau (Pic.1-2-3): the rejection or reinterpretation of academic standards in art, architecture and design, the exploration of literary and

A–4 控制和重点

Dominance and Emphasis

控制和重点与要素在构图结构之内的等级有关，视觉重点就是通过划分构图要素的等级来获得的。秩序的等级是：时间顺序，普遍到特殊，特殊到普遍。

This relates to the hierarchy of elements within the compositional structure; primary and secondary compositional elements establish visual importance. The hierarchies of order are: chronological, general to specific, specific to general.

图1-2-4 范·德·维尔德设计的魏玛艺术学校

实际上，调整手工艺人和工业的复杂关系在德国特别困难，有时还会引发社会和政治矛盾。因此改变设计和艺术教育显得非常重要。设计者或者工匠在工业社会中的作用不但受到挑战，而且要重新审核和讨论。讨论的内容包括创作的自由度与设计人及其教育背景关系，即哪些源自学院派，哪些源自师徒帮带，对传统工艺的压力有多大，需接受德国工业要求的程度有多少，等等。

德国的实用艺术学校发展于19世纪80年代，其目的是为了促进和巩固地方资助人、行会及其有关的地方手工业。因此实用艺术学校的目的与青年风格派（德国的新艺术运动）的目标一致，在柏林、慕尼黑、德累斯顿和魏玛等文化和政治中心发展迅速。[6]

德意志制造联盟于1907年成立于慕尼黑，由代表大型手工艺公司和艺术家团体的12名成员组成，其宗旨是“通过教育和宣传，统一看法，提高商业活动素质，加强艺术、工业和手工业的协作”[7]。它为扶植和贯彻艺术设计和社会关系方面的新思想提供协助。而在其成立以前，德国已有几所艺术设计学校率先采取了与传统的培养艺术家和工匠的教育思想不同的教学计划。这些激进的课程的真正目的不在于它们反对传统的教育方法，而在于改变了艺术家的地位，即艺术家及其职业与社会的关系。课程强调艺术家的个性和自由，同时要求他们通过专注于形和结构，与抽象的自然结合，[8] 注重自然表象后面的规律和原理。

魏玛是当时的“艺术之都”，巴赫、克拉纳赫、歌德、席勒、赫尔德和李斯特等曾居住于此。第一次世界大战前，这里的经济支柱主要是农业和一些小型手工业。1860年成立了一所艺术学校，教授绘画和雕塑。1902年比利时建筑师范·德·维尔德应邀来到魏玛（图1-2-4），试图振兴当地手工艺和工业生产。1907年，他开办了一所新艺术学校，教授印刷、编织、陶瓷、装订和精细铁艺制作工艺。但由于他是外国人，思想过于激进，在开办和管理学校时障碍重重。1915年，作为外国人的他已无法保住职位，辞职前他推举格罗皮乌斯等三人作为他的继任者。7月他去了瑞士，学校随后关闭，车间解体，建筑在战时用作军用医院。[9] 1919年格罗皮乌斯开办包豪斯设计学院。

以上简要历史回顾说明，艺术运动在20世纪初的德国是新设计思想和新工业思想的催化剂。艺术是思想，而设计和生产是思想的实践。

A–5 封闭

看似未完成的构图会激起观众进一步探索的兴趣。面对一个缺少部分视觉信息的形，观者通常会在视觉上“闭合”或完成它——画面上不完整的视觉元素足以使观者想象出完整的形状。

Closure

A composition seemly unfinished can arose viewers interests to further investigate. A viewer has the tendency of to “close” or visually complete a form or figure from which some visual information has been deleted; the remaining visual elements are enough for the viewer to perceive the form as a whole.

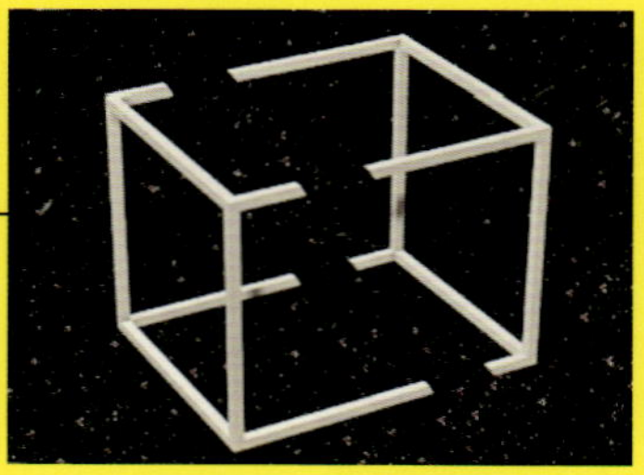

musical analogies, the celebration of the vernacular as well as new spatial and decorative concepts in architecture, and the conviction that art and design were inseparable, reflecting both a social and aesthetic commitment to the "individual value".[5]

However, the uneasy relationship between craftsmen and industry in Germany was particularly difficult and led to political and social tension. This led to demands for changes in the priorities for design and art education. The role of designer or craftsman in an industrial society was challenged, reviewed and debated widely. The issue discussed related to the degree of creative freedom allowed to the potential designer and the nature of his training — how far this was to be academic or divorced from the apprenticeship system, how far the stress was to be on traditional craft skills, and how much acknowledgement was to be given to the demands of German industry.

In Germany, a network of Kunstgewerbeschule (new schools of applied design) was developed in 1880s to inspire and consolidate standards in local craft industries, and was mainly related to local patronage and local trades. Therefore, Kunstgewerbeschule was developed in keeping with the aims of Jugendstil, the German version of Art Nouveau, which flourished in cultural and political centres such as Berlin, Munich, Dresden and Weimar. [6]

The Deutscher Werkbund founded in Munich in 1907 was an association, which composed of twelve representatives of leading handicraft companies and artists, whose aim was the "co-operation of art, industry and crafts in the ennoblement of commercial activity by means of education, propaganda and a united stand on pertinent questions"[7]. It provided a platform for the articulation and implementation of ideas about the relationship of art to design and society. Before its formation, however, several German art and design schools adopted programs that challenged traditional conceptions of the role and training of the artist and craftsman. The intentions of their seemingly radical courses were important not only because of their rejection of traditional methods of instruction and expression, but because they implied a change in the role of the artist and his relationship both to his work and society. They stressed the individuality and autonomy of the artist, but at the same time they urged an empathy with form and structure that united rather than isolated the artists from nature.[8] Or the laws and principles govern the appearance of the nature.

Weimar was predominantly an "art town". Bach, Cranachs, Goethe, Schiller, Herder and Liszt had lived there. Before the First World War, the town's income was mainly derived from agriculture, and had several small, mainly craft-based industries. An art academy had already established in 1860, training both painters and sculptors. In 1902, Henry van de Velde, the Belgian architect, was invited to Weimer to revitalize both craft and industrial production. Van de Velde opened "the school and a new art academy" in 1907, with printing, weaving, ceramics, bookbinding and precious metal workshops (Pic.1-2-4). However, Van de Velde encountered many obstacles in developing and running these new schools as he was a foreigner and his ideas were too avant-garde. By 1915, his position there, as a foreign national, was untenable, and he resigned, nominating Walter Gropius as one of three possible successors to his post. When he left for Switzerland in July 1915, the school was closed, its workshops dismantled and the building was used as a military hospital during the war.[9] Bauhaus, led by Walter Gropius, was founded in 1919.

The point to be addressed from this history is that art movements were seen as generator of new design ideals and ideas for industry. Art was the thought; design and production are the implementation of the thought.

A–6 个性

Identity

个性是指形能打动人并令人难忘的特点，它取决于设计者的创造性。

A form has a unique character, which is striking and unforgettable. It relies on the creativity of designers, who can distinguish themselves from others.

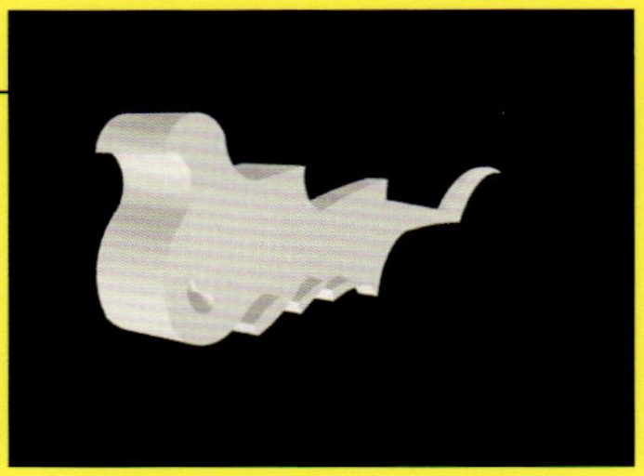

图1-3-1 勒·柯布西耶为斯图加特住宅展览会设计的住宅，1927年

图1-3-2 沙利文设计的洛杉矶某商店立面，1911—1914年

图1-3-3 拉斯金著作中的素描插图：威尼斯窗花（局部）

图1-3-4 莫里斯设计的书页或章节题头字母，1896年

1.3 现代艺术观念

包豪斯设计学院能够维持自身影响力不仅仅因为它与工业化的现实需要相适应，更重要的是它对前卫艺术的信念和实现这一信念的决心。

模仿适用于任何艺术形式。它是表现形式、人的天性，是学习和体验世界的能力之一。[10] 不同的是，现代艺术和现代建筑不是对古典风格或是自然的简单模仿，而是对现实技术环境中操作功能的内在规律的模仿，即机械和机械的运作成为新的模仿对象（图1-3-1）。当然，现代艺术观念并不仅限于此。

19世纪艺术主流可概括为绘画中的“现实主义”和建筑中的“古典复兴”。建筑主要模仿传统，或者重塑与过去的建筑风格相关的视觉效果。这类建筑忽视时代的技术发展，却让艺术家和建筑师能迎合大众的口味。

针对这类轻浮的艺术，一些前卫艺术家和建筑师决定探索新的艺术概念，进行了不同的实验。有些以自然曲线图形为蓝本装饰新结构，如沙利文的著作中曾指出新一代建筑师应继续以合乎大众口味的装饰为设计基础（图1-3-2）。但无论是建筑装饰中植物纹样的模仿，还是后来流行欧洲的新艺术，或是德国的青年风格派都没能体现新的现代主义精神。它们成为“现代”洛可可，不久便令人厌倦。[11] 另一些建筑师试图回到传统和民间建筑中去，作为对工业化非人性社会的批判，这种思想由英国的拉斯金的著作和建筑师威廉·莫里斯的设计为代表（图1-3-3，图1-3-4）。他们开创了英国美术和手工艺运动，但其改良性思想成功实例有限。

在这些不同风格的实验中，一些新艺术思想开始出现，后来发展成为抽象艺术和现代建筑的美学基础。法国象征主义艺术家丹尼斯在评述抽象艺术时说：“一幅画在表物之前，首先是布满色彩的平面，色彩布局规律有序，悦人眼目。”[12] 意指绘画本身是一个物件，从表面元素的抽象组合中人们可以领悟艺术思想，而且线条和色块可直接作用于人的视觉，有时比复杂的形体更有表现力。[13]

早期立体主义以变形而非抽象作为处理自然形状的手法。抽象是一种简化，而早期立体主义却通过分析解构物体，出现了复杂的、扩张的，甚至难以辨认的形象。[14] 出现于1912年的后期立体主义绘画像建筑一样以简洁、巨大的形体为主（早期同类主题绘画图1-3-5和图1-3-6，图1-3-7，图1-3-8的比较）：

A-7　均衡

均衡是指通过构图要素的安排达到视觉上动态或静态的稳定感。构图均衡可以通过对称、非对称或中性配置来实现。在视觉上改变构图形状的物理属性，如形状、质感、颜色、明暗配合和式样等，可以达到均衡。同样的形状和空间相对于一个公共轴或中心点对等分布，称为对称均衡；不同数量和特征的元素在平衡点两边达到视觉重量上的平衡，称为非对称均衡——动态的平衡；消极的，缺乏重点或对比的平衡称为中性均衡，以偶然性和模糊性为特点。

图1-3-5 柯罗《拿曼陀林琴的吉卜赛少女》，1874年

图1-3-6 毕加索《坐着的裸女》，1909—1910年

1.3 Modern Artistic Ideology

Bauhaus maintained its influence not simply in its pragmatic response to the reality of industrialization, but also through its belief of the avant-garde artistic ideology and determination in realizing such visions.

Imitation exists in any kind of artwork. It is a form of expression, natural to people, enabling both learning and pleasurable experience of the world.[10] As Row continues, modern art and architecture are neither the imitation of classical forms nor of nature. "Instead, the objects of imitation were drawn mainly from the contemporary technological environment close to intrinsic matters of makeup and function." He means machine and the functions of machine became the new objects to be imitated (Pic.1-3-1) .However the modern artistic ideology is much more than that.

The prevailing trend in the 19th century art world was primarily "realism" in painting and "revivalism" in architecture, by which the architects simply copied and imitated familiar architectural forms or recombined their visual references to earlier building styles. This kind of art production did not reflect the technological advancement of its age, but certainly provided artists and architects with the greatest assurance of initial acceptance by the observers.

In response to this superficiality of design, some avant-garde artists and architects of the time searched for new art concepts. Various new expressions of this style were experimented with. Some architects experimented with naturalistic curvilinear ornament as a novel embellishment of new types of structure and believed that with it they were achieving at last a new art form. For example, Louis Sullivan's writings indicate that advanced architects of the generation continued to hold, quite as much as their public, that ornament was essential to architecture(Pic.1-3-2). But neither the emulation of plant forms in architectural decoration, nor the later Art Nouveau in Europe and Jugendstil in Germany, faithfully represented this new spirit. They were merely considered as "modern" as Rococo ornament and soon became boring and unfashionable.[11] Other architects strove for a return to traditional or vernacular style as a response to the inhumane conditions of industrialization. This is particularly noted in John Ruskin's writings and the work of his disciple William Morris (Pic.1-3-3, Pic.1-3-4), both in England. Although they initiated the Arts and Crafts Movement, its reformative ideas only received limited success and failed to reach the larger population.

Among these experiments of different styles, some basic assumptions were initially made about the arts, which were later developed, as the aesthetic premises both of abstract painting and of modern architecture. A quotation from Maurice Denis, a French symbolist painter of the generation preceding the development of abstract art: "Before being a representation of anything whatsoever, a picture is a flat surface covered with colours — colours arranged in a certain order and thus arranged to give pleasure to the eye." [12] This stressed the idea that a painting is a material object intended to be apprehended in terms of the abstract organisation of its surface elements. Further, it understood that mere lines of stress or areas of plain colour, appealing directly to the eye, can be as powerfully expressive as more complicated forms. [13]

By the time of early cubism, distortion rather than abstraction seem to be a better word for the painters' way of treating natural forms. For abstraction implies simplification — and in the first stage of cubism the analytical breaking

Balance

The arrangement of the compositional elements can result in visual stability that is either static or active. Compositional balance can be achieved by symmetrical, asymmetrical, or neutral configurations. Balance can be achieved through the visual treatment of the compositional figures or forms by varying their physical attributes such as shape, texture, colour, value and pattern.Symmetrical balance refers to the distribution of equivalent forms and spaces about a common line or point. Asymmetrical refers to the balance of visual weights, while the property and quantity of elements on the two sides of balance point are different. Asymmetrical is a balance of dynamic. Neutral balance is characterized by randomness and ambiguous equilibrium; it is referred to as non-active, lacking emphasis or contrast.

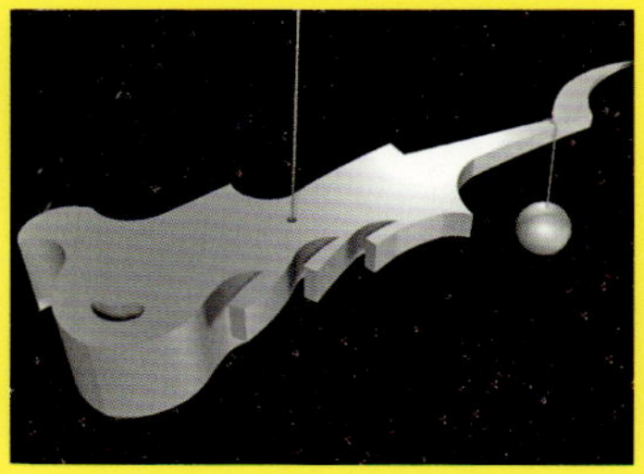

图1-3-7 阿奇潘库《拿扇子的女人》，1914年

图1-3-8 利普奇兹《拿吉他的男人》，1916年

无论这些元素，如在毕加索、布拉克和哥瑞斯的画以及蒙德里安早期作品是从自然物体中“抽象”出来，还是如其他一些法国、俄国和美国的艺术家那里，不代表任何具体物件，战前的现代艺术已经近似于纯设计的研究。[15]

这些绘画体现了对元素关系和布局的认真研究，关注景深但却表现平面效果。不久立体主义画家还通过雕塑或者他们与青年建筑师的关系研究艺术中的“建造”手法。[16] 许多建筑师也尝试将绘画和雕塑的抽象化作为从业过程中艺术培养不可缺少的一部分。代表人物之一当数勒·柯布西耶（图1-3-9）：

我的导师（著名教育家察尔斯·易普拉特耐尔）曾说：“只有自然才是真正的鼓舞着人勇往直前的动力，但不要用风景画法来重现自然，因为那只是它的表面。我们应研究它的起因、形体和活力，再综合起来用于装饰设计。”[17]

对可塑性的研究，对绘画和雕塑的抽象原理的认识，以及将不同艺术形式紧密联系，成为探究新建筑的趋势。而一批流亡艺术家，如荷兰风格派的西奥·范·多斯堡和蒙德里安，俄国构成派（图1-3-10，图1-3-11）和至上主义的莫霍利-纳吉（原为匈牙利人）等人的活动，强化了这一趋势。他们在本国虽不受欢迎，却在外国有一批青年建筑师追随者。

荷兰艺术家和评论家范·多斯堡1917年创办《风格》杂志，和他一起的还有画家蒙德里安和建筑师奥特。他们的目标是提倡一种“国际语言”，它植根于艺术家和社会的新关系，以一种风格体现在所有产品中。[18] 他们认为艺术应协调生活中的矛盾关系。直角和三原色，补以黑、白、灰是艺术表现的基本元素（图1-3-12）。[19] 范·多斯堡在许多场合为他的荷兰建筑师朋友奥特在他的房屋项目中设计了瓷砖地板，彩色玻璃窗和其他装饰配件。1924年里特维德设计的位于乌得勒支市的著名风格派建筑与多斯堡的构成设计相似（图1-3-13）。1925年奥特设计的位于鹿特丹的咖啡店虽没有采用多斯堡装饰，而整个立面却酷似蒙德里安的构成（图1-3-14）。评论家希区柯克指出，这些艺术家影响了包括密斯·凡·德·罗在内的一大批现代建筑师：

范·多斯堡对密斯20年代早期一系列住宅设计的影响体现在平面设计上。即使在他后期的作品中，包括进行中芝加哥的项目，立面上简洁元件布局与蒙德里安严谨的规律相似（图1-3-15，图1-3-16）。他不用强烈色块，而且喜欢古典对称和规律性以保持平衡。他自己却说蒙德里安的影响已经不复存在，而他最倾心的是另一位完全不同的抽象画家保尔·克利。现代建筑与抽象绘画的明显而且神秘的多重关系没有比密斯的作品更有说服力了。尽管他以纯净的数字关系要求他的设计，尽管他常将保尔·克利的画悬挂于他的建筑墙壁，但其实画与建筑毫无关系。而范·多斯堡和蒙德里安的影响仍然体现在他的伊利诺伊工学院的建筑中（图1-3-17，图1-3-18）。[20]

A-8　联想

形是相互联系的，可以根据类型、来源、意义或功能来分组。通过由此及彼的联想来赋予或改变构图的文字释义，这种后天习得的能力称为自由联想。观者对于构图内外的形式进行联想，并由于发现自己的这种能力而得到满足感。

Association

Forms are associated with one another because they can be grouped together according to their type, their family, their meaning, or their function. Free association is the learned or acquired ability to assign and change verbal interpretations of a composition by moving from one to many associations. Viewers have interests to discover their capability to associate forms inside or outside the compositions to achieve a satisfactory.

图1-3-9 勒·柯布西耶《盘子等静物》，1920年

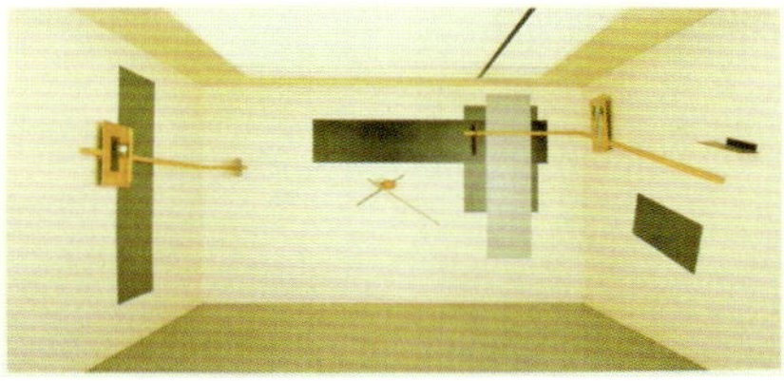

图1-3-10 利兹斯基《布露屋》，1923年

图1-3-11 塔丁《屋角雕塑》，1915年

up of natural objects produced very elaborate and complex images which were usually not readily recognizable.[14] With the next phase of cubism around 1912, as Hitchcock noted, the composition of modern painting became more architectonic again — with simplified and increased scale of the elements of which modern paintings were composed (Pic.1-3-5,Pic.1-3-6,Pic.1-3-7,Pic.1-3-8):

> *Whether these elements were "abstracted" from the forms of natural objects, as they were by the cubists Picasso, Braque and Gris, and also by Mondrian in his early paintings, or whether they were completely non-representational, as in the case of certain other French, Russian and American artists, the most advanced work of the years just before the first European War came very close indeed to research in pure design.* [15]

These paintings reflect a careful study of relations, arrangement of elements, and deal with problems of depth and projection in a non-perspective way. Soon, these cubist painters were also experimenting with "construction", i.e., either through their abstract sculpture, or their close personal association with young architects of their generation.[16] Many architects also attempted abstract painting and sculpture, as a desirable part of the artistic preparation for their profession, one of whom was the most notable was Le Corbusier (Pic.1-3-9).

> *My master (the excellent teacher Charles L'Eplattenier) had proclaimed: "only nature is inspiring and true and should be the support of human endeavour. But do not make nature in the manner of landscape painters, who show nothing but its exterior. Scrutinize in it the cause, the form, the vital development and make the synthesis of it in creating ornaments."* [17]

This trend of exploring new architecture through plastic experimentation and abstract principles of painting and sculpture, and a closer link between these arts was further intensified with the immigration of Dutch de Stijl artists such as Theo van Doesburg and Piet Mondrian, and Russian constructivist (Pic.1-3-10, Pic.1-3-11), and suprematist such as Laszlo Moholy-Nagy (the latter a Hungarian, but much influenced by Russian constructivism and suprematism). These artists were seldom appreciated in their own countries, but were generally welcomed by younger architects in open arms.

Van Doesburg, a Dutch painter and art critic, founded the magazine de Stijl in 1917 with a group of artists including the painter Mondrian and architect J.J.P. Oud. Their aim was the promotion of a "universal language" which would "manifest itself in all objects as a style, born from a new relationship between the artist and society".[18] They believed art should reconcile the great polarities of life. The right angle and the three primary colours, supplemented by black, white and grey, composed the basic elements of expression (Pic.1-3-12).[19] Van Doesburg, on numerous occasions, designed the tiled floors, stained glass windows and other decorative accessories for his Dutch architect-friend Oud in his house projects. In 1924, Rietveld designed and built a house in Utrecht (Pic.1-3-13), which closely resembled van Doesburg's compositions. In 1925, Oud no longer used van Doesburg's design as decorative elements, but designed the facade of his cafe de Unie in Rotterdam with a Mondrian-like composition (Pic.1-3-14). As Hitchcock noted the influences of these painters penetrated many works of modern architects, including Mies van der Rohe:

> *In various house projects by Mies van der Rohe in the early 1920's the influence of Van Doesburg is evident in the pattern of the floor plans. (Pic.1-3-15,Pic.1-3-16) And even in his latest work, now proceeding in Chicago, the arrangement of the extremely simple elements of his facades often seems to approach very closely the rigid discipline of Mondrian. He abjures the accent of strongly colored areas, however, and prefers an almost classic symmetry and regularity to occult balance, so that his explicit denial*

A-9 亲和力

亲和力是观者将不熟悉的形式与比较熟悉的形式相联系的能力。最有效的感知或组织使亲和力无处不在。

Familiarity

Familiarity is the ability of a viewer to associate unfamiliar figures with more familiar figures. The most efficient or effective perceptual organisation universalizes the familiar.

至此，立体主义或抽象艺术原理已不再只是一种方向或是一种尝试。经过长期模仿历史元素和风格的挣扎，一种新建筑精神诞生了，它开创了建筑的新形式。法国的柯布西耶、荷兰的奥特、德国的格罗皮乌斯（图1-3-19）和密斯·凡·德·罗用玻璃和钢丝等新材料创造了新形式，激励着第一次世界大战后的青年一代。

新艺术运动与20世纪初欧洲政治社会的变革关系密切，这是一个社会动荡与现代技术更替和重组交织在一起的时代。在动荡朦胧的世界中，焦躁和疯狂的心理需要找到表现内在规律的抽象艺术来平衡。抽象意味着抽身离开现实，是穿过迷雾寻找基本规律的方法。[21] 为了避开混乱的世界，抽象可以重建一种适当的形式标准。[22] 当时的哲学思想转向客观，沉迷于理性，强调对缘由和规律的思考。柯布西耶指出，现代情感就是几何精神，是建造和组织的精神。他更强调，艺术中的秩序对建立社会公正的重要性："在物欲横流和个人至上的地方，我们主张共处、平常和遏制特殊性。"[23]

现代艺术是包豪斯教育体系中的重要内容，在战后和革命的年代里，格罗皮乌斯将现代艺术思想引入了课程计划。"包豪斯的设计课与当时的现代艺术思想密切相关，其教学明显受立体主义、构成主义和达达主义的影响。"[24]

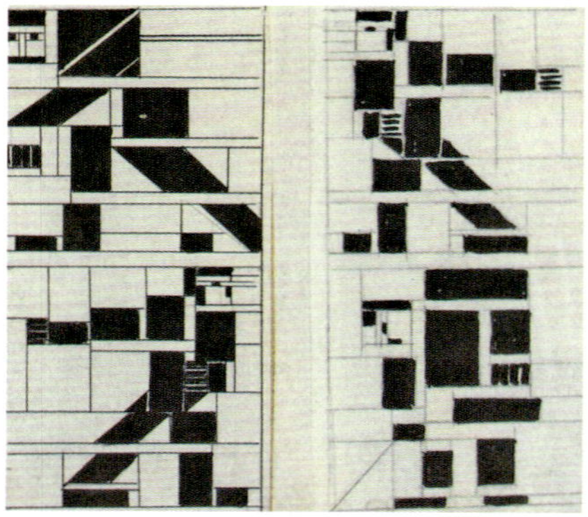

图1-3-12 范·多斯堡的抽象步骤，将凡·高的《播种人》（1889—1890）转变成玻璃花窗图案，1921—1922年

图1-3-13 里特维德设计的施罗德住宅，荷兰乌得勒支市，1924年

图1-3-14 奥特为1927年斯图加特住宅展览会设计的联排住宅

A-10　对比

对比是指以求异为目的的比较。通过属性相反的形式的对比，如构图要素之间或要素群之间在排列上或物理属性（尺寸、重量、体积、数量、形状、简洁性、规则性、颜色、色调、质感、方向性、朝向、连续性或节奏和重复）上的对比，可以创造出构图的重点和趣味。好的构图会有明确的图形与背景的对比，以及在形状属性上饶有趣味的对比。

图1-3-15 范·多斯堡《反建构》，1923年

图1-3-16 重建的密斯·凡·德·罗巴塞罗那展览馆，1929年

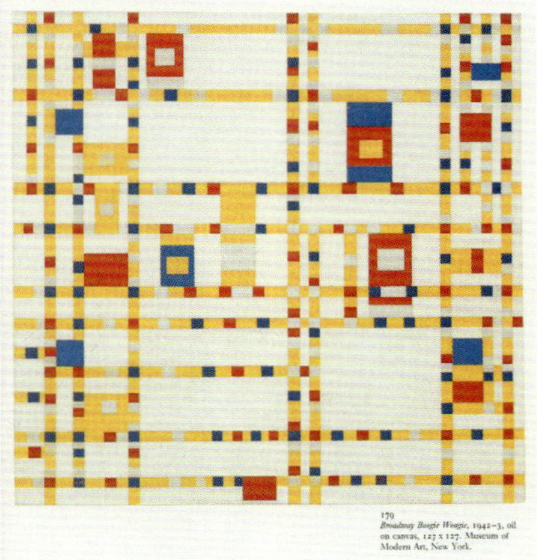

图1-3-17 蒙德里安《布吉伍吉百老汇》，1942—1943年

that this influence continues in his work can be accepted. It is to the very dissimilar abstract art of Paul Klee that Mies remains especially devoted. The subtlety and the mystery of the different possible relationships between modern architecture and abstract painting can hardly be better illustrated than by this fact. Around Mies as he develops his architectural designs in a spirit of Platonic purity and extreme mathematical simplification, hang a score of Klee's paintings, whose influence on these designs it is all but impossible even to glimpse; while the now entirely historical influence of Van Doesburg and Mondrian still seems evident to the observer of his buildings at Illinois Institute (Pic.1-3-17,Pic.1-3-18).[20]

By this time, cubism or abstract arts principles were no longer just a vision or an experimental principle. Years of struggle from imitating the past elements and styles had finally led to emancipation of a new spirit, and development of innovated architectural forms. Le Corbusier in France, Oud in Holland, Gropius (Pic.1-3-19) and Mies van der Rohe in Germany, were developing new expressions with new materials such as glass, steel, etc. This was particularly stimulating to the younger generation after the First World War.

The question is how this art movement related to political and social changes of the early 20th century. It was a period of considerable social change and, a moment at which the modern technical orientation was undergoing radical revision and realignment. Row argued that abstract art arose from feelings of anguish and bewilderment at the instability and obscurity of the world, and reflects an instinctive necessity to turn inward in search of order. Abstraction means drawing away, in the sense of becoming removed from reality. [21] It was clearly necessary in order to prepare the way, sift through the confusion, and get down to basic principles. "In order to deal with an otherwise confused world, and (these principles) are abstract, precisely in order to arrive at an appropriate level of formalism."[22] A philosophical movement of the time also shifted toward subject-centered reason, obsessed by meditation on reason and rationality. Le Corbusier pointed out that the modern sentiment was a spirit of geometry and a spirit of construction and synthesis. He further addressed the order of art is a necessity of social justice. "In the place of individualism and its fevered products, we prefer the commonplace, the everyday, the rule to the exception." [23]

Modern arts were of interest precisely for content of learning and teaching developed in the Bauhaus educational program. Gropius translated these ideas of reform, developed during these periods of revolutionary and post-war years, into the curriculum. "The design classes at the Bauhaus were also concerned with incorporating part of the history of the ideas of the contemporary art of the time. Probably no-one would deny that the teaching was influenced by cubism, constructivism and Dadaism". [24]

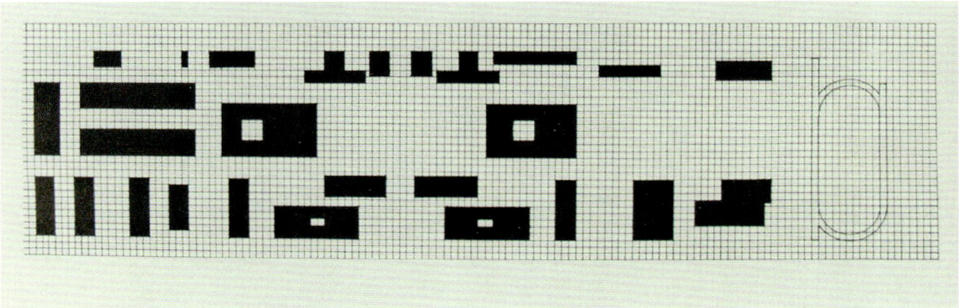

图1-3-18 密斯规划的伊利诺伊工学院总平面，1955年

图1-3-19 格罗皮乌斯和迈耶设计的法古斯工厂

Contrast

Contrast is a kind of comparison where by differences are made clear. Visual contrast can be used to create emphasis and interest through the use of opposing qualities among figures and forms. Contrast between elements or groups of elements in reference to their arrangement or physical qualities: size, weight, mass, quantity, shape, simplicity, regularity, colour, value/tone, texture, direction, orientation, continuity or rhythm, and repetition. A good composition shows clear contrast between figure and ground, and playful using of contrasts in properties of forms.

图1-4-1 包豪斯章程封面

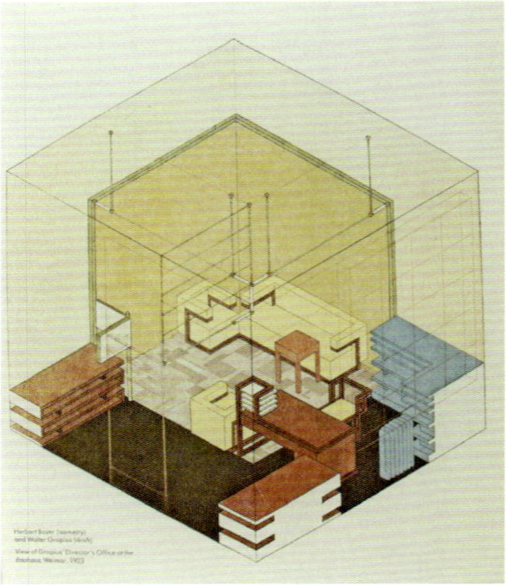

图1-4-2 格罗皮乌斯的包豪斯院长办公室设计图，1923年

1.4 包豪斯

“包豪斯”成了一个代名词，一种受喜爱，或者遭唾弃的风格。它代表着世纪之交的一次突破，一种新精神。教师们的理想和方法直接影响着后来的建筑教育系的理论家们。正如一位评论家所说的，包豪斯的作用是于20世纪早期，以思想鼓励了对设计本质和目的观念的转变。学校从对19世纪工艺思想的继承、改造和摈弃的过程中，发现了与设计和建筑相关的艺术原理。它的根本目的是消除不同社会和不同国家间的隔阂，并建立一套放之四海而皆准的形式语言。[25]

包豪斯章程（图1-4-1）开宗明义，流传广泛，具有前瞻性和革命性：

创作的最终目的是建筑！建筑装饰曾是艺术最为荣耀的功能，艺术离不开伟大建筑。今天它们孤立自娱，只有当所有工艺人认真协作，才能摆脱困境……

旧艺术学校无法实现这种凝聚力，也无此必要。既然艺术不可言传，学校应重新融入车间。图像设计师和实用美术家的世界只有图和画，而这个世界上的有些东西却是建造出来的……

让我们一起渴望、坚信和创造未来的新建筑，它将把所有东西——建筑、雕塑和绘画——融为一体。这个形体是新信念的结晶，将有一天从成千上万的工人手中升起，飞向天堂。[26]

与文艺复兴时期阿尔伯蒂的将艺术、雕塑和建筑合为一体的学校相比，包豪斯似乎继承了阿尔伯蒂的传统。这个章程强调将手工艺师、艺术家和建筑师联合起来创造“未来建筑”。对格罗皮乌斯来说，只有建筑才能将孤立的学科重新整合，“建筑”是社会、精神和象征意义的核心（图1-4-2）。

格罗皮乌斯原想将自己事务所的工程交给包豪斯来设计。这种理想的合作建筑方式——包豪斯的办学宗旨之一，现实中却很难推行。1920年，一个木料商给他们一次机会。这个木料商是学校第一批赞助人之一，希望格罗皮乌斯用他从船上拆下来的柚木造一座房子。当时三名即将留校任教的在校生布劳耶、史密特和阿尔贝斯把这个项目作为业务（而不是教学实验），接下来——布劳耶做家具，学雕刻的史密特负责在楼梯及门上雕刻复杂的象征木材公司活动的图案（图1-4-3），而材料感觉敏锐、富有创造力的阿尔贝斯用抽象图形设计和制作了镶嵌玻璃窗（图1-4-4）。刻工、窗花和室内墙面相协调，结合造型、表现和装饰为一体。所有构件都由包豪斯车间制作。

几种对比

形状对比：几何形与有机形，尖角与非尖角，曲线与直线，面与线，机械与自由，对称与非对称，美与丑，简单与复杂，抽象与具体，原形与变形，等等。

Various contrasts

Shapes: geometric/organic, angular/non-angular, curvilinear/rectilinear, planar/linear, mechanical/calligraphic, symmetrical/asymmetrical, beautiful/ugly, simple/complex, abstract/representational, undistorted/distorted, etc.

图1-4-3 史密特设计的“夏日田园”住宅大门，1921年

图1-4-4 阿尔贝斯设计的彩色镶嵌玻璃窗，1922年

1.4 The Bauhaus

“Bauhaus” is now a catchphrase, a style that is either hated or admired by many. But it also represents a breakthrough and new spirit at the turn of the 20th century. The methodologies and ideologies of its teaching staffs directly influenced many contemporary architectural educators and writers. As Gillian Naylor noted, “What is unique about the Bauhaus is the fact that its ideologies epitomize changing concepts concerning the nature and purpose of design in the early 20th century. The school inherited, reinterpreted and then rejected the craft ideals of the 19th century; it attempted to discover ‘laws’ in art that could be related to design and architecture, and its fundamental aim was to establish a universal language of form that would represent the elimination of social as well as national barriers.” [25]

The Bauhaus Manifesto (Pic.1-4-1), which set out the aims and program of the school and was published throughout Germany, was clearly visionary and revolutionary:

> *The ultimate aim of all creativity is the building! The decoration of buildings was once the noblest function of the fine arts, and the fine arts were indispensable to great architecture. Today they exist in complacent isolation, and can only be rescued from it by conscious co-operation and collaboration of all craftsmen…*
>
> *The old art schools were unable to produce this unity; and how, indeed, should they have done so, since art cannot be taught? Schools must be absorbed by the workshop again. The world of the pattern-designer and applied artist, consisting only of drawing and painting, must at last and again become a world in which things are built…*
>
> *Let us together desire, conceive and create the new building of the future, which will combine everything — architecture and sculpture and painting — in a single form which will one day rise towards the heavens from the hands of a million workers as the crystalline symbol of a new and coming faith.* [26]

It sounds not really novel if Renaissance Alberta’s school which united art, sculpture and architecture under one roof is still remembered. This Manifesto stressed on craftsmanship, and artists and architecture brought together to create the “building of the future”. For Gropius, it was through “building” that previously separate disciplines were reunited again. “Building” became the core of a social, intellectual and symbolic activity. (Pic.1-4-2)

It was Gropius’ original idea to pass on commissions from his architectural office into Bauhaus for design and production. Yet, this ideal of joint work on the “building”, the most important of the Bauhaus goals, proved to be difficult to implement in practice. However, with one rare opportunity, such a goal was almost realized. In 1920, Adolph Summerfield, a timber merchant and one of the first patrons of the school, commissioned Gropius to build a house from teak he had acquired from a dismantled ship. This house provided Marcel Breuer, Joust Schmidt and Josef Albers, three of the students who were to teach at the school, with the opportunity to carry out the commission, rather than experimental work. Breuer, who was a cabinet-maker, designed the furniture. Schmidt, trained as a sculptor, carved complex relieves on the staircases and doors, symbolized the activities of the timber industry (Pic.1-4-3). Albers, who was very sensitive and creative with materials, designed and prepared the stained-glass windows with abstract patterns (Pic.1-4-4). The carving, the windows, and the panelling of the interior all relate to that unity of

尺度对比：大与小，长与短，等等。
Size: big/small, long/short, etc.

色彩对比：明度对比，彩度对比，冷暖对比，等等。
Color: light/dark, brilliant/dull, warm/cool, etc.

质感对比：平滑与毛糙，精致与粗糙，纹理均匀与否，有无光泽，等等。
Texture: smooth/rough, fine/coarse, even/uneven, matte/glossy, etc.

图1-4-5 范·多斯堡设计的艺术之家模型，1923年

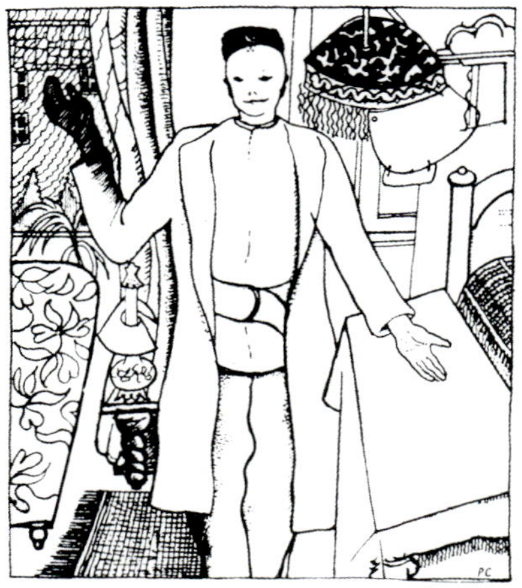

图1-4-6 莫希穿着伊藤设计的包豪斯长衫，1921年

格罗皮乌斯采用建筑师巴特宁的建议，由“房师议会”为首，下分学徒、雇工和房师三个层次，组成学校社会架构，较之现代学校中的“教授”和“学生”，包豪斯似乎更接近“巴艺”的传统。学生受教于造型房师和工艺房师。工艺车间分为雕塑、铁艺、家具、绘画及装饰、印刷和编织等。格罗皮乌斯和“房师议会”一起负责督察车间的教学成果和引入改革项目。开始时，新生可直接进车间工作，后因发现教学效果差，而且浪费材料，议会决定改由伊藤负责为新生上六个月的基础课，只有通过基础课训练的人才可以进入车间深造。[27]

六个月的基础课之后，接下来的三年里还有理论课，包括自然学、布艺、几何、色彩和构成，施工和表现，材料和工具等。[28]

尽管多斯堡从未执教于包豪斯，但作为“风格派”奠基人，他在1921年的魏玛举足轻重（图1-4-5），以至于格罗皮乌斯不得不明言禁止学生偷剪包豪斯定购的风格派杂志，但偷剪事件仍有发生。在风格派的影响下，学生将魏玛校舍礼堂的天花板和墙壁漆成不同颜色。[29] 尽管包豪斯思想与范·多斯堡的思想相似，但在多斯堡的著作和风格派作品清晰的形体构成的影响下，包豪斯发展出新的风格，[30] 主要表现在原形和原色成为设计的出发点，而不是设计的结果。

尽管几乎所有教师都由格罗皮乌斯聘请，但对于艺术一直存在两种看法，由此产生不少矛盾和动荡。以对早期包豪斯影响极大的伊藤为代表的艺术教师认为，艺术是调动学生内在创造性的动力，艺术是哲学，而技术是手段。而以格罗皮乌斯为首的建筑师认为，艺术存在于新技术和新材料当中，存在于学生思想之外。学生必须通过学习新功能、新材料、新建造方式，及其相关的学科才能设计现代建筑，而由此产生的建筑本身就是艺术品。这里，艺术是表现，而技术和科学才是思想。另一位现代大师柯布西耶完全反对以格罗皮乌斯为代表的德国建筑师的观点，他认为功能并不能直接产生美，艺术独行于实用之外。[31] 然而，格罗皮乌斯已决意把学校领向另外一个方向，这也是包豪斯教育模式出现问题的开始。其根本原因是意识形态的问题。

1922年伊藤离开学校，格罗皮乌斯为学校寻求一个新目标。实际上自第一次世界大战以后，德国一直面临资源短缺的问题，德国的研究部门和工业界开始寻找解决的办法，工业标准化便成为出路之一。包豪斯提出新的口号是“艺术与技术：一个全新结合”。[32] 这时期包豪斯的设计强调功能，形式必须随从功能。布劳耶设计了一套茶具，有茶壶、咖啡壶、奶杯和糖罐等，造型各不相同。他说：“既然每个用品满足我们的不同需要，造型和功能的结合就是我们的风格。完美的结合来自于最好地满足独特的功能。”[33] 在1924年莱比锡商业艺术交易会上，新包豪斯设计受到好评。

方向对比：90° 相交的两个方向对比最为强烈。两个不平行的形构成了明显的方向对比。方向对比用于创造一种不安的感觉。

Direction: any two directions meeting each other at an angle of 90 degrees are in maximum contrast. Two forms directly facing each other create a directional contrast of quite a different nature, because they are not unparalleled, although one of them has been rotated a full 180 degrees.
Contrasting directions are used to provoke agitation.

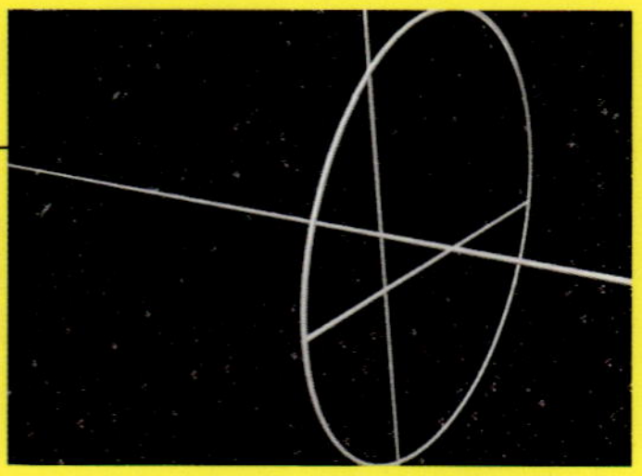

form, expression and decoration. All of the production was made in Bauhaus workshop.

For the structure of the school, Gropius adopted architect Otto Bartning's concept of a "Council of Masters", a preferred echo to the Beaux-Art system instead of using "Professors" and "students" in conventional academia. Here, a hierarchy of apprentice-journeyman-master was developed. Students were to be taught by both a Master of Form and Master of Craft. Different workshops for craft training were formed and could be categorized into sculpture, metal work, cabinet making, painting and decorating, printing and weaving. Both Gropius and the Council of Masters monitored the success and results of workshop training and regularly introduced reforms. For example, the original ruling allowing students to go straight into a workshop was proved to be ineffective and wasteful in materials. The Council of Masters therefore resolved to make Itten's six-month Basic Course compulsory for all entry students. Only students who successfully passed this course could go on to join a workshop. [27]

After the six-month Basic Course the students spent much of the next three years on theoretical work, including studies of nature, fabrics, geometry, colour and composition, constructions and presentations, materials and tools. [28]

Although he did not teach at Bauhaus, the arrival of van Doesburg, one in Weimar in 1921, had a profound influence on the school (Pic.1-4-5). As Droste noted, it even became necessary for Gropius to expressly forbid students from cutting out — as they frequently did — the illustrations from the de Stijl magazine to which the Bauhaus subscribed. The students even painted the ceiling and walls of the Weimar Residence theatre under de Stijl influence.[29] Droste further commented that although the ideas of the Bauhaus and van Doesburg were in many cases identical, van Doesburg's criticism and the clear, constructive forms of de Stijl products served to precipitate and accelerate the Bauhaus' move towards a new style. [30] One of the noted changes was the elementary form and primary colors became the starting-points for design.

Although almost all the teachers were brought together in Gropius' Bauhaus, there were apparently two definitions of art in the school which triggered conflicts and uncertainties. Itten, who was profoundly influential in the early stages of Bauhaus, represented the art teachers who believed art was the driving force behind students' internal creativity. Art was the philosophy, technology, only the medium with which to express it. Meanwhile the architects in the school led by Gropius believed art lay within the new technology and materials themselves, objectively existing outside the student's mind. Students had to learn functions, new materials and constructions and all related sciences to be able to recreate a modern building-as-art work. Here the opposite is emphasized: now art is the expression, technology and science, the philosophy. Le Corbusier, another modernist of the same period, strongly disagreed with Gropius, and other German masters by arguing that functionalism did not necessarily produce beauty, and that art was quite independent of utility. [31] However, Gropius determined to lead the school into anther direction, and so began the problems of Bauhaus as an educational model. The root cause was ideology.

In 1922, the year when Itten left Bauhaus, Gropius sought to give the school a new purpose and direction. In the years following the defeat in the First World War, Germany suffered from lack of essential imports of raw materials. German research and industry gradually concentrated on developing substitutes, and devising and promoting industrial standardization. Therefore, Bauhaus publicized a new slogan: "... art and technology, a new unity..." [32] Bauhaus design of this period was to address the question of function. Form had to be appropriate to its function. Marcel

位置对比：单元形按参考框架的两边安排，用于两组形之间的空间张力。常用的位置对比包括：上与下，高与低，左与右，中心与边缘。

Position: unit forms can be positioned towards opposite borders of the frame of reference, creating tension in between. Common positional contrasts are: top/bottom, high/low, left/right, central/off-centre.

图1-4-7 莫霍利-纳吉摄影作品《面具（自画像）》，1922年

图1-4-8 莫霍利-纳吉《光——空间协奏》，1922—1930年

但观念的变化，特别是要艺术服从工业遭到艺术教师的反对。佐尔格·莫希（图1-4-6）批评道："为工业设计造型，无须有创意的艺术家。形的产生不是通过艺术家对原形和原色的研究，而是来自机器运作。……艺术形体对工业产业来说属于异类。技术的垄断让艺术成为废物。"[34] 1926年莫希与上文提到的莫霍利-纳吉辞职（图1-4-7，图1-4-8）。但内部矛盾并没有因此而解决。格罗皮乌斯1927年在搬进德绍新校舍的一年后辞职。迈耶任校长，此时早期教师中只剩下现代艺术的两位大师康定斯基和阿尔贝斯了。

迈耶敌视所有画家，对他们主导包豪斯的工作十分反感。他始终认为包豪斯应成为一间技术学院。他开设了心理学、社会学和经济学课程。在设计学校里引进心理学家和社会学家，全由迈耶开始。[35] 当他刚到包豪斯任建筑系主任时，他便制定了教学工作的基本思路："我的教学思想是功能、协作和建造，就像ABC一样简单而重要。"[36] 他将包豪斯分为三个历史时期，第一期是在魏玛，在混乱中诞生；第二期是德绍的构成主义时期；第三期始自他任校长之后，包豪斯开始面对"所处地位和社会等真正问题"。[37] 至此包豪斯课程结构大变，建筑学的地位得到强化。但他并没有取消艺术课，他只是通过扩展课程内容以强化建筑学，并且开创了一个介于"科学目的"和"艺术表现"之间的方向。"艺术"一块以阿尔贝斯的基础课程为主。建筑成为科学部的最终课程，其他系最后不得不改变方向配合建筑系的要求。他的设计观点是："建筑是一种组织形式，是社会、技术、经济和心理的组织。"[38] 所以建筑被当成数据的收集计算，一个认真分析出来的结果。这时包豪斯的设计产品也改变了（图1-4-9）。作为包豪斯的建筑教师，迈耶的贡献在于奠定了系统化和科学化的现代教育基础，并在此基础上，他制定设计程序及在实践和理论教学中运用这套程序的方法。[39]

1930年迈耶被解雇，密斯·凡·德·罗被指派为包豪斯新校长。学校也缩小为一所普通建筑学校。在他的领导下，课程重新调整，艺术表现减至最少，心理学和社会学课程被取消，用密斯的话来说，代之以"手工、技术和艺术训练"（图1-4-10）。在此以前一直作为教学思想中心内容的"基础课程"不再作为必修课（图1-4-11）。学生可以不读"基础课程"而直接升入第二阶段，也无须先在手工艺车间积累经验，而直接进入建筑原理工作室。主要建筑课程有建筑法规、统计、采暖和通风、材料、数学和物理。[40]

原来在"房师议会"中的学生代表也被取消，决策权逐渐落在校长个人手中。教学上与一般技校无异，只是更为局限在现代技术内容。在失去往日的原创性和多向性之后，包豪斯变成一所职业培训学校，使其能够应对二战后大量的设计工作。

空间对比：正负形的叠合(减法)是一种创造空间对比的方法。交织的单元形推挤空间，形成张力。叠加的部分也可以处理为虚空，与实体相对比。

Space: the encounter of positive and negative unit forms (resulting in subtraction) is a way of producing spatial contrast. Space can be pushed and squeezed by unit forms which are thrust against each other. It can also be left void, in contrast with congested areas.

图1-4-9 迈耶设计的位于柏林附近的一所学校，1928年

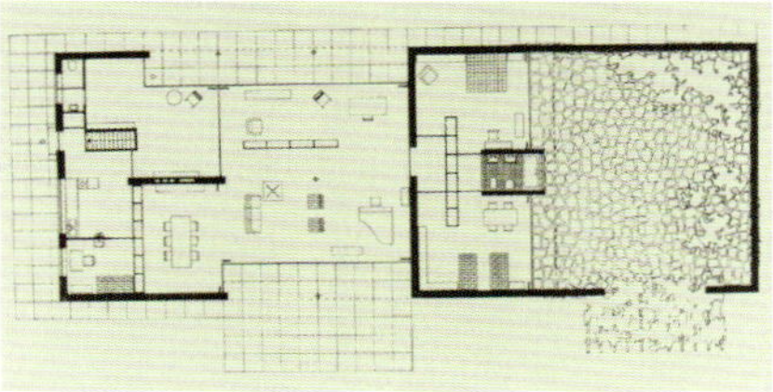

图1-4-10 学生的设计几乎是密斯风格的复制品，设计的主题是开放和封闭的和谐关系，1931年

图1-4-11 学生作业《网和木材垫合》，1930年

Breuer illustrated this principle with examples of a teapot, coffeepot, cream jug and sugar pot, which were completely different. They did not match each other at all. "Since each of them satisfies our requirements without disturbing the other, their combination creates our style. Their overall unity lies in their relatively best fulfilment of their specific functions." [33] This new Bauhaus design was favoured as it had a successful exhibition of its products in 1924 Leipzig trade fair for commercial art.

However, this change of ideology and penetration of art into industry caused much tension among the artist-teachers. Georg Muche (Pic.1-4-6), for example, criticized that "the creative artist was superfluous when it came to designing forms for industry. The form process started not from the elementary forms and primary colors investigated by the artists, but from the working of machine… The artistic form element is a foreign body in the industrial product. Technical requirements make art a useless extra."[34] In 1926, both Muche and Mogoly-Nagy resigned(Pic.1-4-7, Pic.1-4-8). Internal problems of the fundamental nature of the school continued, and Gropius suddenly announced his resignation in 1927, just a year after moving into the new school buildings in Dessau. Of the original staff members, only Kandinsky and Albers remained when Hannes Meyer took over the directorship.

Hannes Meyer was hostile to painters in general and the way they dominated the Bauhaus. He had always felt that the Bauhaus should have become a technical college. He grounded his course in psychology, sociology and economics. "This seems to be the first appearance in any school of design of psychologists and sociologists, entirely at Meyer's initiative. "[35] When he first arrived as Bauhaus' department head of architecture, he immediately laid down guidelines for his teaching activities: "the basic tendency of my teaching will absolutely be functional, collectivist, (and) constructive in the spirit of 'ABC' ".[36] He also noted that the history of the Bauhaus could be divided into three stages: first in Weimar, born out of chaos; the second formalistic phase in Dessau; and the third in Dessau under his leadership, during which the Bauhaus addressed "the real issues of life and society."[37] The program structure at Bauhaus was changed drastically to give architecture a more prominent position. However he never totally abandoned art instruction. He simply attempted to accentuate architecture by expanding the curriculum and by creating a division between a "scientifically objective" and "artistically expressive" direction. The program's "artistic" direction was derived from the Basic Course taught by Josef Albers. The architecture department represented the scientific arm of the program, and all other departments eventually had to orient themselves toward it. His vision of design was: "Building is nothing but organization: social, technical, economical, psychological organization."[38] Therefore, architecture was taught as more or less a collection and calculation of data, an automatic result of careful analysis. There was an obvious switch in the product of Bauhaus design at this stage(Pic.1-4-9). As DrOste noted, Meyer's most significant achievements as an architecture teacher of Bauhaus remain the systematic and scientific bases upon which he placed the design process and its implementation in practical and theoretical teaching. [39]

In 1930 when Meyer was dismissed and Mies van der Rohe was appointed as the new director of Bauhaus, the school had been reduced to a regular academy for architecture. Under his new leadership, the program was revised again with even less artistic expression than before. Psychology and sociology were eliminated from the curriculum and replaced, in Mies' words, by: 'handicraft, technical and artistic training' (Pic.1-4-10) .The Basic Course, which was still considered the ideological core of the training until then, was no longer mandatory(Pic.1-4-11).Students could by pass the Basic Course and, in the Second Stage, could enter directly into the Workshop on Principles of Building with no need to gain experience in the other craft workshops. They were taught construction law, statistics, heating and ventilation, materials, mathematics and physics.[40]

Further, student representation at the Council of Masters was no longer allowed. Final decision-making authority now rested chiefly with the director himself. Overall, teaching increasingly resembled other technical school, but here with narrow focus on modern technology. Losing of all its original creative and multi dimensional objectives, Bauhaus became a job-training school producing graduates who could cope with large design works which followed the Second World War.

图1-5-1 身穿自己设计的包豪斯长衫的约翰内斯·伊藤，1920年

1.5 约翰内斯·伊藤

约翰内斯·伊藤（图1-5-1）在20世纪建筑教育和现代艺术教育史中占有重要的地位。

伊藤出生于瑞士，1908年曾在首都伯尔尼做过小学教师，一年后去日内瓦学绘画。他对当时日内瓦的教育有过这样的回顾："最好的学生是那些模仿导师作品最逼真的学生。"但通过参加吉利亚德的课程，伊藤开始接触到形的几何元素及其对比关系，这成为他后来探索和大量运用到构成练习中的主题。

1913年至1916年，伊藤以斯图加特校外生的身份随导师阿道夫·霍泽尔学习。霍泽尔对伊藤的绘画和教学法影响极大。"他是一位对任何新事物极感兴趣的教师。"[41] 霍泽尔的课不仅有图面构成，而且包括色彩理论和运用原理。他开创了研究"先师"绘画方法，它不是对艺术史背景的分析或者学院式分析，而是对光影塑造、形体的表现力、情感的研究。[42] 伊藤曾说：

> *阿道夫·霍泽尔的课对我影响最大的是向先师学习的重要性。关于他们的工作方法的知识很有用。它告诉我图中的秩序和布局，对韵律和材料的感觉。如果没有谨慎的自我批评，这种学习可能变为发展的障碍，结果是学院式模仿。每次讨论形、韵律和色彩原理时，我都会要求学生分析有关的大师作品，让他们看到不同大师对同一问题的不同处理。*[43]

在霍泽尔的影响下，伊藤于1916年去维也纳开办了一所私立学校，霍泽尔还选送了一些学生到那里。在维也纳，伊藤进一步研究几何形、韵律感、比例问题和图式构成。1919年夏天，他的作品和教学引起了格罗皮乌斯的注意，伊藤应邀去包豪斯任教。

伊藤的"基础课程"是为新生开设的。当时他和格罗皮乌斯都认为这门课对启发对艺术感兴趣而天分还没有被调动起来的学生，强化他们的原创性十分重要。课程的目的是为学生以后的创作活动，如建筑、绘画、雕塑和产品设计打下良好的基础，让学生的天分表现出来，以便他们选择深造的方向。学生的性格和天分各有不同，伊藤的目的是激发每一个人的潜能，调动个人的主动性，建立来自本能的自信，培养创作原创作品所应有的创造力。所以他向格罗皮乌斯建议所有对艺术感兴趣的学生都应该学习这门课程六个月。格罗皮乌斯批准了这个建议而且放手让他组织教学。伊藤的教学不久成了包豪斯教育的核心，其影响范围之大甚至扩展到高年级的车间工作室。用他自己的话说，"基础课程"由三个中心内容组成：创造性、天分多样性和形的基本原理：

重量对比：单元形由高到低坠落，或由低到高堆积，暗示着重力的作用。稳定与不稳定、静态与动态，或是沉重与轻盈的单元形放在一起，形成重量对比。

Gravity: unit forms dropping from high to low positions, or stacking from low to high positions, can suggest a gravitational pull. Stable and unstable unit forms, static and moving unit forms, or heavy and light unit forms can be put together in effective contrast of gravity.

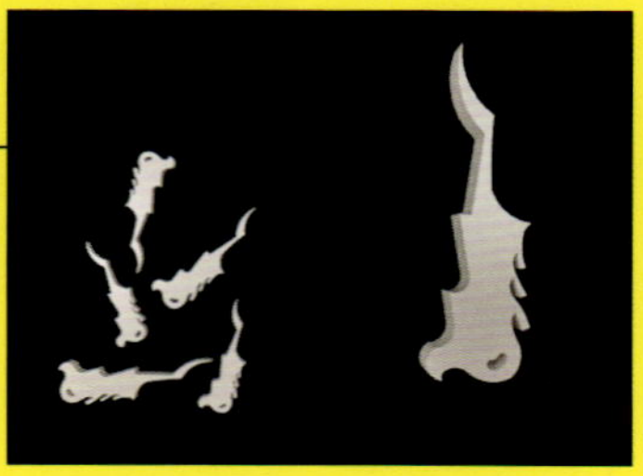

1.5 Johannes Itten

Johannes Itten (Pic.1-5-1) remains the most significant figure in history of both architectural education and modern art education in the 20th century.

Itten was born in Switzerland, trained as an elementary school teacher in Berne. He began teaching children in 1908, and after one year, went to study painting in Geneva. As Itten recalled the trend of education in Geneva at this time, "The star students were those who made the best job of copying their professors." However, through a course run by Professor Gilliard, Itten was introduced to the geometrical elements of form and their contrast, a theme that Itten continued to explore and utilise extensively in his composition exercises later on.

Between 1913 and 1916, Itten became an extramural student of Adolf Hoelzel at Stuttgart Academy. It was Hoelzel who had strong impact on Itten's painting approach and teaching methods. Naylor credited him as a "teacher receptive to anything that was new". [41] The main subject of study in Hoelzel's class was more than pictorial composition, but also on the principles of the theory and practice of color. He initiated studies of "old master" paintings, not within the context of art historical or academic analysis, but as expressions of form, as well as emotion, demonstrated through light and shade. [42] As Itten noted:

> *Adolf Hoelzel's Stuttgart lectures impressed me profoundly with the importance of the study of the Old Masters. Knowledge of their working method is useful. It heightens the awareness of order and disposition in the picture area and the feeling for rhythm and texture. This study can be an obstacle to development and do damage, but only in the absence of a watchful self-criticism, without which only academic copying can be achieved. Each time principles of form, rhythm, or color had been discussed, I asked my students to analyze relevant masterpieces to make them see how different masters solved a given problem.* [43]

Itten must have impressed Hoelzel with his Work as when he moved to Vienna in 1916 and set up a private school, Hoelzel also sent some students over there. During his time in Vienna, Itten spent more time in the study of geometrical and rhythmical forms, problems of proportion and of expressive pictorial composition. In the summer of 1919, Itten's work and teaching caught the attention of Gropius and was invited to teach at bauhaus.

The Vorkurs, or "Basic Course" as Itten called it, was developed for the new students entering into Bauhaus, as Itten, and Gropius at that time, were convinced that it was important to inspire those students interested in art but whose talents were still dormant, and to enhance their originality. The purpose of the exercise was to creating a common basis for different areas of activity—such as architecture, painting, sculpture and product design, and to recognize talent of students and indicate the direction that a student should take in later studies. As every student had different temperaments and talents, Itten tried to help opening up each individual's potentialities, evoking an individual response, and acquiring a natural self-confidence through developing a creative atmosphere conducive to original work. When he suggested to Gropius that all students who showed an interest in art should be provisionally accepted for a six-month term, Gropius agreed and granted him a completely free hand in its arrangement and content. Itten's teaching soon became the backbone of Bauhaus education. Its influence was also to extend to activities in the workshops. In his own words, the Basic Course presented Itten with three core subjects: creativity, diversity of talent

A–11 统一的对比

对比有可能产生混乱、骚动和不稳定，因此需要与其他形式美的原则，如控制、重点、等级等结合运用，才能产生明确和统一的效果。

"我的构图原理本质上就是关于对比的一般理论。明暗对比，材料与质感的研究，形与色的理论，节奏与形的表现，都从对比的角度进行探讨。探索对比的各种可能性是最有意义的课题之一，学生需要从三个方向来理解对比：亲身感觉、物化感觉、综合实现。"（Itten, 1963）

图1-5-2 伊藤的课前操

图1-5-3 伊藤课程练习：形和韵律

1．释放学生的创造力和艺术天分。他们的体验和感知应体现于真正的作品中，由此逐渐摆脱陈规陋习的束缚，获得创作自己作品的勇气。

2．方便学生选择职业。有关材料和质感的练习很有用，要求每个学生很快找到自己最亲切、对自己最有启发的材料，如木、金属、玻璃、石头、陶泥或者编织料。

3．向未来以艺术为专业的学生介绍创造性构成的原理。让学生掌握客观世界的形和色的规律。在工作中以不同方式运用关于形和色的主观和客观的规律。[44]

伊藤的上午课先从“放松”“深呼吸”和“集中注意力”等体操练习开始（图1-5-2），为接下来的大量工作做好精神和肉体准备。[45] 这种节律操也是他从他的老师霍泽尔那里搬过来的，他认为对于有创造力的人来说，体质训练和创造性思维训练同样重要。他说：“我们思考或从事日常生活节奏是和呼吸同步的。在生活中成功的人往往呼吸平稳、缓和，但深入肺腑。呼吸急促的人往往思考和行为也草率急躁。通过练习让学生呼吸平和而深厚，当然练习的效果取决于思想是否集中。”[46]

有评论家指出伊藤的哲学根基来自19世纪的浪漫主义和战前表现主义，表现主义主张经验和表现的融合，[47] 融合需要精神与物质体验同步。如画一个圈之前，学生要体验伸直胳膊在空中前后甩膀子时的感觉（图1-5-3）。画老虎，要先学虎吼。写“怒”字要比写“甜”字下笔重，刚直有力。[48] 他要求学生通过一系列行为，如抚摸、把握、扭曲、对比不同材料，然后根据感觉来画，加深对材料质素的认识。他们用捡来的材料制成拼贴或者无主题的雕塑（图1-5-4）。这些练习让学生直观地了解材料，从而懂得材料。[49] “在深入讨论任何问题时，我总把握住经验—感知—实践能力这条线索。”[50]

伊藤的教学法，可以概括为两个对立面：直觉和方法，或者叫主观经验和客观认知。[51] 发现韵律，协调构成不同的韵律是他的课中经常性的主题，其中分成三个不同研究对象：自然物体和材料、先师作品和人体写生。

研究材料和自然物体的目的是明确不同材料的本质和对比关系，那种儿童时期形成的对物体的感觉通过练习变得成熟，变得敏锐。[52] 练习之外，伊藤也讲授对比、形和色彩理论（图1-5-5）。对比不仅包括粗细、锐钝、软硬等，还包括对材料的感觉。“学生应该从三个方面入手，用感官来体验，用智慧来理解，用综合能力来重组（图1-5-6，图1-5-7）”，[53] 伊藤的形的理论包括基本的几何形，如圆、方、三角等，而且每个形都有一种性格，如圆代表“流畅”和“中心”，方代表“平静”，三角代表“倾斜”。

United Contrast

Contrast may create chaos, turbulence and unstability. To make a contrast clear and unite, some other aesthetical principles may applied, such as Dominance, Emphasis and Hierarchy.

“The basis of my theory of composition was the general theory of contrast. The chiaroscuro (brightness-darkness) contrast, the material and texture studies, the theory of forms and colors, the rhythm and the expressive forms were discussed and demonstrated in terms of their contrast effect. Finding and listing the various possibilities of contrast was always one of the most exciting subjects, was opening up to them. … The students had to approach the contrasts from three directions: they had to experience them with their senses, objectivize them intellectually, and realize them synthetically.” (Itten, 1963)

and basic principles of form:

To liberate the creative forces and thereby the artistic talents of the students: Their own experiences and perceptions were to result in genuine work. Gradually, the students were to rid themselves of all the dead wood of convention and acquire the courage to create their own work.

To make the students' choice of career easier: Here, exercises with materials and textures were a valuable aid. Each student quickly found the material with which he felt the closest affinity; it might have been wood, metal, glass, stone, clay or textiles that inspired him most to create work.

To present the principles of creative composition to the students for their future careers as artists. The laws of form and color opened up to them the world of objectivity. As the work progressed it became possible for the subjective and objective problems of form and color to interact in many different ways. [44]

图1-5-4 不同材料的对比效果

图1-5-5 明暗对比练习

Itten's morning classes usually began with "relaxation-, breathing-, and concentration exercises(Pic.1-5-2) to establish the intellectual and physical readiness, which make intensive work possible," .[45] Again, this "eurhythmic" exercise was something Itten adopted from his teacher Hoelzel. He was convinced that the training of the physical body was as important as the creative mind to a creative person. "As we breathe, so we think and conduct the rhythm of our daily routine. People who have achieved great success in their lives always breathe quietly, slowly and deeply. Those who are short of breath are hasty and greedy in their thoughts and actions. By means of breathing exercises I tried to train my students to breathe quietly and more deeply. All these exercises achieve their proper effect only if they are carried out with thought concentration."[46]

Naylor remarked that Itten's philosophy, at its most basic level, was an extension of 19th century Romanticism and pre-war Expressionism, in that it demanded a fusion between experience and expression.[47] This fusion was achieved through relating the spiritual to physical experience. Before drawing a circle, for example, the students had to experience a circle by stretching, swinging their arms together in opposite directions (Pic.1-5-3). Before drawing tigers, they roared like tigers. The word "anger" was written in a heavier, less rounded hand than the word "sweetness".[48] Students were asked to "absorb" the qualities of materials by touching, handling, blending, contrasting and drawing from memory. "Found" materials were used to create montages, collages and bizarre structure(Pic.1-5-4) .These exercises were meant to provide a "sensuous" appreciation of the qualities of materials that would lead to understanding.[49] "When discussing any subject in depth I always maintained the principle of experience—perception—practical ability." [50]

The pedagogical principle on which Itten's teaching was based can be summarized in a pair of opposites: intuition and method, or subjective experience and objective recognition.[51] The discovery of rhythm and the harmonious composition of different rhythms were among the recurring themes of his classes, which were divided into three main areas: studies of natural objects and materials, the analysis of Old Masters and life drawing.

The purpose of studying materials and natural objects was "to bring clearly to light the essential and contradictory within each material", and thus to develop and refine his pupils' feeling for materials.[52] In parallel with such studies, Itten also taught theories of contrast, form and color, which was a preparation for workshop activities(Pic.1-5-5) .Contrasts included, for example, not only rough-smooth, pointed-blunt, hard-soft, etc., but also a feeling for materials. "The students had to approach the contrasts from three directions: they had to experience them with their senses, objective them intellectually, and realize them synthetically (Pic.1-5-6, Pic.1-5-7) ."[53] Itten's theory of form

A-12 变化

在重复的单元中加入不同的单元，或者对同一单元做少量的改变，而不影响单元特征和整体性。

Variation

Adding some different elements or small changes of existing elements without changes of the character of the whole composition.

图1-5-6 明暗反转构成

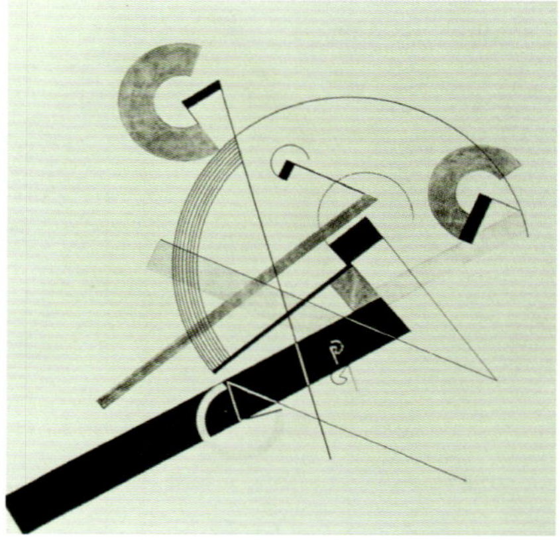

图1-5-7 线形构成

分析先师作品取自他的老师霍泽尔。分析的目的是感受艺术作品中的基本要素（图1-5-8）。人体写生以女性裸体为主，研究韵律。

作为“房师”，伊藤为学生所崇拜。他从维也纳带来的学生们还自发组织了一个团体。青年画家佐尔格·莫希1920年加入包豪斯以减轻伊藤的工作量，他融入伊藤的圈子，并成为伊藤的朋友和崇拜者。他的一个学生这样说：

> *伊藤有一种魔力，作为教师他要么被崇拜，要么被他的敌对者（而且很多）所憎恨，但谁也不能无视他的存在。在我们这个包豪斯的小圈子里，他代表一种光辉。你甚至可称他为圣人（图1-5-9）。他的出现总让我们鸦雀无声，而我们对他无比尊敬。一旦他如朋友般轻松地和我们在一起，我们是那样兴奋，完全被他所吸引。*[54]

在早期资金有限，设备缺乏的包豪斯，伊藤的“基础课程”被认为是“智慧的凯歌”。正如评论家所说：“在这短短的四年中（1919—1923），他的教学手法和对创造性的关注在学校的计划中加入了不确定性，这是对格罗皮乌斯明确自我主张意向的挑战，从根本上动摇了官僚们形成表面的秩序和方向性的要求。”[55] 课程也从此打破了艺术学院里只画静物，如石膏像、装饰品和人体的传统。在那里学生只能模仿技巧，而伊藤则教授色彩和形的理论，构成的创造性设计方法。他的教育直达学生内心深处，帮助他们找到自己的节奏，发展自己的和谐个性。

二战后，伊藤在瑞士苏黎世继续从事教学工作。他的有关色彩理论、形的构成原理等方面的著作被翻译成不同文字（包括中文），在世界各地的设计和艺术学校里被广泛采用。由格罗皮乌斯带到美国的包豪斯资料没有全面反映伊藤的贡献。他注重个人创造性和设计的原创性的教学思想对当今的后工业社会教育极具现实意义。

图1-5-8 伊藤的学生根据14世纪画家乔托的《圣安娜的烦恼》做的练习

图1-5-9 1920年伊藤设计的“白人住宅”方案

took the elementary geometric shapes of circle, square and triangle and each shape was assigned to a certain character. Hence, circle was “flowing” and “central”, the square “calm” and the triangle “diagonal”.

“Analysis of Old Masters”, an exercise which Itten adopted from his master Adolf Hoelzel. The theme of this analysis was to experience works of art in their profoundness (Pic.1-5-8). The life drawing was usually female nude studies, which concentrated upon rhythm.

As a “Master”, Itten was greatly revered by his students. The original students he brought with him from Vienna at the beginning of Bauhaus years formed an influential group at the Bauhaus. The young painter, Georg Muche, who joined the Bauhaus teaching staff in 1920 to relieve Itten’s workload, also attached himself to Itten’s circle and became his friend and admirer. As one of his students Paul Citroen described:

> *Itten had something demonic about him. As a Master, he was either profoundly admired or, by his opponents (of whom there were many), equally profoundly hated. Whatever else, it was impossible to ignore him. For those of us within the Mazdaznan circle — a special community within the Bauhaus — Itten had a very special aura. You could almost call him saint(Pic.1-5-9); his presence practically reduced us to whispers, and our respect for him was overwhelming. Should he treat us in a friendly and relaxed manner, we would be enraptured and inspired.* [54]

Itten’s Basic Course was considered as “a triumph of ingenuity” with the limited resources and lack of facilities of Bauhaus had in its early years. Itten taught at Bauhaus from its conception in 1919 till 1923. As Naylor commented, “during those four years his (Itten’s) approach to teaching and his conception of creativity reinforced the ambiguities of the school’s program, challenging Gropius’ attempts both to clarify his own priorities, and at the most basic level, to establish some semblance of the order and direction required by the bureaucrats.”[55] The course was also innovative that it broke away from the teaching at conventional art academies where only set objects such as plaster figures, ornaments and nudes were drawn. Students thus acquired most of their skills through copying. Itten, on the other hand, taught his students the fundamentals of colour and form theory, composition and design. His teaching, aimed at the inner being of the students, helped them to find their own rhythm and develop a well-tuned personality.

Itten remained active in teaching after the Second World War in Zurich, Switzerland. His books on colour theory, principles of composition of form and design have been translated into many languages, including Chinese, and widely used in design and art school worldwide. Itten’s Bauhaus was overshadowed by Gropius’s Bauhaus after the War. Itten’s teaching philosophy focused much more on personal creativity and design originality than Gropius. These qualities are extremely significant in current education of post-industrial society. They remain treasures to be rediscovered.

B-1 点

点标志着空间中的位置，它没有长度、宽度或深度，因此是静态、无方向性和中心化的。
点被置于可视区域时，可以被感知。如果把点放置在所处环境的中心，点是静态和安定的，并成为区域内的统治因素，组织起周围的元素。两个以上突出于环境的点创造出张力或运动。

图1-6-1 阿尔贝斯自画像，1917年

图1-6-2 阿尔贝斯《人体》，1921年

图1-6-3 阿尔贝斯课上的报纸剪贴练习，1931年

1.6 约瑟夫·阿尔贝斯

和伊藤一样，约瑟夫·阿尔贝斯原是小学教师。1913年辞职，入柏林皇家艺术学校学习，准备毕业后当中学美术教师。两年后在小学重执教鞭，同时兼读埃森应用艺术学校课程。他花了一年半时间在慕尼黑参加佛朗兹·施图克的绘画班。他这时期的自画像（图1-6-1）和雕塑作品明显受到表现主义、慕尼黑装饰艺术和布鲁克绘画小组的影响。但阿尔贝斯一直努力走一条与表现主义不同的道路，他说：“我不相信表现主义是艺术的动力和目的。”[56]

受包豪斯的将艺术与工艺相结合的课程吸引，1920年阿尔贝斯来到包豪斯求学，想成为一名画家。1923年他成为包豪斯首位留校任教的学生。他做“房师”直到1933年移居美国。在这期间他开始发展自己的艺术主题和表现。施皮斯在《阿尔贝斯》一书中作过这样的记载：

> *读完伊藤的六个月课程之后，阿尔贝斯被安排入壁画班，而他自己却想入玻璃车间。他不顾学校安排独自做玻璃工艺，他拿起玻璃钳和锤子，捡垃圾里的碎玻璃开始工作。格罗皮乌斯对他说，你要么学壁画，要么离开包豪斯。六个月过去了，阿尔贝斯展示了他的玻璃作品（图1-6-2），他以为这是他在包豪斯的最后一件作品，没想到却收到房师议会的一封信，不仅要他留下来，而且要他来重组包豪斯的玻璃车间。*[57]

阿尔贝斯对材料的兴趣在1928年执教基础课程之后更趋强烈。他以反常的方法探索材料的应用，极力反对材料处理的个性化。[58] 在之前伊藤的课上，学生可以选用任何材料。而阿尔贝斯则要求学生在某些阶段只能研究和试验几种材料，如玻璃、纸、金属、草、波形纸板和铁丝网等（图1-6-3），在其他阶段研究材料的组合，从而获得对这些材料的理解和经验。阿尔贝斯认为：“材料的运用应该避免产生任何废料，即经济性是首要原则。形应该体现材料剪裁和折叠后表现出的张力（图1-6-4）。”[59] “如果一个形体中仅有某些部分有用，这说明计算出现了错误，或者形中的偶然性无法解释，无法证明。进一步说，由习惯导致的结果是没有意义的。”[60] 用减法而不是加法来做设计的思想，与密斯的“少即多”的观点一样。用最少的东西获得最大效果，虽然表现形式不同，却是阿尔贝斯终生的研究方向。

通过从材料到形的变化，阿尔贝斯的练习让学生开发“建构思想”和“空间的想象”。他说：“最佳的学习方法是个人的经验，试验比学习更重要。”[61] 在基础课程中他指导的学生作品表现出对材料处理的高度想象力（图1-6-5）。形的塑造直接来自对材料的质素和潜力的研究，而且他主张对材料的建构而不是表现——成果来自自我约束，而不是自我表现。在学生的试验建构过程中，每个决定都需要有依据，即他常说的“对我们自己，对材料和对工作都要负责，要自

Point

A point marks a position in space. Conceptually, it has no length, width, or depth, and is, therefore, static, directionless, and centralized.
A point makes its presence felt when placed within a visual field. At the center of its environment, a point is stable and at rest, organizing surrounding elements about itself and dominating its field. More than two points distinguished from the context can create tension or movement among them.

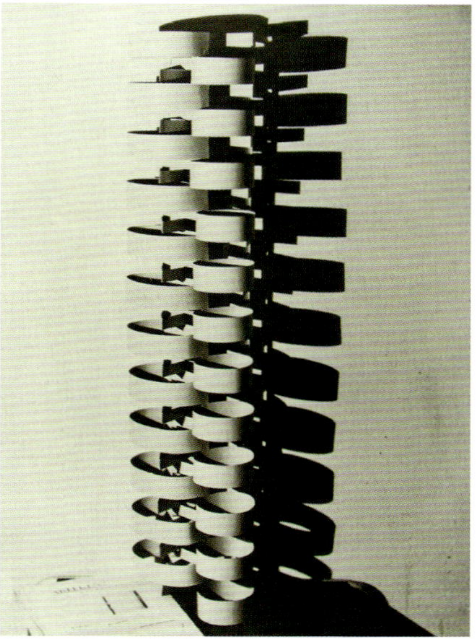

图1-6-4 1928年阿尔贝斯课上的纸造型，经过精心地设计和剪裁，纸张没有一点浪费

图1-6-5 学生作品《梳子和乒乓球》，时间早于1938年

1.6 Josef Albers

Josef Albers, like Itten, began his career life as an elementary school teacher. In 1913, he interrupted his career and attended the Royal Art School in Berlin to be trained as an art teacher at secondary schools. But after two years, he resumed his elementary school position and at the same time took courses at the School of Applied Arts in Essen. He spent another eighteen months in the painting class of Franz Stuck in Munich. His self-portraits (Pic.1-6-1) and other woodcut works at this time were most evident of the influence of expressionism as well as of the graphic art of Munch and the painters of the Brucke group. However, Albers always strove to break away and develop a different approach to expressionism: “And I very much distrust expression as a driving force as well as an aim in art.” [56]

Albers was attracted by the Bauhaus program, which aimed at the union of arts and crafts. In 1920, he entered Bauhaus as a student and hoped to be a painter. Instead, he later became the first of the Bauhaus students to become a “master” in 1923, and continued in this position until 1933 when he immigrated to the United States. It was in Bauhaus where Albers started to develop his own theme and expression of arts. As Spies wrote:

> *After the first six-month term with Itten he was supposed to enter the class for wall painting while he himself preferred to get into the glass workshop. He disregarded his assignments and occupied himself with working with glass. He took a knapsack and hammer and collected fragments of bottles and glass in rubbish dups. During this term Gropius reminded him of his obligation to devote himself exclusively to the study of wall painting since otherwise he would have to leave the Bauhaus. At the end of the second six-months term there was an exhibition at which Albers showed various studies in glass (Pic.1-6-2): “I thought that this would be my swan song at the Bauhaus.” But instead he received a letter from the Council of Masters, in which he was admitted to further study and even asked to reorganize the glass workshop of the Bauhaus.* [57]

Albers’ interest in the study of materials was further emphasized after taking over the teaching of Basic Course in 1928. Here, Albers explored various applications of materials in an unorthodox manner, and “he depersonalized a working material to the extreme.”[58] Previously, when Itten was teaching the course, students were permitted to work with any materials they wished during the class. Now, the class was re-formatted and students had to explore and experiment with specific materials (glass, paper, metal, straw, corrugated cardboard, wire mesh, etc.) at certain stage (Pic.1-6-3) , and a combination of different materials at another stage, so that they had a thorough understanding and working experience with these materials. Albers believed that “materials must be worked in such a way that there is no wastage: the chief principle is economy. The final form arises from the tensions of cut and folded material(Pic.1-6-4).” [59] “If in a form there is something that is not utilized, then the calculation has been wrong, for coincidence then plays a part and that is unjustified and unjustifiable. Moreover, it is senseless because it usually results from habit.”[60] The idea of design with reductions instead of with additions, echo to Mies’s point of “less is more”. This idea of achieving maximum effect with minimum of means turned out to be his life-long search through various forms of expression.

Through Albers’s exercises, students were encouraged to develop “constructive thinking” and “spatial imagination” through the transformation of material into form. Albers wrote: “The best education is one’s own experience. Experimenting surpasses study.” [61] The works created by his students under his guidance in the Basic Course were

B–2 线

人们将长度远远大于宽度的形认知为线。线可以用来连接、支撑、包围，或切断其他视觉元素，可以描绘面的边界，赋予面形状。线能够在视觉上表现方向、运动、和增长。
线可以指向任意方向，可以是几何形，也可以是非几何形。

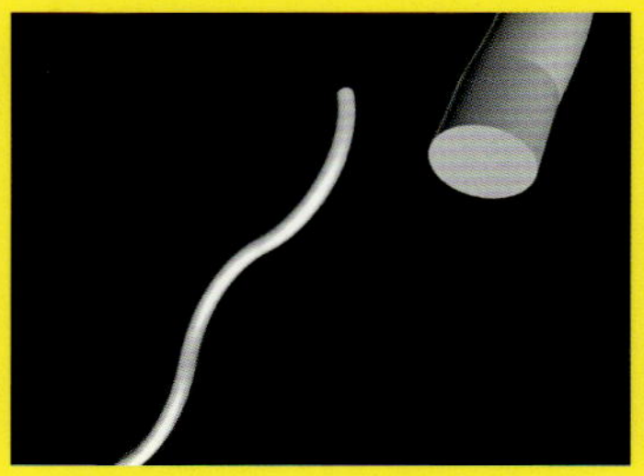

制。”[62] 对材料极限的长期关注也是密斯的建筑设计特点。尽管在密斯领导下的包豪斯，基础课程不再是必修课，作为艺术教师的阿尔贝斯仍使包豪斯有别于其他的技术学校。

除了大量的关于材料研究和材料极限测试之外，阿尔贝斯也从事对二维空间感知的研究。他自己的作品体现“看”和“感知”的复杂关系。在1931年作品《台阶》（图1-6-6）中，他改变了观者视觉：在背景中的台阶看起来在前景，台阶看似向下，实际却向上。这里没有确定的图像，不同的视觉无优劣之分。施皮斯对这件作品有这样的评述：

> *阿尔贝斯通过加入互不兼容的矛盾的解象给观众一个不确定性。观者一直受此困扰，不知哪种解象更好。也许暂时喜欢一个而试图努力注意它。而这种注意一旦消失，画面又给他另一个不确定的结构。看画的踌躇不决，感知的游移动荡正是此画的真正含义。*[63]

在后来的另一幅作品《结构星座》（1957）（图1-6-7）中，阿尔贝斯不仅挑战人的视觉，而且挑战对感知内容的理解和解释。观者看到的是层次和空间。所见与所释不停地转换，而这种复杂效果却是以简单而节制的手法获得。在这些作品中，阿尔贝斯让观者自己开发“看”的经验，从而产生启迪心智的效果。

阿尔贝斯还用色彩叠加和色彩造型研究视觉感知。他的耶鲁大学教科书《色彩互动》概括了他的色彩理论。与伊藤的色彩理论不同，阿尔贝斯更关注色彩心理和视觉训练。书中介绍了他课上的练习。学生通过不断试验，经历和学习实际颜色与心理颜色之间的关系和差别。练习的内容包括图底转换、色彩密度、色彩形象、补色、透明感、层次强化和边界消失等。阿尔贝斯不是机械地传授知识，而是启发空间感知（图1-6-8）。他的作品《对方形的敬意》（图1-6-9）也许正完整地概括了他终生研究、试验和教学的成果。

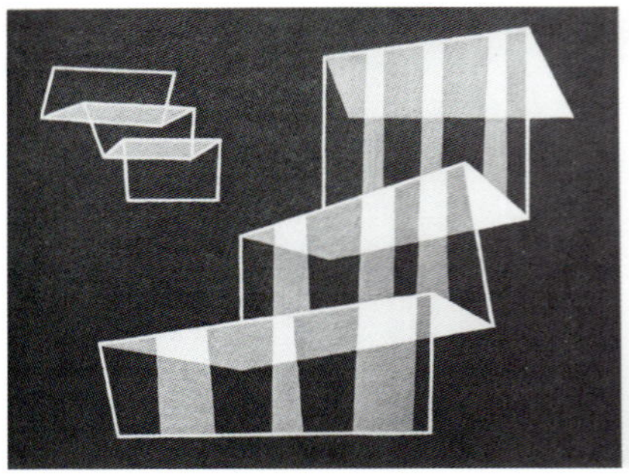

图1-6-6 阿尔贝斯《台阶》，1931年

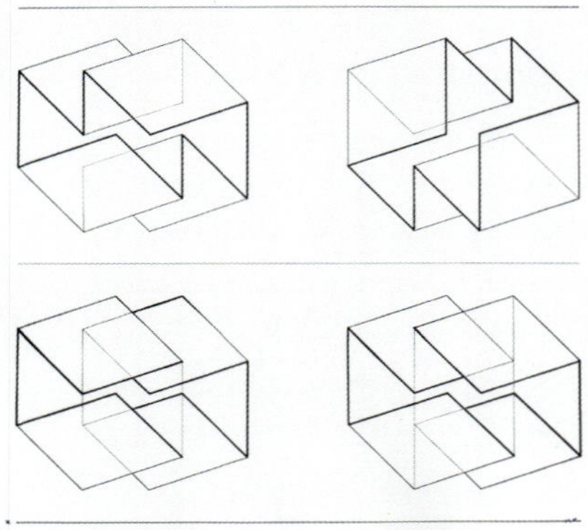

图1-6-7 阿尔贝斯《结构星座》，1957年

图1-6-8 阿尔贝斯《俄克拉何马城的砖墙》，1963年

Line

A form is recognized as a line because either its breadth is extremely narrow, or its length is quite prominent. A line can serve to join, link, support, surround, or intersect other visual elements; describe the edges of, and give shape to, planes; and to articulate the surfaces of planes. A line is capable of visually expressing direction, movement, and growth.
A line can be geometrical or non-geometrical, towards any direction.

图1-6-9 阿尔贝斯《对方形的敬意》，1959年

distinguished by an exceedingly imaginative handling of the material (Pic.1-6-5). The approach to form was based on the exploration of the qualities and potential of materials — and Albers emphasized on the constructive rather than the expressive nature of materials, and results were achieved through self-discipline rather than self-expression. Justification was needed for every decision and process involved in the students' experimental constructions, since this encouraged "responsibility and self-discipline — towards ourselves, the material and the work."[62] Consistently focusing on the limits of materials and pushing these limits to extreme were, not coincidentally, characteristic of Miesian architecture. Although the basic course was not the compulsory in Mies's Bauhaus, Albers remained an active teacher of art, which was complementary to the otherwise very technical school.

Apart from doing extensive and exhaustive studies on different materials and testing on their limits, Albers was also preoccupied with investigations in perceptual and spatial problems with two-dimensional means. Some of his work demonstrated this complicated method of "seeing" and "perceiving". In his *Steps* (1931) (Pic.1-6-6), Albers fooled the observer's perception: what seems to be in the background steps forward, what seems to descend, actually ascends. There is no definitive illustration, and not one interpretation is any better than the other. As Spies commented on this work,

> *Albers provokes in the spectator an uncertainty by superimposing contrary interpretations, which are mutually exclusive. The spectator remains uncertain — he is incapable of deciding in favor of one interpretation or the other. He may momentarily prefer one and may make an effort to concentrate on it. But as soon as this concentration diminishes, the picture offers him further, indecisive structures. This vacillating attempts to read the picture, the uncertainty and turbulence of perception — that is the actual content of the illustration.* [63]

In a later example, *Structural Constellations* (1957) (Pic.1-6-7), Albers challenged not only the observer's seeing, but also his understanding and interpretation of what was perceived. The observer reads the drawings between his perception of level surfaces and perception of space. Seeing and understanding alternated consistently, and this effect was achieved with simple and restrictive means. In these works, Albers insisted the observer to develop his "seeing" experiences into experiences of himself, which in turn, produced an intellectual and psychological effect.

Albers continued to play with this visual perception theme by using, juxtaposing and forming different colors. In his book *Interaction of Color* , a textbook he used in his teaching at Yale University, summarizes his theory of color. In contrast to Itten's teaching on color theory, Albers taught more on the psychology of color and visual training than actual color theory. The book introduces exercises Albers used in his class. Through various experiments, students experienced and learnt the conflict between the physical reality and psychic effect of colors. Themes such as inverse background, color intensity, after-images, simultaneous contrasts, illusion of transparency, enforced contours, vanishing boundary, etc. were introduced and discussed. Here, Albers did not teach the mechanism of knowledge, but helped one to develop an understanding of spatial perception (Pic.1-6-8). Albers' *Homage to the Square* (Pic.1-6-9) probably is the best example to summarize all the quests and achievements, experiments and teachings which Albers sought after in his career life.

B-3 面

在二维平面上，非点非线的平面形便被认知为面。面可能有各种各样的形状：几何形、有机形、线形、不规则形、曲线形、随机形。在视觉构成中，面用于定义空间或体积的边界。

Plane

A form is recognized as all flat forms that are not commonly recognized as points or lines on a two-dimensional surface. It may have a variety of shapes: geometric, organic, rectilinear, irregular, curling, or accidental.
In the formation of a visual construction, a plane serves to define the limits or boundaries of a space or a volume.

练习四　空间和实体：加法和减法

目的：

建筑构成包含两种基本元素：空间和实体。一个三维的划分成4×4×4的立方体空间可以理解为由一组1×1×1的小型立方体组成。立方体的间隔分布，在其间形成小型立方体空间。这个练习集中训练我们空间造型最基本的方法：加法和减法。

方法：

1. 立方体模型的尺寸是16厘米×16厘米×16厘米。概念上划分为4×4×4网格，用木条框定一半的空间。

2. 用卡纸做至少32个立方体（4厘米×4厘米×4厘米），如儿童积木，在模型内搭出不同空间和实体效果。用已掌握的构成原理来分析和研究不同的组合方式。通过加进或者取出一些立方体研究不同的视觉效果。

3. 从中选出一种“最佳”的组合方式，用胶水将小立方体和模型底板固定在一起。

注意事项：

1. 这个简单的练习是图底转换在三维空间中的运用。立方体是空间中的“图形”，同时又是形成“底”的空间的元素。

2. 构成的视觉整体感来自概念网格和统一尺寸的立方体。在制作和比较不同的组合方式的同时，练习的目的是不断强化整体感和个性。

3. “空间”不是画出来的，而是做出来的。“做”的动作包括插入、抽取、叠加、挖空和元素之间黏合。

工具和材料：

1. 白色卡纸；
2. 模型用木条；
3. 做底板用的瓦楞纸；
4. 刀具和胶水。

成果：

一个16厘米×16厘米×16厘米的立方体模型。

Exercise 4. SPACE AND VOLUME: ADDITION AND SUBTRACTION

Objective:

All buildings consist of two basic elements: space and volume, or void and solid. A three-dimensional cube space based on a 4×4×4 grid is reinterpreted by a set of small cube elements, the volume. Organization of these elements creates the spaces in between. We will deal with the basic skills of making forms in the space: addition and subtraction.

Methods:

1.The model occupies a cubic volume measuring 16cm×16cm ×16cm. It is conceptually divided into a 4×4×4 grid. Half of the space is framed with wood rods.

2.Make 32 cube elements (4cm×4cm ×4cm), or more, with cardboard. Playfully arrange the cube elements within the model space and study the effect of form and space. Use the principles of visual quality learned in the previous exercise to evaluate each variation. We can add or reduce a few cube elements and test the result.

3.Choose a “best variation” from several variations and make a final object by gluing the cube elements firmly to each other and fixing them on a baseboard.

Notes:

1.With this simple exercise we learn about the figure and ground effect in three-dimensional design: the cubes are figures in the space, and at same time they frame and surround the background spaces.

2.The visual quality of unity and wholeness of the composition is made with aid of the grid and the standardized cube elements. Our effort is to enhance such unity-making, comparing and evaluating different variations.

3.Space is made by actions, not by drawing. The actions here are insertion, subtraction, addition, excavation, element edge-tracing.

Tools and materials:

1.White cardboard;
2.Wooden sticks;
3.Corrugated paper panels;
4.Knife and glue.

Presentation:

One model within the maximum dimensions of 16cm×16cm×16cm.

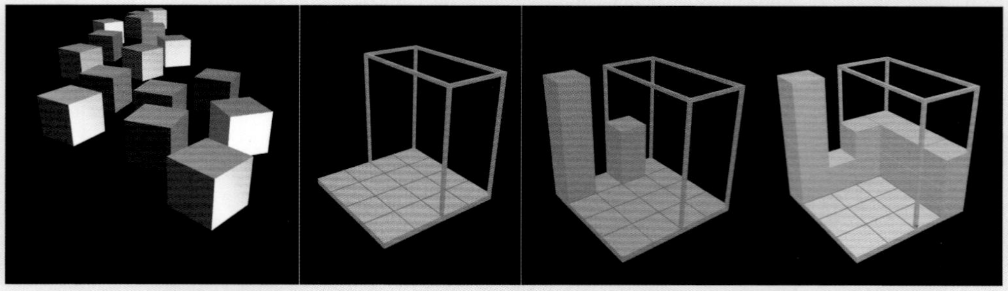

Ang Bing Hung
Lo Man Sze

练习五　用木条和纸板划分空间

目的：

建筑的形体可以看作是构成原理作用下的结果。这个练习要求学生用纸板和木条将蒙德里安的二维绘画转换成三维的结构。

方法：

1. 构成原理介绍。这些原理包括一组质素的对立和平衡，如大和小，宽和窄，多和少，水平和垂直等。

2. 运用这些原理分析和讨论蒙德里安绘画。大师作品都体现形体构成的高超技艺，通过分析这些作品，我们在不同形态中找到基本的构成原理。

3. 从艺术作品中抽象出框架，用木条表现这三维的框架（24厘米×24厘米×24厘米），规则和模度在形体和空间中建立一种秩序。这个练习进一步强化学生运用网格来做空间设计的方法。这个步骤的目的是研究如何将绘画中的网格转变成为三维空间的网格。

4. 根据这个网格，用纸板和木条设计框架并制作一个三维空间结构。研究网格如何在模型内外建立一种秩序和整体感。作品应具有一定的手工质量。

注意事项：

练习过程中要注意观察一个二维的视觉图形如何转变成一个三维的结构。原图中的线变成木条或者板块，点变成了柱，板块变成体量或者空间。我们进一步体会网格的作用，及其与最终成果中多样性和整体性的关系。

工具和材料：

1. 瓦楞纸板；
2. 木条；
3. 胶水等。

成果：

一个24厘米×24厘米×24厘米的立方体结构。

Exercise 5. DIVIDING SPACE WITH STICKS AND PANELS

Objective:

Architectural forms can be generated according to certain principles of composition. This exercise requires the student to transform a two-dimensional Mondrian painting to a three-dimensional structure, using corrugated paper and wooden sticks.

Methods:

1. Introduction to the principles

These are balances and contrasts between: large and small; broad and narrow; more and less; horizontal and vertical.

2. Oral analysis of Mondrian's painting with these principles

Masterpieces all have combinations of these form-composition principles. By analyzing these works, we are encouraged to distinguish generic principles from variations.

3. Using wooden sticks to make a three-dimensional framework (24cm×24cm×24cm) based on the grid abstracted from the painting.

Rules and modules create regularity and order in form and space composition. This phase emphasizes the design process, in which students study the utility of grids in creating a box. Study how the grid lines in the painting transforms into a three-dimensional framework.

4. Following such framework, a three-dimensional structure can be divided.The structure based on the framework is divided and constructed by panels and wooden sticks. Study how the framework creates a harmonious form in all directions both inside and outside of the box. The structure should be neat and of a handwork quality.

Notes:

Always observe how a two-dimensional visual pattern can be transformed into a three-dimensional structure, by redefining lines as a stick or a panel, a point as a pole, and a plane as a volume or space. We learn more about the function of grid and its relation to the varieties and regularity of final products.

Tools and materials:

1.Corrugated paper panels;
2.Wooden sticks;
3.Glue.

Presentation:

A structure within the maximum dimensions of 24cm×24cm ×24cm.

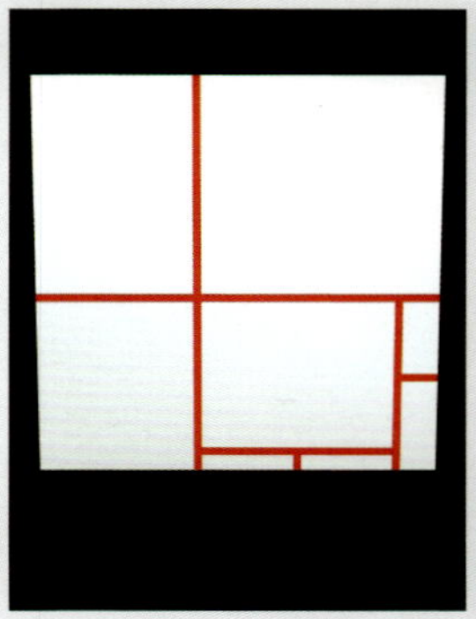
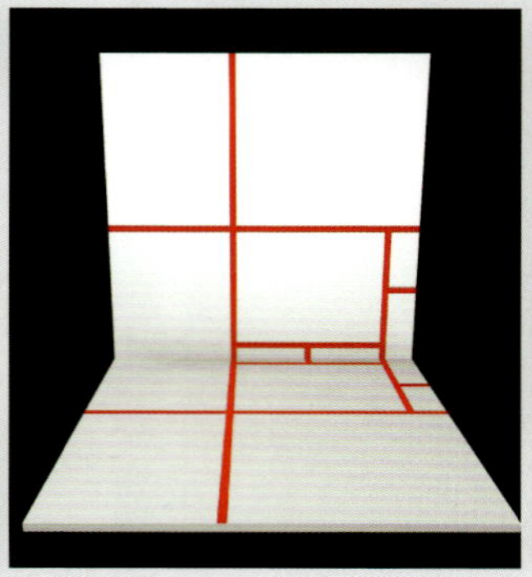

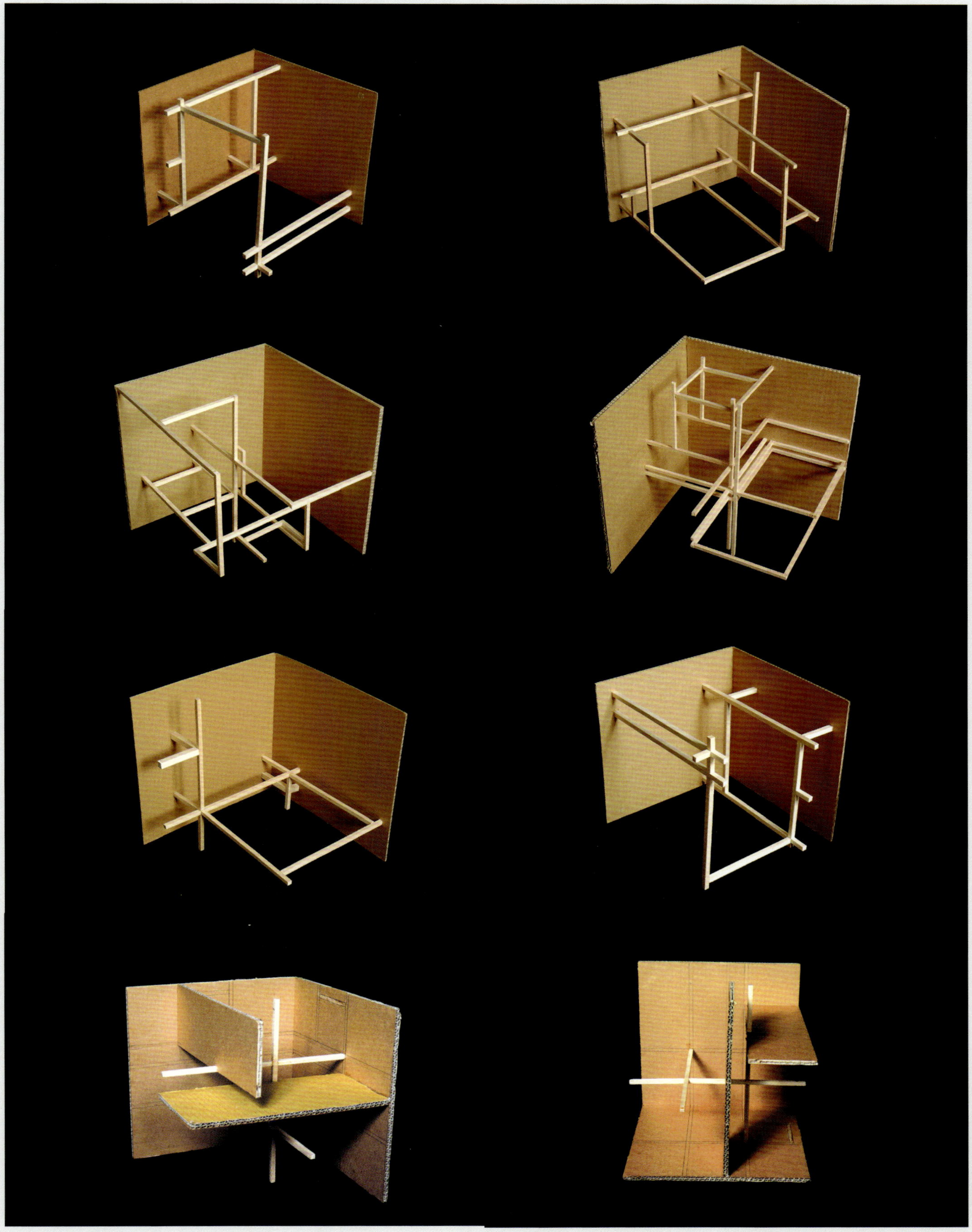

H L Poon
T Gunawan
M K Lin
(Unknown)

练习六　蒙德里安的方盒子

目的：

我们将用纸板和木条做一个盒子，其内部用板材和实体分隔和构造。我们先自己设计一个网格，根据网格做一个盒子。然后用蒙德里安的绘画网格做第二个盒子。比较两者的区别，体会如何将设计变成艺术。

方法：

1. 设计一个二维网格，然后发展成一个三维的网格草图。
2. 在做第一个波纹纸（瓦楞纸）盒子之前用卡纸做一个10厘米×10厘米×10厘米的草稿模型。这个盒子的空间水平分为等高的三层，并且必须要有至少一个垂直的体积和与三层水平空间垂直的交叉结构。
3. 研究蒙德里安的抽象画，并由此设计一个三维的网格。
4. 根据蒙德里安的网格做第二只盒子。
5. 比较两个盒子的异同，记录你的体会。

注意事项：

1. 研究一个方形平面网格怎样转换成三维空间网格，以及网格如何在各个方向上，包括内部和外部形成和谐的整体。
2. 模型的元件结点和纸板的厚度在设计中要综合考虑。
3. 研究瓦楞纸的结构和质感，并将其引入设计构思。
4. 一般来说，第二个盒子比第一个盒子更生动，更多样，更有个性。注意到第二个盒子具有的艺术美。
5. 我们要注意并理解设计的质量始于设计过程的最初始阶段，即网格的设计。

工具和材料：

1. 草图纸；
2. 瓦楞纸板、木条；
3. 铅笔、切具和胶水等。

成果：

两个尺寸为26厘米×26厘米×26厘米，制作精良的盒子。

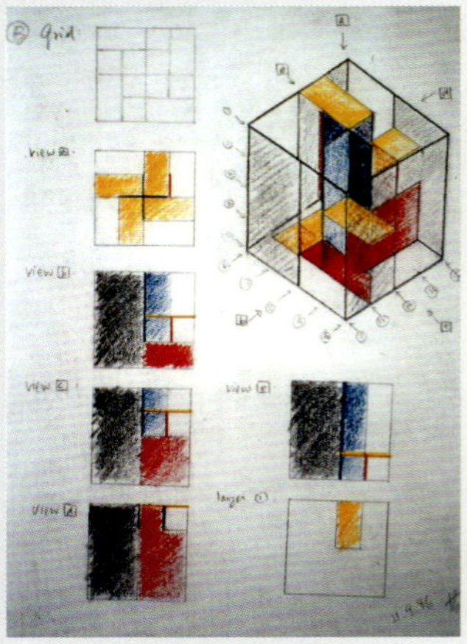

Ang Bing Hung
(Sketch Book)

Exercise 6. A MONDRIAN BOX

Objective:

We will make a box with corrugated paper and wooden sticks. The box interior is divided and constructed by panel elements and solid volumes. We first design a grid and make the first box based on this grid. Then we use a Mondrian painting grid to make a second box. By comparing the two we understand how a design can become a work of art.

Methods:

1.In a sketch book, design a grid and make it three-dimensional. Do one's best to make the grid as neat and visually pleasing as possible.
2.Make preliminary test models of 10cm ×10cm ×10cm with card paper before making the first box of corrugated paper. The box space is divided horizontally into three layers with equal heights. At least one vertical volume and one vertical which crosses the three horizontal spaces are required.
3.Study the Mondrian grid painting. Based on this, design a three-dimensional grid in the sketch book.
4.Make a second box based on the Mondrian grid.
5.Compare the two and write down your understandings.

Notes:

1.Study how the square pattern on the plane transforms into a 3D-space grid, and how the grid makes a harmonious form in all directions, including inside and outside.
2.The joints between elements and the thickness of paper should be well considered.
3.Examine the texture and structure of corrugated papers and try to integrate them into design.
4.We notice that the second box is more dynamic, lively and unique than the first one. The second one is more beautiful than the first one.
5.We understand that the quality of design starts from the very beginning of design process, the first line we lay for the grid.

Tools and materials:

1.Sketch book;
2.Corrugated paper panels and wooden sticks;
3.Pencil, knife and glue.

Presentation:

Two boxes (each 26cm×26cm×26cm) should be neat and tidy, and showing good handcraft quality.

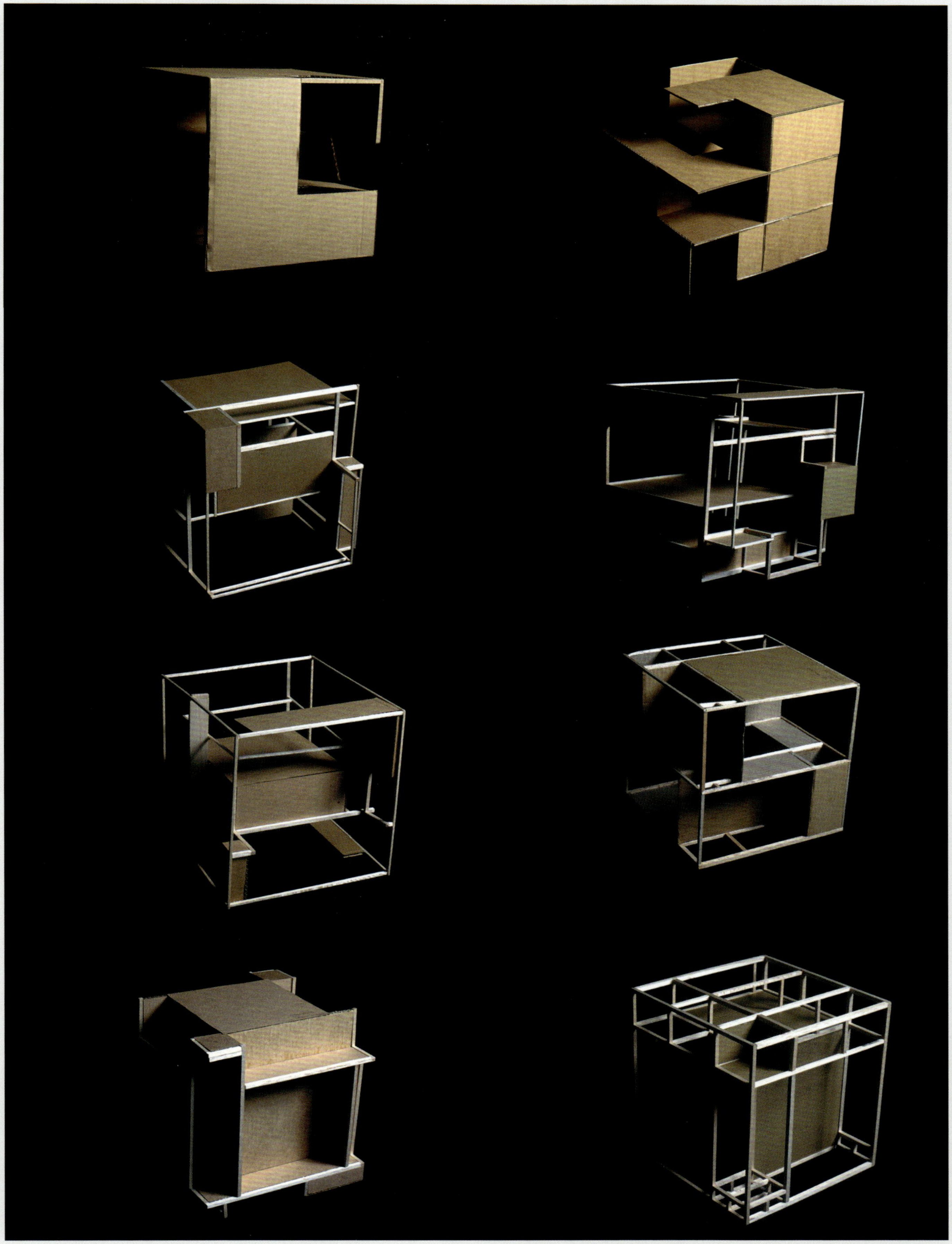

Wong Ming Tak
Chung Ho Wai
Law Sin Hang
Sin Yee Man
Leung Tik Man
Lee Pok Man
Lam Yee Lap
Sharon Tsang
Chan Yat Chun
Leung Tak Yin
Lawrence

图1-7-1 格罗皮乌斯于1920年

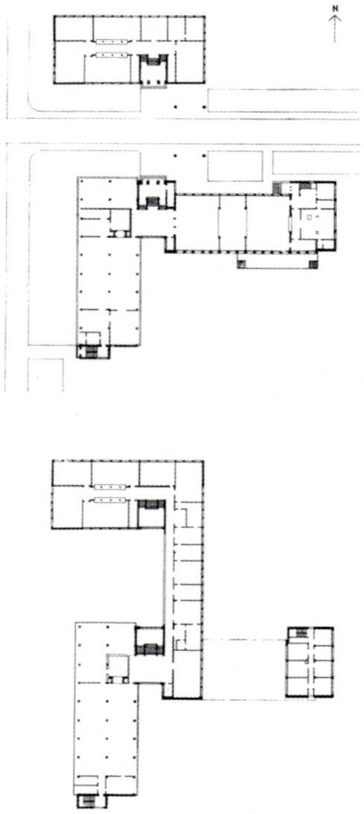

图1-7-2 德绍包豪斯校舍平面，1925—1926年

1.7 瓦尔特·格罗皮乌斯

20世纪60年代中期，当格罗皮乌斯回顾一生时，他说他从没有改变过自己的基本观念（图1-7-1）。而对他一生的职业生涯回顾可以发现他一直在修正他的基本观念，一种新的“多样统一”的观念，协作观念和在教学与实践中反对风格的观念。[64]

在他1916年发表的《关于建立一个将艺术发现融入工业、贸易和工艺教育学院的建议》一文中，他号召用新风格、新文化来表现时代的整体性。“文化最终是各种生活形式中艺术及风格的凝聚体，真正的文化是风格的整体。”[65] 1916年筹建的包豪斯这所前卫风格的学校，正是格罗皮乌斯在1910年以他的法古斯工厂和德意志制造联盟为例的演讲中所提倡的新“德国文化”的代表。1918年战败后的德国经济崩溃，革命一触即发，迫切需要一种新的文化，而新文化的目的和方法还很模糊。格罗皮乌斯的思想即使不是先锋，也处于社会和经济变化的中心。

1919年的包豪斯将“艺术与工艺相统一”的意义和目标写入校章，即艺术与工艺的统一。目标核心是通过教育形成跨阶层的新的社会统一。所以格罗皮乌斯的教育理论强调学生要既向艺术导师学习，也要向手工艺师傅学习。传统实用艺术学校是贵族式的，已经过时，他需要的是新的综合艺术。他聘用的第一批教师都来自当时德国的激进艺术团体，这说明他不仅需要有“个性”的艺术家，而且需要有理想的艺术家。他甚至将教学计划置之一旁，让教师制定开发自己的教学方法，让学生试验和探索自己的方向。他在1923年著的《艺术和技术：一种新统一》一文中说：“包豪斯至高无上的理想是统一，它来自人本身，依附于朝气蓬勃的生活，将所有艺术、时代趋势和理论结合成一个不可分割的整体。”[66]

1926年包豪斯迁至德绍之后，格罗皮乌斯为学校设计了新校舍（图1-7-2，图1-7-3，图1-7-4，图1-7-5）。建筑充分展现了包豪斯和格罗皮乌斯的建筑哲学。他在《包豪斯建筑》一文中说，平面组织完全根据功能等现实要求，朝向取决于对阳光的需要，互相间交通便捷，不同建筑体又有一定独立性，空间灵活适应功能改变。[67] 他最关心是功能的多样性、清晰性和统一性。在《新建筑和包豪斯》一文中他说：“新建筑的意义来自其自身有机体的需要和活力。它是真实的，逻辑鲜明的，没有谎言和庸俗，是对我们机械化和快速变迁的现实世界的直接肯定。”[68]

很明显，格罗皮乌斯的“统一”转向了机器和工业。“长期与新技术、新材料和新的组织方法相结合，一个有创意的人可以将设计带入活跃的现实，从而产生设计的新观念。”[69] 1919年，他批判任何形式的机器观点，而唯独主张回到手工艺。1922年至1923年，他仍信手工艺，但开始主张与技术结合。1924年他写道：“手工艺是人类生活的必要手段，但过去的工艺已经不存在。

B–4 实体：形

Solid Volume: Form

体是面运动的轨迹。体是三维的，有空间位置，被面所限定。也称为形体。

A volume is the path of a plane in motion (in a direction other than its intrinsic direction). It must be three-dimensional object and has a position is space and is bound by planes. It also called form.

图1-7-3 包豪斯工作室及主入口

图1-7-4 包豪斯学生宿舍

图1-7-5 包豪斯工作室及学生宿舍

1.7 Walter Gropius

When looking over his long life in the mid-1960s, Gropius once declared that he had never had to alter his fundamental views (Pic.1-7-1). A quick review of his career life illustrates how he had repeatedly reformulated his basic idea of a new "unity in diversity" — teamwork and collaboration, and taught and practised against any notion of style. [64]

In his *Proposal for an establishment of an educational institution to provide artistic advisory to industry, trade and craft* of 1916, Gropius called for an expression of his age in a new unity of forms, into a new style, a new culture. "Above all, culture is the unity of artistic style in all of a nation's expressions of life, true culture is therefore unity of style." [65] The planned Bauhaus of 1916 was a forward-looking school of style for the expected new "German culture" as proclaimed by Gropius in lectures since 1910, of which his Fagus works and Werkbund factory were examples. The German defeat of 1918, the economic collapse, revolution, and founding of the republic deepened the yearning for a new culture, but the ends and means had to be reformulated. Gropius' idea was right in the centre of the social and economic changes, if not leading such changes.

In 1919 when Bauhaus was formally established, the meaning and intention of "unity" was explicit clearly in its manifesto — a unified work of art, a unity of art and crafts. The essence of this goal was to achieve a new social unity, crossing all class barriers, by educating for a new community. Hence, students taught by artists as well as craftsmen were fundamental to Gropius' theories of education. He saw the methods of the Kunstgewerbeschule as elitist and outdated, and he strove towards a synthesis of the arts. Most of his first appointments to the staff were drawn from Arbeitsrat or Novembergruppe circles indicated that he was trying not only to attract artists of "character", but artists who were sympathetic to ideals. Gropius decided "to leave everything (the program) in suspension," so as to allow the teachers to formulate and develop their own pedagogical approach, and the students to experiment and explore their visions. Gropius wrote an essay *Art and Technology: A New Unity* for the Bauhaus exhibition in 1923. "The overriding idea of the Bauhaus is therefore the idea of unity, the assimilation of all the arts, tendencies, and manifestations into an indissoluble whole, rooted in man himself and only meaningful in a vital life." [66]

When Bauhaus moved to its new location in Dessau in 1926, it moved into the new building facilities designed and built by Gropius' office (Pic.1-7-2,Pic.1-7-3,Pic.1-7-4,Pic.1-7-5). The new buildings bore with them an architectural manifesto of the school and Gropius. As Gropius wrote in *Bauhausbauten*, his aim in his organisation of the plan was traced to simple functional and pragmatic reasons: proper orientation to achieve maximum natural light; easy and quick access from one area to another; a clear separation of the various "components" of the building, and the ability to change or adapt the spaces for possible variations in use.[67] Gropius was more concerned with the variety, clarity and unity of the activities that went on inside it. "A modern building", he wrote in the *New Architecture and the Bauhaus*, "should derive its architectural significance solely from the vigour and consequence of its own organic proportions. It must be true to itself, logically transparent and virginal of lies or trivialities, as befits a direct affirmation of our contemporary world of mechanisation and rapid transit." [68]

It is now clear that Gropius' interpretation of "unity" evolved with his changing attitude to machine and industry. "Through constant contact with newly evolving techniques…new materials and new ways of putting things together…

广义而言，所有可见之物皆有形。狭义而言，形是自成一体的，在空间中可以与背景相区别。形可以根据内容大致分为表现形式和抽象形式两大类。表现形式即包含特定主题，可与观众进行视觉以外交流的形，包括自然形式、人工形式、和语言形式。抽象形式（或非表现形式）即不包含可认知主题的形，分为徒手形、有机形和几何形。

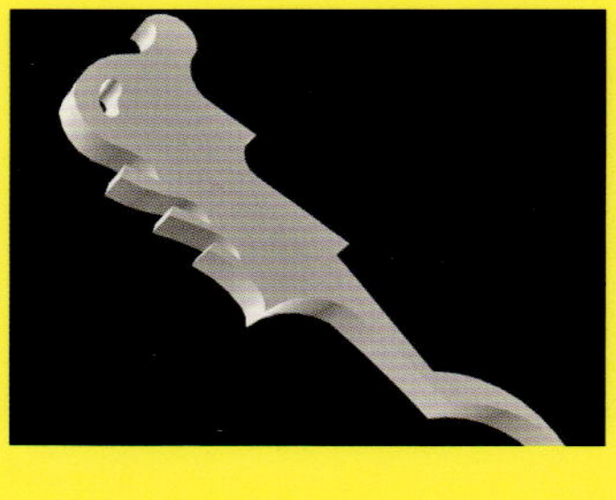

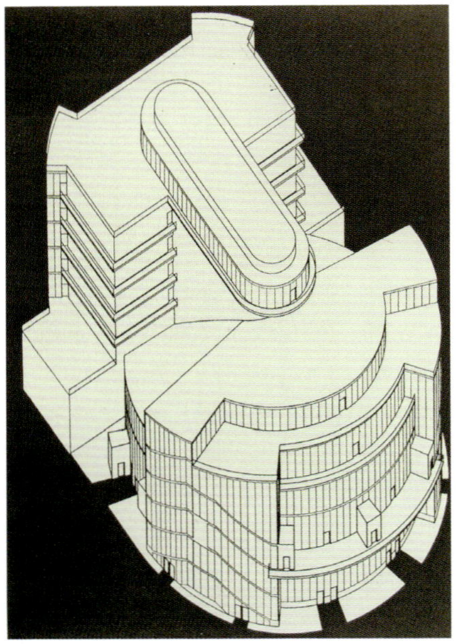

图1-7-6 格罗皮乌斯的剧院设计，1927年

图1-7-7 格罗皮乌斯设计的哈佛大学研究生院，1949年

回到手工艺就像人类的返祖现象一样是病态，工艺和工业应该在一个新的工作环境中统一。”[70] 随着经济实力的增强，设计任务（包括格罗皮乌斯自己业务）的增多，及与工业界合作的增强，包豪斯不断修正思路。从过去由“新统一”而建立新文化的目标，逐渐变为与技术、机器和进步的统一，甚至迷恋。理性和经济原则主导格罗皮乌斯事务所的建筑设计。他和迈耶都认为建筑教育的基本内容是“功能、协作和建构”（图1-7-6）。

尽管在20世纪20年代末“包豪斯风格”一词已经普遍用来形容设计和装饰中的几何形体，但格罗皮乌斯坚持自己，否认想制造风格。在他的《新建筑和包豪斯》（1935）一书中他写道：“包豪斯的目标不是宣传一种风格、体系、教条、章程或者风气，而是尽力发挥对设计有力而活跃的影响…… ‘包豪斯风格’一词实际上等同于承认失败。”[71] 然而从历史角度评价，格罗皮乌斯的包豪斯的确推行一种方盒子式建筑，在二战后盛行于世。二战后的环境，如大量性建设和快速建设的需要和相对拮据的经济条件，使格罗皮乌斯在20年代开始主张的工业效率、标准化生产成为唯一方向。他甚至说：“从整体上看，大多数人的生活必需条件是一样的。家和家具都是大量性商品，其设计应基于理性而不是热情。”大量性生产不可避免导致单一性，就像高效率生产线和机器要求稳定精确的生产环境一样。工业化、标准化、大量性生产和为每一个人创造一个由理性和科学控制的世界，是格罗皮乌斯教学思想的核心。这里，没有艺术、热情、历史和个人创造性的空间。这也是其他一些长期以来从事艺术活动的建筑师无法苟同之处。柯布西耶曾说：“帕提依（神庙）并不取悦于所有人，伟大的艺术不是大家都接受的艺术……艺术仅让人有所触动……帕提依有力地打动每一个人，包括那些不高兴的人；最重要的是是否具有唤起情感的力量。”[72]

格罗皮乌斯移居美国后，一下成为建筑教育改革和美国现代建筑发展的中心人物。1936年他概括了建筑教育的一系列原则，主要内容是：

1．“柏拉图绘图桌”是“巴艺”绘图艺术工具之一，应取消，学生应直接画施工图，做模型，教育应将设计变成理性和系统的过程。

2．课程设置改革：削减艺术史课，最终变成选修课。格罗皮乌斯认为，过多的艺术史知识会削弱青年人的创造力，所以学习先师的作品应在学生毕业之后。[73]

Broadly speaking, all that is visible has form. Form is everything that can be seen. In a narrow sense, forms are self-contained, positive shapes that occupy space and are distinguishable from a background. Forms can be broadly classified according to their particular contents. A form that contains a recognizable subject communicates with viewers in more than purely visual terms. This is called a representational form, which includes natural, man-made and verbal forms. When a form does not contain a recognizable subject, it is considered non-representational or abstract. Non-representational forms may be classified as calligraphic, organic and geometric shapes.

that the creative individual can learn to bring the design of objects into a living relationship with tradition and from that point to develop a new attitude towards design."[69] In 1919, he condemned any form of machinery and rigidly demanded a return to handicraft. In 1922—1923, he still believed in handicraft but now he wanted to unite it with technology. In 1924, he wrote that "handicraft was an invaluable means to harmonise man, but the craft of the past does not exist any longer … A return to craft would be an atavistic error … Craft and industry will dissolve into a new working unit."[70] With the increasing consolidation of the German economy, increasing commissions as an architect, and closer co-operation with industry, the Bauhaus concept was continuously remodelled. In place of the old goal of achieving unity as the basis for a new culture, there was now an aestheticization (and in part, fetishization) of technology, machines, and progress. Rational and economic principles guided the architectural designs of Gropius' office. Both Gropius and Meyer agreed that the basic tendency of architectural education should be "functional—collective—constructive"(Pic.1-7-6).

Although by the late 1920s, the term "Bauhaus style" had become popular and was applied to any expression of geometrical form in design and decoration, Gropius tried to distant himself to such connotation as he denied any intention of developing a particular "style". In his book *The New Architecture and the Bauhaus* (1935) he wrote: "The object of the Bauhaus was not to propagate any style, system, dogma, formula, or vogue, but simply to exert a revitalising influence on design… A 'Bauhaus Style' would have been a confession of failure."[71] However, historically speaking the Bauhaus demonstrated by Gropius did encourage a uniformity of box-like buildings worldwide after the Second World War. Taking into account the great demand for new buildings and rapid pace of construction on the one hand, and economic constraints and confidence in industrial efficiency on the other, standardization was the answer, as Gropius tried to promote in the Bauhaus in the early 1920s. As Gropius remarked: "on the whole, the necessities of life are the same for the majority of people. The home and its furnishings are mass consumer goods, and their design is more a letter of reason than of passion." Mass production virtually guaranteed uniformity in products, just as efficient throughput and a well-functioning technocracy required precise and unchanging definition of specific task environments. Industrialization, standardization, and production the masses as a means to achieve a perfect future world, governed by rationality and science, stood in the centre of Gropius' educational program. There was no room for art, passion, history or individual creativity. This was what many architects, who associated tightly with art and creativity, could not stomach. Le Corbusier once said, "The Parthenon is not pleasurable to anyone. Great art is not art of agreement … art has the sole duty to move us… The Parthenon moves everyone powerfully, even those whom it displeases; what counts is the intensity of the provoked emotion."[72]

When Gropius arrived the United States, he found himself amidst widespread reform in architectural education as well as a burgeoning popular interest in modern architecture nationwide. In 1936 he proposed a set of principles on architectural education, a few of which were:

1.The "platonic drawing table", that is the Beaux-Arts drawing virtuosity, was given up; by learning to make working drawings and models, the whole education got a more rational systematic approach to design.

2.The curriculum was changed: the courses on art history were reduced year by year, and eventually became electives. According to Gropius, too much knowledge in art history limited the creative forces of young people and therefore they should learn about the work of their predecessors only at the end of their studies.[73]

图1-7-8 格罗皮乌斯和贝聿铭等设计的上海华东基督教大学方案，1948年

格罗皮乌斯在美国哈佛大学的设计研究生院教学的时间（1937—1953）比在包豪斯的时间还长（图1-7-7，图1-7-8）。他的许多学生后来成为著名现代建筑师。尽管他的思想在美国许多学校极受欢迎，但也有些建筑师开始质疑他的教育哲学的核心。20世纪50年代的得克萨斯建筑学院就是其中之一，这将在下文讨论。有评论家在批评格罗皮乌斯的教学改革时，将他的课程计划和问题归纳为三个主要方面：

1. 强调建筑为民主思想服务。

2. 强调郊区而不是城市作为人的居住中心。

3. 实用主义偏见。[74]

由于实用主义的具体化，思想、造型和社会等方面内容在设计中被忽视。设计的重要源泉之一的历史作品的学习被压制，作为建筑教育一部分的历史课被取消。设计过程变成研究和计算的机械过程，不允许主观思想介入。这种方法有人戏称为“由以下因素计算之结果”的设计模式。

从历史大框架中考察，顽固或者幼稚地相信和追求建筑中的量化的因果关系可能是包豪斯对建筑设计的最有害的影响。[75]

有人甚至挖苦说：“格罗皮乌斯带到美国的没有多少包豪斯的精华，相反大部分是包豪斯的糟粕。”[76]

B-6 形状

形状是由外轮廓界定的区域，具有体积和厚度。根据角度不同而变化的形状，是形的属性之一。形状是从不同角度、不同距离描绘出的形。

Shape

Shape is an area easily defined with an outline. Form has a shape that is given volume and thickness and that can exhibit different views. Shapes are forms depicted at particular angles, from particular distances.

Gropius eventually taught longer at Harvard's Graduate School of Design (1937—1953) than at Bauhaus (Pic.1-7-7,Pic.1-7-8). He had educated generations of architects who are now best known in modern architecture. Apart from its popularity and adoption into many American schools of architecture, there were other contemporary architects who questioned the essence of its teaching philosophy. The Texas School of Architecture in the mid-1950s was one, which searched for alternatives, and we shall look into it in the latter part of this paper. In The Decorated Diagram, Herdeg criticised Gropius' reformed curriculum, and identified three main characteristics as they were represented in the official course descriptions and in a random selection of class problems:

1.An explicit commitment to architecture in the service of democratic ideals.

2.An implicit preference for suburbia over the city as the proper locale for human habitation.

3.A bias in favour of pragmatism.[74]

The pursuit of pragmatism had become so literal that the considerations of design development in areas of idea, form and social content were simply ignored. The study of historical precedents as possible resources for design development was discouraged; in fact history as a legitimate part of architectural education was left out completely. The design process was conceived as a neutral activity characterized by impersonal research and calculations, as against any personal interpretation. Herdeg followed a similar approach as did Hannes Meyer's design diagram "The Plan Calculates Itself from the Following Factors" which he used during his term at Bauhaus. He further noted:

> *In a larger, historical frame of reference, the unrelenting, if ultimately naïve, pursuit of literal and presumed measurable cause-and-effect relationships within pairs of architectural entities may very well be among the most destructive of Bauhaus contributions to architectural design.*[75]

As Vincent Scully once remarked cynically: "Gropius brought with him most of the few weaknesses and few of the many virtues of the Bauhaus."[76]

B–7　空间

空间可以分成三类：正空间、负空间、灰空间。正空间是形所包围的部分。负空间是包围形的部分。灰空间是部分被包围、部分包围的形。

Space

Space can be divided into three categories, positive space, negative space and in-between space. Positive space is what surrounded by a form. Negative space is what surround a form. In-between space is what partially surrounded and partially surrounding a form.

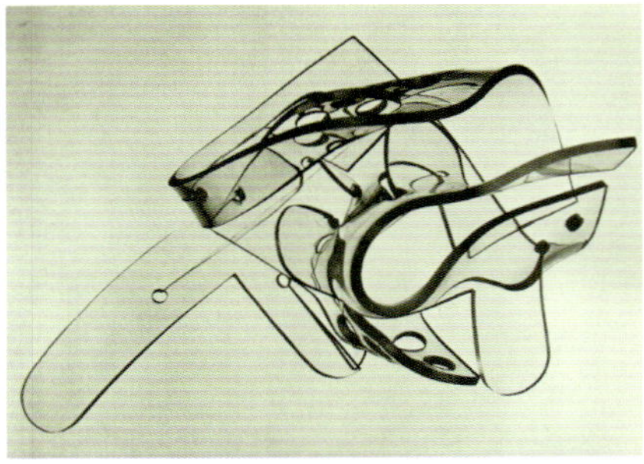
图1-8-1 莫霍利－纳吉《构成CH7》摄影作品，1941年

图1-8-2 阿尔贝斯为哈佛研究生院做的砖雕

图1-8-3 学生作业《质感》，1941年

1.8 得克萨斯建筑学院

由格罗皮乌斯及其在美国的同事所代表的包豪斯教育体系在20世纪50年代受到一些青年建筑教育家、史学家和艺术家的挑战。尽管当时他们势单力薄，但却对后来美国，甚至是欧洲影响巨大。他们重新提倡为包豪斯所摒弃的价值观，而且实际上一直是建筑学核心问题，如历史、空间和艺术。建筑教育理论家布罗德本特认为建筑教育自古希腊和古罗马开始就分为理论和实践两个方面：理论，包括维特鲁威人的比例问题等；实践，即建筑技术方面的职业训练。“在许多地方和不同历史时期，理论教育和实践训练齐头并进。”[77]

二战为美国输入了大量欧洲移民，包括许多思想家和专业人才。尽管伊藤等一些早期包豪斯教员仍留在欧洲，但其他人如格罗皮乌斯、密斯·凡·德·罗、阿尔贝斯、布劳耶等（图1-8-1）都移居美国，重开各自教学和设计业务。如前文所述，格罗皮乌斯改革了哈佛大学设计研究生院的课程。阿尔贝斯继续绘画事业，并在当时属于先锋派的芝加哥黑山学院教书，后来任职于耶鲁大学设计系（图1-8-2）。密斯创办了伊利诺伊工学院建筑系。

密斯将教学大纲分成三个部分：方法、目的、计划和创造。[78] 他所说的方法指的是几种有限的材料：木、石、砖、钢和混凝土；目的指的是建筑类型，如住宅、医院、图书馆等；而计划和创造，密斯认为取决于时代。和格罗皮乌斯一样，他认为“形”产生于组织和运作方式，但他仍坚信建筑、绘画和雕塑应结合成一个“创造性整体”（图1-8-3，图1-8-4）。他的学校重新强调绘图，特别是对木结构、砖及其他建造材料的细部描绘。学生在完成必修功课之外的探索机会非常有限（图1-8-5，图1-8-6）。密斯以专断而闻名，甚至说如果学生不喜欢，可以转到其他学校（图1-8-7）。实际上他的学校代表了新的现代建筑教育取向。

在二战以前，美国的建筑学院分为两种源流，但都是来自欧洲。一是美国学院派，即传统的“巴艺”模式。除了折中主义风格之外，这种教育体系的主要问题是建筑与新技术和新材料的结合薄弱。另一种模式是格罗皮乌斯由包豪斯课程发展而成的设计研究生院。[79] 尽管当时还是新建筑精神代表，但其中已存在许多问题，其中最主要的是否定理论和学术课程的重要性。格罗皮乌斯认为，设计课是通过摒弃历史、先例和流行做法来释放学生的创造力的。对包豪斯来说，明确被认为是一种“客观”的教学方法，也允许设计的自我表现；但同时也否认过多的方法设计上的“学术性”。虽然“现代风格”被越来越多的学生所欣赏和运用，但其真正的内容和演变仍有很多未被检验。[80]

B-8 形限定空间

三维形可以限定周围空间的体积，创造出一个自己的影响区域。可限定空间的形有多种：线性元素（柱体）、单个面、L形平面、平行平面、U形平面，以及各种有机元素（围合）。

Form Defining Space

A three-dimensional form will articulate the volume of space surrounding it and generate a field of influence or territory which it claims as its own. There are various of forms defining space: linear element (column), single plane, L-shaped plane, parallel planes, U-shaped planes and four planes, and various kinds of organic elements (closure).

图1-8-4 学生作业《交叉的平面》，1947年

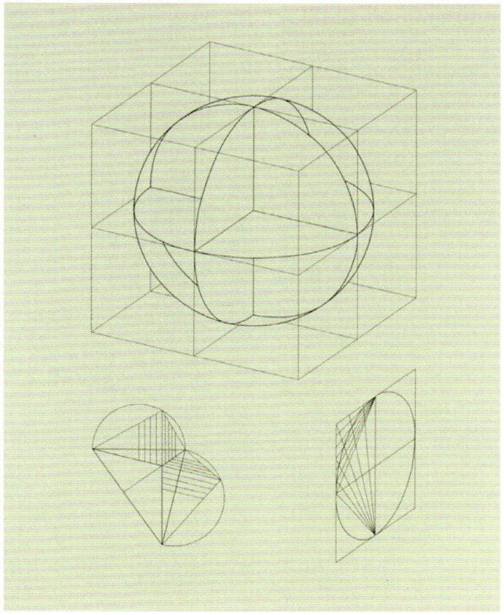

图1-8-5 学生作业《线描几何运用》，1951年

1.8 Texas School of Architecture

The Bauhaus education system, as represented by Gropius and his colleagues in United States, was challenged by a small group of young educators, historians and artists in the 1950s. The challenge was initially weak, especially in the United States, but increasingly influential in Europe with passing time. They demonstrated the values of what the Bauhaus neglected, but had always stood in the centre of architecture: history, space and art. Broadbent observed that architectural education in ancient Greece and Rome had two aspects: theory, which for Vitruvius included proportion, and practice, or pragmatic, which meant training "on the job" in the actual technicalities of building. "At most times (in history) and in most places, too theoretical an education and practical training have taken place simultaneously." [77]

The Second World War brought an influx of the European immigration, with their brilliant minds and expertise to the United States. Although some former Bauhaus staff remained in Europe (such as Johannes Itten), most of them, such as Walter Gropius, Mies van der Rohe, Josef Albers, Marcel Breuer, Moholy-Nagy (Pic.1-8-1) and Bertrand Goldberg, came to America to launch new professional or academic careers, and continued to impact the architectural scene. Gropius, as we previously discussed, reformed the architecture program at Harvard University's Graduate School of Design. Albers continued his painting and teaching profession at the avant-garde Black Mountain College in Chicago, and later on, at the Department of Design at Yale University(Pic.1-8-2) .Mies founded and built the architectural department at Illinois Institute of Technology.

According to Broadbent Mies' syllabus was divided into three parts: studies of means, of purposes, and of planning and creating.[78] By "means" he had in mind a set of limited materials: wood, stone, brick, steel and concrete; "Purposes"meant building types: dwellings, hospitals, libraries etc., and by "planning and creating" Mies meant dependence on the current epoch. As for Gropius, "form" developed out of organisation and working methods, but he insisted that architecture, painting and sculpture were to be joined as a "creative unity" (Pic.1-8-3,Pic.1-8-4). In his school, drawings were emphasized once again. Highly detailed perspectives of timber frame, brick and other forms of construction characterized his approach. Students had little opportunity to explore beyond what was required of them(Pic.1-8-5,Pic.1-8-6). Mies had the reputation of requiring students to work his way. If they did not wish, Mies would suggest them to go to another school (Pic.1-8-7) .His school represented new approaches in modern architectural education.

In United States, European academic hegemony in American architecure schools before the end of World War II took two predominant streams. The former was the American Academy, which was derived from Ecole des Beaux-Arts model as previously described. Besides its stylistic eclecticism. The major problem of this educational system lay in its failure to integrate new technology and new materials. The latter model was derived from Gropius' Graduate School of Design; itself assimilated from his earlier Bauhaus program. [79] Although Gropius' model remained popular, Gropius himself was still considered a hero of the new architectural spirit, there were numerous problems inherited in this model, too. The essential problem was its rejection of theory or intellectual content. Its design studio was, as Gropius argued, "aimed to release the creative powers of the students" by rejecting history, precedent, or convention.To Bauhaus, this was considered an "objective" approach to teaching which also permitted the self-expression of design; but at the same it also denied an explicitly "intellectual" design approach to design. Though the "modern style" had come to be admired and employed by an increasing number of students, its formal content and its antecedents remained largely unexamined.[80]

B-9 形与空间

两组相对的要素：正要素——感知为形体，负要素——感知为形体的背景。引人注意的形体（正要素）不能脱离背景而存在，因此形体与背景不仅仅是相反的要素，而且共同构成不可分割、相辅相成的整体，如同形与空间共同构成建筑一样。形与背景的关系可以反转。

在相应的构图中，形的负空间和灰空间以及参考框架都成为背景，这时形被看作“形体”。构图是图形与背景交互作用构成的视觉效果。

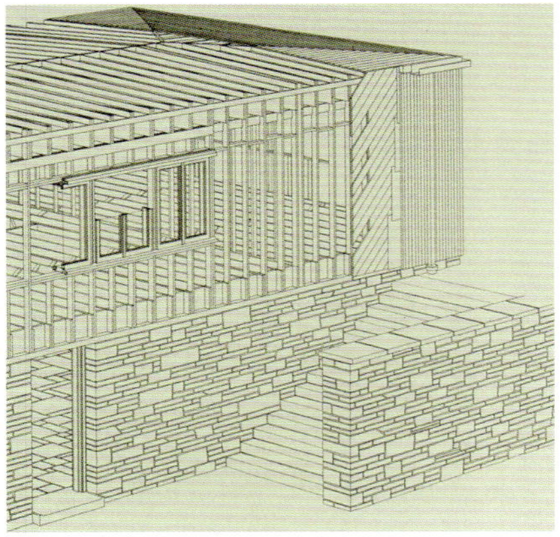

图1-8-6 学生作业《材料和建造》，1961年

图1-8-7 密斯于四年级教室，伊利诺伊，摄于1939年

图1-8-8 哈里斯设计的哈罗德住宅，1949—1950年

到了20世纪50年代早期，包豪斯的基础课程已为美国的建筑院校普遍采用，和伊藤的课程一样，这些基础课程一般由艺术家执教，旨在让学生回到儿童般的天真心态，开发学生内在的对创造性的感知能力。[81]

1951年得克萨斯大学建筑系从工程学院中独立出来。开始时，教学中混合了学院式和包豪斯两种体系。设计课以建筑类型为基础，美术课延用“巴艺”传统，画石膏像，练习石炭笔素描、水粉和水彩，为设计作业打好表现技能之基础。和格罗皮乌斯的课程一样，设计课中的历史课被取消，体现将所谓现代建筑与历史建筑分开的取向。设计课中历史研究和幻灯片讲座的教学法尚未出现。[82] 一位早期学生，后来成为建筑师和作家的卡拉哥纳这样评论当时的教学计划：“在教学计划中，教学内容直奔预设的结果，根本无法培养学生的分析、组织和发明的智慧和能力。学生只能根据既定题目做设计，并将其发展为适当的建筑图。”[83] 在这个体系中，“青年学生的好奇心和热情不断受到压制，直到变得枯燥、冷漠，夹杂着厌恶和失望。学生被动地上完设计课程，希望以毕业作为解脱。”[84] 整个学校弥漫着一种“反智慧的实用主义，自我保护性艺术，天真保守主义夹杂着长期繁殖能力丧失……一种对实验和创新的抗拒”。[85]

1954年学校聘请了洛杉矶的国际著名建筑师哈威尔·哈里斯为新系主任（图1-8-8），瑞士建筑师伯恩哈德·赫茨里也于同年来到学校。针对教学计划中存在的问题和低效率，哈里斯委托赫茨里改进教学计划。1954年他们聘请了多位来自欧洲和美国东岸的青年建筑师，包括英国建筑师和理论家柯林·罗，纽约建筑师约翰·海杜克，画家鲍勃·斯路斯基和李·希尔舍。凭着对建筑教育的热情和相互交流激发的灵感，这些人开始形成新的教学理念和方法，对后来的美国和欧洲的建筑教育产生重大影响。

1954年柯林·罗任教之后，赫茨里请他参与制订下学期的课程计划。赫茨里和柯林·罗之间的交流讨论在哈里斯的记录中有详细记载。

这个记录提出了新课程的三个重要方面。

首先它明确指出学校的建筑教育不仅是为职业需要，更重要的是确立一种学术地位。

> *建筑学校是一个学院，本质上服从学术。它建立在对知识的信念和对教育理论的尊重上。它强调文化的重要性。教学计划不应以个人的观点、主张或兴趣为基础，而必须来自对一些普遍原则的理解和尊重。这些普遍原则是一种参照体系，教师间合理的不同观点可以并存。所以首先要做的是建立一个参照体系。*[86]

Form and Space

Two opposing groups distinguish elements: positive elements that are perceived as figures, and negative elements that provide a background for the figures. The figures, the positive elements that attract our attention, could not exist without a contrasting background. Figures and their background, therefore, are more than opposing elements. Together, they form an inseparable reality, a unit of opposites, just as the elements of form and space together form the reality of architecture. The relationship of figure and ground can also be inverted.
Forms are seen as "figures", and the space behind forms and the space between them and the frame of reference as "ground" or "background" in the resulting "composition". A composition is the visual effect that is generated by the interaction of figures and ground.

In the early 1950s, abstract exercises in basic design already applied in many American schools taught by artists. Former students and teachers from the Bauhaus assumed that basic design training in architecture would free the student's innate creative sensibilities. Basic design provide a common basis to all the visual arts and that the experiences would find their way into the design process of the students, whether in graphics, industrial design or pattern making.[81]

In 1951, the Architecture program at University of Texas was split from the College of Engineering, and an independent faculty was established. In its early years, the pedagogical approach at Texas School of Architecture was a mix of the Academy and Bauhaus traditions. The design problems were type-driven. Drawing classes still used classical casts and busts as models with various media such as charcoal, pastel renderings and watercolors as in any typical Beaux-Art school. These classes were mainly for acquisition of presentation skills for future design studios. Further, in following the precedent of Graduate School of Design, study of history as an integral portion of the design studio was dismissed, a decision reflected in the tendency to separate so-called modern architecture from the architecture of previous periods. Historical research and slide lectures as a component of design studio were unheard of.[82] The program was, as the former student, architect and writer Caragonne comments, "considerably less able to train students intellectually in the ability to analyze, to organize, and to invent. In the very formulation of the program, the elements pointed to the expected solution; it only remained for the student to elaborate a specific theme and to produce from this elaboration an appropriate architectural drawing."[83] Under this system, "the curiosity and enthusiasm of the young students were progressively dampened until boredom and apathy combined to produce frustration and disillusionment. The student, haplessly and mechanically plodding through his studio courses, sought only a release through graduation."[84] The overall spirit of the school was filled with "a pragmatic anti-intellectualism, a self-defensive 'artiness' and native conservatism combined with tenured impregnability ... a resistance to experimentation and innovation."[85]

In 1954, the School invited the internationally renowned Los Angeles architect Harwell Harris to be the new director (Pic.1-8-8). Another young Swiss architect, Bernhard Hoesli was also hired on the faculty in the same year. They also saw the shortcoming and ineffectiveness of the program, and Harris commissioned Hoesli to introduce a more satisfactory educational program. Subsequent to this, in 1954, they also recruited other younger architects from Europe and East Coast into the faculty, such as the British architect and writer Colin Rowe, New York architect John Hejduk, painter Bob Slutzky and Lee Hirsche. With their passion in architectural education and stimulating exchange of ideas and thoughts, these people started to formulate a teaching ideology and methodology, which impacted the later development of architectural education in both U.S.A. and Europe.

Following his arrival in Texas in January 1954, Rowe was invited by Hoesli to devise a new curriculum for the coming semester. A series of exchanges and discussions between Hoesli and Rowe resulted in a memorandum for Harris.

The memorandum identified three important aspects for the formation of the new curriculum. Firstly, it stated clearly the architectural education at Texas School was not simply for training students for the mechanics of the profession. Rather, it existed mainly as an academy:

> *An academy — and a school of architecture is an academy — is, by its nature obliged to be academic. It is in consequence committed to a belief in knowledge and a respect for theories of education. It assumes cultural self-consciousness to be a virtue. It can exist only by reference to a body of ideas. Its educational program cannot be founded upon irresponsible opinion, private preference, or individual fantasy, but must be rooted in the understanding and respect for certain general principles. These general principles can form a frame of reference within which legitimate differences of opinion among faculty can exist. It is necessary to consider what frame of reference we legitimately assume to be our own.*[86]

图1-8-9 哈里斯的建筑画，1956—1957年

第二，记录指出“巴艺”和包豪斯都不是唯一的方向，应结合两者的长处。“这既不是‘巴艺’复兴，也不是新包豪斯创立。既然两者都对我们深有影响，就不应忽视，我们要做的是通过实验在其废墟上建立更有意义的东西。”[87]

第三，他们坚信现代建筑是可教的，通过对现有现代建筑实例的认真分析和理解，可以产生一套实用的建筑理论。这就是新教学计划的思想基础：

1. 设计本质上是对特定现状的批判。

2. 培养学生的举一反三和抽象概括的能力。

3. 设计取舍和决策要有理有据。

4. 学院以知识为基础，有一个基本立场。[88]

新教程建立了对建筑意义和内容的思想探索的框架，同时让教师发挥各自的智慧和兴趣。各年级的设计课有一个共同的目标，但各设计组也体现教师和教学小组的不同个性。[89]

新教程引起了学生们的广泛兴趣和热情，这从他们的作业质量中也反映出来。但一些年纪较大、较保守的教师对教程中思想性、理论性和鲜明的学术性不习惯，甚至不满。哈里斯和他的朋友很快成了有关办学方向上争论的焦点。他和一些老教师间的争斗使他不得不于1955年辞职（图1-8-9），柯林·罗、海杜克、斯路斯基和希尔舍也于一年后辞职。只有赫茨里和几位新教师，约翰·沙、李·霍奇登和维尔纳·西利哥曼继续教新教程，直到三年后对政治争斗彻底失望一起离开了学校。

他们后来被冠之以“得克萨斯游击队”之名。尽管他们的新教程在政治争斗中只施行了几年，却使这些探索者用智慧心灵建立了一套新教学观念和方法。20世纪50年代后期，这些“游击战士”在各地大展拳脚。赫茨里回到欧洲任教于瑞士联邦苏黎世高等工科大学（以下简称“苏黎世高工”）（ETH），一代欧洲学生受教于他在得克萨斯开创的课程。柯林·罗在纽约的库伯联盟和克耐尔大学相继任教，几年后回到英国剑桥大学。但他仍心系美国，1962年他回到克耐尔开办城市设计专业，不久发表影响巨大的重要著作《拼贴城市》。海杜克和斯路斯基回到美国东部，不久任职于库伯联盟，海杜克后来升为院长直至90年代末去世。斯路斯基成为著名画家。

B-10　几何形

几何形由直线、平面、圆创造出来。平面可以进行加、减、演绎、复合、分割、缩放、遮盖等操作。大部分几何形是规则的、或由连续或规则排列的元素组成。对称形是左右两部分相对于某一直线轴镜像对称的规则形。

Geometric Forms

Geometric forms are created using straight lines, flat planes, and circles. Planes can be manipulated by adding, subtracting, interpenetrating, multiplying, dividing, varying sizes, folding. Most geometric forms are regular, or have components with consistent or orderly positions and directions. Symmetrical forms are regular shapes whose left and right halves are mirror images. An invisible straight line, an axis, divides the shape equally.

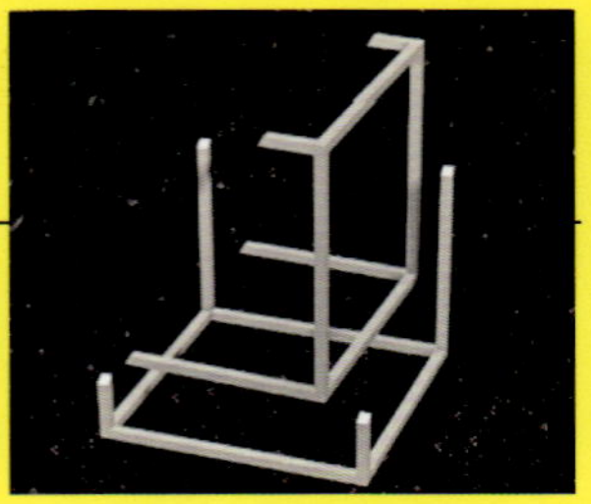

Secondly, it stated neither Ecole des Beaux-Arts nor Bauhaus program were a pedagogical approach to follow; rather, the School should devise an approach by adopting strength from both traditions. And so there was a new opportunity drawing upon both traditions, "neither to revive the Beau-Arts nor to erect a new Bauhaus, but merely to indicate that since in the recent past both have affected us, neither can be overlooked, and that from the remnants of both it is possible that by a process of trial and error something of significance might be constructed." [87]

Thirdly, it stated its conviction that modern architectural design could be taught; and through careful analysis and understanding of the existing examples of modern architecture, a useful body of architectural theory could be derived. It laid the intellectual foundation of the new program:

1.That the process of design is essentially the criticism of a given situation.

2.That the power of generalization and abstraction (in the student) must be aroused.

3.That the act of selection assumes a commitment to certain principles.

4.That an academic institution should offer an essential knowledge and an essential attitude. [88]

The new curriculum laid the foundation for an intellectual investigation of the meaning and content of architecture, and also allowed individual faculty members to bring their distinctive talents and interests to the school. The objectives of each year's studio courses were designed to function within an integrated system or plan. However, the conduct of any particular studio would bear the imprint of individual faculty member or team of faculty members. [89]

The new curriculum received great interest and enthusiasm from the students, and there was a noted improvement in their work. However, the older and more conservative faculty members were uncomfortable and resentful with the intellectual, theoretical and unabashed academic bias of the program. Harris and his faculty soon found themselves in increasingly bitter conflict over the direction in which the School of Architecture was to proceed. A string of disputes between Harris and the older faculty finally led to Harris' departure in 1955 (Pic.1-8-9), and Rowe, Hejduk, Slutzky and Hirsche also left the following year. Hoesli remained and continued to teach with the new curriculum, with combined efforts of new staffs John Shaw, Lee Hodgden, and Werner Seligmann, for another three years until they too left due to the frustrated political struggle at school.

The title "Texas Rangers"was later used to term this group of young architects/artists pioneers at Texas School of Architecture. Although there was much political struggle to keep the newly devised program alive for a few years and was eventually cut out from the School, it provided a breeding ground for these adventurous and intelligent minds to formulate and mature their pedagogical ideology and approach. In the next few years in late 1950s, there was a good deal of moving around for these "Texas Rangers". Hoesli returned to Europe and settled in Zurich at the Eidgenossische Technische Hochschule, where a generation of European students was in turn to discover through his teaching many of the lessons of Texas. Rowe first taught at New York's Cooper Union and then Cornell University to the north in Ithaca. A few of years later he returned to Cambridge University in England. However, he admitted he was "always more at home in the colonies"; he returned to Cornell University in 1962 to establish its urban design program. He published most influential book Collage City soon after. Hejduk and Slutzky also returned to the East Coast and, after a brief period, settled at Cooper Union. Hejduk eventually became the dean of Cooper Union, while Slutzky continued as a successful painter.

B-11 有机形

有机形由光滑曲线连接而成，很少有直线。由直线和曲线连成的形既具有几何性，又具有有机性。

Organic Forms

Organic forms are formed of smoothly flowing curves with imperceptible transitions or project connections. Straight lines are rarely present. A shape created with curves and straight lines exhibits geometric as well as organic characteristics.

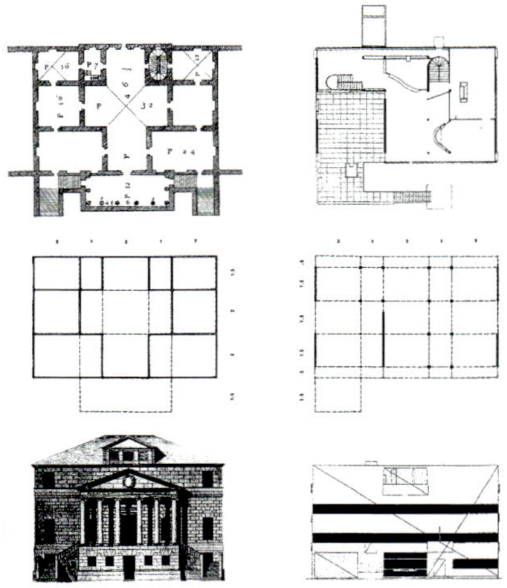

图1-9-1 柯林·罗对帕拉蒂奥的马康藤塔住宅和柯布西耶的加西斯住宅的比较分析

1.9 柯林·罗和他的艺术家们

在1945年至1947年间，柯林·罗跟随伦敦沃堡学院的鲁道夫·维特阔克学习，打下了坚实的历史知识基础，具备了极高的洞察力和评论能力。维特阔克的结构分析方法运用在柯林·罗的著作中，这些著作直接影响得克萨斯建筑学校的教学法。

> *他（维特阔克）认为文艺复兴时期的建筑是对“某些特定意义”的图解，所以各种要素，如平面、立面、剖面等都包含这些意义。对这些建筑的解读，即“阅读”密码是维特阔克的重要贡献。他运用光学和格式塔心理学概念解读文艺复兴建筑的立面、平面和内空间。“解读”，即帮助读者了解格式塔的线索或者建筑的基本思想。从平面、墙体和剖面来解读建筑空间是维特阔克的重要发明，是观察理解空间和形体的新方法。*[90]

在学维特阔克之后，柯林·罗在耶鲁大学跟随希区柯克学习了一年。之后他在美国旅行并参与一些设计项目，直到1953年受聘于得克萨斯大学。他的同事罗伯特·马克斯韦尔对他有这样的评价：“在头五个学期里，他不仅通过引进欧洲模式而改革了建筑设计教学，而且改变了美国人对自己传统的看法，他高度评价得克萨斯州洛克哈特市的城市价值，并由此指出美国住区的多样性和美国古典复兴的历史价值。”[91]

此时的他年仅33岁，已是一位有成就的建筑评论家。他参与二年级和三年级评图，讲授意大利文艺复兴。卡拉古纳曾对柯林·罗对历史事件的广博知识有这样的评述：“他引证大量鲜为人知却又和建筑密切相关的东西，向学生灌输当时设计课中没有的学术和理论。”[92] 他和赫茨里有不少相似之处，两人都有深厚的欧洲和英国建筑传统背景，对分析立体主义的建筑有浓厚兴趣，熟悉并喜爱柯布西耶作品中的理论质素（图1-9-1）。

柯林·罗在耶鲁大学时，约瑟夫·阿尔贝斯的学生作业给他留下的印象很深，斯路斯基和哈希尔都是阿尔贝斯的学生，他们到得克萨斯大学和柯林·罗的极力推荐有关。作为画家，斯路斯基一直关注建筑和绘画的关系，尽管自己并非建筑师，他对立体主义、风格派和现代建筑的关系兴趣浓厚。他在耶鲁大学的毕业论文直接受到20世纪艺术和格式塔视觉心理学的影响。他和柯林·罗之间的思想共鸣无疑得益于这种背景，他们合写了“透明性”理论。当然，斯路斯基和哈希尔的首要工作是向学生传播阿尔贝斯的绘画和色彩理论。

B-12 质感

质感可分为触觉质感和视觉质感两类。触觉质感是三维的，可以用手感觉到。视觉质感是二维的，通过眼睛来感受，但可以引发触觉，可以通过绘画、印刷、替换、擦揉、喷漆、泼墨、染色、拼贴等方法获得。

Texture

Texture can be divided into tactile texture and visual texture. Tactile Texture can be felt with the hand. It rises above the surface of a two-dimensional design and approaches a three-dimensional relief. Visual texture is a two-dimensional texture that is seen by eye although it also may evoke tactile sensations. It may be achieved through drawing, painting, printing, transferring, rubbing, spraying, spilling, pouring, staining, dyeing, collage, etc..

1.9 Colin Rowe and His Artists

Between 1945—1947, Colin Rowe studied under Rudolf Wittkower at Warburg Institute, London, during which Rowe built a solid foundation in history and developed an extraordinary power of observations and criticism. An influence of Wittkower's structured analytical approach is evidenced in Rowe's writing, which has later impacted the educational methodology of Texas School of Architecture.

> *He (Wittkower) proceeded from the assumption that the architectural productions of the Renaissance were iconographic, imbued with "particular meaning", and therefore that each of their manifold aspects — plans, elevation, section — was also imbued with that meaning. The decoding of that architecture, the "reading" of that code, is Wittkower's equally considerable accomplishment. Through the application of optical and Gestalt psychological concepts, Wittkower shows us how building facades, plans, and the internal space of Renaissance architecture may be "read". "Read", in the sense of imparting to the observer a particular meaning, a clue to the Gestalt or the essential idea of the building... The reading of architectural space via plans, walls, and sections — this extraordinary invention of Wittkower's — is a new way of seeing or interpreting space and form.* [90]

After completing his study with Wittkower, he spent another year on a scholarship at Yale, studying with Henry-Russell Hitchcock. In 1952, he travelled in the United States, worked on a number of architectural projects before accepting a post at the University of Texas in 1953. As his colleague Robert Maxwell later remembers his contribution, "During only five semesters when he taught there he not only revolutionized the teaching of architectural design by bringing in European models, but he altered the American attitude toward its own heritage by his praise for the city of Lockhart in Texas and generally, by pointing to the dynamic quality of American settlements, and the American revitalization of the Classical." [91]

Rowe was 33 years old when he taught at Texas School of Architecture and was already an accomplished architectural critic. He was assigned as a critic in the sophomore and junior studios, and a lecturer on the Italian Renaissance. Caragonne notes that Rowe possessed a prodigious memory for historical fact and example. "With an astounding recall of the most obscure but unfailingly relevant architectural scheme, he imparted to his students a level of scholarship and theory exceptional in the design studios of the period." [92] Here, he shared many commonalties with Hoesli. Both of them were thoroughly grounded in the European and British architectural traditions, had an intense interest in the architectural nature of analytical cubism, and were also familiar with and attracted to didactic possibilities of Le Corbusier's work (Pic.1-9-1).

The hiring of Slutzky and Hirsche was due to Harris's inclination and Rowe's prompting. But it was Rowe who was very impressed with the work of Josef Albers' students during his year spent at Yale. Both Slutzky and Hirsche had studied under Albers. As a painter, Slutzky remained permanently fascinated with the relationship between architecture and painting. Although untrained as an architect, Slutzky had had an interest in the connection between cubism, the de Stijl movement, and modern architecture. Significantly, he had also completed a thesis at Yale inspired by the relationship of twentieth-century art to Gestalt perception psychology. Such a background readily lent itself to that significant exchange of ideas between himself and Colin Rowe and, subsequent to that, their collaboration on the

"在包豪斯，我有很多套色彩系列的样品，用来测试触觉质感。学生要闭上眼睛，用手指去感觉这些质感系列。很快他们的触觉就大大提高了。于是我让他们进行材料质感对比的综合练习。学生创作出各种别出心裁的构图，周围的一切都被重新发现了——粗糙的木头和刨花、钢丝、长金属线和绳，光滑的木头和羊毛、羽毛、玻璃和锡箔、网格和各种织物、皮革、皮毛以及发光的铝罐。学生们发现了新的手工技术和新的质感。一个创新的手工艺时代开始了，刚被唤醒的敏感开发出了无穷的质感以及组合的可能性。"（Itten, 1963）

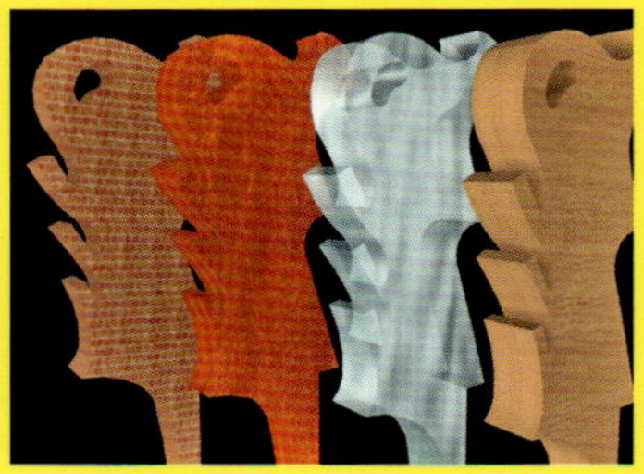

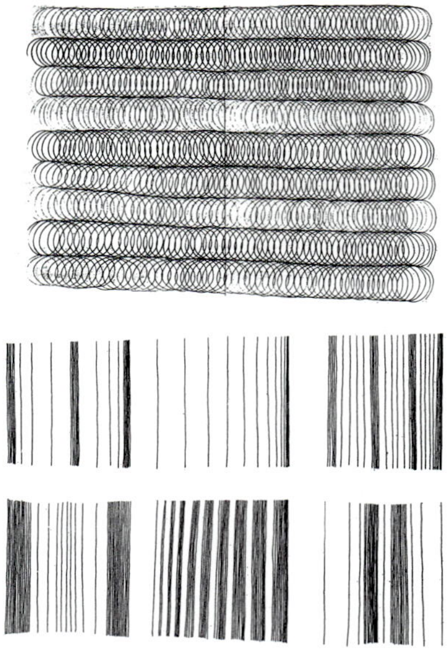

图1-9-2 斯路斯基和哈希尔的美术课绘画基础练习

图1-9-3 绘画练习：家庭日用品

在新教程中，一年级绘画课的目的是培养学生清晰观察和准确描述的能力。他们强调观察、线条和组织，而不是简单的徒手写生。他们主要画单线条（图1-9-2）。禁止使用图画式的和夸张的表现手法，甚至不允许使用明暗和阴影。体量、深度和形体细部都要求用连续的单线条来体现（图1-9-3，图1-9-4）。这样学生必须仔细观察，画画时要信心充沛，并培养心、眼、手的协调。这种严格的线条画同时也培养了学生简练的工作态度，尽量用一条线表述通常十条线才能表述的东西。他们也教一些空间的表现技巧。

课中还教概念素描和“负空间”刻画。概念素描引自伊藤的练习，让学生根据记忆和想象而不是实物作画。大量此类训练开发学生的抽象和选择能力，这是一般绘画达不到的。对物体之间的“负空间”的刻画训练采用了阿尔贝斯关于感知模糊性的教学法（图1-9-5），旨在增强学生的观察能力，但更主要的是加强学生对物体和空间在视觉上快速转换的能力。在实体和空间，物体和背景之间的慧眼转换，让学生更清楚地看到各部分之间的关系和比例。这些课程练习不仅提高了学生的绘画技巧，而且培养一种“观察”空间和物体的能力，这正是设计的基本技能之一（图1-9-6，图1-9-7）。

斯路斯基和哈希尔同时根据阿尔贝斯的色彩互动理论改革了色彩课程。阿尔贝斯的色彩课让学生把色彩看作互动关系，“一般的理论将色彩分类研究而忽视它们的真正生命——色彩在环境中的表现方式，阿尔贝斯正是要突破这类理论”。[93] 斯路斯基和哈希尔照搬阿尔贝斯的课，让学生集中注意色彩的感觉和效果，他们不采用一般绘画方式，而是让学生“发现”色彩和形体，如以剪贴画板而不是作画来训练色彩感觉。每节课都有特定的主题，如色块边际线的清晰和模糊，色彩强度、补色、色彩透明度的使用，空间表现，光的“混合”作用和模式变换等等（图1-9-8）。[94] 和阿尔贝斯一样，他们将色彩课作为实验，与新教学计划要求的以平面色块为主的建筑表现是一致的。

> *课程的哲学基础——色彩表象的相对性，多样性和转换性，模糊性和艺术的关系以及摒弃各种色彩‘原理’（阿尔贝斯的教学和作品的主要思想）都和柯林·罗的思想密切相关，即强调‘观察’的重要性，避开所谓的抽象理论。在这些方面，斯路斯基和哈希尔的课程都进一步强化了新课程大纲的思想和目标。*[95]

"At the Bauhaus, I had long chromatic series of material samples made for the tactile assessment of the various textures. The students had to feel these sequences of textures with their fingertips, their eyes closed. After a short while their sense of touch improved dramatically. I then asked them to make texture montages of contrasting materials. Fantastic structure were produced and their effects were completely novel at the same time. . . The whole environment was rediscovered — rough pieces of wood and wood shavings, steel wool, lengths of wire and rope, polished wood and sheep's wool, feathers, glass and tin foil, grids and weaves of all kinds, leather, fur, and shiny tin cans. Manual skills were discovered and new textures found. It was the beginning of a period of fantastic 'handicraftsmanship', and the newly awakened sense of discovery found inexhaustible treasures of textures and possibilities of combination." (Itten, 1963)

Transparency essays. However, the first step Slutzky and Hirsche took was to introduce students to the Albers color theory and methods of drawing.

Under the new curriculum, the drawing segment of the first year was to be devoted to the development of the student's ability to see with clarity and to draw with accuracy. Therefore, Slutzky and Hirsche emphasized more on observation, line and composition, rather than simply freehand drawing in perspective. The new approach was based on a preference for, but not limited to, the single expressive line as a method of drawing (Pic.1-9-2). Picturesque or expressionist representations of reality were prohibited as were the use of shading and shadows. The fullness, depth, and detail of forms were taught to be found within the discipline of the single, continuous line (Pic.1-9-3,Pic.1-9-4). This taught students to observe carefully, to draw with conviction, and to develop a co-ordinated mind, eye and hand. This strict reliance upon line drawing taught the student an economy of means: to avoid ten lines when one would do. Other drawing techniques to represent spatiality were also emphasized.

图1-9-4 绘画练习：鞋

图1-9-5 椅子的图底空间研究

图1-9-6 学生作业：单色及其变化的构成

Other concepts introduced to the class were the gestural drawing and delineation of negative space. The gestural drawing was adopted from Itten's exercises, in which students were asked to draw without reference to the subject, by memory and by intuition. The rigorous application of this new discipline stimulated students to develop a power of abstraction and selection that ordinary drawing could not provide. The exercises on the delineation of negative space adopted Albers' teaching on the ambiguity in perception (Pic.1-9-5) .The effort to draw the "negative space" defined by the object was a seminal exercise designed to increase the student's skill in observation and, most importantly, to enhance students' ability to shuttle visually back and forth between the subject/object itself and the space it occupied. This oscillation of the mind's eye between solid and void, foreground and background acted as a self-correcting device that enabled students to see more clearly the actual relationship of parts and their true proportions. These drawing classes, apart from improving students' skill in drawing, also encouraged them to develop an ability to "see" space as well as objects, an essential skill in design (Pic.1-9-6,Pic.1-9-7) .

Slutzky and Hirsche also restructured the color course based on Albers' theories of color interaction. As Werner Spies described, Albers' color course was designed to teach his students to see color as interactive; to "liberate the teaching of color from conventional theories, which codify colors but analyze them into oblivion by ignoring that which gives them life — the way they are perceived in context". [93] Slutzky and Hirsche adopted the same format as in Albers' class. In order to allow the student to concentrate on the perception of color and its effects, and avoid reliance on conventional painting technique, "found" colors or objects such as cutouts from magazines were used instead of paint. Each class focused on a specific issue each time. Here, they instilled students with concepts such as border or non-border line between colors, color intensity, simultaneous contrasts, and manifestation of color transparency, spatial illusion, and optical "mixing" and disrupted patterns (Pic.1-9-8).[94] Like Albers, Slutzky and Hirsche conducted the color course experimentally, moving into areas that were consistent with the new architectural program's preference for the use of flat, colored planes in architectural presentations.

> *The philosophical basis of the course — the relative, variable, transmutable nature of color perception; the correlation between ambiguity and art; and the avoidance of color "theories" (all of which Albers himself demonstrated in his teaching and work) — was closely akin to Rowe's own philosophical stance, the importance attached to the "specifics of observation" and the avoidance of so-called abstract theory. In all of these areas, the course as taught by Slutzky and Hirsche had the effect of amplifying those ideas and*

B-13 建筑空间的属性

Properties of Architectural Space

空间的属性由下列空间围合的特性所决定。

Spatial qualities depend on the following properties of the enclosure of a space.

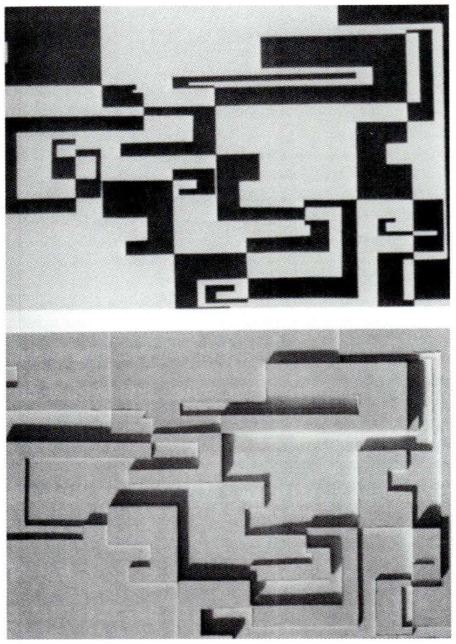

图1-9-7 图底转换构成：ETH 1959至1960年设计基础课中的基本练习

图1-9-8 网格上的透明性练习

总之，他们的课程成功地引进了线条、色彩和构成的基本原理，以及和建筑空间的关系。他们鼓励学生通过绘画达到观察、动手和思考的统一。正如柯林·罗后来指出的一样：“这些学生的绘画，用阿尔贝斯的体系来看，表现了高度精练的素质，而今天在我看来，得克萨斯短暂而辉煌的教学成就直接来自这些新生作品，这种素质在学习过程中不断强化。这实际上直接与斯路斯基冷静而热情的教学方式有关。”[96]

海杜克一直和赫茨里一起从事建筑设计教学，他在得克萨斯的主要贡献之一就是发明了九宫格练习（图1-9-9），这个练习直到今天还被一些学校采用。而实际上在这之前，斯路斯基和哈希尔已经用九个立方体在他们的设计组做了相似的三维练习，他们用纸板围合、分隔、定位和组合一系列的空间元素，然而这个练习与建筑关系不够紧密。作为建筑师，海杜克将垂直和水平元素定义为柱和梁，从而形成框架结构，由此发展下去，底板变成平面，垂直的和半高的板块成为空间分隔墙，而由梁支撑的水平板块则为屋顶。这种由一系列基本建筑构成练习组成的教学法，如九宫格练习，和赫茨里主张的以实用形体组合做抽象设计的思想完全一致。不久海杜克自己继续对框架形体做了进一步研究，发展成为后来著名的得克萨斯住宅。这些住宅设计，和同时期的学生作业，将九宫格增加到了2层（18个立方体）或3层（27个立方体），这种看似简单的练习包含了无穷变化。一方面它是“现代”的、流行的，体现了密斯风格；而在另一方面，它又好像超出纯粹的思想，跨越时间、场所和风格。[97] 用海杜克自己的话来说：“九宫格和风格无关。因为九宫格的空间变化无穷。”[98]

围合特性
Properties of Enclosure

- 大小dimensions
- 形状shape
- 组合configuration
- 表面surface
- 边界edges
- 开放度opening

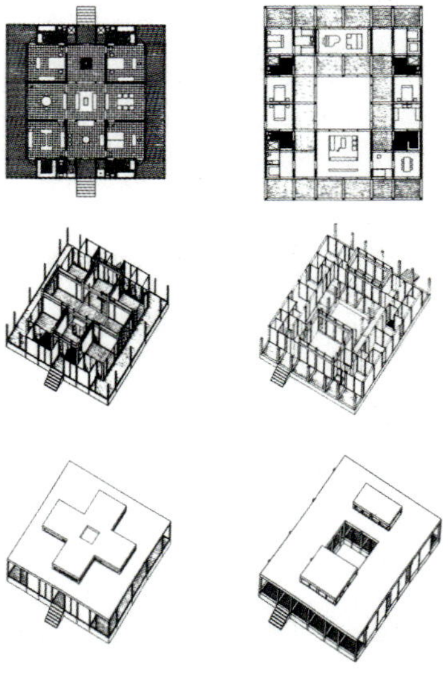

图1-9-9 海杜克的九宫格设计

objectives outlined in the new program. [95]

On the whole, Slutzky and Hirsche's courses were successful in introducing these basic principles of lines, color and composition and their relationship to architectural space. They encouraged students to keep on drawing until the act of observation and the activity of one's hand and mind became inseparable. As Rowe commented later on, "The drawings the students made, under Albers' dispensation, were of an economy which was outstanding; and, today, I would say that it was from these arrivals that there began the great brilliance of a very brief Texas performance. A performance where the students were excessively stimulated; and where, I suspect, they particularly responded to the passionately cool teachings of Slutzky." [96]

Hejduk had been working closely with Hoesli in the design studio, but one of his major contributions during his tenure at Texas was his invention of the nine-square grid exercise (Pic.1-9-9), which continues to evolve in various architectural schools today. During that time, Slutzky and Hirsche devised a similar three-dimensional exercise in their design course for their students with a grid of nine equal cubes. Here, panels of board were used to enclose, divide, define and configure a number of elementary spatial effects. However, the process did not quite relate to architecture yet. When Hejduk came along, as an architect, he reinterpreted the verticals and horizontals as post and beam, and thus, a frame structure emerged. From this, the base would signify the plan, vertical panels and half-panels would be space-defining partitions and the horizontal panels supported by the "beams" would represent the roof. This rationale for a series of elementary architectural exercises, titled the Nine Square Grid Exercises, became fully in line with Hoesli's idea of an integrated "useful" form of abstract design. Hejduk himself soon became engaged in an independent investigation of the frame, through a series of studies that would later come to be known as the Texas Houses. In these projects, and simultaneously in the work of his students, the nine-square grid exercise was expanded into two-storey (18-cube) or three-storey (27-cube) formats. This apparently straightforward exercise did not hinder its wide spectrum of various interpretations. On one level, it was undeniably contemporary and "modern", with a definite Miesian orientation, and therefore congruent with the academic rationale developed by Hoesli and Rowe: Yet, on another level, it seemed to exist as pure idea, transcendent of time, place and style. [97] In Hejduk's own view, "the nine-square has nothing to do with style. It is detached: The nine-square is unending in its voidness."[98]

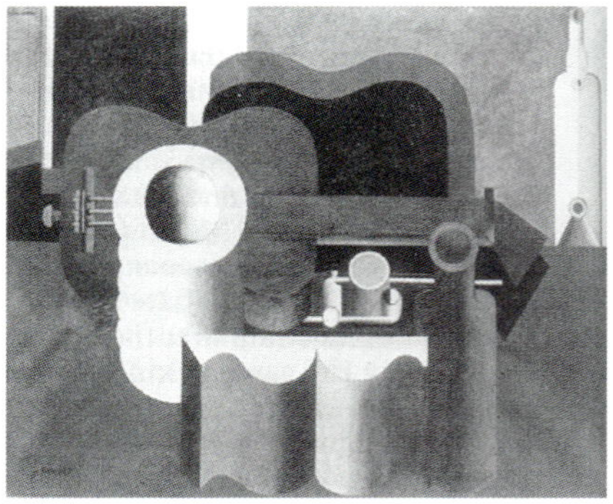

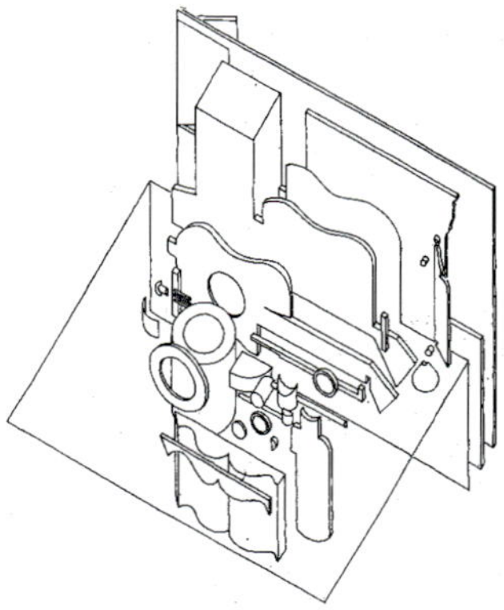

图1-10-1 对柯布西耶绘画的空间解析

图1-10-2 布拉克《葡萄牙人》，1911—1912年

1.10 透明性理论

柯林·罗等人认为，在设计课里加入建筑历史，对启发学生思维至关重要（图1-10-1）。他将设计组的作用视为“一个剧院，而不仅是实验室。在剧院里，教师、学生、各种材料、谜语、先例和个人价值应结合、碰撞，但最终通过具体的艺术方法，像一台戏一样，完整地演绎出来”。[99]

柯林·罗和赫茨里一样，主张重建设计方法学的学术地位，以建立正统的现代建筑评论框架，反对格罗皮乌斯的自我表现主义。

除了伊藤的向先师学习的练习外，包豪斯的“客观”教学法排斥对历史先例的研究，主张“内在冲动的表现”，柯林·罗对此不以为然。他要在设计课里形成一种气氛，一种质疑精神和对意义的追求。在几年后写的一篇文章中，柯林·罗这样来回顾他的建筑教育目的：

> *我认为建筑教育是一个非常简单的事情，教育工作者的任务可以简单地描述如下：*
>
> *1．鼓励学生坚信建筑学和现代主义建筑；*
>
> *2．鼓励学生质疑建筑学和现代主义建筑；*
>
> *3．由此让学生以热情和智慧去操作自己信念和怀疑中的主观和客观内容。*[100]

由柯林·罗和斯路斯基在这个时期完成的论文集《透明性》（1955—1956）概括了他们在得克萨斯的思想和教学法。卡拉哥纳认为他们“是在所有人中真正奠定了这个学校的学术思想和共同观念基础的人”。[101] 赫茨里认为：“这本书用实例证明了以现有经验足以奠定一套理论。”[102] 这是自希区柯克《走向建筑的艺术》（1948）之后的第一本分析立体主义绘画和现代建筑关系的重要著作。但即便是文集中最早发表的《透明性：实际与现象》这篇文章，也是直到1963年才得以在耶鲁大学的建筑刊物《视野》上发表。这些文章集中反映了柯林·罗的分析思路和体验，与斯路斯基在现代艺术和格式塔心理学关系方面的学识。

柯林·罗和斯路斯基开篇以吉奥吉·凯佩斯的双重定义来解释“透明性”一词。“如果你看到两个或者两个以上的人形叠在一起，这些人形具有透明性……然而透明性还不局限于视觉，而是有着更广泛的空间秩序。透明性指同时看到不同空间位置上的表象。空间不仅远去，而且在一个连续的活动中起伏不定。透明人形的位置有多重解释，就像它既在前面，又在后面。”[103] 因此，柯林·罗和斯路斯基将“实际透明（如玻璃幕墙一样的物质特性）”和“现象透明（一

图1-10-3 莫霍利－纳吉的构成，1947年

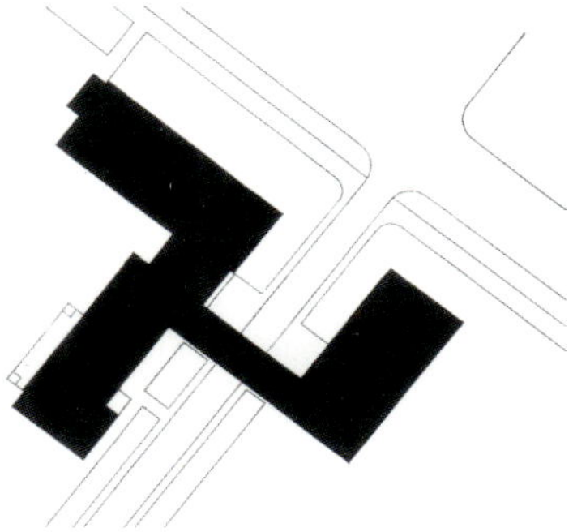

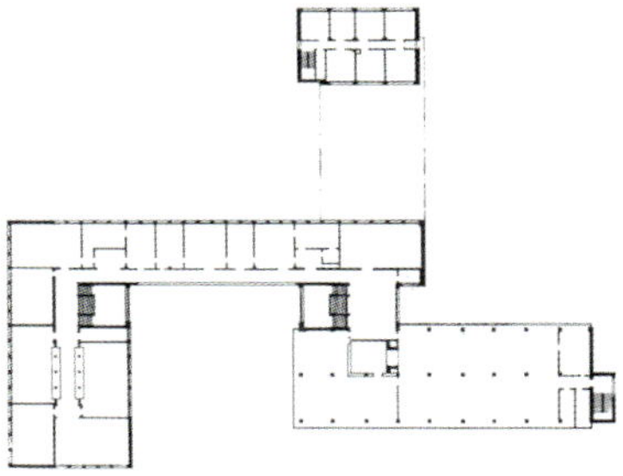

图1-10-4 柯林·罗分析的包豪斯平面

1.10 The Theory of Transparency

Primarily, Row and his friends found it essential and critical to reintroduce architectural history in the design studio as a vital and practical stimulus to students (Pic.1-10-1). To Rowe, the role of the design studio "esembles less a laboratory than a theater or, if you will, a scene within a theater in which teacher, student, material facts, myth, precedent, and personal values are encouraged to combine, clash, and ultimately find approximate expression through the manufacture of a specific, tangible, artistic work". [99]

Further, Rowe also echoed with Hoesli's belief in restoring the intellectual approach of design and in reestablishing a legitimate form of contemporary architectural criticism, as opposed to Gropius' approach of self-expressionism.

It is this Bauhaus' "objective" teaching approach, that no historical precedent, except Itten's exercise of learning from masters, was allowed to follow and reliance on "innate budding expression", which Rowe found unnecessary and denied. On the contrary, he sought to establish in the design studio a particular mood, a spirit of inquiry and a search for meaning. In an essay he wrote some years later, Rowe reflected on the subject of architectural education:

> *I presume architectural education to be a very simple matter; and the task of the educator I am convinced can be quite simply specified as follows:*
>
> *1. To encourage the student to believe in architecture and modern architecture;*
>
> *2. To encourage the student to be sceptical about architecture and modern architecture;*
>
> *3. And then to cause the student to manipulate, with passion and intelligence, the subjects or objects of his conviction and doubt.* [100]

An important series of essays which Rowe developed with Slutzky during this period, *Transparency* (1955—1956), demonstrated the ideology and pedagogy Rowe held onto during his tenure at Texas School of Architecture. As Caragonne describes, they were " … more than any other, responsible for providing an intellectual thrust and a common understanding for that 'school' within a school". [101] In Hoesli's words: " … it demonstrates by way of example that theoretical bases can be obtained from what has been developed empirically."[102] This was the first significant analytical work on the study of Cubist painting and Modern architecture since H-R. Hitchcock's *Painting Toward Architecture* (1948). However, the first of these essays, *Transparency: Literal and Phenomenal*, was not published until 1963 in Yale's architectural journal Perspecta. These essays combined both the analytical minds and experiences of Rowe with Slutzky's knowledge of the relationship between modern art and Gestalt psychology.

From the outset, Rowe and Slutzky furnished the term "transparency" with Gyorgy Kepes' dual definition."If one sees two or more figures overlapping one another, … the figures are endowed with transparency … Transparency however implies more than an optical characteristic, it implies a broader spatial order. Transparency means a simultaneous perception of different spatial locations. Space not only recedes but also fluctuates in a continuous activity. The position of the transparent figures has equivocal meaning as one sees each figure now as the closer now as the further one." [103] Hence, Rowe and Slutzky distinguished "literal transparency" as "an inherent quality of substance, as in a glass curtain wall", such as Braque's *Le Portugais* (Pic.1-10-2), Moholy-Nagy's *La Sarraz* (Pic.1-10-3) and Gropius' Bauhaus School at Dessau (Pic.1-10-4) ; and "phenomenal transparency" as "an inherent quality

C-1 相似

如果形式只是相像而不完全相同，则不是重复，而是相似。视觉上常常将元素根据特征、轮廓，或对称分组。观者通常将相似的形状和图案视为一组。主要相似的特性包括色彩、质感、色调、图案等，被认知为一组。

相似形式的集合保持了一种强烈的秩序感。在设计中的相似可以通过单元形在形状、尺寸、色彩、质感的轻微变化而达到。相似不等于重复，但是可以与重复、放射、渐变等结合运用。

图1-10-5 毕加索《单簧管演奏家》

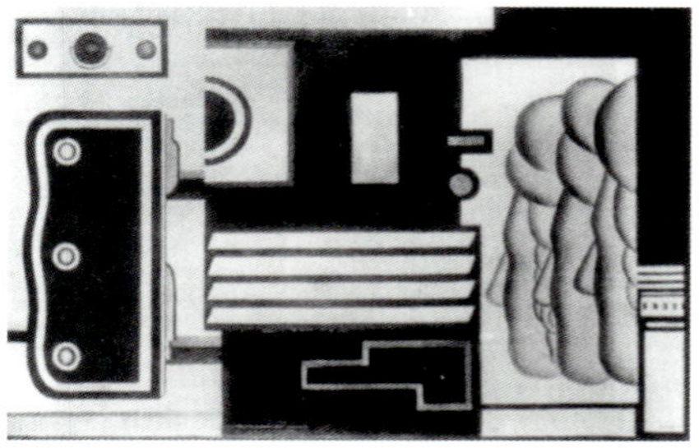

图1-10-6 费尔南·莱热《三张脸》，1927年

种组织关系特性）”区别开来，[104] 前者体现在布拉克（图1-10-2）和莫霍利-纳吉的绘画（图1-10-3）以及格罗皮乌斯的德绍包豪斯校舍（图1-10-4），而后者则体现在毕加索《单簧管演奏家》（图1-10-5）和费尔南·莱热的《三张脸》（1926）（图1-10-6）以及柯布西耶的加西斯住宅（图1-10-7）上。两者词义相近，但却代表两种不同的状态。由此，柯林·罗和斯路斯基彻底研究这些实例，特别是格罗皮乌斯和柯布西耶的作品。包豪斯校舍体现所有实际物质上的透明性：如悬挑的玻璃幕墙，光洁的外表，虚化的转角等。此外，空间上不存在“空间尺寸上的矛盾”，“没有运动的取向”，多层面的建筑形体“并不体现在内外空间中的多层次结构”。[105] 总之，柯林·罗和斯路斯基认为格罗皮乌斯的设计没有现象组织式的透明性中的复杂性，如空间层次，如空间延伸，或者内空间穿过平整外墙扩张到外空间，在深度空间的真实和浅显空间的延续之间对话和张力，以及形体关系的多重不同解释。[106]

《透明性》一文中最主要的观点是建筑空间可以通过空和无，而不是材料来“构造、支撑和塑造”（图1-10-8）。[107] 这种对建筑空间的新理解方法也是这些教师的共识，即得克萨斯建筑大学新教程的理论基础。

Similarity

If forms are not identical, they are not in repetition. They are in similarity. Elements are visually grouped according to like features, contours, or symmetries. Viewers tend to see similar shapes and figures as one group. Figures with similar color, texture, value, and pattern are more dominant and are perceived as one group.

Similar forms resembling each other maintain a strong feeling of regularity. Similarity of forms in a design usually refers to shapes of unit forms, which can be created by slightly verifying the shape, size, colour, or texture of unit forms in a composition. Similarity is not repetition. However, it can combine with repetition, radiation, gradation, and etc. as one composite tool in arrangement of forms.

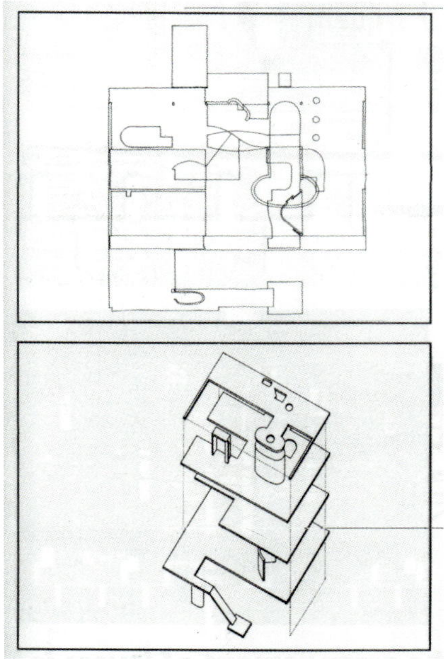

图1-10-7 赫茨里对加西斯住宅的分析

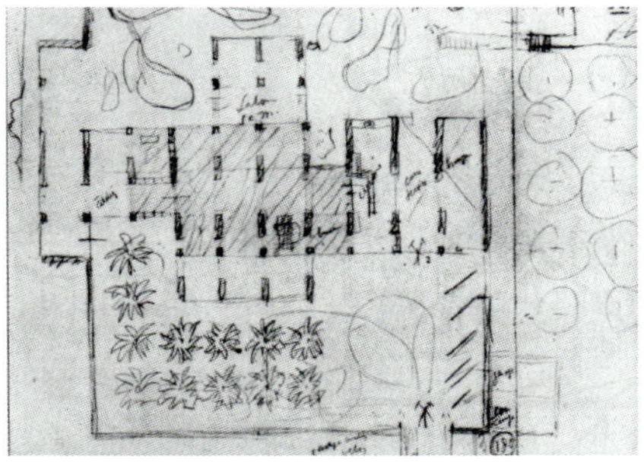

图1-10-8 柯布西耶的平面草图，说明透明性如何使规整的结构具有空间灵活性

of organization", [104] such as Picasso's *Le Clarinettiste* (Pic.1-10-5) , Lèger's *Composition with Three Faces* (1926) (Pic.1-10-6) and Le Corbusier's Villa a Garches (Pic.1-10-7). The terms look similar, yet, each of them points to a fundamentally different reality. From this, Rowe and Slutzky thoroughly examined these examples, especially projects of Gropius and Le Corbusier. The Bauhaus was presented as embodying all the characteristics of a literal, material transparency: suspended glass walls, polished surfaces, dematerialized corners. Apart from these features, the space was lack of "a contradiction of spatial dimensions", "no preference of movement direction", the layerlike character of the blocks failed "to suggest a layerlike structure of either internal or external space",[105] On the whole, Rowe and Slutzky found no evidence of sophistication as found in a phenomenal, orgainizing transparency, such as spatial stratification: a deep extension or enlargement of interior space behind a flat, unassuming exterior; a continuous dialectic and tension between the reality of deep space and the inference of shallow space; and multiple interpretational possibilities of formal relationship.[106]

One of the most significant ideas from this Transparency essay is Rowe and Slutzky's proposal that architectural space could become "constructed, substantial, and articulate"(Pic.1-10-8),[107] not from the material object, but from the mere emptiness or void. This promulgation of spatial interpretation of architecture reflected the consensus of the young faculty and formed the theoretical basis of the program at the Texas School of Architecture.

C-2 接近

指元素之间的距离的接近。相互靠近的元素在构图中被看作一组统一体的“成员”。当形体的位置很接近时，即使并不相似，观者也会倾向于将它们归为同一组。将位置上接近的形体联系起来，成为一组大面积元素，具有更强的视觉吸引力。

图1-11-1 伯恩哈德·赫茨里，1983年

图1-11-2 费尔南·莱热《手和帽子的构成》，1926年

1.11 伯恩哈德·赫茨里

伯恩哈德·赫茨里1923年出生于瑞士（图1-11-1）。他将一生全部智慧贡献给建筑设计过程的规律性研究和以形体作为设计手段的探索。[108] 他毕业于苏黎世高工，在画家费尔南·莱热（图1-11-2）的画室短暂工作一段时间后，加入柯布西耶事务所。他参与的柯布西耶的两个设计项目——他任项目监理的建成于1949年的马赛公寓（图1-11-3）和建成于1948年的巴西克鲁彻特住宅（图1-11-4），对他后来的教育和设计思想有很大影响。他后来经常以巴西克鲁彻特住宅这个城市加建项目为例在课堂上讲解空间分析。在柯布西耶工作室的两年经历，使他既具备教师应有的学术能力，又具有职业建筑师的现实态度。但1950年他却突然离开了柯布西耶，到美国旅行参观赖特的建筑。这次旅行又一次激发了他对学术的兴趣。旅行期间他申请了得克萨斯大学的教师职位，1951年任教，当时他才27岁。

开始时，他主要教三年级设计课和规划课。然而，当时的教学体系缺乏对建筑空间和形体的生成、意义和内容的研究，教学计划忽视历史课，这令具备深厚历史知识的赫茨里十分不满。他将自己的不满与哈里斯谈了，两人都有同感，决定制定一个新的教学计划，1953年他负责重组设计组。

赫茨里的教程来自“巴艺”和包豪斯。他强调方法和对先例的研究源自“巴艺”学院派，而他坚持探索、实验，尊重个人选择和表现的理念则来自早期的包豪斯。[109]（这是他的教学体系一开始就存在的问题，我们会在后面加以分析。）课程内容应该是典型的设计步骤(或)段落，例如功能阐述，安排，现场空间布置，环境，结构选择等。他的教程由一系列二维和三维抽象空间练习组成，通过简化设计问题和有关讲座，教授学生空间组合的基本方法，建筑绘图方法和设计的思想过程（图1-11-5）。他要求学生在设计过程中记录自己的思考和发现。有时他强调的问题太过复杂，导致学生的进度达不到要求，以及存在设计组过大等问题，但他不停地修正教学方式，同时重视学生的设计过程。从1953年到1957年，他详细记录了每天的活动，学生的进度、反馈，设计的结果和他自己对过程的反思与评价。他强调学生和教师间的相互切磋。“只要求学生做而不教学生怎样做是个严重的错误，这样，评图成了单向的筛选，而不是对学生的给予或者关怀。”[110] 他说：“我们不应该忘记先给予然后才能索取这个道理。”教学法实验的制定和选择都是为了“在学年结束的时候能够看到并鼓励学生精神方面的成长”。[111] 根据头八个月的教学实验，他逐步明确了引入建筑基础课的思路和内容，在后来的几年他也在不停地调整这个课程：

Proximity

It is about distance between elements. Elements that are nearer to each other in a composition will be seen as “belonging” together as one group of unity. When figures, even not similar, are located in close proximity to each other, viewers tend to see them as belonging to the same group of figures. Because of the visual attraction of mass, viewers relate or connect figures that are located closer together than those that are located farther apart.

图1-11-3 马赛公寓底层入口

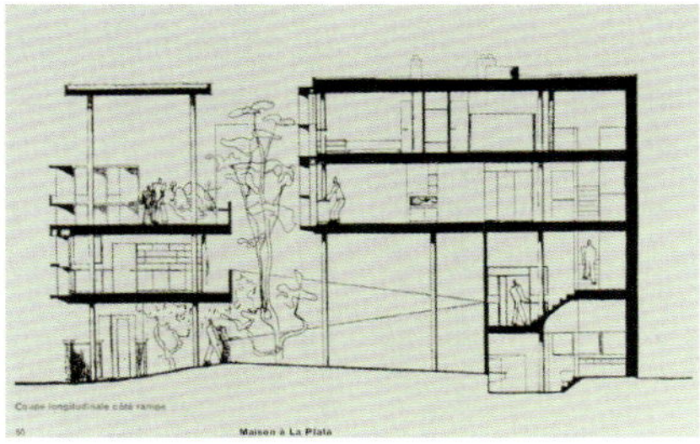

图1-11-4 克鲁彻特住宅剖面

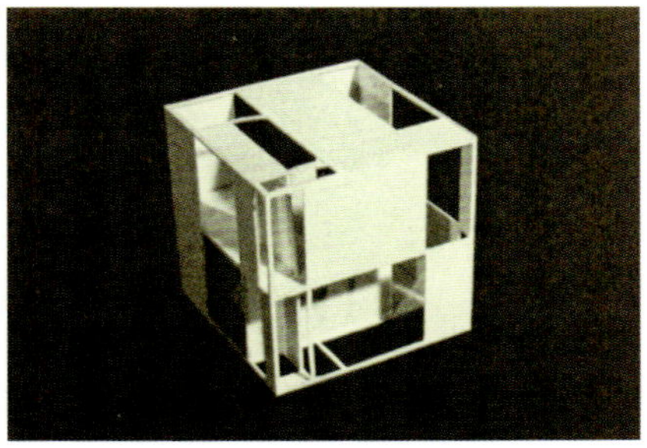

图1-11-5 “方盒子”练习，1956—1957年

1.11 Bernhard Hoesli

Bernhard Hoesli was born in Switzerland in 1923 (Pic.1-11-1). His highly intellectual mind underpinned his life-long search for a common denominator in architectural design process, and his exploration of forms as an instrument of design. [108] Following his graduation from ETH, Hoesli worked briefly at the atelier of painter Fernand Lèger (Pic.1-11-2), after which he worked as an assistant at Le Corbusier's office. There, Hoesli was assigned two projects that were influential to his later thinking as a teacher and an architect. He worked on the design of the Villa Currutchet, Brazil in 1948, and was later appointed as a project architect in the United'Habitation, Marseilles in 1949 (Pic.1-11-3). The Villa Currutchet, a small urban infill project, was later referred repeated by Hoesli in his lecture as a subject of spatial analysis (Pic.1-11-4). These two years of practice in Le Corbusier's office trained him as a teacher a strong intellectual and methodical bias tempered with the pragmatic attitude of the practitioner. In 1950, Hoesli abruptly left Le Corbusier's office and travelled to U.S.A. to see the work of Frank Lloyd Wright (the trip was intellectually stimulating and exciting to Hoesli). At the same time he applied for a teaching opening at the University of Texas and was subsequently accepted in the spring of 1951, at the age of 27.

Hoesli began his career at Texas teaching planning and the junior-year studio. However, the limited exploration into the development, meaning and content of architectural space and form, the denial and dismissal of historical precedent in the program were against Hoesli's intellect (as he had a strong sense of history) and felt much dissatisfied with the system. His frustrations were discussed and shared with Harris, and sought to resolve them by introducing a more satisfactory educational program. In 1953 he proposed a restructuring of the design studios.

Hoesli developed his new program from both the Beaux-Arts Academy and the Bauhaus: its reliance on method and the employment of example resembled the Academy's tradition, while its insistence on investigation, experimentation, and personal choice and expression resembled the philosophy of the early Bauhaus. [109] (This is where the problem of his teaching system began, which will be analyzed later.) Through a series of two- and three-dimensional exercises, simple design problems and lectures, he introduced fundamental principles of space and composition, presentation of architectural drawings, and design thinking process (Pic.1-11-5).Students were asked to keep design notebook of which they kept a record of their thinking and discoveries in design process. At many times, Hoesli might have devised too complex problems for his students, frustrated over the progress of students' work, and lamented over the size of studio. Yet, he never gave up in refining his teaching approach and in maintaining a high awareness of his students' progress. From 1953 to 1957, he diligently recorded the daily activities of the class, the progress of the students, their response to the teaching, the result of their work, and his own reflections and conclusions. He stressed the importance of interdependency of teachers and students. "A great mistake is committed when we only 'demand'from the students without giving; when the function of the critique is understood as only extracting, not as giving, as caring."[110] "We forget,"says Hoesli, "that we have to put something in the student before we can ask something of him." Experimental, methodical, and selective as his teaching method was, he evaluated at the end: "It is encouraging to realize at the end of a year that this method, which was developed while working, provides a means to provoke and, at the same time, observe mental growth." [111] These eight months of teaching experience defined some ideas with respect to the conduct and content of the introductory course to architecture, which continued to evolve in the following years:

C-3 重复

同样的形在一个设计中多次使用，称为重复。重复对于视觉和谐感的创造具有立竿见影的效果。重复可以有形状的重复、尺寸的重复、色彩的重复、质感的重复、方向的重复、位置的重复、空间的重复和重量的重复等。然而太多的重复可能会损害构图的活力。这时可以在方向和空间上作一些变化——如形以各种方式相互叠加、穿透、组合，或正负形的结合等。
元素组的重复可以产生节奏。

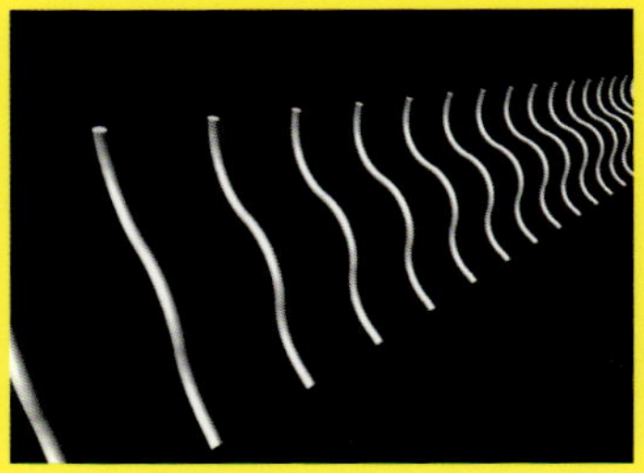

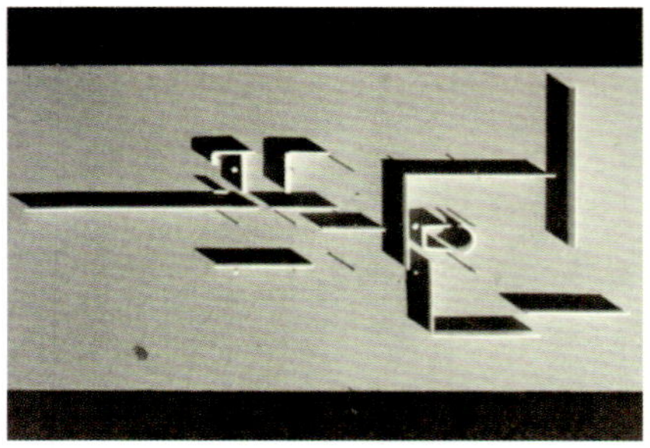

图1-11-6 赫茨里做的密斯住宅模型，1956年

图1-11-7 赫茨里做的教学模型，1956年

图1-11-8 a.古罗马哈德里安住宅遗迹

在设计中引入逻辑体系，即赫茨里的设计程序，结合空间建筑这个强有力的思想，5年里新教程改变了学校的课程计划，并成为后来35年中欧洲和美国的建筑教育研究的中心和素材，影响深远。[112]

新教程的教学方法之一是将大量现代建筑实例引入建筑教学。实例“分析”的教学方法，是得克萨斯学校的一个首创，这个练习让学生关注并发现所分析建筑的组成要素，然后用统一的格式简单直接地表述自己的发现。这些建筑一般是现代建筑大师，如柯布西耶、密斯·凡·德·罗或者赖特的作品（图1-11-6，图1-11-7）。这些研究让学生用空间去思考建筑，培养学生在作业完成后积极参与讨论的能力。

赫茨里相信，设计活动应分步进行，如确定题目、分类，用智慧不断修正设计。当一个建筑概念确定后，他要求学生通过一系列对话和讨论，把概念塑造成建筑形体。这个过程解决了在一般评图过程中“为什么你这样做”之类问题所引起的学生自我保护心态，而“你的概念是什么”等更重要的提问却可以让学生回到学习的状态中。赫茨里让学生体会到，建筑答案是在理性和分析的过程中“演进”和“出现”的，即在“设计开始前，答案并不存在”。[113]

“赫茨里要求设计问题要像‘每日一题’一样清楚地列出来，这直接影响出设计题的方法。每道设计题都分为问题、要求和目标，每次发设计题的同时，对需要运用的设计原理和方法做专门讲解。”[114] 程序化的设计过程，结合一系列关于现代艺术和建筑历史发展的讲座。正如他的设计手册指出的，这些讲座是为了阐明建筑和艺术（如绘画和雕塑）的关系，介绍现代结构方法和功能之外的空间逻辑。这些讲座也介绍概念的产生，如立体主义及其与现代建筑的关系。这些讲座让学生看到在不同大师如赖特、密斯和柯布西耶作品中，有一个建筑空间的“公分母”。赫茨里在他为柯林·罗和斯路斯基的《透明性》一书所写的前言中，用传统建筑实例，如哈德里安住宅遗迹、阿尔伯蒂设计的圣·安德里亚教堂（图1-11-8）和帕拉第奥的伊莫别墅，指出这种空间解析既是理解历史建筑，又是指向未来建筑的有力工具。

赫茨里回到瑞士以后，一直主持一年级设计课。同样他也革新了传统的课程计划。“苏黎世高工建筑系的基础课程不是包豪斯那样简单的艺术感知训练，更不是如‘巴艺’艺术和绘图技巧训练，而是在八学期的大学教育的一开始就教新生做建筑设计。”[115] 他对建筑、空间组合艺术的兴趣浓厚，决定取消其他艺术课。尽管他也曾想开设如阿尔贝斯或者斯路斯基在得克萨斯开的与建筑紧密结合的艺术课，但没有成功。实际上，赫茨里认为伊藤的基础课毫无必要。伊藤在包豪斯的课程旨在激发学生创造力，从大量不同原始材料和资源中寻找、发现艺术形体，而赫茨里的

Repetition

Same form appears more than once in a design, we use it in repetition. This visually conveys an immediate sense of harmony, and can be applied as repetition of shape, size, color, texture, direction, position, space, and gravity. More elements in repetition, stronger the sense of order, unity and harmony. However too much repetition may destroy the vitality of composition. Variations are possible through directional and spatial (forms encountering one another in a multiple of interrelationships such as overlapping, interpenetration, union, or positive and negative combinations) variations.
Repetition of elemental groups can provoke quality of rhythm.

图1-11-8 b.阿尔伯蒂设计的圣·安德里亚教堂，约1470年

The investment of a logical system—Hoesli's process of design—with a truly powerful idea—the vision of an architecture of space—utterly transformed the course of the school over the next five years and, when that program was abruptly terminated, continued to supply sufficient interest and material to influence the course of architectural education in both the United States and Europe over the following thirty-five years. [112]

One of the principle elements both Hoesli and Rowe inserted into the new curriculum was a belief that a great body of work within the modern movement was a resource to be integrated into the teaching of architecture. The "Analysis" problem, one of the original developments from the Texas School, introduced the students to focus and observe the architectural properties of an assigned building, and to present his opinions in concise words and simple models. These assigned buildings were usually works of masters of modern movement, such as Le Corbusier, Mies van der Rohe, Frank Lloyd Wright, etc.. These problems motivated students to think spatially, and stimulated discussions following their presentations (Pic.1-11-6,Pic.1-11-7).

Hoesli believed that the activity of design could be arrived at with a step-by-step process — the identification, classification, and intellectual appropriation of the design. After identifying the architectural idea, Hoesli encouraged students to develop their ability in articulating the idea into an architectural form through the process of dialogue and discussions. This approach opposed to the critic system when students were in a defensive role in answering question like "Why did you do this?". Instead, they were put in a learning role in answering more important question like "What is your idea?" . Hoesli showed that the architectural solution was "evolved" and "emerged" through this rational and analytical process and "does not exist as a pre-established fact. It is not pre-existent at the beginning of the design act." [113]

"Problems were stated with utmost clarity and according to Bernhard as 'lessons for the day'. This affected the way design problems were issued to the student. Each programme was divided into problem issues, requirements and objectives, followed each time by explanations of the particular principles or methods to be applied."[114] This conviction of an orderly design process was complimented with a series of formal lectures on the recent historical development in arts and architecture. As described in the design manual, the theme of these lectures was to illuminate the relationship between architecture and plastic arts (including painting and sculpture), to introduce students to contemporary structural organizations and to demonstrate that spatial logic was independent of functional necessity. These lectures also traced the origin, development of Cubism, and in turn its relationship with modern architecture. This led Hoesli to propose that there was a "common denominator" in the architectural space in the work of Wright, Mies, and Le Corbusier. Further, in his commentary to Rowe and Slutzky's Transparency essay, Hoesli drew architectural examples from pre-modern periods, such as Hadrian's villa, Alberti's Sant'Andrea (Pic.1-11-8), and Palliadio's Villa Emo, to demonstrate that this spatial interpretation could become a powerful tool in understanding earlier architecture, and even pointing towards the future development.

After Hoesli arrived in Zurich, his teaching focus was on first year design studio. He also fundamentally changed traditional teaching programs. "A basic course in the architectural department of the ETH could neither simply be an artistic sensitising of the student (as in Bauhaus), nor serve the training of visual design capabilities and manual skills (as in Beaux-Art), but must right away, as part of the mere eight-semester-long educational programme, introduce the beginner systematically to the design of buildings."[115] His interests in the art of architecture, or of spatial composition, quickly ruled out a possibility of integration with teaching of art. Although he hoped to establish an art course similar to Albers or Slutzky's program in Taxes, which was oriented to architecture, proved a failure. Actually, Hoesli saw

C–4　重复构图

重复可以是任意重复，也可以在一个固定的参考框架内重复。运用固定的参考框架，可以建立规则的构图——所有的元素按照一种数学秩序来组织。重复包括在一个设计中复制同样的形，或根据无形的网格按照一定间距放置形。
线性重复：按同一方向、同样间距重复形体。
二维重复：多行的单元形或组规则重复。
三维重复：产生空间和结构网格系统。

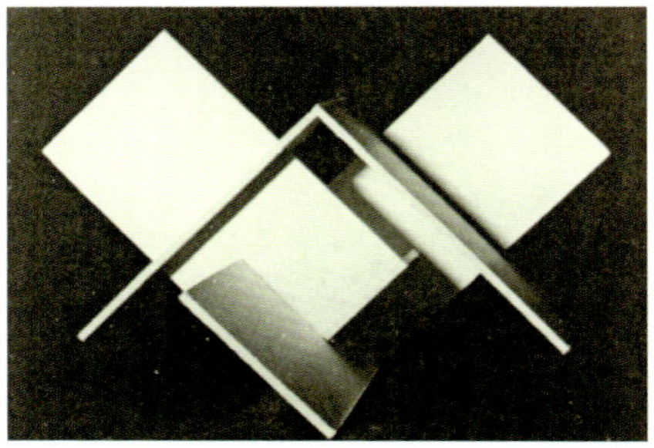

图1-11-9 空间造型练习："L"形纸板及其构成

图1-11-10 "建造方式运用"

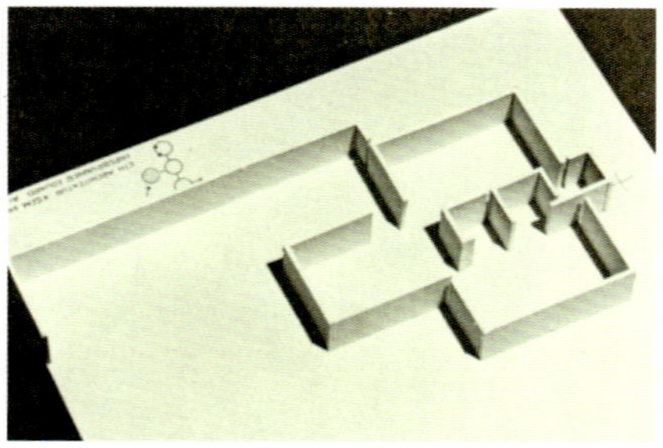

图1-11-11 "平面上的空间"

练习在这种感知训练方面自由度非常有限，却强调利用已确立的现代建筑形体概念。[116] 伊藤认为，艺术是探索未知的工具，赫茨里则相反，认为现代建筑的答案是现成的，学生要做的是遵循教学步骤将这些形体重新组合。"1959年，现代建筑已经成为独立的观念和知识体系，具有自己的原则，特别重要的是，有自己的操作模式。我坚信现代建筑是可以教的，设计是可以讨论的，以过程为中心的教学可以将设计程序制度化……"[117] 赫茨里的设计基础课一般由一系列形体和空间组合练习组成：

1．三维空间形成：由教师选择空间限定元件（如板块，"L"形或者"U"形元件），并让学生根据元件联结规则（如元件之间不能以角相连等）做一个三维空间（图1-11-9）。

2．构造利用：用木条和斜拉线做一个立方体，竖向木条也可以用板材替代，练习要求学生认识空间类型与细部构造的关系（图1-11-10）。

3．平面上的二维空间：练习要求学生在一个平面上做一系列的空间，研究空间的性质，如围合度、尺寸、形状和区域划分等（图1-11-11）。

4．空间中的空间：一个空间体既无上下之分，也无前后之别，像是浮于空中，在无限的空间中限定出一个空间部分，要求学生用不同的构造方式，如板材与木框架相结合，或者用木条分布来限定空间。

5．连续的空间：这是一种环境中的设计，设计的空间既是一个独立个体，也能与设计前或者设计后的环境空间结合成为一个整体（图1-11-12）。

6．作为方法的形：用现代建筑的"语汇"来做形体练习；同时形体也应体现和限定空间元素的构造方式（图1-11-13）。

……

从以上对基础设计练习的简述可以看出赫茨里的哲学思考和对建筑教育的重要贡献。首先，设计练习与建筑类型，如住宅、学校、工厂、医院等无关，这与格罗皮乌斯和密斯的课程组织很不同，赫茨里的练习是按问题类型组织的，如交通体系、体块布局、内外空间的过渡方式、形的开始与结束等。对格罗皮乌斯来说，功能决定形的组合，而赫茨里的形体组合原则却超越具体功能，适用于任何建筑，无论"现代"还是"传统"的。课程内容应该是典型的设计步骤(或)段落，例如功能阐述，安排，现场空间布置，环境，结构选择等。[118] 其次，赫茨里将现代建筑特征之一的创造性转换成学院式方法传授给学生——通过讲座和设计练习来传授其设计原理，而不是个案。19世纪的"巴艺"强调的是比例、轴线、光影等原理，以及新古典主义风格。而赫茨里注重的是空间组合原理，采用的是抽象元件，如板、木条、抽象的空间等现代建筑的语汇。两种教学体制有许多相似性，如都忽视社会变革和不断出现的新思想、新技术和新结构。赫茨里同建立于20世纪建筑学教

Compositions with Repetition

Repetition can be random or within a definite frame of reference. With a definite frame of reference, a regular arrangement could establish — all elements are organized in a kind of mathematical order. Repetition involves reproducing the same shape in a design as well as placing the shapes at intervals, which can be determined with lines forming an invisible structural grid.

Linear repetition: It repeats the figure in the same direction the same distance (interval) each time.
2-D repetition: rows of unit or groups of forms are repeated regularly, creating a pattern like design.
3-D repetition: results in a spatial and structural grid system.

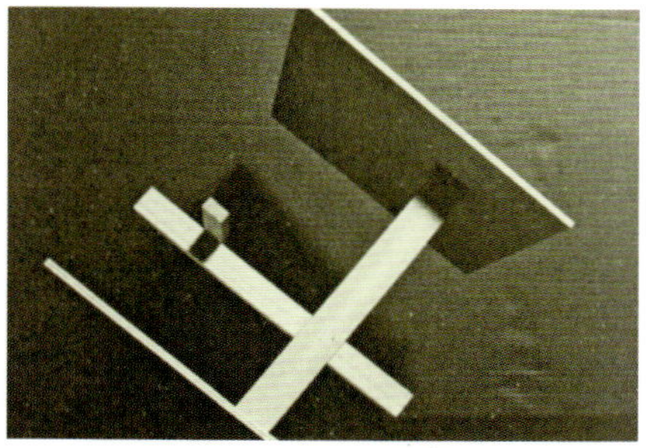

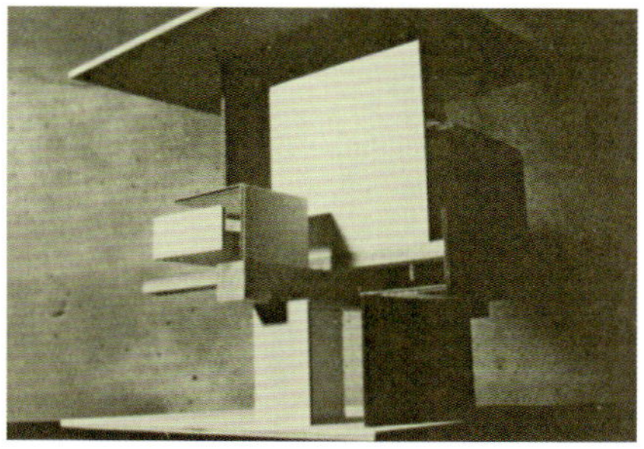

图1-11-12 “环境中的空间”，给定的环境（上图）和衍生出的设计（下图）

图1-11-13 ETH基础课中的练习，1967—1968年

Itten's basic course as unnecessary for architectural students. In Itten's pre-course at the Bauhaus, the students had to develop an object from a large variety of materials and resources by using their creative ability. Bernhard Hoesli's exercises were far less free from such sensitizing studies, but instead were much more clearly defined tasks with an established modern architectural form.[116] For Itten, art is about exploration into unknown. In contrast, Hoesli believed answers to modern architecture were already there and what was left for art was the composition of form following a teaching procedure. "In 1959, Modern Architecture appeared as a distinct body of knowledge of perceptions, principles and above all, a prototypical model of an approach. I was convinced that Modern Architecture had become teachable, that design was accessible to discursive argumentation and that process-orientated teaching could be ordered into typical design steps…" [117] A typical Hoesli "basic design course" consisted of a sequence of formal and spatial composition exercises:

1. Forming (3D) Space: A single space had to be set up by space defining elements (slabs, L-shaped and U-shaped elements) provided by teacher, as well as a principle of joints with the condition that elements should not touch each other at the corners (Pic.1-11-9).

2. Implication of Construction: A cube was set up with struts having the necessary braces; vertical struts could be partially or completely replaced by panels. Students should recognize relationships in the type and method of construction of details (Pic.1-11-10).

3. (2D) Space on a surface area: The students had to organize a certain number of spaces on a plane using variations of spatial properties, such as enclosure, size, shape and zoning (Pic.1-11-11).

4. Space (with-) in Space: A spatial object had no above or below, no front or back, floating weightlessly in space to delimit a defined space from the unlimited continuum. Student had to try several constructions, such as panels glued to a strut lattice, or wood struts positioned as a means of defining space.

5. Space within space: This was a design within context. Each space designed as itself as well as in unison with space created before and after (Pic.1-11-12).

6. Form as Means: Using the architectural "language" of the Modern Movement to generate form; but also generating form through choice of space-defining elements and the means of construction (Pic.1-11-13).

……

A brief introduction to the studio exercise illustrates the philosophy and the significant contribution Hoesli made for architectural education. Firstly, the studio projects were not selected according to building type — housing, schools, factories, hospitals, etc. as in Gropius and Mies' schools. The projects should be arranged by Problem Types —as systems of connection, volumetric arrangement, type of transition from external to internal, beginning and end of a form, etc. Gropius saw function as the generators of building forms; however, Hoesli universally applied form composition principles to any building whether it was "modern" or "traditional". Course contents should be "typical design steps (or) passages, as for example, functional interpretation, arrangement, spatial disposition on site, and in context, the choice of structure, etc.."[118] Secondly, Hoesli finally transformed the creation of exclusively modern architecture into an academic approach, in which its design principles, rather than building examples, were taught in lectures and trained in studios. Whereas the Beaux-Art emphasized principles of proportion, axis, light and shadow, and the Neo-classicist style, Hoesli addressed space composition principles with abstract forms of panels, struts, voids, etc: in other words, the Modernist language. Both approaches paid little attention to the prescient social changes, new technologies and structures that would eventually come to be. Hoesli did nothing less than build a 20th century Academy of architectural education. His third contribution was to make architectural knowledge more effectively "teachable" by only a handful of few teachers—to large numbers of students. The traditional studio teaching led by

C-5 中心构图

多个二级和三级构图形体或空间围绕一个主要构图形体或空间的构图，成为中心化。作为中心的主要形体通常为一个更吸引人的形状。中心构图是稳定的、集中的、平衡的构图。中心构图也可以通过一些次要空间围绕着大的、占主导地位的中心区域来构成。中心的形没有方向性。中心构图可以用于营造空间中的点或场所，可用于结束轴线构图的收束，也可作为一个在固定区域或空间内的存在物。

育学院一模一样。赫茨里的第三个贡献是将建筑知识有效地在大学里“传授”，以少量教师教大量的学生。传统的设计教学由“巴艺”的“房师”领导，这种传统在包豪斯，格罗皮乌斯的哈佛（建筑）设计学院和密斯的伊利诺伊工学院被逐步取消。为了提高教学效率，用我们今天普遍采用的授课方式，替代传统的由几个大师在工作室直接面对面地和少量学生交流的方式。这和20世纪50年代、60年代的经济环境有关，当时少数建筑大师对大量巨型工程项目应接不暇，用于教学的时间极少，而当时市场也急需大量的建筑系毕业生，在这种形势下，尽管大学逐渐沦为“职业培训学校”，赫茨里的体系化教学方式仍然大受欢迎。

赫茨里的教学体系的问题在他退休前已经出现，在可教的组合原理和学生个人的感知之间存在一定距离。换句话说，在限定的工作程序、限定的问题和提供的有限元素中，学生的个性和创造性被限制。随着他的退休，原来他从得克萨斯带来的教师也分别离开苏黎世高工，一年级的设计教学的问题更加严重：

> *当我离开苏黎世时，一年级的气氛已开始改变，这也许是大量新生入学的原因。我发现教学变得更无个性。要想在瑞士能迅速形成像在得克萨斯一样的探索精神，没有一批有共同目标且活跃的青年教师的集体努力是不可能的。苏黎世长期缺乏得克萨斯的那种艺术、视觉设计和历史课教学的中坚力量。*[119]

如果将赫茨里放在以效率和大量性生产为中心的快速增长的工业经济环境中考察，他的教育体系的长处和缺陷并不是唯一的。这个体系可以看作是工业社会中的一个产物。为了在较近的距离内（课堂或者学校）最有效地传授信息和知识，在最短的时间内培养大量的人才，大学更倾向于采用被动接受式学习方式。他们要求学生最快地牢记一些知识，而且，基于工业化的分工来提高效率的观点，将这些知识划分为各自独立的课程，思想和观念的争论往往被忽视。学习的目的是使学生尽快地进入实践领域就职，而不是对一般的思想和做法提出挑战。学生交流技能在既定教学程序（赫茨里称为按部就班）里没能得到很好的训练。[120] 在工业社会的教育模式中，学校是学习的工厂，毕业生（及其作业）是标准化的产品。20世纪的教学概念和方法本源于此。卡尔·罗杰斯在他的《学习的自由》一书中，对这种大量生产性教育制度作了形象的描述：

> *在美国东岸、中西部甚至整个美国的城市中，学校、工厂和监狱不仅看起来雷同，而且运作方式也一样。它们都用20世纪初的同样材料，以国家工业发展为目标。大多数学校建筑和工厂、监狱一样，像是大盒子里装了许多小盒子（教室）。……公立学校的教程是以就业环境的需要，而不是学生的需要为基准的。*[121]

Centralization

They are characterized by a single dominant compositional figure or space, around which a number or secondary and tertiary compositional figures or spaces are arranged. The primary or dominant figure in a centralized organization usually is a shape that is larger, denser, more attractive than other figure. It attracts the attention of the viewer. A centralized organization is a stable, concentrated and balanced composition. that consists of a number of secondary spaces grouped around a large, dominant, central space. The centralized form is inherently non-directional. Centralized organizations can be used to establish points or “places” in space; terminate axial compositions; serve as an object-form within a defined field or volume of space.

the Beaux-Art "masters", in the Bauhaus, in Gropius' Harvard School of (Architectural) Design and Mies' Illinois Institute of Technology was ultimately undermined. Teaching efficiency was increased by replacing studio teaching, where a master talked with individual students, with the large-scale lecture delivery we currently take for granted. Bearing in mind the circumstance of the 1950s and 1960s, when a handful of "master architects" were busy with large and many commissions but had little, if any, time for teaching, and when the markets demanded a large amount of professionals graduated from university, Hoesli's educational system was well suited. Universities were perceived as, and meant to be, "job training schools".

The problems of Hoesli's education system became obvious even before his retirement. There was a gap between the composition principles and the student's individual perceptions. In other word, individuality and creativity was limited, if not discouraged, in the constrained working format, limited problems defined and elements provided for students. This problem in the first year design studio worsened after Hoesli's retirement, by which time the original Texas colleagues already left.

> *When I left Zurich the atmosphere in the first year course had already changed. It might have been due to the much larger number of entering students. I observed that the teaching became increasingly impersonal. It was improbable and foolish to expect that a similar spirit of discovery and collective contribution and shared objective by a group of vital, young faculty could be created instantly in Switzerland. The natural support that existed in the areas of drawing, visual design and history at Texas was lacking in Zurich for quite some time.* [119]

The merits and problems of Hoesli's educational system was not unique, if it is put back to the educational mode of an fast growing industrial economy, which was centered on efficiency and mass production. The system can be seen as a product of industrial society. To be more effective in conveying information and knowledge over a short distance (such as a lecture room or within a school) and therefore produce as many human resources as possible within a short period of time, universities encouraged students to take a passive approach to their education. They required students to memorize large amounts of information as quickly as possible. In addition, as knowledge is taught in divided subjects, for the sake of industrial efficiency, there is little integration, let alone debate of different thoughts and views. Students were prepared to quickly take up jobs in any practical field, instead of developing any challenge to conventional thought or practice. Communication skills were under-emphasized in favor of rote learning, (or step-by-step, a term used by Hessle) and students are not encouraged to learn or use critical thinking.[120] The educational mode of an industrial society school changed into a learning factory, and its graduates into industrial mass products of an average standard. This presupposition led to all modern teaching concepts and methods common to the 20th century. Carl R. Rogers in his work *Freedom to Learn*, described the mass-produced education as such:

> *In the cities along the East coast, and throughout the Midwest and across the Unites states, schools, factories, and prisons look remarkably alike and often function in the same way. They were built out of the same material at the turn of the 20th century and served the purpose of responding to the industrial development of the country. Like their factory and prison counterparts, most schools appear as large boxes subdivided by many smaller boxes—the classroom. … The public school schedule was adapted to the needs of the work environment, not for the learner.* [121]

练习七　水平地域中的空间

目的：

在建筑艺术中，实体和空间的对比一直是最强烈的。然而艺术美还取决于如何处理在这两个极端中间的微妙变化。这种微妙的空间变化，不同程度的封闭和开放正是练习中所要研究和表现的。另一方面建筑又可以看作是在一个连续的地域中紧密相连的个体，这个练习也同样研究个性和连续性的关系。这个练习还将介绍和试验“叠加”和“穿插”两种空间塑造方法。

方法：

练习的第一步是将一个实体逐步分解，最后变成空间。

1. 在一块底板上画出6厘米 × 6厘米的网格。

2. 在网格的一角做一个6厘米 × 6厘米 × 6厘米的立方体，在其对角线的网格另一端，做一个想象的空间。

3. 用空间围合和限定元件，如竖直板块、柱和顶板，每隔一个方格做一个不同围合度的立方体空间。研究从实体到空间过渡中不同的变化。

练习的第二步是根据给定的要求做一种空间模式，然后用“叠加”和“穿插”的方法将其转变成另一种模式。

1. 将另一块底板分成12厘米 × 12厘米的网格。

2. 将每一块格子分成均等的三块条形，分别想象成一个实体，一个空间和一个半实体（半空间）。高度皆为4厘米。

3. 在每一个方格子中插入同样的三条实体、空间和半实体（半空间），但与前一种垂直，研究两种模式叠加后的视觉变化。

注意事项：

1. 在第一步练习中，要注意不同程度的围合效果。这种不同围合效果都是用墙、柱和顶盖这三个基本元素实现的。

2. 空间不同程度的围合直接影响我们的方向直觉和形体空间的整体效果。

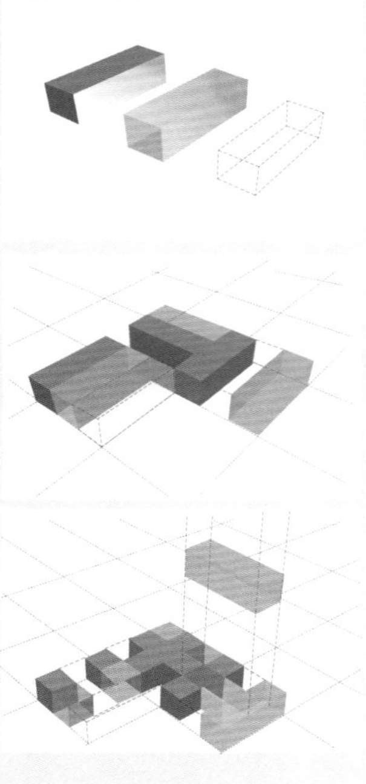

工具和材料：

1. 两块软木底板（60厘米×45厘米）；
2. 白卡纸;
3. 木条模型;
4. 切具、胶水。

成果：

两块水平状连续的空间。

Exercise 7. SPACE WITHIN HORIZONTAL FIELDS

Objective:

In the art of architecture, the contrast between solid form and empty space is among its strongest expressions. However, beauty depends on refined and sensitive gradations between these two poles. Therefore these need to be investigated. Differences in degree of solidity and emptiness need to be presented clearly. On the other hand, architecture integrates individual objects within a continuous field. This exercise investigates the visual relationship between individuality and continuity. Overlap and Penetration as methodologies of space creation are introduced and tested here.

Methods:

The first step is to study how to “degrade” solid form into empty space.

1.Divide a baseboard into a grid of 6cm × 6cm.

2.Choose one corner square as a complete enclosure of a cube (6cm × 6cm × 6cm) and the diagonal opposite corner as a complete open space.

3.Build a series of cubic structures in every two squares and explore the varieties of space enclosure with wall elements, columns and covers.

The second step is to create a spatial pattern by following a given requirement and then transforming it into a new pattern through the actions of Overlap and Penetration.

1.Divide a baseboard into a grid of 12cm × 12cm.

2.Subdivide each square into three parallel pieces of equal dimensions. Build a solid, a void and a semi-solid (or semi-void) in the three pieces of each square, but in different order. The model height is 4cm.

3.In each square, place an object consisting of a true solid or a semi-void, which also intersects the existing three elements.

Notes:

1.Always concentrate on the visual effect of space enclosures, and in their different extents. These are consistently made with the three basic construction elements: wall, column, cover, etc..

2.The degree of enclosure of a space has a significant impact on our perception of the orientation and overall form of the space.

Tools and materials:

1.Two based boards made of soft wood (60cm×45cm);
2.White cardboard;
3.Wooden sticks;
4.Knife, glue.

Presentation:

Two horizontal models showing the two steps of this study.

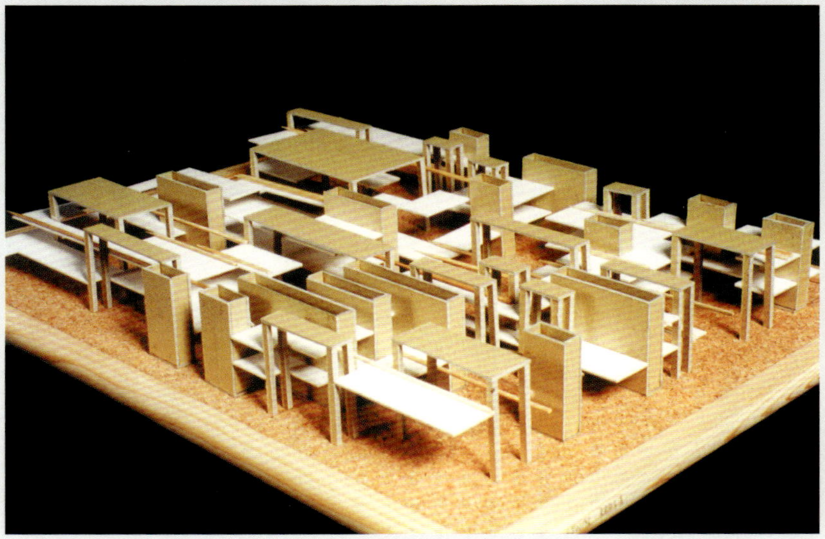

Chung Ho Wai　　Lo Man Sze　　Tsang Boon Chi

Unknown　　Chung Ho Wai　　Chan Yuk Hong

练习八　形、尺寸和比例

目的：

所有复杂的形体和空间都是由秩序和对比组成的。这个练习旨在训练一系列对比原理及其在三维组合中的运用。我们将认识各种对比关系，如大和小，厚和薄，宽和窄，多和少，水平和垂直，直角和斜线，曲线和直线，等等。

基本形包括方形、三角形、圆形，线形、点、球体等。我们将研究这些基本形的尺寸和比例的变化，我们也要讨论和运用层次、渐变和相似性等构成方法。

方法：

1. 用人体运动来体会形的特征。如甩开膀子，旋转身体来表现弧形的运动感。

2. 熟悉一些基本形，如立方体、球体、圆锥和圆柱，用手感知其三维状态。

3. 通过比例变化做几种不同的基本形，同时研究1:2:4:8:16:32或者1:3:9:27:81等比例关系，“黄金比”和等边三角形等。

4. 运用构成原理将不同形状组成水平雕塑。

注意事项：

1. 用感觉和对比的敏感性来掌握比例的均衡变化。

2. 对比是相对的。长是相对于短来说的，反之亦然。当用对比作为构成手段时，相对性则十分重要。

3. 形体和空间是通过划分和增减现有底板上的元素形成的。由简单的划分开始，底板上会出现一系列的形状。图底形状的完美来自深思熟虑的设计。

4. 构成作品中的主要元素分布直接影响视觉效果的质量。

工具和材料：

1. 卡纸、瓦楞纸板；
2. 不同尺寸的木条；
3. 软木底板（A2）；
4. 铅笔、刀具和胶水等。

成果：

一个在软木底板上做出的水平空间构成。

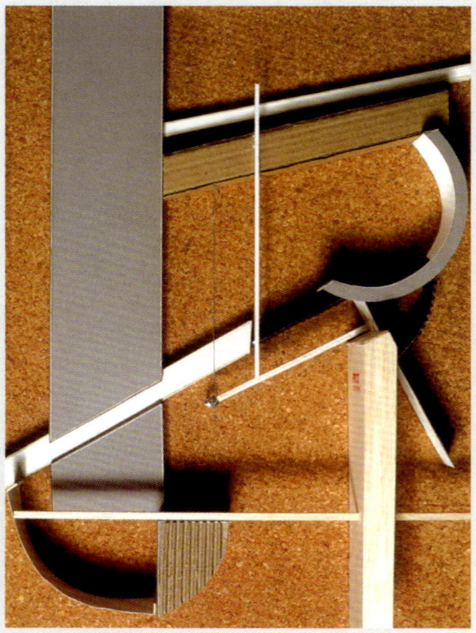

Tsang Pui Lai

Exercise 8.　SHAPE, DIMENSION AND PROPORTION

Objective:

Any complex form and space are created by regularity and contrasts. This lesson concentrates on the principles of contrasts and applying skills in 3D composition. We become aware of the contrasts between large and small; thick and thin; broad and narrow; much and little; horizontal and vertical; orthogonal and diagonal; curved and straight,etc..

The basic forms, such as the square, the triangle and the circle, line, point, ball, are all “focused” forms. Variations of these basic forms are tested changing of dimension and proportion. Composition skills such as hierarchy, gradation, and similarity are implied and discussed.

Methods:

1.Use body movement to perform the characters of form. For instance, performing a circle movement can be done with a motion of swinging and rotation of one’s body.

2.Familiarize oneself with model cubes, spheres, cones and cylinders. Feel their three-dimensional geometrical forms with one’s hands.

3.Make several variations of the basic form by changing their proportions. Proportions of 1:2:4:8:16:32 and 1:3:9:27:81 are to be investigated and represented. The golden section and the proportions of the harmonic triangle are introduced and tested.

4.Using composition principles, make a horizontal sculpture with various kinds of forms.

Notes:

1.Simultaneous changes in proportion can be judged with perception and sensitivity to contrasts.

2.All contrast effects are relative. A line appears long or short in relation to a shorter or a longer line. If a composition is to be based on a certain contrast, this relativity plays an important role.

3.Both the space and form are made by dividing and reducing existing settings such as the baseboard. Starting from one of these basic divisions one can find a large number of other forms. The positive-negative congruent forms are the most precise means of dividing an area.

4.Proper distribution of the accents in a composition largely decides the quality of visual effects.

Tools and materials:

1.Cardboard, corrugated paper;
2.Wooden sticks in various sizes;
3.Soft wood baseboard (A2-size);
4.Pencil, knife and glue.

Presentation

A horizontal composition settled on an A2-size notice board.

练习九　材料和质感

目的：

形是由材料做成的。这个练习强调在构成设计中培养对材料的敏感度。用语言描述材料的性能对建筑师来说是远远不够的，视觉和触觉的体验与表现是非常必要的。不仅要看到光滑和粗糙等材料特性，而且要将体验到的感觉有效表达出来。

方法：

1. 在抽屉里，厨房里，垃圾桶里，建筑工地上和五金店里收集各种材料，如木板、玻璃、织物、橡胶、毛发、电线、绳子、羊毛、胶水、金属材料、石头和各种编织材料等。
2. 闭上眼睛，用手感觉这些材料的不同质感。不一会儿，你的触觉灵敏度就会显著提高。即使这些材料不存在了，你也会对它们的触感记忆犹新。
3. 在一块A2底板上做一个材料构成，体现以下对比效果：光滑和粗糙，硬和软，轻和重，反光和亚光，透明和不透明，旧和新。

注意事项：

1. 这个练习的目的是重新唤起人对材料世界天生具有的敏感。它是手工活的基础。发现新事物的能力是在无穷多样的质感、操作技术和组合方式中培养起来的。
2. 练习中会出现一些新的结构，给人以惊喜。
3. 在练习过程中也会发现或发明新的材料质感，如刷子、筛网、油污或者干了的胶水等。

工具和材料：

1. A2大小的软木底板；
2. 任何材料。

成果：

在A2底板上构成的材料拼装。

Chung Ho Wai

Exercise9. MATERIAL AND TEXTURE

Objective:

Form is made of material. This lesson enhances sensitivity toward material selection while preparing a collage presentation. Mere knowledge of the words describing the properties of materials is far from enough for architects; it is necessary to experience and demonstrate their visual and tactile character. Contrasts such as smooth and rough, hard and soft, light and heavy, shiny and mat, transparent and opaque, old and new are not only be seen, but also be felt and demonstrated.

Methods:

1.Collect all the materials, wood, glass, fabrics, bark, furs, wire, rope, wool, foil, weaves of all kinds, glues, metals and stones, which you can find from your drawers, kitchens, rubbish dumps, building sites, and hardware stores.

2.Feel these sequences of textures with one's fingertips, and with one's eyes closed. After a short while one's sense of touch will dramatically improve. One can retain the memory of a tactile experience even when the material is not present.

3.Compose the materials onto an A2 board according to the contrast effects:

—Smooth and Rough;
—Hard and Soft;
—Light and Heavy;
—Shiny and Matte;
—Transparent and Opaque;
—Old and New.

Notes:

1.This exercise re-awakens a sense of discovery of the material environment. This is the beginning of craftsmanship. A sense of discovery can be found in the inexhaustible treasures of textures, skills of operation and possibilities of combination.

2.Fantastic structures are produced and their effects are completely novel at the same time.

3.New textures are invented with brushes, strainers, oil and glue.

Tools and materials:

1.An A2-size baseboard;
2.Any materials.

Presentation:

A collage of collected materials is fixed to an A2-size board.

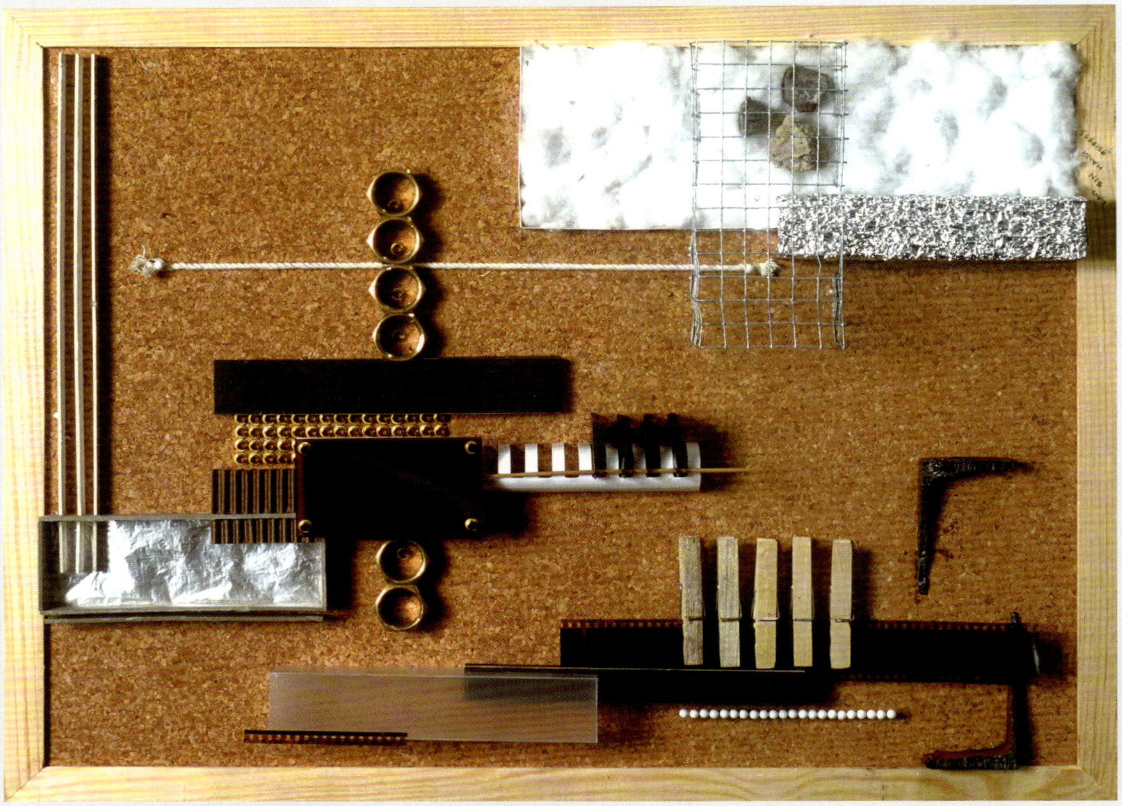

Law Sin Hang　　Tsang Boon Chi　　Unknown
Hui Lung Nin　　Lee Kui Sim(Sketch book)

练习十　韵律和动感：曲径通幽

目的：

人的空间体验是基于时间和空间序列的。简单重复的空间如果没有韵律的调剂会显得单调枯燥，而韵律过强且没有变化，也会带来同样的问题。这个练习研究的是表达空间韵律美感的技术。

特征的重复性，线条、体块和场所的协调都是构成韵律的基本要素。形的韵律是靠空间的时挤时松来表现的。不同的挤迫感也影响人的运动速度。

方法：

1. 中国书法本身具有韵律和动感，选一个书法字形，研究其笔画和韵律。
2. 按照字的笔顺设计一个行走空间。这个空间应是连续的，运动并不因空间特征的不同而打断。空间的构成来自三个基本元件：铺地、柱列和墙体。
3. 模型高度为3厘米。

注意事项：

这个练习综合运用先前几个练习研究的构成原理。

材料：

1. A3板；
2. 木条；
3. 卡纸、瓦楞纸板；
4. 胶水。

成果：

在A3大小的底板上用一个水平的空间模型来表现运动路线。

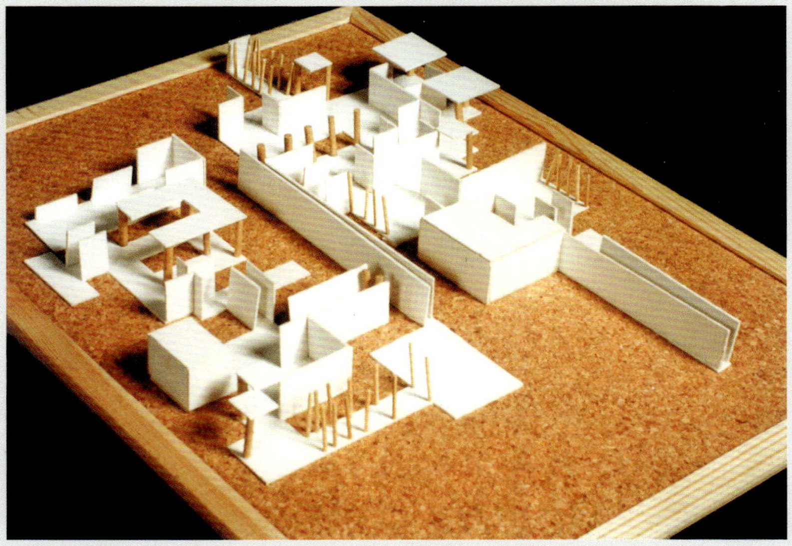

Chan Hau Man

Exercise 10.　RYHTHM AND MOTION: A WALKWAY

Objective:

Our spatial experiences are based on the sequence and time. Repetition can make a space boring and chaotic if there is no rhythm there. At the same time a rigid, unchanging kind of rhythm can also be boring. The skills of presenting the beauty of rhythm in space are studied in this exercise.

Repetitions of features, harmony of lines, bodies and areas, are all subjects for rhythm. The rhythm of form is presented with stressed and unstressed spatial volumes. Different stresses scan the progress of movement. The experience of a flowing movement in space is impressive whenever the forms are continuously related in a rhythm of unison.

Methods:

1.Choose a word written in Chinese calligraphy which has an inner rhythmical motion. Study the rhythms in the stroke movement.

2.Create a space sequence (a walkway) following the strokes of the calligraphy. Produce a space sequence in an unbroken flourish, an uninterrupted movement of by making different space definition. The space is defined by three elements: pavement, rows of columns, and wall pieces.

3.The height of the model is 3 cm.

Notes:

This exercise is a synthesis of all we have learned through previous exercises.

Tools and materials:

1.A3-size base board;
2.Wooden sticks;
3.Card paper, corrugated paper;
4.Glue.

Presentation:

A Chinese character, written in a horizontal model space, is shown on an A3-size board.

练习十一　演绎和转型：一个雕塑

目的：

绘画艺术杰作完美地运用了构成原理。通过分析我们可以找到这些原理，再通过运用这些原理，我们可以把绘画作品转换成雕塑作品。

方法：

1. 从绘画作品中抽象出其基本造型元素（包括图形和背景）。
2. 找到各元素之间的结构关系，如控制线、模式、韵律和动感等。将这些隐藏在画面背后的关系在草图纸上表现出来。
3. 注意这些元素的色彩。在雕塑上，色彩也许以不同的方式来表现，如各种材料。
4. 在A2底板上将这些元素和关系用三维构成设计表现出来。

注意事项：

1. 与先前练习不同的是，底板要竖直放置，做构成于其两侧，底板面积的约四分之一要开通，让两侧的构成设计连成一个整体。
2. 认真地选择模型材料，仔细设计构成的结构。
3. 作品应表现学生的创造性，所以无须刻意模仿原画。
4. 充分体会和享受二维艺术转型成三维空间构成的乐趣。

工具和材料：

1. 一块A2大小的软木底板；
2. 学生自定材料。

成果：

一个嵌在A2底板两侧的抽象空间雕塑。雕塑应有精细的制作质量。

Exercise 11. INTERPRETATION AND TRANSFORMATION: A SCULPTURE

Objective:

Fine arts masterpieces show all the form-composition principles. By analyzing these works, we trace out these principles and transform a painting into a sculpture by implying pushing these principles into a higher dimension.

Method:

1.Identify the formal elements (both figures and ground) in the given painting.
2.Find out the relations among the elements, the grid, pattern, rhythm and movement, which may not be apparent at first glance. Make these relations obvious in an analytical sketch.
3.Pay attention to the colors of these elements. They may not be represented differently in sculpture; for instance, as different materials.
4.Transform the elements and relations into a three-dimensional composition on an A2-size board.

Notes:

1.The sculpture must be constructed on both sides of the board. The board will stand vertically. At least 1/4 of the board should be cut off and removed; and the sculpture should penetrate the board.
2.Choose the material sensitively, and the carefully design the structure of the composition.
3.The sculpture shows our creativity! Do not rigidly adhere to the original painting.
4.Feel and enjoy the process of transformation from the original 2D "picture space" into the actual 3D "sculpture space".

Tools and materials

1.A2-size board;
2.No restrictions on materials for the sculpture.

Presentation:

A sculpture fixed on an A2-size notice board. The sculpture must be neat, tidy and show good-quality handwork.

Mok Hei Lun
Lee Kiu Sim
So Hoi Yan
Tsang Boon Chi
Sze chun nga
Law Sin Hang

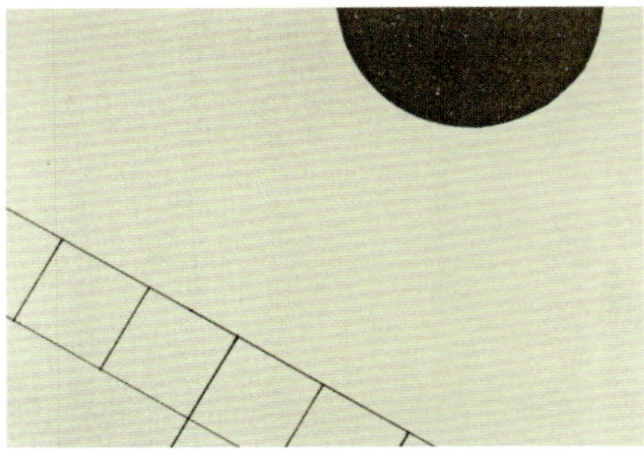

图1-12-1 赫茨里做的拼贴练习，从起始条件（上图）到最终作品（下图）

图1-12-2 耶尼的装置艺术作品

1.12 彼得·耶尼

赫茨里似乎已经感到没有艺术家的参与，他的教程一直有个缺憾（图1-12-1）。当他看到彼得·耶尼受聘教一年级视觉设计，而且将其发展作为必修课后，像是松了一口气。“赫茨里对我说，苏黎世高工开设了一门与得克萨斯不同的视觉设计课，但同样令人振奋，有价值，而且同样意义重大。”[122]

彼得·耶尼，一位苏黎世视觉交流艺术家，自1977年开始在苏黎世高工教授视觉设计基础（图1-12-2）。和斯路斯基不同，他的课似乎从没有和设计课相结合，他以对包豪斯的强烈认同感，独自向那些对特定教学内容和目标之外的东西有兴趣的学生传授一种思想。他的理论思考、哲学和如何培养创造性的方法集中反映在他1991年出版的《设计的视觉基础》一书中。

和伊藤一样，他首先认为艺术在我们所有人的心中，或者说人人都是艺术家（图1-12-3）。[123]因为人人都需要交流、秩序和美，尽管方法不同。大多数人之所以没能成为艺术家，是因为被动地接受我们看到和听到的东西，实际上已失去了看和听的官能。“……在这样一个我们不得不快速吸收（的社会中），图像工业（也是最积极的工业之一）的所有产品，已经快要将我们的头脑压爆，失去主动的视觉官能是很自然的事。”[124] 但每个人都有权进入“艺术殿堂”，就像每个人都有权获得本属于自己身体的一部分。只要人真正地关心自由，关心创造性以及他和环境的关系，艺术就不仅存在于艺术馆，而且存在于人的每个活动。[125]

其次，艺术活动的目的，包括艺术学，都是为了让人的心灵充满创造精神。教艺术就是教人怎样去创造。艺术教育不应仅仅教既定的，或者以前做过的艺术，而且要告诉学生未来是充满潜力、充满条件、充满创造的空间的。按部就班地延续过去的经验、原理和答案不可能创造一个未来。[126] “未来大量的可能性藏在暗处”，需要用艺术思想和艺术活动来探求（图1-12-4）。这和赫茨里将现代建筑语汇和原理视为现成的，问题是怎样让学生去掌握的观点完全相反。耶尼批判当时的学校（也许也暗指当时的一年级建筑设计教程）过于追随商业兴趣，假装让学生有备于未来。“在纯艺术中，以现在的角度看，未来在黑暗之中。教学生或者让学生学看一个看不见的未来，怎么可能？”[127] 创造性是一种在黑暗中看东西的视觉能力，或者说是一种想在黑暗中探索的心灵。“设计基础教学应是一种形成思想感觉，和形成一个让创造性可以重温萌芽时期的方法。”[128] 这种观点似乎让人想起伊藤的课前体操、深呼吸、情感绘画等为新生准备的课程练习。

第三，耶尼认为艺术反对抄袭，其作品应永远是特殊的、唯一的，而不应是满足大众的迂腐的兴趣。这和后期包豪斯、格罗皮乌斯与密斯时代大众的艺术观念不同，而更接近柯布西耶主张

C–6 线性构图

线性构图的特征是几个构图形体或空间安排为一个线状的序列。元素通过距离和大小的重复互相联系。竖向、横向或任何给定角度的一行元素都可以产生线状。行不一定是直的，可以扭转或弯曲。这种构图具有动感。
在建筑上，线性的空间序列包括一系列可以直接相互联系或通过一个单独的线状空间相联系的空间，通常为相似功能空间的重复。

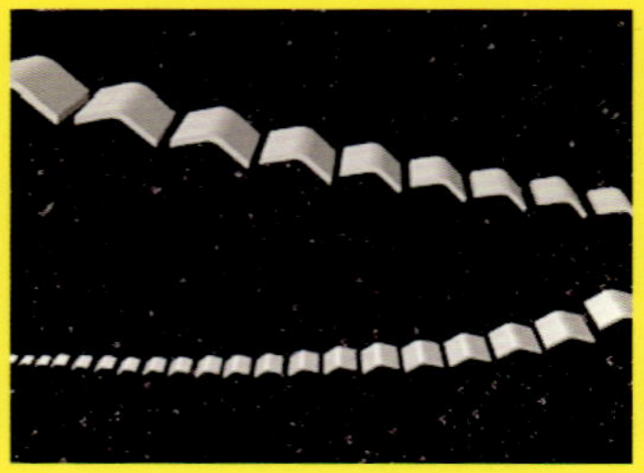

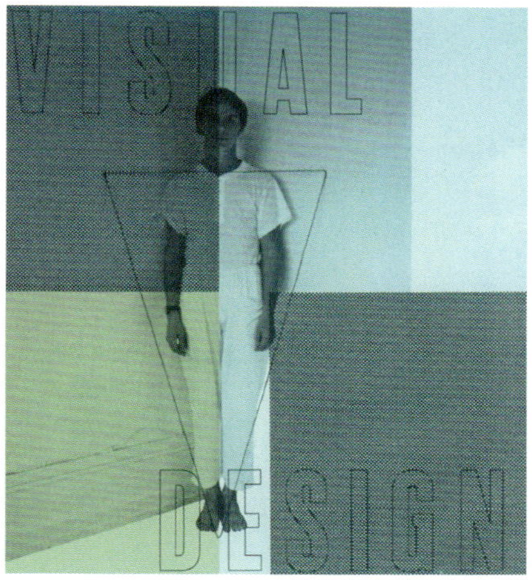

图1-12-3 耶尼的拼贴作品

图1-12-4 学生作业《模式构成》

1.12 Peter Jenny

It was likely that Hoesli has always felt his program was handicapped because no artist participated in it (Pic.1-12-1).He felt relieved when Professor Peter Jenny was appointed in teaching visual design to first-year students as a compulsory course. "Bernhard commented to me that the direction in visual design at the ETH had taken a different but very exciting and rewarding course—very different from Texas, but equally significant." [122]

Peter Jenny, an artist of visual communication in Zurich, has being taught Fundamentals of Visual Design in the Architecture Department at ETH Zurich since 1977 (Pic.1-12-2). Unlike Slutsky at the University of Texas, there was lack of evidence that Jenny had any collaboration with studio teaching. He seems to have launched his program alone, with a deep sense of commitment to the Bauhaus, introducing a body of thought to the students whose interests lie above and the objects of specific classroom study. His thinking, philosophy and his methodology of teaching creativity were compiled in his book *The Sensual Fundamentals of Design* published in 1991.

Firstly, similar to Itten, Jenny was convinced that art could be found within us all: everybody was an artist.(Pic.1-12-3) [123] This is simply because everyone has a desire for communication, for order, and for beauty but in different ways.The reason why many of us are not artists is because we are not active, but instead, passive when we watch and listen. We have literally lost our senses of sight and hearing. "Understandably, for were we to react to and absorb all that the picture industry—the most assiduous of all industries—has to offer, our minds would be filled to bursting point".[124] Every one has right to enter the "Palace of Art" as he has the right to long for substance, a right inherent in every individual. Art is a special property not only in art museums but also in every human activity, if he really concerns with freedom, creativity and contextual connections. [125]

Secondly, the only object of art activity, including teaching art, is to keep the minds of people immersed in a spirit of creativity. Teaching art is teaching how to be creative. Art education should not simply about anticipated art, or the artwork done before. Instead, it should tell students the future is full of possibilities, offers and unclaimed space. This future could hardly be possible to create with a logical continuation of the past experience, principles and answers.[126] "A great many conditions of future design are hidden in darkness" which need to explore in art thinking and art activity (Pic.1-12-4). This statement is opposite to Hoesli's—that principles and languages of modern architecture were already there, and the question was how to let students know them. He criticized conventional schools, implicitly possibly including the first-year program of Architecture in ETH, for they are dominated by business interests and pretending that they prepare the future for students. "In the fine arts, the future—seen from the present – lies in darkness. How, then, is it possible to teach and learn for the future when the future is unforeseeable?"[127] Creativity is a capability of eyes, which can see in the darkness, or a mind which can explore into the unknown. "The teaching of the fundamentals of design is a methodical attempt to form the thinking senses and to create a climate in which centres of creativity can once again remember their embryo stages."[128] This statement reminds us again Itten's physical exercise before class, of deep breathing and drawing of personal emotions.

Thirdly, he believed art is the opposite of copying, is always exceptional and unique, and not for common or cross interests. This is different with the late Bauhaus and Gropius and Mies' idea of art for the epoch. It is more attached to

Linear

Linear organizations are characterized by the arrangement of several compositional figures or spaces into a linear sequence or series. Elements relate to one another primarily through the repetition of distance and size. Linear forms resulting in rows that can extend vertically, horizontally, or at any given angle. The row does not have to be straight, but crooked or curved. However, it always convey a feeling of movement.
In Architecture, a linear organization consists essentially a series of spaces, which can either be directly related to one another, or be linked through a separate and distinct linear space. It usually consists of repetitive spaces with similar functions.

的尼采哲学，即艺术不是为了寻找美和快乐，而是个性和情感：“对艺术的评价因人而异……所有对艺术作品的价值讨论都是错误的……伟大的艺术不需要共识……艺术总是令人感动……帕提依神庙让所有人感动，包括不喜欢它的人，这里重要的是唤起情感的力量。”[129]耶尼认为“艺术的特征正是一种力量，一种对特殊性的追求，这正是设计的榜样”。[130]“……艺术将永远作为特例而存在（图1-12-5）。”[131]

绘画的问题不是关于是否能像照相一样准确，而是怎样处理参照物（如，一个苹果）和艺术作品（一幅关于苹果的画）之间的区别（图1-12-6，图1-12-7）。在绘画或者设计过程中，苹果会改变，在某人手里它是一个苹果，而在另一个人那里却成了一幅画，一个物体，或者一个空间形体。两者不同之处在于，前者强调艺术过程的开始，苹果仍是过程开始时的那个苹果；而在后者则强调过程结束，苹果变成另一个东西（图1-12-8）。

因此，耶尼的教学内容和形的组合原理无关，这和“巴艺”、包豪斯和赫茨里的教学模式都不同。他关注的是一种哲学思考，感知（与伊藤和阿尔贝斯相似），和处理恰当性和差异性的方法。对感知的训练不能脱离哲学。教育应把听觉、嗅觉、触觉和视觉结合为一个整体。“从感觉元素中形成一个整体的看法需要观念。”感觉开始时局限于眼睛，然后延伸到各种联系，如质感和皮肤，色彩和舌头，形体和手，空间和嘴等。[132] 这种对形体感觉的训练，是基于人人都有的感觉和体验（图1-12-9）。教育的目标应是基础性的、简单的，在学生的能力范围之内。其目的是让学生通过对视觉元素的实践和创造，让心、意、手都兴奋起来。[133]

培养创造性的方法对耶尼至关重要。教师有责任提供一个产生和训练的教学环境，这种方法要让人认识到关系和差异，并清楚地表现出来。[134] 他的教学方法之一是鼓励学生在任何地方，寻找和利用任何东西，将其发展成为艺术形体（图1-12-10）。“天才的教科书和垃圾一样到处存在，丢在街上，粘在墙上，或者长在废墟中的霉斑上。”要将它们视为新艺术的资源、材料和

图1-12-5 学生练习《图像空间》

图1-12-6 学生练习《色彩质感》

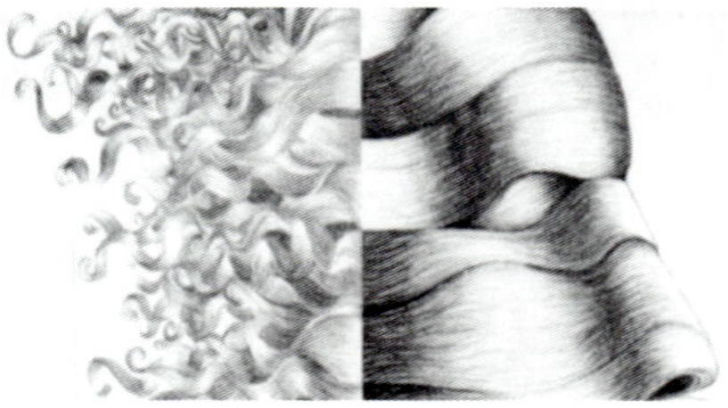

图1-12-7 学生练习《黑白质感》

图1-12-8 名作转型练习（左图为利希滕施泰因原作）

空间序列的意义也可以通过其位置来强调，如线性序列的终点、分出旁支，或多个线性序列的交汇点等。线性序列具有明显的运动、延伸和增长的趋势，表达一种方向性。为了限制它的增长，可以用一个主要空间、一个精致的入口、另一个建筑的形式或地形来结束线性序列。弯曲的和分散的线性空间在凹面内围合了一定范围的外部空间，其内部空间的方向指向这片外部空间的中心。在凸的一面这些形式成为正面，对其外部空间有排斥作用。

图1-12-9 质感和可塑性练习

图1-12-10 物体转型练习：将货物照片（下图）抽象为艺术（上图）

Le Corbusier's Nietzschean philosophy that man does not look for beauty or pleasure in art, but rather character and emotion. "Judgement (on art) varies with each individual … all discussion based on the worth of a work of art was thus vicious …Great art is not art of agreement … art has the sole duty to move us… The Parthenon moves everyone powerfully, even those whom it displeases; what counts is the intensity of the provoked emotion."[129] Jenny says, "The distinguishing characteristic of art is its intensity, this desirable exception to which we owe exemplary statements about design".[130] "…Art will continue to come into being as an exception (Pic.1-12-5)." [131]

The problem of painting is not about copying something with photographic accuracy, but a matter of how differences and deviations are handled between the reference object (an apple, for instance) and his work (a painting started from the apple) (Pic.1-12-6, Pic.1-12-7). During the drawing or design process, the apple may change; with one person it will remain an apple, with another it will develop into a picture, an object, and a spatial entity. The difference between these two is that the former person exaggerates his entrance into the artistic process: the same apple remains as when the process started. Meanwhile, the latter exaggerates his exit from the same process: the apple disappears or becomes something else (Pic.1-12-8).

Therefore the content of his teaching is not about principles of composition, as those can be traced back to the teaching model of Beaux-Arts, Bauhaus, and Hoesli. Instead the content of his teaching is philosophy, sensuality (similar to Itten and Albers) and methods of recognizing the relationship, appropriateness and difference. Training of senses can not separated from philosophy. The education should promote a unity between hearing, smell, touch and sight. "Concepts are necessary in order to develop an idea of a whole from elements of perception." Sense is limited at first to the eyes; it extends to include connections between textures and skin, between colours and tongues, between shapes and hands, between spaces and mouths.[132] This kind training, a training of form-perception, is based on sensual experience values which are available to everyone (Pic.1-12-9).However, the teaching goal must be modest, simple, in the capability of students, because it cannot independent from existing talent. The goal is to allow students to create forms of communication that delight the mind, heart and hand, by practicing with visual elements.[133]

The methodology of teaching creativity was important for Jenny. The teacher is responsible for creating conditions which permit the development of methods and tools, so relationships and differences can be recognized and presented clearly.[134] One of his teaching methods was to let students find and use anything, in the anywhere and develop it into artistic form(Pic.1-12-10). "The educational sketchbook of genesis and decay is found lying on the street, sticking to walls, mildewing on crumbing masonry." Using them as resources, materials and generators of new products, instead of treating them as final products. A second method was to prolong the process, or make an endless actions of seeing, perception, drawing and recreation. In the process, every step is a divergence from the previous step; this makes clear that invention occurs in the act of seeing or drawing (Pic.1-12-11). So invention is always an integral part of seeing, perception, and re-presentation.[135] Another methods are to allow students to design drawing instruments and test them with pictures drawn by that same instrument. The concept is to demonstrate no difference between the tool and the product; or between the means to an end and the end itself.[136] Recognition and discovery are creative activities, and therefore highlighted through various exercises of observation. "Collecting things which other people do not recognise means choosing from an unseen abundance…"[137] New creation occurs when new forms are found. The objective is to allow eyes to select that which is not immediately apparent. Much of what is regarded as new is nothing but variation and recycling. That which is new (designed) and that which already exists (recycled) make use of a game

Significance of a sequence space can also be emphasized by their location: at the end of the linear sequence, offset from the linear organization, or at the pivotal points of a segmented linear form. Linear organisation express a direction, and signify movement, extension, and growth. To limit their growth, linear organizations can be terminated by a dominant space or form, by an elaborated or articulated entrance, or by merging with another building form or the topography of its site. Curved and segmented linear organized forms enclose a field of exterior space on their concave sides and orient their spaces toward the centre of the field. On their convex sides, these forms appear to front space and exclude it from their fields.

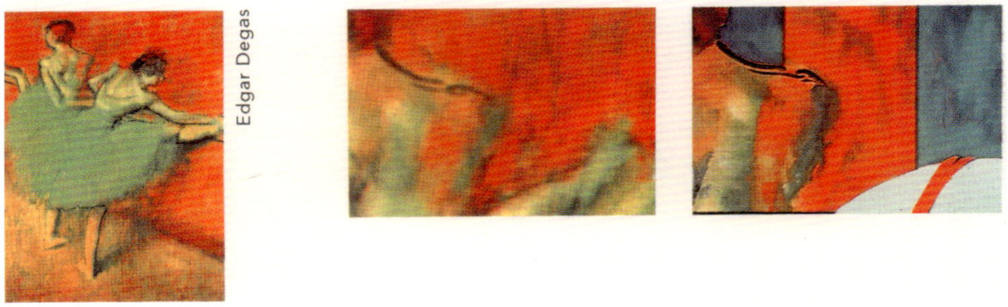

图1-12-11 名作转型练习：将德加原作（左图）的局部（中图）转变为新作品（右图）

源泉，而不是产品的最终结果。他教学的另一个方法是延长创作过程，或者说将创作视为观察、感知、绘画和再创作等一系列无止境的行为。过程中的每一步都是对过去的离异。发现产生于看和画的行为中。（图1-12-11）看、感知和再现等行为是发现的过程。[135] 耶尼的另一个练习是让学生设计绘图工具，并通过工具所作的图来检验工具的质量，其背后的概念是在工具和作品之间，或者说方法和目标之间并无区别。[136] 认知和发现都是创造性活动，所以耶尼的练习也都强调观察的重要性。“收集别人认识不到的东西意味着在黑暗中选择……”[137] 找到新的形体意味着创造。所以观察训练的目标是培养能在混沌中搜寻的眼睛。新东西常常不过是旧东西的变化和循环利用，研究新（设计）的和已有的（再循环）关系可以培养选择和摒弃的能力，这种能力和设计能力同样重要。任何现有的事物中都有未被探索的东西，它们都是教学的重要组成部分。[138] “现实中许多被遗忘的领域，其中丰富的形象都有探讨价值。”[139] 同阿尔贝斯的练习一样，耶尼的练习中也常利用极少材料，用细小的变化和差异形成强烈的形象变化。

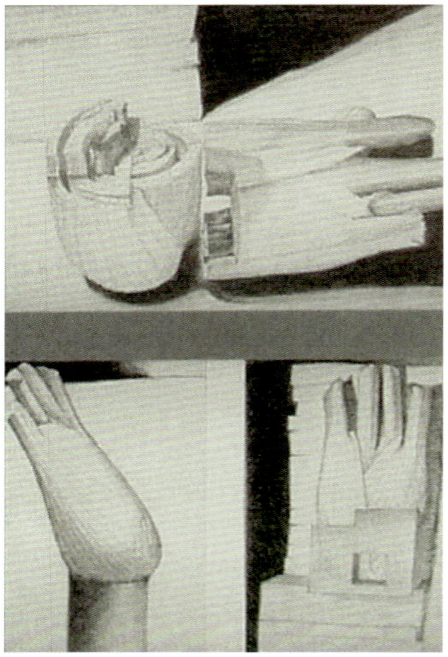

图1-12-12 形体和质感：通过思辨视角分析物体

耶尼采用的另一种创造方法是改变视点。环境中的所有东西都可以从不同视点来考察，从而发现多样的形体和新的色彩组合（图1-12-12）。[140] 埃森曼曾指出，如果把波洛克的画放在地上，是一个“野蛮人作品”，如果从地上放到墙上，马上变成“当然”的、“学术化”的、“新注册”的艺术品（图1-12-13）。[141] 但和斯路斯基的单线白描不同，耶尼鼓励学生充分利用双手，在观察的过程中，去画，去撕，去剪贴、重组和错置物体或图像。他称之为“会看的手”。手的行为可以深化看的方式，激发人的好奇心，只有这样视觉思考才会有意义。

图1-12-13 波洛克《灰色海洋》，1953

最后，耶尼还有一个教学方式是鼓励学生去犯错。（图1-12-14）他对完美并无兴趣，他要的是挑战性、潜力和对现有的超越，他欢迎错误。“错误引人关注，给发展以意义，错误是我们的巨大资源，因为我们的目的是超越自己。”错误是创造和探索未知“黑暗”或者未来的过程和经验（图1-12-15）。在创造的过程中，学生应对如履薄冰的情形习以为常，要自然而快乐地游戏于其中。只要能在漫无目的的游戏中找到乐趣，人人都是创造型艺术家。

C-7　放射

放射原理创造出的形式以中心轴和中心形为特征。单元形环绕一个中心分布，产生一种向心的动势，如风车形和其他放射状构图都暗示着向心的旋转运动。
放射与其他构图原理结合运用可以产生多种构图形式，如完全放射、部分放射、平移放射（膨胀）等。运用扩张的旋转技法使得扩张的形式在旋转过程中出现细微的形状变化。平移放射由移动的单元形旋转而成，也可形成螺旋形构图。

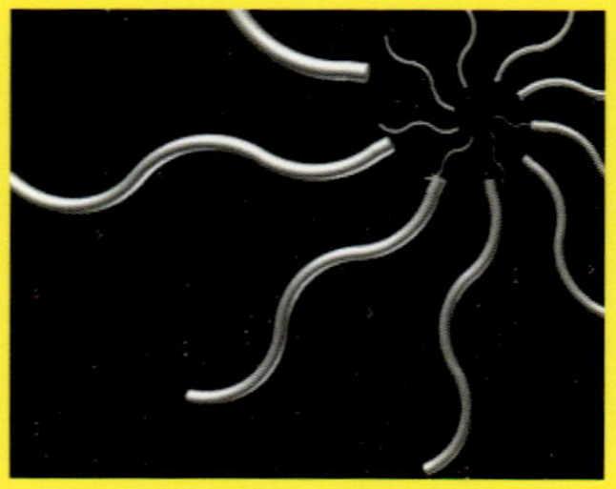

图1-12-14 学生作业《对物体不同方面的观察和素描》

图1-12-15 学生练习《铅笔图像空间》

in which the ability to choose and reject is just as important as the ability to design. The unexploited possibilities inherent in existing elements of everything which is available for use is called for school in criteria.[138] "In reality we too have our forgotten areas which contain a wealth of images worthy of more than a fleeting glance."[139] Similar to Albers' exercise, practice with small materials, small changes, and little differences that provided sufficient changes in perspectives were also used in Jenny's program.

Another creativity method introduced by Jenny is a change of views. Almost everything in the environment is open to a different way of seeing that perceives new interactions in the existing variety of form and colour.(Pic.1-12-12) [140] When the view changes, new properties and new values of the objects are found. When a Pollock painting is placed in a horizontal position, it is a "savage work". But the moment the canvas is taken off of the floor and moved to a vertical position on the wall, it becomes "naturalized", re-institutionalized and re-inscribed into the discourse of painting(Pic.1-12-13).[141] In contrast with Sluzky's exercise, in which only single line drawings are allowed, Jenny encouraged the full use of one's hands to draw, tear, cut, paste, arrange, dislocate objects when engaged in the act of seeing. He called it "seeing hands". The actions of one's hands can deepen the way of seeing and guiding interest and curiosity, so that the visual contemplation becomes more meaningful.

Last, but not least, is a methodology Jenny felt was important was to encourage students to make mistakes (Pic.1-12-14). He was not interested in completion and beauty, but challenging, resourcefulness and excess of that which already exists. And he did welcome mistakes. "Mistake triggers perception, signifies development. Mistakes are our greatest resource because our intentions are always in excess of our ability." Mistake is the process and resources of creation and exploration into the unknown, the "darkness", or the future(Pic.1-12-15).In the process of creation, students should be familiar with uncertain situation, and be comfortable and joyful with play in uncertainty. Everyone is a creative artist only when he can play and enjoy with uncertainty.

Radiation

Radiation principles creates the forms which characterized by a centralized axis and figure. Forms around and move towards a common center. It is a pinwheel pattern, a variation of radial organization, visually suggests a rotational movement about the central space.

There are various forms of compositions with radiation associated with other organisational principles, such as Full radiation, Segmentary radiation, Translation Reflection: Dilation. Translation in radiation composed of translated unit forms which are rotated to achieve radiation. That Rotation works with Dilation make a dilated forms with slight variations of shape appears in rotation. This can result in a spiral arrangement.

图2-0-1 黑尔佐格和德·莫罗设计的巴塞尔铁路信号楼，1995年

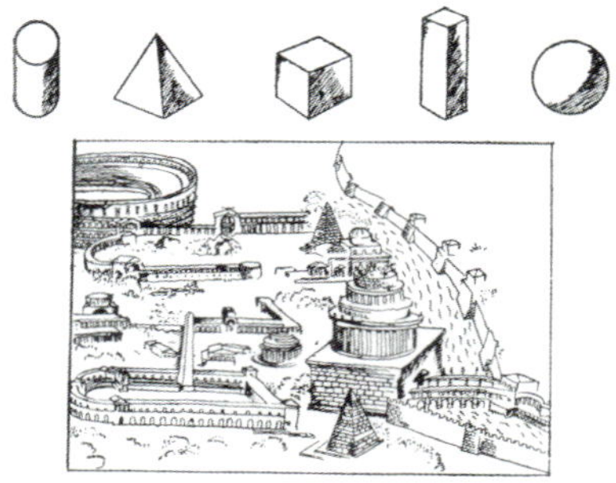

图2-1-1 勒·柯布西耶速写，1920年

2. 形的生成与信息

无论学习还是创作，建筑都是很有趣的东西。它给混乱的世界以秩序，并通过对其存在的感知，调动参观者和使用者空间的精神体验。最好的是，建筑会激发我们对于一个更美好世界的希冀。形和内容都与建筑密切相关，但孰先孰后则无定律。建筑内容相对来说更具体、更重要，因为它包括许多复杂的东西，如程序、环境、社会、文化、功能和活动等。然而建筑的形是理性主观的创作，是一种交流和表现，在只有一个设计者的情况下更是如此。对一个有创造性的设计者来说，形的生成是实现一个梦想，是一个创造的行为，一种交流的方式，一次思想的表现，或者个人世界观的体现，也是社会和文化价值的物化，以及对未知领域（如结构和材料的极限等）的探索。建筑构成原理正如语法让思想以秩序和相互理解的方式传达。当然创造性地使用语言与机械地交流不同，因为它将作者的个性、情感和特质带进了语言。真正有创造性的设计者是那些将综合知识与艺术完美结合的人，这种结合体就是需要探索的未知（图2-0-1）。此章试图探讨他们的创作源泉、创作过程，特别是与现代艺术的结合方式。这些探讨揭示了在决策、组织、建立新秩序和有意识地探索新形体的各种不同方法。

艺术已不再是社会的象牙塔，由于上个世纪中，艺术领域和范围不断扩大，现实生活中的所有事物都可以用不同艺术方式来表达。同样，自20世纪中期开始，建筑已不再像以前那样孤芳自赏。

2.1 几何形和几何形之后

几何形

几何形是20世纪现代建筑形体构成的基石。

在这以前，几何的哲学思想和实用功能，和其数学化的秩序已长期运用在建筑中，但直到20世纪初才真正地被研究并发展成为抽象几何形体。“形式至上”，自古代以来，哲学家和建筑师的主题，即形的神圣不可侵犯，作为人统治自然的体现而被进一步开发，立方体、球体、锥体、金字塔和圆柱体等便由此而生（图2-1-1）。

几何形在建筑中的运用主要有以下几种方式：

在建筑中，中心空间通常在形式上居于主导地位。具有相似的形式和长度的线性分支可以保持构图整体的规律性，但也可能根据各自的功能需求和环境的差异而互不相同。

In architecture, the central space is generally dominant in form. The linear arms may be similar to one another in form and length and maintain the regularity of the organization's overall form,or they may be different from one another to respond to their individual requirements of function and context.

2. Creative Formation and Information

Architecture is both a fascinating subject of study and object of creation. It brings order into a chaotic world with a sense of presence, evoking in the observer and user a unique spatial and spiritual experience. At its best, architecture inspires us with hope of a better world. Although there have been numerous debates on which comes first – form or content – both, in fact, are what architecture relates to. Architectural content is comparatively more objective and significant than form, though the former also relates to complex issues such as programme, context, society, culture, functions, and activities. Architectural form, on the other hand, is predictably subjective, communicative and expressive, especially if proposed by a singular designer. For the creative individual, form generation is a realization of a dream, an act of creation, a tool of communication, a manifestation of the designer's thoughts, an expression of a personal ideology, a materialization of social and cultural values, and an exploration of an untested or unknown boundary (such as structural or material limits). Here, architectural composition principles are the linguistic grammar, which help us to communicate our thoughts in an orderly and understandable manner. Creative use of language, on the other hand, goes further then the mere mechanics of communication; it delivers the character, emotion, and uniqueness of the author. Truly creative designers tend to be those who can best synthesize intellect with the arts in what might be called research into the unknown(Pic.2-0-1). The following study intends to explore their creative origins, as well as the creative processes themselves, especially in the way such processes deal with contemporary art. These approaches offer a variety of ways to organize decisions, to provide new orders, and to consciously generate forms.

Art is no longer autonomous in society. Because the realm and scope of art have so widely expanded over the last century, everything in contemporary life can, in one way or another, be readily interpreted in artistic terms. Similarly, since the mid-20th century, architecture no longer stands aloof as the discrete and independent entity it was previously understood to be.

2.1 Geometry and Beyond Geometry

Geometry

Geometry is the foundation of 20th century modern architectural form.

The philosophical and pragmatic qualities of geometry and mathematical order have been applied in architecture for centuries. However these had not been explicitly explored and maturely developed into abstract forms until the early 20th century. "Formal un-deniability"—the divine nature of forms, a central theme for philosophers and architects since antiquity—has been considered and studied as a reflection of man's conquest over nature. Cube, sphere, cone, pyramid and cylinder were developed along the way(Pic.2-1-1).

Geometry may be applied in architecture at several levels, namely:

C–8 簇群构图

簇群构图是以空间和集中组群安排的关系为基础的。这种分组不需要任何几何秩序，十分灵活。组群中的要素可以在形状、大小、形式或表面等属性上有某种程度的相似。

Cluster Organizations

Cluster organizations are based on the relationship of space and the concentrated placement of a group of forms. This is a flexible grouping because it doesn't require any geometrical order. The elements in the cluster may or may not have a similar character in shape, size, form, or surface attributes.

图2-1-2 博塔设计的卢加诺公寓办公楼

图2-1-3 勒·柯布西耶速写《伊斯坦布尔》，约1920年

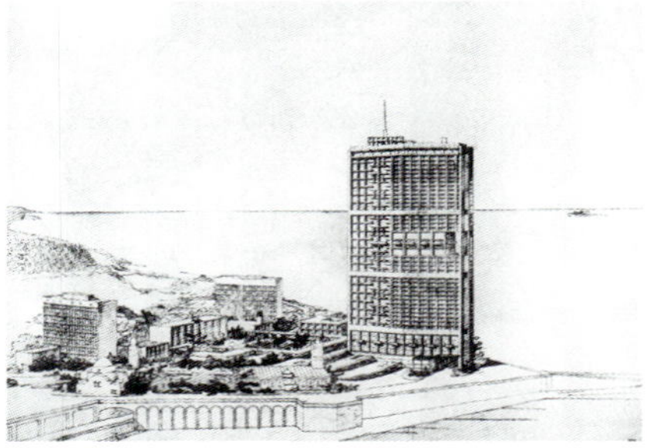

图2-1-4 勒·柯布西耶所绘的位于阿尔及尔的建筑方案

1. 几何形建筑体量。以一种简单明确的几何形，如立方体、棱柱体或者穹窿作为建筑基本的形体元素，其他较小的形体只是附加于其上或者其中（图2-1-2）。

2. 用几何形将整体与部分相结合。相同的几何形重复使用，或者以几种不同几何形组成建筑群的整体性。

3. 用几何强调结构秩序和韵律。建筑的结构以其本身要求和存在形成空间的几何秩序。而这种几何秩序可通过模式、布局及空间和体量的组织而进一步强化。

4. 几何空间的象征模式。不同的几何形状和体量通过不同的精神需要调动不同的空间感，同时形成秩序、整体和韵律感。穆斯林的清真寺以简单有力的几何形实现功能作用（图2-1-3），而早期的基督教堂则用高度精确的十字形平面。这种布局是文化与材料本身的要求结合的产物。

柯布西耶等20世纪早期的建筑师和艺术家用几何形来探索满足现代人需要的新建筑。“（现代）人应走直线，因为他有一个目标，知道走的方向，他要去一个地方，所以直接走过去。只有小圈子里的驴子徘徊不前，它的不发达的脑子犹豫不决，受不同的风格影响，走起来弯来转去……”[142]柯布西耶相信现代思想就是几何精神，由此反对个人主义，由此为所有被几何形控制的人（现代人）创造一个完美世界。“精确和秩序是这个世界的基础……站在个人主义及其浮华的产品的对立面，我们主张时时刻刻地共处，主张对特例的标准化……”[143]“人是几何动物”是他最著名的口号之一。

许多早期现代主义艺术家和建筑师都用规则线条来组织形体和空间。柯布西耶自1911年开始就用这种方式做设计和作画。但这种方式只用来做最后加工，在设计方案完成之后，用来推敲各部分的比例：“将造型完美化。”有时他的建筑构思来自他早期绘画中的规则线条。他曾这样描述他在1938年设计阿尔及尔商业中心时的情形（图2-1-4）：

当我推开门进入我的画室，一幅1931年的画背面有一些规则线条吸引了我的注意。我一下明白了，这种比例框架正和我自1930年思考的阿尔及尔高层建筑形态一致，八年来我一直在思考用我的“笛卡儿”摩天楼来代替纽约和芝加哥的非理性的高层建筑，它告诉我内在的生物性、结构和布置方式应该是怎样的……从那天起，思想成为现实：比例——整体、多样性和韵律。[144]

他有时将几何用于线、圆、方等形体元素，但更多地将其用于控制线、规则、模数或者整体与局部关系比例协调，即在各部分间建立强烈统一感，部分随从整体，或者整体遵循局部。一个整体可能由一个或者多个部分组成（图2-1-5），部分可以是空间也可以是形体，包括使用空间、

在建筑中，簇群式布局可以在大的主体建筑或空间之外添加附属物，也可以用“近似”的手法来联系以表现单体的体积感，还可以紧密联系成为一个多面的整体。簇群构图可以容纳大小、形式和功能相似而不相同的空间。簇群构图内的空间没有重要性之分，具有一种超脱于社会或经济等级的民主精神，因此建筑或空间可以灵活适应功能的改变。

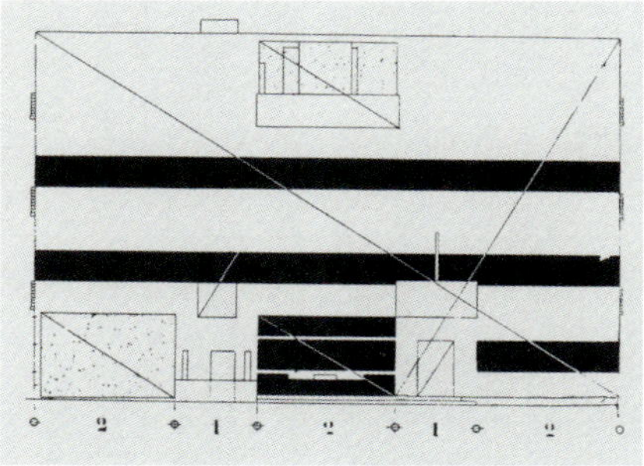

图2-1-5 勒·柯布西耶设计的斯泰因住宅立面，1926年

1.To create the overall massing and configuration. A basic describable and recognizable geometric form, such as a cube, prism, or dome, is used as the significant, dominating or perceptible element. Other forms may be added, overlapped or incorporated as smaller components to this basic form. (Pic.2-1-2)

2.To establish the underlying relationship between parts and whole. Elements may be laid out and scaled in proportion to the overall composition to strengthen a sense of unity.

3.To emphasize structural order and rhythm. Building structure, by its nature and expression, creates a sense of order in space. However, such order is further emphasized through the pattern, layout, and intervals of solid and void.

4.To generate and maintain geometric fields. Different geometric shapes, forms and solids offer different psychological stimuli, which in turn evoke a range of different feelings. Yet they also offer a fascinating possibility for order, unity, and rhythm. Muslim mosques, for example, incorporated strong, simple geometric shapes to achieve functional results (Pic.2-1-3) whereas early Christian churches utilized a highly articulated cruciform plan. Such arrangements were the combined result of cultural concerns and the nature of available materials.

Le Corbusier accompanied by many other early modern architects and painters took geometry as the way to search for new forms, which address the needs of modern man. "Man walks in a straight line because he has a goal and knows where he is going; he has made up his mind to reach some particular place and he goes straight to it. The pack-donkey meanders alone, meditates a little in his scatter-brained and distracted fashion, he zigzags…"[142] Le Corbusier believed that modern sentiment is a spirit of geometry, which is anti-individualism and the path towards a perfect world for everyone governed by orders. "Exactitude and order are its essential conditions… In the place of individualism and its fevered products, we prefer the commonplace, the everyday, the rule to the exception…"[143] It is therefore not surprising that "Man is a geometrical animal"became one of his well-known statements.

Regulating lines had been widely used as a tool to compose elements and spaces for early Modernist artist and architects. For example, Le Corbusier had adopted this tool in his architectural work since 1911, and in his paintings since 1919. But these tools served only purposes of refinement; he used them after the design had been drawn up, and only then to make its proportions more exact: "to perfect the composition". There were also incidents when the design of an architectural project was inspired by the regulating lines of his earlier paintings. Le Corbusier shared this experience in his 1938 design for a business center in Algiers (Pic.2-1-4):

As I opened the door into the studio where I did my painting, my eye was caught by a set of regulating lines painted straight on to the canvas on the back of a 1931 painting. Suddenly I saw the whole thing clearly in my mind: here was the framework of proportions which would fit into the landscape of Algiers the skyscraper of which I had been thinking since 1930, that is, for eight years. For eight years I had been building up in my mind the idea of the 'Cartesian' skyscraper as opposed to the irrational sky-scrapers of New York or Chicago: internal biology, structure, general position … On that day, suddenly, the idea became reality: the proportion — unity, variety, and rhythm.[144]

"Geometry", for Le Corbusier, sometimes meant such elements of form as lines, circles and square; more often it referred to guidelines, rules, modules or a proportional agreement between the parts and whole, one in which everything is in agreement with everything else, where parts follow the whole, and vice versa. A whole may comprise

In Architecture, a clustered buildings or spaces can be attached as appendages to a larger parent building or space. They can also be related by proximity alone to articulate and express their volumes as individual entities. They can also interlock their volumes and merge into a single form that has a variety of faces.

A clustered organisation can accept within its composition spaces that are dissimilar in size, form and function, but related to one another by proximity. Since there is no inherent place of importance within the pattern of a clustered organization, the buildings or spaces can be flexible and adaptable in terms functional changing, and democratic without imposing social or economical hierarchy.

结构元素、体量，以及这些元素的组合体。部分可以结合、叠加，也可能是分开的，而各元素与整体的关系则以几何来强化。

图2-1-6 a.帕提侬神庙

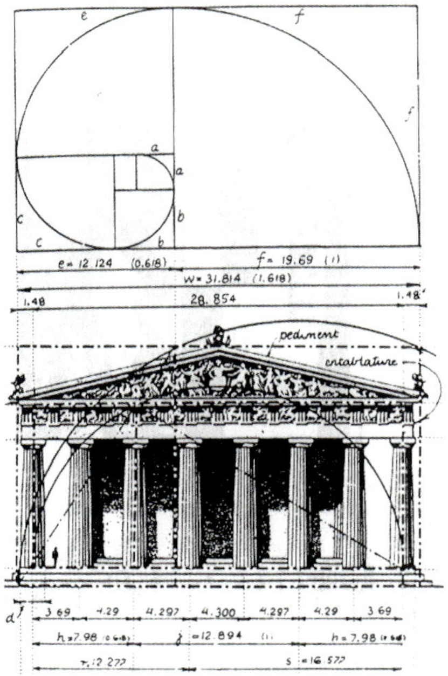

图2-1-6 b.比例分析

几何比例体系的巧妙运用，可以有效组合结构，产生视觉上的整体感。例如安德利亚·帕拉蒂奥的别墅设计广泛运用了“3-4-5”毕达哥拉斯勾股定理，并体现在许多房子的长、宽、高上。每座建筑的比例体系都有一个特定的协调机制，使每个建筑都有一种个性。这完全是构成的需要。另一种广泛运用的和谐比例就是直角黄金比，其长宽的比例按ϕ数（1.618……）递进。对古希腊帕提侬神庙（图2-1-6）的许多研究都发现，其立面设计依据的是黄金比。帕提侬的空间非常简单。两层柱廊环绕中堂，柱上架着巨石，上面是三角形山花。当时的建造大师有意调整视差以达到理想的抽象几何，让人真正体验空间、秩序和光感。建筑各个部分及其组合都调整到体量和空间感的最佳状态。陶立克柱式上的竖向凹槽在希腊灿烂的阳光下形成条形阴影，强化了柱体浑圆的感觉，每根柱子都由几块上小下大的柱石建成，柱石的线条精确流畅。柱子中部稍稍鼓起，由柱础和基座组成的底部向上呈弓形，从而视觉上矫正了垂直体量会看起来太细弱的问题。其效果是让神庙看似平稳地放在基座上，而且好像轻轻腾空而起。其他的视觉调整还包括，角柱跨距稍小，角上三陇板也不在柱体的中心。使建筑成为激情、明晰和美的样板的不仅是组成形体的元素，而且是它们之间的特殊关系——部分与部分之间的整体性，部分与整体之间的统一。

模数制

第二次世界大战之后，欧洲急需大量住宅建设。由于机械化生产技术的进步，大量生产标准化建筑构件成为解决一时危机的方法。这一时期，柯布西耶开发了一套比例体系，希望可以广泛采用在设计和建造业中。这种体系，后来称之为“模数制”（图2-1-7），它是一种比例网格，将建筑中的所有构件，从房门、家具到房间建筑都标准化。只要按体系设计和建造，建筑及其组成部分不仅直接表现现代工业，而且无限多样，比例和谐。

柯布西耶相信人体与潜在空间的和谐基于某些规律和数学关系，他以一个高举左手总高为2.2米的人体为基本模数，以此为出发点实现一种“和谐的建筑”。他相信，如果设计和产品都能以这个人体需要为基础，则可以适合所有不同高度人的需要。通过一系列与人体和黄金比有关的控制线，可以找到一系列具有斐波纳奇数学关系的数字，即两个相邻数字之和等于下一个数字（1，1，2，3，5，8，13…）。（这些有趣的数字关系可以在自然和艺术作品中找到，它和黄金比也有一种特殊关系：三个数字之后的任何两个相邻数字的比例是1:1.1618，与黄金比相同。）这些数字可以用作尺度，也可以用来量度人作息和阅读等的活动空间，从而成为所有设计的基准。通过

C-9　框架网格

网格是一种包含一系列等值空间或对称尺度的空间体系。它在形体、形式和空间之间建立起一种视觉和结构上的联系。形式和空间的位置及其相互关系通过三维网格来限定。
网格的构图能力来自所有要素之间的规则性和连续性。大小、形式或功能上不尽相同的空间，可以通过网格建立起连续的秩序或参考区域，从而产生普遍联系。

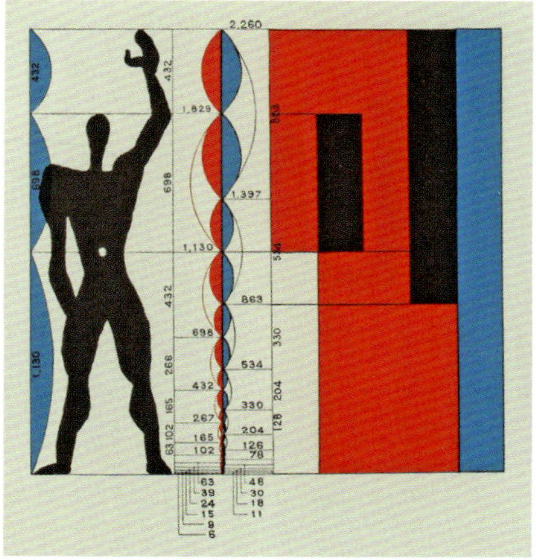
图2-1-7 模度图式

of one part, or aggregation of parts(Pic.2-1-5). Parts may be spatial or formal entities, which correspond to user-spaces, structural components, massing, volume, or combinations of these elements. Parts may adjoin, overlap or be separate from each other. The relationship of parts and whole is reinforced by geometry.

Geometrical proportion systems, when skilfully applied, provide structural organization and visual unity to the building. For example, the "Pythagorean 3-4-5 right triangle" is widely used in Andrea Palladio's villa and it occurs in the height, width and length of its many rooms. Each of these proportion systems has within itself a specific kind of equilibrium, which in turn gives each one its own character. They are chosen based on the demands of the composition itself. Another geometrical system widely used to develop harmonious proportions is the golden section rectangle, whose long and short sides are in the proportion of the transcendental number phi (Φ= 1.618…). Many studies of the Greek Parthenon show that the frontal elevation design has been ordered according to the golden section rectangle (Pic.2-1-6). The basic organization of the Parthenon is very simple. A double row of columns surrounds a central room and supports spanning stones, which in turn support a triangular pediment roof. The master builders further adjusted its ideal abstract geometry to deepen our experience of space, order, and light. Each part, and the whole ensemble, was lovingly modelled to intensify our sense of its mass and space. For example, the Doric columns' vertical grooved fluting reveals the roundness of their cylindrical shafts through the shadows cast in the brilliant Greek sunlight. The sticklike columns are actually stacks of carved stone drums, shaped to flowing lines in every dimension. The columns' subtle swelling and the slight upward bowing of the stylobate and plinth that compose the base of the building correct one's eyes' tendency to find straight forms too thin or weak. As a result, the Parthenon rests easily on its base, and seems to leap into the sky. Additional devices counteract other optical illusions: column spacing at the corners is reduced; and the triglyphs at the corners are not centred on their supporting columns. What make the building a clear example of passion, clarity and beauty is not simply the shapes of the elements, but the special relationship between them—the unity between the parts, and between parts and whole.

The Modulor

During and after the Second World War, there was a sudden and great demand for housing in Europe. With the advancement of machinery and technology, mass production of standardized building components seemed to offer a timely solution to the crisis. During these years, Le Corbusier developed a system of proportion, which he hoped could be adopted by the design and construction professions. The Modulor, as it was later called, was meant to be a proportioning grid, which would standardize all objects in the construction of building, from the design of a door and furniture, to the design of a room and building(Pic.2-1-7). If this system was accepted and built, resultant buildings and their components would not only directly express modern industry, but also offer an unlimited variety of harmonious designs and scales.

With the conviction that certain laws and mathematical relationships linked the human body with potentially harmonious spaces, Le Corbusier initially developed a human figure with his left arm raised to a height of 2.20 meters as his starting point. This was a height at which Le Corbusier felt was very much in agreement with the human scale, hence the beginning of a "harmonious architecture". It was his belief that if the manufactured goods or designs satisfied the physical requirements of the tallest man, then these goods and designs would also be suitable for use by people of any height. Through establishing various regulating lines, relating with the golden section and the

Structural Grid

Grid is a spatial system consisting of a series of equal spaces or systematically defined dimensions. It establishes a visual and structural relationship between figures, forms, and spaces. Positions of forms and spaces in space and relationships with one another are regulated by a three-dimensional grid.
The organizing power of a grid results from the regularity and continuity of its pattern that pervades the elements it organizes. Its pattern establishes a constant set or field of reference points and lines in space with which the spaces of a grid organization, although dissimilar in size, form, or function, can share a common relationship.

不断实验，柯布西耶后来根据6英尺高的人开发了英尺模数制。他认为这是经验和厘米公制之间的联结体，因此适用更广。

有意思的是，柯布西耶发现了模数制的数学关系之后，他又发现一些古代建筑也运用这种协调方法，如巴黎附近的拜占庭时期的切利斯教堂，伊斯坦布尔大清真寺的入口和其他一些例子。“模数制”首先运用在柯布西耶的马赛公寓（图2-1-8，图2-1-9），贯穿设计的各个方面，从单元设计、建筑立面、室内木作、家具，甚至到开工奠基石。模数制还用在其他规模迥异的项目上，如地形研究、移动展厅、墙板，甚至巴黎规划。

需要指出的是，模度只用于建立秩序，增加清晰度，与设计中的诗意、情感色彩和构思无关。它只是用来平衡各部分的关系。尽管柯布西耶发明了“模数制”，他的设计却表明他自己并不受其制约，如果“模数制”让设计不好看，他马上放弃这个工具。“要知道你的眼睛才是最终裁判……‘模数制’是工具，一个精确度的测量仪，或者说钢琴键盘，音色已调好，但要弹得好，完全靠你自己。”[145]

图2-1-8 勒·柯布西耶设计的马赛公寓电梯间外墙上的模度图式

图2-1-9 马赛公寓室内

图2-1-10 香港的生态系统一角

几何形之后

在标榜几何重要性的同时，柯布西耶也知道其局限性。他要求用“眼睛”和“演奏”来做最后标准。他暗示了几何仅仅是建筑形体内容之一，而不是全部。彼得·戴维森（1997）在他主编的杂志中以一篇题为《几何之后的建筑学》的文章明确分析了几何的目的和局限。[146] 建筑之所以“需要”几何，是因为一种物理和感知科学的要求，是对抽象的和清晰的形的需要。在前者，几何方便尺寸量度，易于形成感知世界中的形象；在后者，几何是一种主观控制，凌驾于感知世界之上（图2-1-10）。对于像早期现代大师这样坚信未来在于创造的人来说，几何是建筑造型的依据，并成为形本身。换句话说，几何要素（网格、轴线、对称等）来自现实之外，因形体组合的需要而强加在现实之上。

第二次世界大战后的城市开发都体现了几何控制下的城市状态（图2-1-11）。它们由于单一化、重复性和社会僵化等问题而遭到各方面的批评。现代城市是由各种因素作用的结果，几何只能是其中之一。马克·安吉利尔发现促进城市发展中的基本因素实际上是一些各行其是、相互矛盾的体系，它们叠加在一起，在一个城市区域内共存。[147] 城市可以看作不同，甚至矛盾的控制原理结合后的形体。与传统几何形的“欧几里得”和“笛卡儿”城市相反，“城市自己看来从未要实现某种完整的秩序”。

网格可以根据不同的构图要求进行修改，如可以删减、增加或分层；可以处理成不规则的，创造出一系列不同大小、比例和位置的等级模式；可以进行比例的渐变，以改变视觉和空间的连续性；可以被主要空间或基地的自然特征所打断；可以在基本框架之内取走或旋转部分网格；还可以在基地内改变视觉意象——从一点逐步变为线、面或体。

human figure, a Fibonacci series of inter-related numbers was found in which the sum of two consecutive numbers equals the following number (1,1,2,3,5,8,13 …). (These numbers have interesting properties and are often evident in nature and art. It is also worth noting its unique relationship with the golden section rectangle: the ratio of any two adjacent numbers in Fibonacci series after three is approximately the same as the proportional ratio 1:1.1618 found in the golden section rectangle.) This series of numbers was translated into a scale or a measurement related to human activities, such as sitting, leaning, etc., and was used as the basis of all designs. With further experiments, a foot-inch Modulor was later developed, based on a six-foot human figure. Its inventor saw this as a tool bridging both worlds of the imperial and metric measurements, and hence, universally applicable.

It is interesting to note that since Le Corbusier discovered the mathematical relationships of his Modulor, he found other ancient examples with this underlying harmonious principle: Abbaye de Chaalis near Paris; an ancient Byzantium church in Kahrie; and the doorway of the Grand Seraglio at Istanbul, among others. The Modulor was first put into practice in Le Corbusier's Unite d'Habitation at Marseilles (Pic.2-1-8,Pic.2-1-9). Here, the Modulor was widely applied: in the planning of apartment units, development of building elevations, the design of interior woodwork, furniture, and even the stone used for the opening ceremony of the project. The Modulor was applied in other projects of diverse scales: typography, travelling exhibition, and wall panels – even a plan for the city of Paris.

It is important to note that the system was used only to establish geometrical order and clarity. It neither carried poetic or lyrical overtones nor inspired any overall theme. Its existence merely established a balance. Although Le Corbusier invented the Modulor system, his projects and designs proved that he was not enslaved by it. If the Modulor produced designs, which looked displeasing, Le Corbusier was willing to drop the tool aside and scrap the system. "Your eyes are your judges, the only ones you should know…The 'Modulor' is a working tool, a precision instrument; a keyboard shall we say, a piano, a tuned piano. The piano has been tuned: it is up to you to play it well."[145]

Beyond Geometry

While he celebrated the importance of geometry on the one hand, on the other Le Corbusier did understand its limitations; he called for "your eyes" and "your play" to make the final decision. He implicitly argued that geometry was only one of several aspects of architectural form. Peter Davidson (1997) in his edited journal "Architecture after geometry" more clearly analysed the purposes and limitations of geometry.[146] Architecture's "desire" for geometry rests in a need for both a material and sensory discourse, and an abstract and cognitive formation. In the first instance, geometry provides the measure and image of a sensed world; in the second, geometry is the conceptual ordering which affirms its relevance in spite of the sensory world. For millennia, geometry acted in the formation of architecture, ultimately providing its proper form. In other words, geometric figures (grid, axis, symmetry, etc.) pre-exist reality (Pic.2-1-10), but are further imposed by the designer in his conscious desire for organized form. As previously mentioned, this geometric preoccupation reached a climax in the early Modern era.

Cities constructed after the second world war show a typical consequence of geometrical order (Pic.2-1-11) ,they have been broadly criticized for both their repetitive, monotonous forms and social sterility. Contemporary cities are formed by multiple forces, and geometry is but one of them. As Mark Angèlil observed, the primary forces involved in city development operate autonomously, each for and of itself. Incompatible systems are juxtaposed with one

Grid can be modified to meet different composition requirements. It can be subtracted from, added to, or layered, and still maintain its identity as a grid. A grid can made irregular and create a hierarchical set of modules differentiated by size, proportion and location. It can also undergo other transformations: portions of the grid can slide to alter the visual and spatial continuity across its field; a grid pattern can be interrupted to define a major space or accommodate a natural feature of its site; a portion of the grid can be dislocated and rotated about a point in the basic pattern; and the grid can transform its visual image across its field from a pattern of points — to lines, to planes and to volume.

图2-1-11 20世纪50年代巴西利亚的住宅

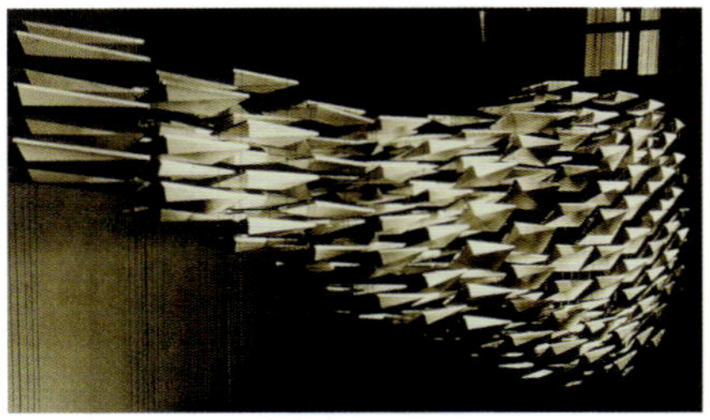

图2-1-12 基普尼斯设计的陈列体系

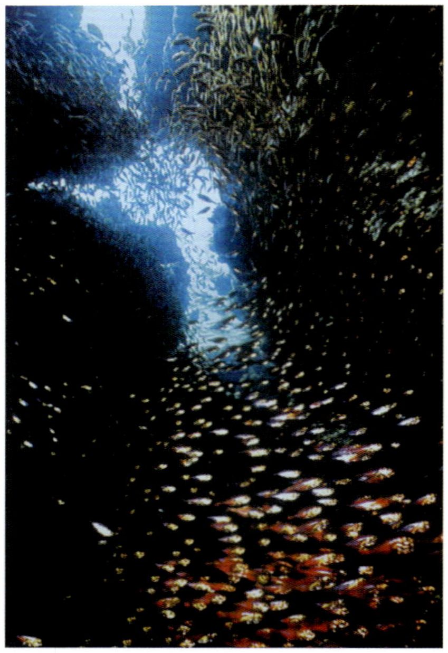

图2-1-13 液态空间

杰夫·基普尼斯指出，没有一种文化像建筑那样受制于几何和技术条件。这是由于经济和结构等因素的制约，也是由于现代主义大师坚信几何形体和组织必须凌驾于人的想象之上。实际上，几何仅仅是建筑空间创造因素中的一部分，形、材料、光以及使用程序都对空间感知有重要影响。几何本身对建筑并不太合适，而且几何在塑造今天新社会、新政治和不断出现的新结构方面已经捉襟见肘。基普尼斯自己的艺术装置作品体现另一种秩序，看起来统一但实际上完全不同（图2-1-12）。“图像空间，液态空间，肌理状，模式感和地域形态”可能更接近这种秩序。这些作品没有对形体一致性的肯定，也不是想象的综合，“总之，我对鱼群感兴趣，它是庞大的，有组织的，又是转瞬间即逝的，永远有形，永远变形（图2-1-13）”。[148]

正如彼得·戴维森所说，“几何之后”并不是要反叛或者漠视建筑中的几何作用，而是在结合和推进新技术和新形式，或新秩序和形体组织过程中，需要对几何的批判性认识。他说：“建筑和几何的结合是先验的，专横的。”因此对几何之外的探索需要打破几何的专制，排除先入为主的观念（图2-1-14）。他强调说，建筑师在将地球重力因素简单地转变为垂直的直角空间模式时要三思而后行。

C-10 渐变

渐变通常用于在构图内创造逐渐变大的多个形。这些形通常按规则间距排列，也可以按照增加或减小的密度来排列。渐变也指一个形在形状、位置、方向或比例系统上的转换。

Gradation

It is a principle which usually creates a composition consisting a number of increasing size of forms. The forms are usually set at regular intervals or percentages, and can be determined systematically through different proportional systems. The forms can also be positioned with increasing or decreasing density. Gradation also refers to the systematic alteration of the shape, position, direction, or proportion of a form.

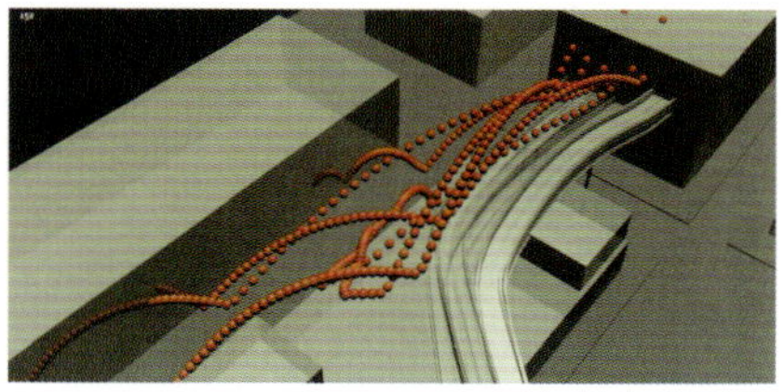

图2-1-14 在林恩设计的海港管理局入口项目中，形、结构和帐篷式立面是通过计算机模拟人的运动而设计出来的非几何形态

another, co-existing within the same urban territory.[147] The city could thus be considered a hybrid form derived from multiple, or even contradictory, ordering principles. In contrast to traditional "Euclidean" or "Cartesian" cities founded largely on geometric coherence, "new urban developments instead appear to disclaim any attempt at a unifying order."

Jeff Kipnis pointed out that no cultural practice is more indebted to technical solutions than architecture is to geometry. This is because of practical reasons such as economy and structure, and the Modernist belief that geometric form and organization should prevail over imagination. On the contrary, it should be noted that architecture's major spatial innovations have not been solely enabled by geometry; form, materials, lighting and programming all contribute to a complex spatial sensibility. Geometry by itself is inadequate here. Most important, geometrical ordering is no longer sufficient to embody or project the new social, political and cognitive structures emerging around us. Kipnis' art installations presented other types of orderings, which are visually apparent but materially indistinct (Pic.2-1-12). "graphic space, liquid space, texture fields, pattern effects and field conditions". In these works there is no formal ratification by means of correspondence and eidetic resemblance. "Of late, however, I have become more interested in schools of fish: immense, composite, ephemeral, always in form, but always changing form." (Pic.2-1-13)[148]

As Peter Davidson said, "Beyond Geometry" is not based on an overturning or annihilation of geometry in architecture, but a critical speculation on the incorporation and expansion of new techniques and tactics for architectonic ordering and organization of forms. He claimed, "The linkage of architecture and geometry is based on a transcendental imperative." To explore what is left by geometry is to break that imperative and therefore to evaporate this transcendentality (Pic.2-1-14) .He argued that architects should remain critical when they translate simple ideas of a uniform gravity emanating from the earth into simple static models of vertical and orthogonal space.

形状的渐变：形在内部和（或）外部的变化。
尺度的渐变（膨胀）：形的放大或缩小。
位置的渐变：在重复的框架里，活动的结构线拦截或部分切断形。

Gradation of Shape: vary a form internally and/or externally.
Gradation of Size (dilation): enlarge or reduce the form.
Gradation of Position: this is possible in a repetition structure with active structural lines that intercept and partially crop forms.

图2-2-1 赫茨伯格在荷兰设计的比尔公司总部，1968—1972年

图2-2-2 20世纪30年代英国人对汽车技术的迷恋

2.2 转型和解型

建筑和建造本身就是一个不断转型的过程：从概念到图，从图到建筑。建筑师自己也处于转型的过程，因为他不可避免地处于现实和抽象，人工和自然，现在和未来的不同位置上。约翰·海杜克曾说，艺术源自现实而终止于抽象，而建筑作品则相反，源自抽象概念，形成于现实。然而，“一个好的建筑师应能让建成的作品尽量接近原始设计概念”。[149]

一般形的转变来自三个方面的需要：

1．外部条件：包括自然环境对建筑的影响，如风、地形、景观、朝向等；

2．内部需求：如建筑法规、规划要求、活动内容、投资等建筑本身的条件；

3．艺术取向：建筑师在根据各种因素要求基础发展和操作建筑形体时的能力、观念和意愿。

20世纪的建筑形体和组织直接体现前两种因素。这种单纯对实际要求的考察，自然带有局限性，平淡而功利。以有限的方式，根据不同限制条件的最佳综合要求，从开始想象的体量到最终的建造的转型过程不可避免地机械生硬。最后的答案总是固定的几种，真正有差别的极少。转型的讨论主要关于建筑师在功利之外的思想和处理各种条件和制约因素的方法。乔治·西尔维蒂将转型定义为：

对脱离原始的、平常的或者规范要求之外的对现状的加工，通过扭曲、重组、再造或者更改，使形与原始状态有一定关系而同时又正在形成新意义。[150]

转型可以通过增加和减少，或者一个形与另一个形的关联而转变。增加方式指将同样的单元体组合在一起，易于形成视觉上的整体（图2-2-1）。减少方式正相反，从完整的形体抽出一部分，而同样会有一种整体感。在两种操作过程中，建筑形体处于多向延续的过程，直到获得满意空间质素，作为从初始状态派生出来的形当然也是多种多样的。

转型也可以从某种建筑模式开始，这种模式的结构和元素关系可能有适用性和合理性，但需要一系列的操作将其转变以适应某项设计的特殊条件和环境要求。这种转型要求对先前的样板或模式的体系有充分的认识和理解，在一系列的变化和转换过程中，初始的设计概念应不断强化和清晰化，转型是建设性的而不是相反。比如柯布西耶将希腊神庙的几何体系——以及它的意义、清晰性、精确性、不可替代的诚实和经济严谨——转型后，引入他的作品，最后还带入并引入整个现代主义运动。他和其他一些现代主义大师还直接将机器特征从形象和原理两方面引入建筑（图2-2-2）。柯布西耶曾将建筑标准化比喻为打字机：“自打字机发明后，打印纸也标准化了，这种标准也

方向渐变：在一个平面上左右旋转一个形，或在三维空间内前后旋转一个形，同时保持其形状不变，其效果是方向上的变化。

Gradation of Direction: rotating a form from left to right on a flat surface, or from front to back in three-dimensional space, while maintaining its shape, effects a change in direction.

2.2 Transformation and Deformation

Architecture and construction, by their nature, undergo a constant process of physical transformation, from concept to drawings, and from drawings to buildings. Further, architects themselves are constantly under a process of transformation; they unavoidably exist between the multiple poles of reality and abstraction, of the man-made and the natural, of present and future. John Hejduk noted that a painter starts from the real world, and works towards abstraction; an architect works the opposite way. However, "a significant architect is one who, when finished with a work, is as close to that original abstraction as he could possibly be". [149]

Transformation is moulded by three major factors:

1.External Constraints: This refers to natural, environmental constraints imposed on a building, such as wind, topography, view, exposure, orientation, etc.;

2.Internal Requirements: This refers to conditions applied to a building, such as building code, planning issues, program requirements, budget, etc.;

3.Artistic Response: This refers to the ability, attitude and will of the architect in developing and manipulating built forms based on the above factors.

Throughout the 20th century, building form and configuration typically evolved out of a direct response at least the first two of these factors, based solely on programmatic conditions could be quite restrictive, predictable and utilitarian. The overall transformation of an initially imagined solid "mass", given a permitted number of incremental transformations which respond to optimum combinations of constraints, will generally yield mechanical results. The range of ultimate solutions will be virtually fixed, with only some subtle differences. However, the transformation process introduced here will depend largely on the architect's interpretation and/or response of these constraints beyond a utilitarian approach. Transformation, as Jorge Silvetti defined,

By transformation we mean those operations performed on the elements of a given existent code which depart from the original, normal, or canonical usage of the code, by distorting, regrouping, reassembling, or in general altering it in such a way that it maintains its references to the original while tending to produce a new meaning. [150]

Forms may be transformed through additive and subtractive processes, or through an association of one form to another. An additive design grows from an assemblage of identifiable units, and hence, has a perceptually dominant whole (Pic.2-2-1). Subtractive design, on the other hand, develops out of removing parts from a recognizable totality, and hence, it also has a perceptually dominant whole. In either case, the overall massing or image of the building form is massaged in a dynamic, continuous process until the desirable spatial quality is obtained. The resultant whole may or may not be identifiable as a derivative of the original.

A transformation may start from a prototypical architectural model whose formal structure and ordering of elements might be appropriate and reasonable, and to transform it through a series of discrete manipulations to respond to the specific conditions and context of the design task at hand. Transformation requires first that the ordering system of the prior, or prototypical, model be perceived and understood, so that through a series of finite changes and permutations,

比例的渐变：在渐变的框架中缩小或放大部分要素。

Gradation of Proportion: the narrowing and widening of subdivisions in a gradation structure might demand the narrowing and widening of forms.

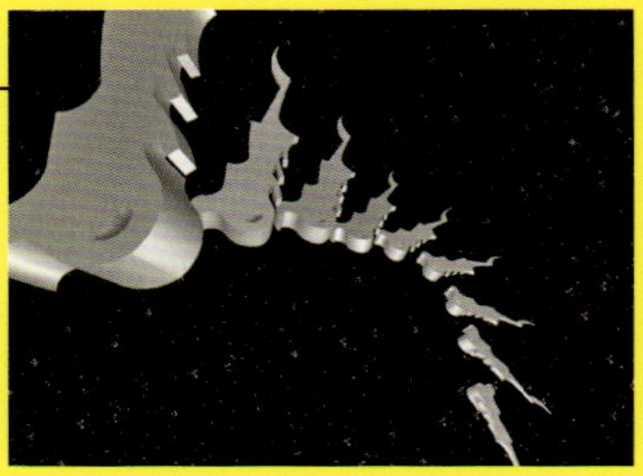

对家具产生巨大影响，打字机成了一种模式，一种商业方式，其他东西的尺寸将不再是随意的了。”[151] 这种以非建筑元素为素材进行转型的方法还将在下文中继续讨论。

图2-2-3 赫斯扎尔将凡·高绘画中（上图）的色彩关系运用在德·阿伦舒夫住宅的卧室设计当中（下图），荷兰，1919年

图2-2-4 a.蒙德里安《蓝色和黄色构成》，1922年

图2-2-4 b.巴塞罗那展览馆

将艺术形体转为建筑形体

转型可以出自一种抽象的概念，它也许来自建筑以外的领域，如绘画、雕塑、科学、数学或者其他工艺品。对其他物体特征的借用和重新解读可称为“图像转换”或者“图式隐喻”。而我们讨论的并不是简单的转型，而是探索和推动新思想的过程（图2-2-3），形体和空间在生长过程应注入新的含义或者新的解释。

对建筑影响最大的依然是蒙德里安的作品，许多现代建筑师都曾借鉴他的作品。密斯·凡·德·罗在设计著名的巴塞罗那展览馆时就借鉴了蒙德里安的《百老汇布吉伍吉》（一种爵士乐钢琴奏法）等系列作品（图2-2-4）。

集建筑、美术和雕塑天才于一身的阿尔瓦·阿尔托认为艺术和建筑有许多共同点，可以相互借鉴（图2-2-5）。两者的共同基础之一是在潜意识层面上形成的思想。当面对许多错综复杂的建筑问题而难以理性地解决时，阿尔托习惯于转用其他方式发展自己的概念，他会把面对的问题先放在一边，投入绘画等抽象艺术活动中，让创作灵感重获自由。“突然间一个原始的思想产生了，它是一个将许多相互矛盾的元素结合为一个整体的起点。”[152] 在设计维依普里图书馆时，阿尔托将大多数时间用在作“儿童画”，画不同形状的山上阳光普照。这些画后来发展成图书馆的基本构思，几个不同层面上的扇形平面借阅室，好似山坡高低起伏，主要功能围绕着圆锥形天窗，好像太阳系里的行星（图2-2-6）。

弗兰克·盖里以他的高度敏感和用雕塑方式来处理建筑的设计方法而闻名。他常以特殊的空间效果给人带来惊喜。正如他的艺术家朋友库西·范·布鲁金指出：“盖瑞自己认为对建筑实践

图2-2-5 a.阿尔托油画作品

图2-2-5 b.阿尔托设计的垃圾桶，1936年

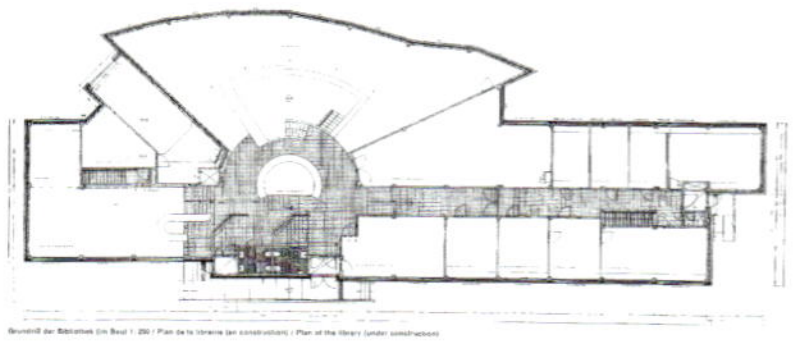

图2-2-5 c.阿尔托设计的图书馆平面，1963—1965年

C-11 集中

集中是指形的密度的分布方式。形可能在某一区域中密集分布或在其他区域少量散落。这种分布通常是不平均和非正式的。集中的效果可以通过以下几种方式创造出来：
空白：设计中的空白可以引起单元形的不规则分布，并在部分场所集中。
位置变化：已占有空间相对于未占有空间的比例消长。应避免规则的渐变。
量变：应避免规则的渐变。

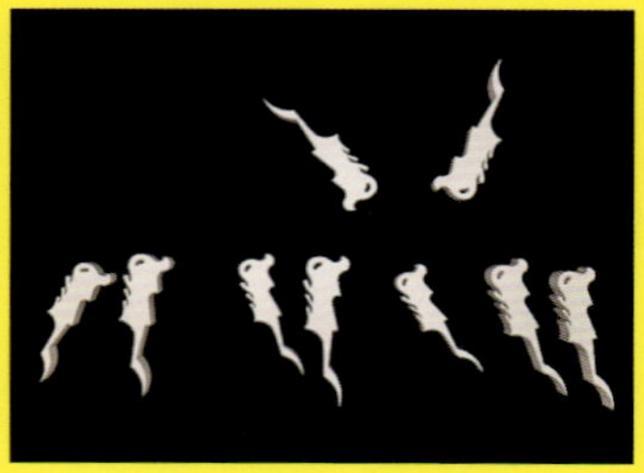

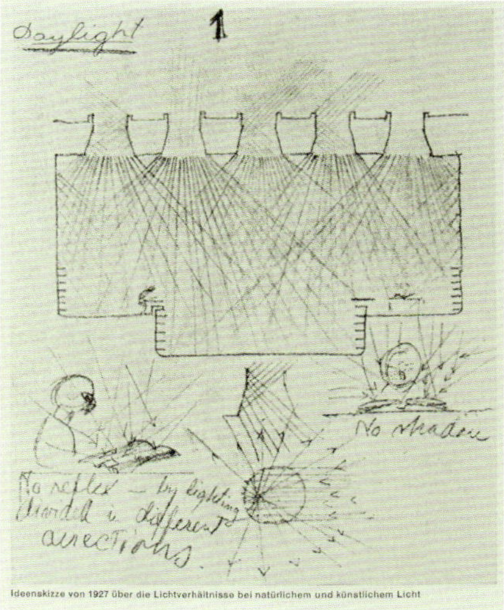

图2-2-6 a.自然采光研究草图

图2-2-6 b.大阅览室

the original design concept can be clarified, strengthened, and built upon, rather than destroyed. As we have understood, Le Corbusier transformed the geometrical order of the Greek temple — its meaning, clarity, precision, implacable honesty, and economic severity — and incorporated these into his own buildings and ultimately the larger Modern movement. Le Corbusier and other Modernist architects also transformed the literal machine-character into machine-architecture, either for its superficial image or its deeper principle (Pic.2-2-2). Le Corbusier once elaborated on architectural standardization by taking typewriter as an example. "When the typewriter was invented, typing paper was standardized; this standardization had a considerable repercussion on furniture, it "established a module, that of the commercial format … this format was not an arbitrary measure." [151] The inspiration for transformation may come from varied sources besides architecture, as discussed further below.

Transforming Art to Architecture

Transformation is frequently evolved from an abstract idea or concept, which itself may be borrowed from fields outside architecture, such as painting, sculpture, science, mathematics, or other artifacts. This kind of borrowing and interpreting the properties of the object is called "pictorial transfer" or "pictorial metaphor". The kind of transformation we refer to here is not simply a modification of an original, but a process, which explores and expands a new idea (Pic.2-2-3). Form and space are evolved and injected with new meaning and interpretation.

Piet Mondrian's work has been most influential on and adopted by many contemporary architects. Mies van der Rohe captured the spatial qualities of the former paintings of *Broadway Boogie Woogie* series, when he developed the Barcelona Pavilion (Pic.2-2-4).

Alvar Aalto, who by talent was an architect, painter and sculptor, felt that art and architecture shared many commonalties. He was able to exploit both worlds to his benefit (Pic.2-2-5). One of the shared foundations between both disciplines was the process of conceiving the idea on a subconscious level. When bombarded by an architectural problem — affected by numerous and complicated factors and could hardly be resolved rationally, Aalto turned to other means to develop his concepts. He abandoned all the immediate problems from the board and his mind, and busied himself with drawing, painting and other abstract art to free up his creative instinct. "Suddenly, the basic idea is born, a starting point which links the numerous, often contradictory elements and brings them into harmony with each other."[152] When designing the Municipal Library in Viipuri, Aalto spent much time making children's drawings: several suns shining around an imaginary mountain of varied profile and typology. These drawings later became the concept for the library, which translated into a group of fan-shaped lending and reading rooms on different levels, recalling the mountain with its different slopes; and its functions revolved around the conical skylights, recalling the orbiting planets of the solar system (Pic.2-2-6).

Frank Gehry, who excels in his sensitive and sculptural approach to architectural problems, always surprises us with the unexpected spatial qualities of his buildings. As his artist-friend Coosje van Bruggen comments, "Gehry feels that his main contribution to the practice of architecture is the direct implementation of an image or form he is in search of. It is this unique hand-to-eye coordination, a process of transforming intact a sketch into a model into a building, that comprises the building."[153] His continuous inclination to befriend and collaborate with artists began early in his school years. He has worked with Claes Oldenburg (Pic.2-2-7) and Coosje van Bruggen as early as 1984

Concentration

Concentration refers to a way of distribution and density of forms which may be thickly gathered in certain areas or thinly scattered in other areas. The distribution is usually uneven and informal. The effect of concentration can be created through:
Frequent Absences: this can result in uneven distribution of unit forms, leading to concentration in certain places in a design. The pattern of absences can be irregular or quite regular.
Positional Changes: the increase or decrease of the proportion of occupied space as against unoccupied space. Regular gradational changes should be avoided.
Quantitative Changes: regular gradational changes should be avoided.

图2-2-7 奥登博格《开关》，1964年

图2-2-8 盖里和奥登博格设计的“乔·日·莫”住宅，1991年

图2-2-9 安德烈《杠杆》，由137块防火砖组合而成，1966年，纽约

的主要贡献是将自己研究的形和图像直接变为建筑，正是通过特有的眼手协调，在转型的过程中把草图变成模型，模型变为建筑。”[153] 在读书时候盖里就开始和艺术家为友，他在1984年与克丽斯·奥登博格（图2-2-7）和布鲁金合作设计了好景夏令营，后来和其他艺术家设计了罗约拉法学院（1978—1984），和乔·日·莫（1991）住宅（图2-2-8）。他的许多构思直接来自或者受他朋友的绘画和雕塑的启发，建筑成为这些思想的实验。1966年他偶然走进卡尔·安德烈的装置艺术品，两排137块防火砖（图2-2-9）。他后来回忆说：“当时我正在研究链条式的物体，这件作品吸引了我。我一直在寻找电话线式的建筑，你可以叫一个人来，告诉他一些规则，他们就可以将它建起来，这太有意思了。这让我思考处理某种材料时候的体验。”[154] 他这一时期设计的温斯顿旅社（1982—1987）（图2-2-10），一座监狱方案（1983）和伍斯克住宅（1981—1984）都受乔吉奥·莫朗迪的《静物》的影响（图2-2-11），“我是这样开始想的，如果我做一个静物，一个莫朗迪，如三个瓶子和两个罐子，或者三个大瓶子和三个小瓶子，如果每个东西内部都塞进功能，它一定有缝，一定是由几个部分组成的，不可能是一个整体。”[155] 盖里感兴趣的是把绘画放进另一个领域时出现的问题。当三维空间里并列一组形体，如何解决建筑中的问题。“与在空间中排列不同，静物画中最有意思的是物体间距离和关系是灵活的，是形成立体雕塑的过程（图2-2-12）。”[156]

扎哈·哈迪德的建筑画实际上更像艺术，建筑好像脱离地球引力，腾空而起，它表现爆炸式的动感和多重能量。这是结构的图像研究，也是艺术品——抽象、失重（图2-2-13）。形体本身好像很轻，但是确定的，实际上来自现代建筑的“语汇”。哈迪德的雄心正是不向世俗低头，行似艺术家。她的作品也体现了创作源泉：马里维奇、列昂尼乌夫、维斯宁、伊尔·里西斯基、梅尼科夫等苏联20世纪20年代的一批至上主义和构成主义的新派建筑师。她说：“当时在一个巨变的世界中的试验品，现在应该可以建起来了。”[157] 哈迪德的构成似一种空间爆裂，充满动感和张力（图2-2-14）。她的第一座建成作品是坐落在莱茵河边的维特拉家具公司总部的消防站，很好地体现了这种空间感。她的空间组合既无内空间的围合，也无外空间的延续，而是像用刀在欧几里得几何形的“紧身囚衣”上划出的一道道的口子（图2-2-15），每划一道同时出现一系列动感体量，或是向上拱起，或是向下弯曲。

常见的集中类型有：

· 相对于点的集中：设计中单元形围绕一个中心点聚集，点所在的位置聚集密度最大，向外逐渐稀疏。

· 向一条线集中：设计中单元形围绕一条中心线集中。线周围密度最大，相对于线的集中产生渐变的效果。

· 自由集中：不同密度分布的单元形自由分组，完全非正式的构图。

图2-2-10 盖里设计的温斯顿旅社，1982—1987年

图2-2-11 莫朗迪《静物》

图2-2-12 盖里的温斯顿旅社构思草图

in the Summer Camp Good Times projects, with other works such as Loyola Law School (1978—1984), Chiat/Day/Mojo (1991) that followed (Pic.2-2-8). Many of his ideas are inspired and generated by paintings and sculptures of his contemporaries, and he relates these inspirations with what he is experimenting in architecture. During a 1966 exhibition, he "walked into" Carl Andre's installation serendipitously: a lined-up, double-row of firebricks, a total of 137 pieces (Pic.2-2-9). This triggered Gehry to think: "At the same time, I was starting to work with chain-link, and I was fascinated. I was looking for an architecture that you could dial up, phone in. You could call somebody and describe the co-ordinates, and they could build the thing. That was a fantasy … It made me think about the experience of working with materials." [154] His Winston Guest House (1982—1987) (Pic.2-2-10) and other work of the same period such as Prison Project (1983) and Wosk Residence (1981—1984), were very much influenced by Giorgio Morandi's Still Life (Pic.2-2-11) . " That's when I started thinking, well, if I made a still life, if I made a Morandi, with three bottles and two pots, three big bottles and three little bottles, in order for each piece to retain its object hood, the thing had to have the crack, it had to have the separation, it couldn't be a continuous structure." [155] That which fascinated Gehry in the realm painting became a new problem for him to resolve in the realm of architecture: juxtaposition of forms in three-dimensional space. " … And the wonderful thing with the still life, as opposed to just lining them up, is that the distances and the alignments among the parts become mobile, forming a sculptural composition(Pic.2-2-12)." [156]

Zaha Hadid's architectural drawings are more often like paintings than working drawings, which express an architecture so free that it appears to escape gravity. They portray an experience of explosive movement and dynamic energy. They are graphic studies of structure, yet they are clearly the realms of art—abstract and weightless(Pic.2-2-13).The forms are light but well defined, taken from the vocabulary of the Modern Movement. Hadid's boldness lies precisely in the fact that she does not compromise with conventions but behaves as an artist. The designs clearly reflect Hadid's source of inspiration: Malevitch, Leonidov, Wesnin, El Lissitzky, Melnikov—the entire contingent of Russian Suprematist and Constructivist revolutionaries from the 1920s. "The explosive world designs (of that era)," Hadid claims, "were all abandoned experiments, which must now finally be realized" [157]. Hadid's structures came close to an experience of space exploding with tension and movement(Pic.2-2-14). Her first realized building project, the firehouse for the Vitra headquarter in Weil am Rhein, is such an example. Hadid's spatial composition produces neither closed interior spaces nor continuous exterior structures. Rather, it is virtually as if these compositions were carved out of the rigid Euclidean geometrical straightjacket with a knife (Pic.2-2-15). Each of the moving surfaces represents simultaneously an ascending and curved, a convex and descending, mass of movement.

Frequently appeared concentration types:
· Concentration Towards a Point: the unit forms crowd around a pre-established conceptual point in a design. The density reaches the maximum where the point lies and gradually thins down in surrounding areas.
· Concentration Towards a Line: the unit forms crowd around a pre-established conceptual line in a design. Maximum density occurs along the line. Concentration towards a line approaches the effect of gradation.
· Free Concentration: the unit forms are grouped freely with varying density and scantiness in the design. Organization is completely informal.

图2-2-13 a.哈迪德为香港山顶缆车站方案作的表现图《跳水者》，1982—1983年

图2-2-13 b.伦敦特拉法哥亚广场主楼方案表现图《公共平台和塔楼》

图2-2-14 哈迪德设计的日本季风餐厅，1990年

图2-2-15 哈迪德设计的莱茵石（地名）消防站

形的削弱

转型的方式多种多样，只有当形在转变过程中逐渐消失，转型才会结束。而这也正是一些当今先锋派建筑师所认为的，21世纪建筑的开端。拉菲尔·莫耐奥说：“今天时代需要的是没有形的世界，它反对用显而易见的形象来体现（图2-2-16）。”[158]

这种倾向出现于20世纪60年代的艺术运动。大量室外雕塑的普及意味着原来的艺术场所，建筑室内不再重要。这些室外艺术品有时将整个城市作为图底，而最常见的是将一个广场或者整座花园作为艺术品，这些广场和花园好像是室内空间的延伸。这些作品也可看作是对大地或城市空间的改造行为，空间本身像是物体被形体所分隔。通过一系列操作，形，如大地，开始转变，原有特性消逝，新的含义产生。“单个物体的堆砌被整体开放的气氛代替，一个永久性的设置被短暂的侵入行为替代。”[159] 这时不仅单体建筑的边界变得模糊，而且城市要素叠加在一起的质素，如运动、变化、密度和强度开始显现。有些艺术品甚至更通过视觉游戏，故意表现转瞬即逝的现象，它需要的是记忆，而不需要永久性展示（图2-2-17，图2-2-18）。

当代一些前卫建筑师认为，建筑业也应参与到当今城市中的动态的、时常是非物质的转型力量当中。传统单纯的、固定的、永恒的形体和结构已无法适应当代城市和其所包含的活动需要。[160] 建筑概念应重新确定，因为城市被视为一个多样性的整体，其特征是靠力而不是形来体现的。过

C-12 旋转

旋转是将形体围绕一个固定的轴或中心点旋转的法则。旋转时，形相对于中心的距离不变。旋转的量或对称性由形之间的间距决定。轻微的形的性质的变化给正统或严格的构图增加了活力。

Rotation

Rotation is a principle that turns the figure about a predetermined axis or a central point. It is a round and symmetry operation. The form remains at a fixed distance from the central. The interval or space between the forms rotate about the axis determines the quantity or symmetry value of the rotation in 360 degree.Slightly change of form property contribute a vitality to a otherwise very formal and rigid composition.

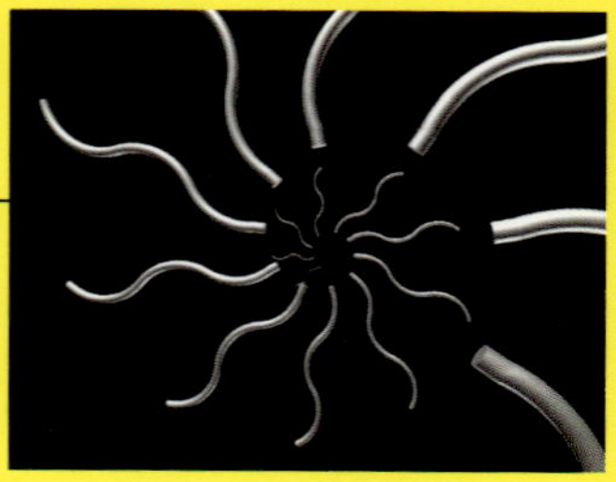

De-formation

Transformation approaches can be many but there is an ending when a form is evaporates in the process. That is, as some avant-garde architects believe, where the new architecture of 21st century starts. Rafael Moneo said, "What the zeitgeist suggests is a world without form, a world that resists being represented by recognizable images (Pic.2-2-16)." [158]

The trend originated in the artistic movements of the 1960s. The fact that outdoor sculpture became popular indicated that the former context of art, traditionally indoor architecture, was now defunct. With the emergence of outdoor sculpture, sometimes an entire urban area became "domesticated"; in the best examples a sculpture garden or plaza became seen as a kind of extended interior. These works could be seen as an act performed on the land or urban space. The space itself came to be read as a positive artefact onto which form has been applied. With the investment of formal manipulations, form—i.e. the land—is now transformed, deformed, and informed. "An accumulation of individual objects is replaced by an all-enfolding atmosphere, and a permanent installation is replaced by a transient intervention."[159] Here, not only does the edge or boundary of a discrete building becomes blurred, but also overlapping urban qualities, such as motion, change, density and intensity now come to the fore. Some artworks engage in perceptual games where they are deliberately temporary and ephemeral, made only to be memorable, and not as permanent displays (Pic.2-2-17, Pic.2-2-18).

Some avant-garde architects today believe that architecture needs to participate in the mobile, often immaterial, shaping forces of the contemporary city. The classical models of pure, static, timeless form and structure are no longer adequate to describe the contemporary city and the activities it supports.[160] Architecture must be conceptualised and modelled within an urban field that is understood as dynamic and characterised by forces rather than forms. Traditionally, urban questions are often questions of large-scale forms or fabrics. "In order to address patterns of organisation on the urban scale that differentiate subtly, it is necessary that architects begin to design using dynamic

图2-2-16 莫耐奥设计的巴塞罗那音乐厅，1988—1999年

C-13 反射

Reflection

反射产生镜像效果，从而得到一对完全相同的形。反射轴的位置决定了镜像图案的位置和相互距离。

A mirror effect generating a pair of forms opposite to each other, being same in any aspects except one rotates 180 degree. An axis of reflection can be placed in any position relative to the figure. Its placement determines the resulting pattern and the distance between the pair of forms.

图2-2-17 展厅成为艺术作品的一部分

图2-2-18 艺术家八个星期的临时住所成为艺术作品，苏黎世，2000年

图2-2-19 林恩用废弃工厂改造设计的朝鲜移民教堂，纽约

去城市研究局限在大规模形体或者肌理上，“为了体现不同的城市规模组织模式，建筑师必须开始用多样化城市作用力与区域相似体系进行设计（图2-2-19）”。格雷戈·林恩主张建筑多少应似液体状，体现流动和变化等水的特征。

丹尼尔·利比斯金为柏林兰德堡大街做的获奖方案采用与传统规划理论不同的方法（图2-2-20）。传统的城市设计要么以功能效率为中心，如柯布西耶的现代城；要么围绕形体系统化组织，如传统的西方城市。利比斯金旨在探索新的形态，它既无功能分区，也无形象塑造，却可以适应和满足不确定因素的需要——一种灵活多样化的组织体系。

“异类办公室”事务所一直在研究城市环境和交通系统中的建筑形体弱化，近年曾获得多个国际建筑竞赛大奖。在韩国釜山火车站方案竞赛中，他们的方案改变了传统车站“城市大门”的模式，形成以大量性交通为核心，如基础设施一样的建筑形态（图2-2-21）。“这种结构所服务的人流量与50年前相比是巨大的。”[6] 为了满足大量上下火车人流和分流的需要，并和其他交通系统和服务设施有效连接，他们提出在公路和铁路上建一个人工的地面，火车站的屋顶变成海边花园，将原本被铁路分开的城市和海岸连接起来。他们的设计将传统的雕塑式的建筑——建在地面以上的，有明确的形体和边界的建筑——转变为城市区域，或者交通网络，将高速公路、人行天桥和起伏的花园结合成一个整体（图2-2-22），而一般意义上的建筑却已消失得不见踪影。

C-14 连续

Continuation

图形或图形组沿一定方向连续排放。

A figure or group of figures is arranged in such a way as to have direction and seem to continue.

simulation systems of urban forces and fields(Pic.2-2-19)." Greg Lynn calls for an architecture, which is more or less a liquid medium with aqueous characteristics of flow and transformation in time.

A winning project by Daniel Libeskind for the Landberger Allee in Berlin shows a departure from traditional planning discourse(Pic.2-2-20). Traditional urban designs have concentrated on either functionally efficiency, such as Le Corbusier's modern city, or as the point of departure for the systematic organization of form, derived from the classical Western city. Libeskind, however, aims at an alternative morphology, the result of which would be neither the discrete zoning of functions nor the prescription of forms, but which would allow for, and support, the unpredictable—a flexible and dynamic organization. Foreign Office has investigated de-formed architecture in the urban context and networks of motions with a few winning transportation projects.

In the scheme of Busan Railway station, South Korea, Foreign Office changed the traditional station type, a city gate, into a new typology of mass-transportation infrastructure(Pic.2-2-21). "The volume of passenger flow that a structure like this now requires, compared to the volume required, say, 50 years ago, is enormous."[161] With its differentiated arrivals and departures and its efficient interfaces with other transportation systems and leisure facilities, their scheme provides an elevated urban ground over both road and railway lines. It turns the terminal roof into an artificial waterfront park, which connects the city and sea front, which otherwise would be cut off by the railway lines. In this project sculpture-like architecture—a building emerging from the land with clearly defined forms and boundaries – is transformed into an urban field or a traffic network, combining such elements as automobile highways, flyover passages or a sloping park(Pic.2-2-22). The building, in the conventional sense, has disappeared.

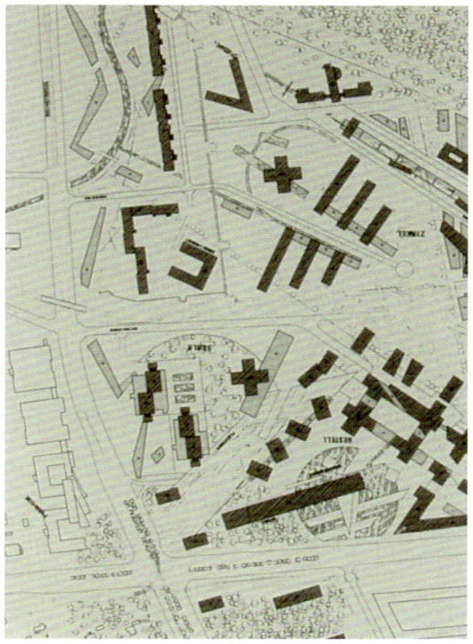

图2-2-20 柏林兰德堡大街规划（局部），1994年

图2-2-21 车站规划轴测图

图2-2-22 a.车站屋顶花园

图2-2-22 b.车站大厅

练习十二　寻找和发现

目的：

世界是由形组成的。我们无须发明新的形状，只要在一片混沌的世界中寻找并完善有意义的形体。我们周围到处都有许多能带来惊喜的形体，我们之所以熟视无睹，是因为不知道正确的观察方法。

这个练习的目的是掌握观察周围环境，发现新形体的方法，并通过运用构成手法将形体变成艺术。

方法：

1. 将教师给定的（或者学生自己寻找的）照片复印放大，将照片中的图形、轮廓、背景和不同色块的分界用粗笔描一遍。顺着粗线将照片剪成碎片，涂黑。

2. 观察照片中的背景，即元素之间的空白部分，如何变成一个图案，同时保持和原照片中元素的关系。

3. 将这些碎片，按照尺寸、形状、类型、规律性或者大小分类排列，从中选出十个较新颖的形状，这些形状应各有不同，但有一定相似性。

4. 再从中选三至四个形，确定不同尺寸和色彩之后，用叠加、图底转换、对称、重复、韵律和层次等构成方法，将它们排列组合成一幅抽象画。

5. 作画时注意研究工具的性能，如纸、粉笔、油画棒、水粉、油画色等。

工具和材料：

1. 水彩纸;
2. 速写本;
3. 铅笔;
4. 彩色炭笔、粉笔、油画棒、墨水笔等（由学生自选）。

成果：

1. 在一张A2大小的白纸上排列一组黑色的形。
2. 一张A2大小的彩色抽象画。

Exercise 12.　FINDING AND DISCOVERY

Objective:

The world is made of forms. As designers, we actually do not have to invent new forms. We can find and develop stimulating forms out of any big mass.

There are already enough existing and surprising forms everywhere. If we do not see them, it is because we do not know how to see them.

The aim of this lesson is to introduce a way to find forms from our everyday surroundings and develop these into artworks while also exploring new composition principles.

Method:

1.Enlarge and copy the given photos (or any photos we choose). Frame the forms (or form sets) in the copy, based on figures, outlines, backgrounds, and color edges. Cut out all these forms and paint them in black.

2.Study how the negative space – the space between elements or objects in the photo – become figural, and with an original character.

3.Organize the forms we find in a sequence according to the size, shape, composition type, regularity, plan or line type. Choose ten most existing and surprising forms, which are different, but also have a similar feature.

4.Choose three or four forms. Define the colors and sizes for each of them. Draw a graphic by arranging them with composition principles, such as overlap, figure and ground, symmetry, repetition, rhythm, hierarchy, etc..

5.Draw the painting by exploring the potentials of painting tools, such as paper, chalks, oil paste, gouache, oil painting, etc..

Tools and Materials:

1.Watercolor paper;
2.Sketchbook;
3.Pencils;
4.Color charcoals, chalk or oil paste, ink pen, etc..

Presentation:

1.Formal elements in black on a sheet of A2-size paper .
2.A colored graphic painting (A2-size).

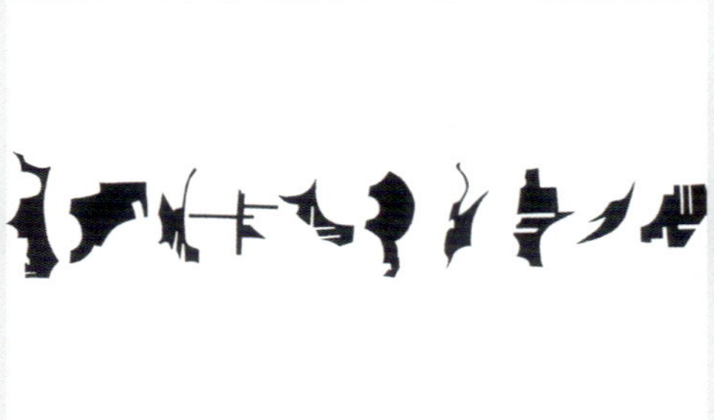

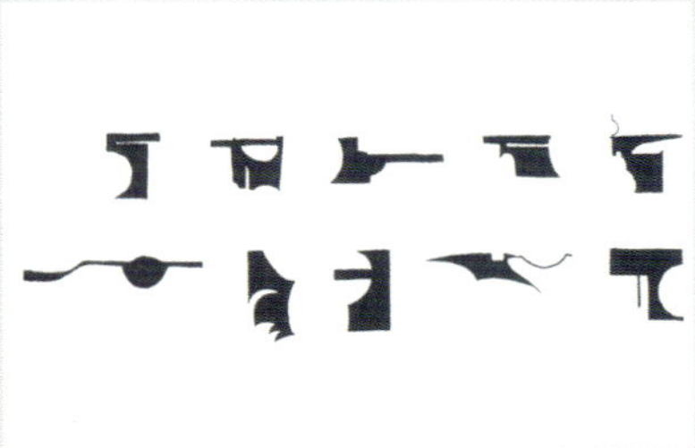
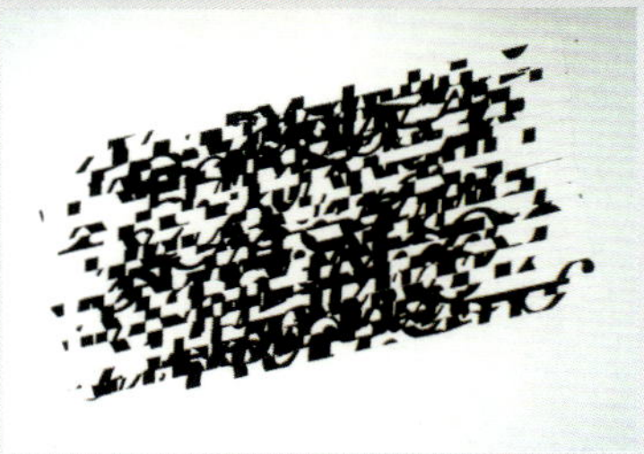

Law Sin Hang
Yeung Mei Nai
Lee Kiu Sim
Yu Ka Wah
Chung Ho Wai(Sketch Book)
Wong Ming Tak
Tsang Boon Chi
Mok Hei Lun

练习十三　观形和造型

目的：

我们将继续学习观察事物的方法，进一步开发我们的眼睛、手、工具和身体对形的感知能力。写生的目的不是复制，也不是绘画的完成状态，而是对事物观察、思考和绘画的过程——重要的是行为而不是作品。

在绘画过程中，我们要努力寻求原来没有观察到的，或者隐藏着的新的形体。绘画不是描画，而是造型。

在这个练习中，学生先对校园里的任何东西做一次写生，然后对写生作品再进行一次设计、重组等加工过程，作一幅彩色抽象画。

方法：

1. 选择校园中的任何东西，如台阶、走廊、建筑局部等，进行速写和写生。

2. 写生的目的是探索对象的特征和特性，为了探索，应从不同角度对同一对象进行多次写生。

3. 视点的改变包括视角（观察对象的角度）的改变：时而鸟瞰，时而平视，时而内视。视点的改变也包括视距的改变：时而远视，只画轮廓线；时而近视，刻画对象的细部。

4. 写生的表现手法和内容也应不断变换，有时画对象，有时画对象的背景，有时将三维画成二维，有时改变对象的质感，有时改变它的环境，也可以画抽象或者是想象的对象。

5. 在写生过程中，我们鼓励尝试使用不同的绘画工具，或者综合运用不同的工具。同时鼓励表现个人情绪，如愤怒、恐惧、快乐、平和、迷惑等。

6. 在练习的第二阶段，我们对写生的资料进行裁剪、扭曲、撕碎等加工，然后进行重组。作一幅多视点、多信息的抽象画。

7. 在这一过程中，对这些碎片的重组是建立在新的秩序基础上的，这些碎片之间要形成新的关系，目的是通过简化和组合，创作出一幅动人的抽象画。最后的作品应是精心设计之作。

注意事项：

1. 抽象绘画比写实绘画在形体组织方面有更多的自由。在写实作品中对象的形体只可以有少量的夸张，而在抽象作品中我们通过想象、变形和夸张手法表现全方位的认识。

2. 充分体会一个三维空间如何通过一系列的操作方法以二维图像空间方式表现出来。

Exercise 13. LOOKING AND SHAPING

Objectives:

Following the previous exercise, here we continue to learn the skills of looking at things by exploring all the possibilities with our eyes, hands, tools, and bodies.

What is important in sketching a thing is neither the thing itself, nor the final drawing (whether it looks like the thing or not), but instead the process of looking, the process of thinking and the process of drawing—actions, not objects.

In a process of drawing, we find things which are unknown, which are covered, which are new. Drawing is not copying, but shaping.

In this exercise, we sketch any built form in the university campus and then make a color graphic, based on the sketches, with actions of shaping, design and creation.

Methods:

1.Find one set of objects on the University campus, such as steps, corridors, buildings, entrances of buildings, etc., and record it with a sketch.

2.Sketching something is a way of exploring the features and properties of the thing. To explore, you need to sketch the same thing many times by changing your "view point".

3.Changes of "view point" include change of our standing points of looking, such as bird's-eye view, ground view, interior view, etc.. It includes change of distance between oneself and the objects (such as viewing the object's outline, as opposed to viewing its detail).

4.It also includes change of figure and ground, change between 3-dimensions and 2-dimensions, change of texture, change of location of the object, and other methods of abstracting the objects through imagination.

5.In sketching, we encourage ourselves to explore different tools, combinations of different tools, colors, and ways to express one's emotions, such as anger, fear, joy, calm, confusion, etc..

6.In the second step, we distort, break down, reconnect and restore our sketches through cutting, breaking, and montage-making. Combination of different information in one presentation provides multi-level viewpoints, which means one's attention is not fixed on any single object.

7.It is necessary here to organize several picture fragments by connecting fragments and tearing them apart. Simplify and arrange shapes creatively to make a visually interesting abstract design. The final product is a graphic drawing with a carefully designed pictorial space.

Notes:

1.We have more latitude in the arrangement of shapes in an abstract picture than in a representation of reality. In the realistic picture, we can make only minor adjustments to the shapes of the subjects. In the abstract picture, we can take liberties with the image, distorting it, exaggerating it, but not losing it entirely.

2.Enjoy the feel how actual space is presented in the picture space of multiple strategies.

工具和材料:

1. 水彩纸;
2. 速写本;
3. 铅笔、彩色炭笔、粉笔、油画棒、墨水等。

成果:

1. 拼在一张A2图纸上的10张对同一对象的速写稿。
2. 一张A2彩色构成绘画。

Tools and Materials:

1. Watercolor paper;
2. Sketchbook;
3. Pencils, color charcoals, chalk or oil paste, ink pen, etc..

Presentation:

1. Ten sketches about a same set of objects on a piece of A2 paper;
2. A colored graphic painting in A2-size.

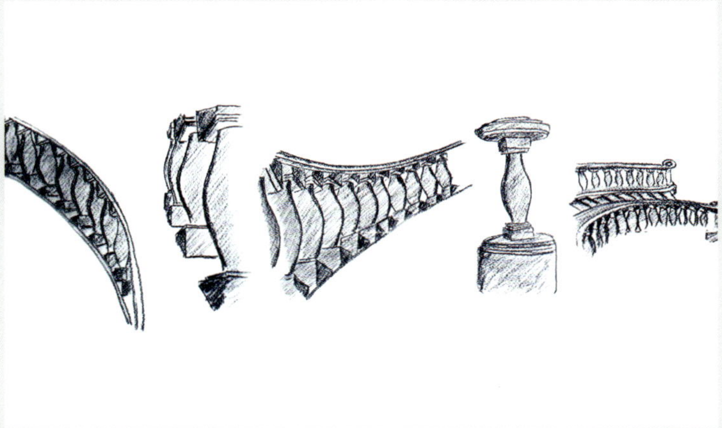

Tsang Pui Lai
(Sketch Book)
Law Sin Hang

Ang Bing Hung
(Unknown)
Lau Pui Chuen
Yeung Mei Nai
Hui Lung Nin
Mok Hei Lun
Chan Hau Man
Sze Chun Nga
Chung Ho Wai

练习十四　作品和工具

目的：

创作受不同因素的制约。艺术家传达内心世界的表现方法就是这些因素之一。建筑依赖于建造技术。而技术的革新反过来激发形的创作。这个练习将通过实验探讨工具与形体之间的关系。

方法：

1. 用家庭常见的用具或者玩具，如陀螺、鞋子、厨房用品，甚至录音机，设计制作画笔。

2. 用这个画笔作一幅形态上直接体现画笔和画笔运作特征的画。

3. 画笔与画的关系应尽可能清晰，也可以表现人手或者身体与画笔的关系。如果画笔是机械自动的，就应更直接表现画笔的特征。

4. 对于任何事物，我们都要保持批判的态度，而不断地改进。

5. 最重要的事情是开始，做一次冒险——为创作而撇开习惯中的陈规陋习。先做而不是先想。

注意事项：

1. 从工具和操作工具过程入手，是一种创作概念：形体出自工具。

2. 试验是创造性活动的重要组成部分。也许还有许多事物没有人尝试过。对于艺术和建筑史中没有的东西无须恐惧。实际上没有做过的事情很多。

3. 也许有人会问：“这个工具能画些什么杰作呢？”这个问题并不重要，重要的是我们能体会和享受这个过程。

工具和材料：

没有限制。

成果：

1. 一件新发明的画笔。

2. 一幅A2大小的用这件画笔作的抽象画。

Exercise 14.　PRODUCTS AND TOOLS

Objective:

Creation is dominated by different factors. The medium of expression through which the artist translates his inner world is one of these factors. Buildings are constructed with certain building technologies. And technological innovations can stimulate the creation of new building forms. This exercise is an experiment to create new forms through the invention of new tools.

Methods:

1.Design a drawing instrument with any household objects such as a top, shoes, kitchen utensils, or even a tape recorder.

2.Make a drawing or sketch, which is unique to the instrument and its operation process.

3.The drawing made by this instrument should exist and show direct relation to the instrument. It should also show the movement of hand, body, or the instrument itself, if it is automatic.

4.As we try new things, we have to be critical of the thing we make and try to improve it continuously.

5.The important thing is to begin. This is an adventure — open one's mind to creativity and make things happen.

Notes:

1.The relation between tools and procedures allow a new concept in form creation: a form starts from a mechanical tool.

2.Experimentation is a vital component of creative process. There are probably great many things we have not attempted yet. We do not need to be afraid of something that has never been done in the history of art or architecture. There is not much that has really been done yet.

3.One may ask oneself, "What can this instrument do?" It does not matter. It is important for us to enjoy and have fun in the process.

Tools and materials:

No restriction.

Presentation:

1.An invented instrument.

2.A drawing on A2-size paper produced by the instrument.

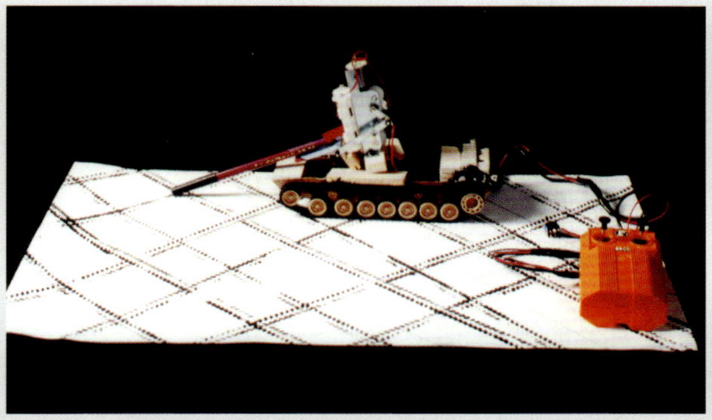
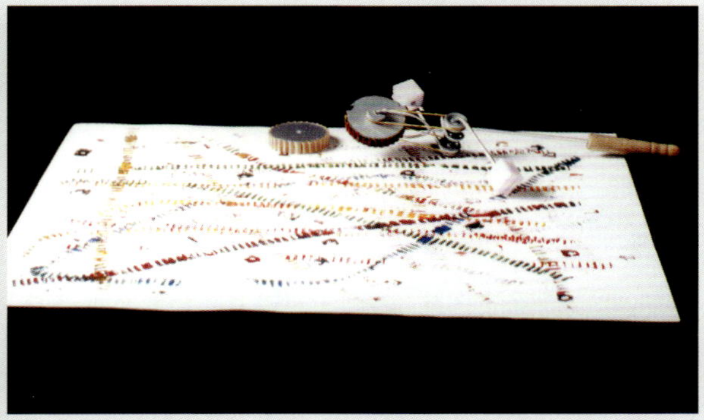
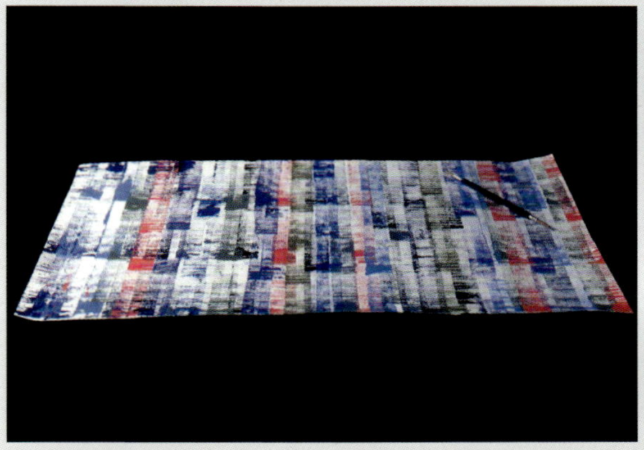

Sze Chun Nga
Law Sin Hang
Mok Chung Shun
Lan Pui Chuen
Woo Ching Hang
Lau Pui Chuen
(Sketch Book)

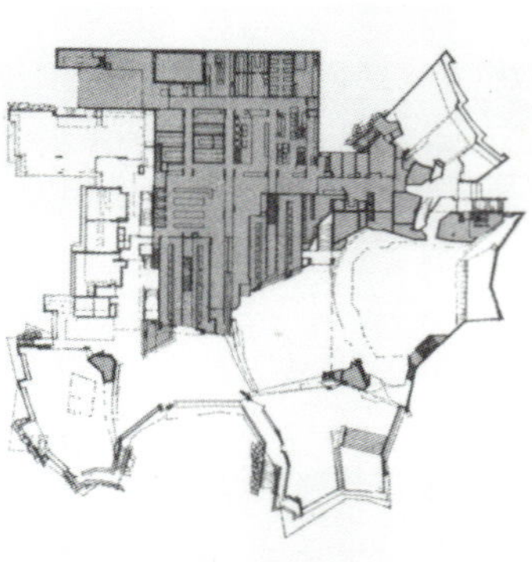

图2-3-1 皮亚蒂拉设计的学生中心，1961—1966年

图2-3-2 埃森曼设计的阿若诺夫设计艺术中心，1989—1996年

2.3 形的隐喻

隐喻广泛地运用在文学、音乐、哲学中，贯穿整个文明史。隐喻有如寓言，灵活、特点鲜明、富有表现力，是一种艺术创作工具。路易斯·康在语言和建筑两方面都有很高造诣，他将深沉和光的关系比喻为“孪生兄弟”，表达准确完美，又让读者去想他说的意思。设计中的隐喻让人用不同的眼光来看待一件作品，令人深思，发人深省。形体和空间的组织更具表现力，更富有感情，更开放。不管通过简单的图表还是复杂的空间的质量，隐喻都有象征意义，从而与使用者交流，触动他们的思虑和感觉，最后让他们走进设计者的内心。

隐喻可以直接来自现象或者物体。波普建筑，如拉斯维加斯的热狗店和冰激凌小卖铺等，这种符号简单、直接、明了，却含义肤浅，无法进入现象背后的深层意义。

自然的启发

自然是许多隐喻的主题，其自然元素特征和组织象征宁静、严酷、崇高等不同思想。芬兰建筑师瑞玛·皮亚蒂拉将自然形体运用于建筑。赫尔辛基奥塔柏米大学学生会中心是他早期建筑之一（图2-3-1），构思源自“原始洞穴”，象征学生，或者现代原始人在里面探索知识和真理。以“原始猎人”自居的皮亚蒂拉将创造性视为生存本能，建筑师实际上是在思想丛林中搜寻，他的其他一些建筑看起来像洞穴，像波光粼粼的湖面，像起伏的沙丘，或者像旋风。[162]

当自然本身被重新定义后，自然的隐喻也就变得复杂抽象。彼得·埃森曼的阿若诺夫设计艺术中心与场地形态相互呼应，建筑表现为人工园林，其思想是将环境作用力，如风、重力、交通和园林等结合为一个整体的结构（图2-3-2）。物质体系推到秩序和混乱的交界处，象征地壳承受巨大压力。建筑形体前倾后斜，叠加在一起形成不断强化的动感。这些建筑形体里面的视线也是扭曲的（图2-3-3）。“这里没有观赏的最佳视点。”[163] 在另一个作品，州岛艺术和科学学院设计中，埃森曼将“地球深层形态”的特征发展成晶体结构，在集舟、船、人流和公共汽车于一体的交通节点上，叠加一个由半透明玻璃和钢构件组成的螺旋体，交通流线是形体根据之一，但风和水也起了重要作用。这个构思似乎也受到了多面的由相似体块组成的隐形战机的影响。切线拼接成的曲面让建筑看起来像是石头上结了一层层冰体（图2-3-4, 图2-3-5）。这种形象也隐喻了设计的另一个构思，即在原有的轮渡码头——石头上建了一个新的博物馆，其参观流线盘回曲折而上。

C–15　对称

对称是一种重复图形构图中控制位置和方向的特殊规则。
对称值是指图形的构架。非对称图形不能进一步划分成全等的几部分，对称值较低；对称图形可以划分成全等的组成部分，对称值较高。对称值的定量可以由全等组分的数量所决定。（如六边形可以分解为六个三角形，因此其对称值为6。）

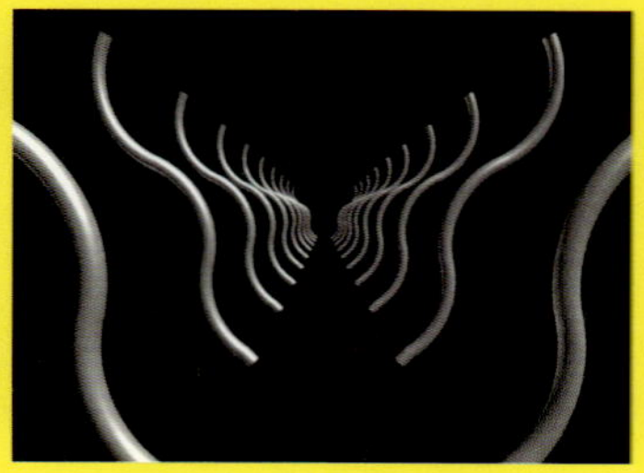

2.3 Form as a Metaphor

Metaphor has been used and treated repeatedly throughout the history of civilisation, in literature, music and philosophy. Metaphor, like parable, is a creative tool, which is very plastic, individualistic and expressive. Louis Kahn, who was very skilful in both verbal and architectural expression, described the close relationship between silence and light as "twin brothers". This description is precise and conclusive, but at the same time, encourages and challenges the readers to think about what he means. In the design world, metaphor allows the designer to see the contemplated work under a different light and probes new questions and concerns with new interpretations. The form and organization of spaces may become more expressive, emotional and explicit. Metaphor carries in itself symbolic meaning, either simply through visual appearance or spatial quality. It communicates with the users, probes their queries and feelings, and encourages them to walk into the mind of the creator.

Metaphor can be developed strictly from visual or material elements. Pop architecture, such as a hotdog stand or ice cream parlour in Las Vegas, is one such example. This brand of semiotics offers simple and literal interpretation, but is very weak in communicating anything beyond its superficial appearance. It fails to transcend its visual resemblance to deliver a deeper symbolic meaning.

Inspirations from Nature

Nature is a source of many metaphors. It lends its characteristics and ingredients for contemplation of such varied qualities as serenity, harshness and sublimity. Finnish architect Reima Pietila, has used natural metaphor for some of his buildings, and he frequently resorts to literal interpretations of natural forms. One of his earliest examples is the Dipoli student union at the University of Otamiemi-Helsinki (Pic.2-3-1), which was inspired by the "the primitive cave", a shelter where the student, a contemporary primitive, searches for knowledge and truth. Pietila, a "primitive hunter" himself, views creativity as a case of survival; the architect is in search of game in the jungle of ideas. Several of his buildings look like caves, undulating lakes, waving sand dunes and spiralling winds. [162]

Nature metaphors become more complex when the Nature itself has to be redefined. Peter Eisenman's Aronoff Centre for Design and Art (Pic.2-3-2) is designed to respond to the topography of the site. It is an expression of architecture as an articulated landscape, an idea that the environmental forces–wind, gravity, the flow of traffic and the landscape—all work together in a cooperative tectonic activity. Material systems are pushed to the threshold between order and chaos, recalling the earth's tectonic plates under immense compression. Forms are tilted back and forth, overlapping each other and stepped to accentuate the sensation of movements. Perspective views inside these building forms are distorted (Pic.2-3-3). "There is no preferred place for the viewer to understand", as Eisenman says. [163] In another project, the Staten Island Institute of Arts and Sciences, he has pushed the now-characteristic deep landform building in a more crystalline direction. White spirals of translucent glass and steel ratchet their way over a dense traffic intersection of boats, pedestrians, and buses. The flow of traffic becomes one generator of the forms, while wind and water also play a role. Here, the idea was inspired and formulated by the multifaceted, self-similar fractal shapes of a military Stealth Fighter. It rises and curves in tangents, like an ice-flow bent around a rock (Pic.2-3-4,Pic.2-3-5). This metaphor reveals something about the design since the old ferry terminal—the rock—makes the new museum and circulation space twist and tilt.

图2-3-3 艺术中心室内

图2-3-4 埃森曼设计的纽约州岛学院

图2-3-5 州岛学院

Symmetry

Symmetry operation refers to the specific rules that govern the position, orientation, and action of a figure as it is repeated to create a compositional group or pattern.
Symmetry value refers to the structural composition of a figure. An asymmetrical figure that cannot be subdivided into smaller, congruent parts has a low symmetry value; a symmetrical figure that can be broken down into a number of congruent parts has a higher symmetry value. The numerical quantity of the symmetry value is determined by the number of smaller congruent parts. (e.g. a hexagon is a symmetrical figure that can be broken down into six congruent triangles; therefore, the symmetry value is six.)

图2-3-6 a.哈德里安庄园遗迹

图2-3-6 b.路易斯·康速写

"建筑不能没有意义。"[164] 建筑师在设计建筑时不能有墙而不懂墙的意思，反之亦然。建筑中到处是墙，它是符号也是工具。和艺术不同，建筑既有意义，同时也反对意义，因为它必须有功能。这种对意义的反抗正是埃森曼的兴趣所在，他设计的目的并不是建起一座建筑本身，而是要建筑成为表达隐喻的手段，而这种隐喻需包含多种多样的甚至主观夸张的意思。为了达到这一目标，要人为地分开意义和建筑之间的关系，分开形和功能。这种"开放"化，他称之为"解构"，使一个意义产生另一个意义，以至无穷。正是将这种建筑自然关系解构了，意义才可以不断变化，这才是建筑区别于其他艺术的关键。他的建筑形体与现代建筑不同，因为现代建筑是根据美学和意义上的机械关系，即"形式随从功能"。埃森曼的建筑一直在挑战对形态和社会两方面的教条式理解。他的建筑形式反映这种目的，并正由于它们在隐喻上的模糊性而自成一体。

历史符号

正是由于隐喻的灵活性和多意性，隐喻成为设计手段。隐喻像自然有机体一样不断生长变化。不断研究同一个隐喻，通过演绎和转换，可以产生新的形体空间和意义。

路易斯·康一直在把历史建筑综合融入新建筑。他曾多次去罗马和希腊，都是为了研究和画古代建筑遗迹，不久他就以不同方法运用吉萨金字塔和卡尔纳克的阿蒙神庙于自己的设计中。自萨克研究院之后一系列作品，都体现了一种深思熟虑地将这些古代神庙创造性转型为新设计的创作手法。[165] 在1950年于意大利旅行时给同事一封信中，康写道："我坚信意大利的建筑将是未来设计的思想源泉。……我们要做的是将它与我们的建筑知识和需求结合起来，对这些意大利建筑要重新理解。我对恢复重建（这种理解）没有兴趣，我指的是将这些建筑作为起点，通过不同设计者的改造，创造新空间，从中体现出设计者的个人价值。"[166] 他在哈德里安庄园大浴场的彩色粉笔画直接影响他后来几何形的设计方法（图2-3-6, 图2-3-7）。[167] 他的一种石灰笔素描表现了一面墙上开了一系列砖拱，直接影响他在伊克塞特图书馆设计中对窗和墙关系的处理。

象形隐喻

在柯布西耶早期的一些艺术作品中已出现一只张开的手。在20世纪30年代的绘画中，手和脚缠在人体周围，手形日益突出，成了一个魔力象征，甚至要超出整个画面。1934年的一幅画出现了一个固定手势（图2-3-8）。[168] 在巴黎的瑞士学生宿舍的壁画中，一个展开翅膀的女人体浮在一些半透明的几何和有机形体的上面，右翼支撑在一只巨大的张开的手上面（图2-3-9）。[169] 在

图2-3-7 路易斯·康设计的宾夕法尼亚大学化学系教学楼

图2-3-8 柯布西耶《教堂中的女子》，1934年

图2-3-9 柯布西耶设计的巴黎的瑞士学生宿舍壁画

"Architecture cannot be without meaning".[164] One cannot have the wall without the sign of the wall and vice versa. Yet in architecture there will always be the presence of walls, walls that are both icon and instrument. Thus, unlike art, architecture both requires a meaning and resists the meaning, because it has to function. This resistance alone is of interest to Eisenman. His long-term design objective has not been to create architecture per se but to create architecture as a means of expressing metaphors—here, metaphors that imply manifold and ambiguous meanings. To achieve this, the natural relation between meaning and building, or form and function, have to be artificially separated. This opening up, or "deconstruction" as he calls it, creates the possibility to generate one meaning after another. It is the deconstruction of this natural relationship that establishes constantly changing meaning. This is what is unique to architecture. His architectural form differs from previous architecture based on an instrumentality of aesthetics and meaning, or "form follows function" as 20th century modernists believed. Eisenman's architecture must always overcome normative typological and social gestures. His architecture not only achieves this but also continues and maintains itself precisely because of its metaphorical ambiguity.

Motifs from the Past

Metaphor is characterized for its flexibility and versatility as a design tool. Metaphor is organic in nature as it grows and is ever-changing. The same metaphor may be re-investigated and re-studied, but through evolution and transformation, fresh forms, spaces and meanings may still be generated.

Louis Kahn always sought to synthesize new architecture from historical precedents. He made several trips to Rome and Greece simply to study and draw the architectural ruins he found there. Soon he was making use of the Pyramids at Gizeh and of the Temple of Ammon at Karnak in various ways. Beginning with his Salk Institute onward, his buildings represented a thoughtful and inventive transformation of these ancient examples. [165] In a letter to his office staff during his trip in Italy 1950, Kahn wrote, "I firmly realize that the architecture in Italy will remain as the inspirational source of the works of the future... What is necessary is the interpretation of the architecture of Italy as it relates to our knowledge of building and needs. I care little for the restorations (that kind of interpretation) but I see great personal value in reading one's own approaches to the creation of space modified by the buildings around as the point of departure." [166] His pastel drawing of the Large Baths at Hadrian's Villa inspired Kahn's approach to geometry and interplay of mass and space in strong light and deep shadows(Pic.2-3-6,Pic.2-3-7). [167] Kahn's charcoal sketch of a Roman wall pierced by arched openings can be related to his understanding of relationship between windows and wall, as in his Exeter Library.

Metaphor as an Icon

Even in Le Corbusier's early painting, the icon of the open hand could be found in a number of his works. In his paintings of the 1930s, the human form was apt to get its hands and feet entangled — so much so that the hands tended to stand out of the pictorial context and become a sort of magic sign.[168] His 1934 painting, Portrait de la femme a la cathedral de sens (Pic.2-3-8), for example, the hands are shown in an affirmative gesture. On the fresco of the Swiss Pavilion in Paris, a winged female creature is placed floating above a landscape of transparent geometric and organic forms, and its right wing lightly supported by a large, half open hand (Pic.2-3-9). [169] At Chandigarh, this hand-symbol was eventually translated into an open-air sculpture and became a public icon. Long before the construction of the city had begun, the sign of "open hand" had become the trademark of the town (Pic.2-3-10). Yet

变形是指一系列保持、加强和建立建筑概念或建筑秩序的操作方法。形式和空间可以通过相接、穿透、联合、减法、剖切、重合、简单分离、 叠加、合并等方式相组合。某些形会使人产生前进或后退的感觉，平面或三维的感觉，正或歪的感觉。

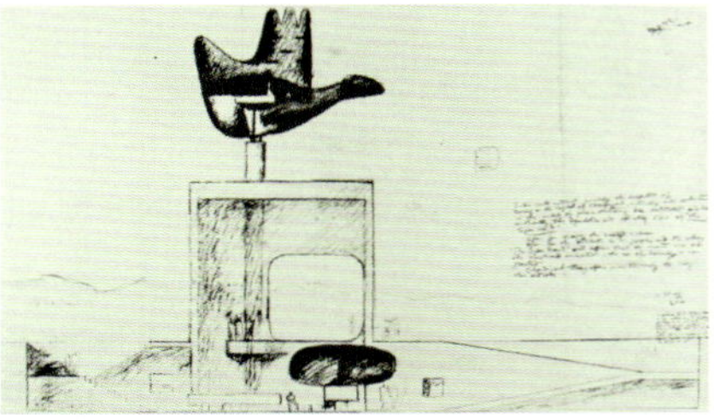

2-3-10 柯布西耶设计的《张开的手》纪念雕塑

2-3-11 柯布西耶设计的朗香教堂室内

图2-3-12 朗香教堂室内

图2-3-13 朗香教堂西立面

昌迪加尔，这个手的形象做成了一个室外雕塑，一个公共场所纪念物，在由柯布西耶设计的这个城市建成前，这个雕塑，一只向上张开的手，一直是这座城市的象征（图2-3-10）。这只手的雕塑构思早在1948年就出现在柯布西耶的速写本上。他不仅将其视为个人观念的体现，而且要它成为昌迪加尔的隐喻，即“新印度的神庙”。“将一只张开的手的象征符号立在正在建设中的昌迪加尔首府的机关部门的广场中间，对印度的意义也许是迎接新的繁荣，并将这种繁荣贡献于人民。张开的手标志着机器时代的第二阶段：一个和谐的时代的开始。”[170]

一个隐喻雕像可以超过时代和文化的局限。由于意义是象征性的，对于它的形体和空间有不同的理解，使得一座建筑更有意思。在设计朗香教堂的过程中，柯布西耶的目的是塑造一种进入建筑的特殊感觉，造访者先要爬一段缓缓的山坡，就像过去朝圣一样，但进入教堂之后却发现没有传统基督教，或者天主教教堂中的中殿和后殿。随意开在一面厚重的墙上的彩色的洞将自然光线带入室内，效果奇特。洞的布局如星座，猎户、金牛、昴星、白羊都可以找到（图2-3-11）。[171] 像是魔法变幻，渲染出室内空间，形体、景象和气氛，让人仿佛身处自然岩洞或者中世纪修道院。屋顶的设计灵感据说来自纽约长岛上的蟹壳。“壳体放在刻意加厚的墙体上，墙体内包着混凝土柱，壳体放在柱头上，但和墙体间空着一段距离。”[172] 天花板像是浮在墙体顶部射入的光环上面（图2-3-12），天花板表面为素混凝土，没有粉刷。地面随着山顶地形自然隆起。东南面墙的表层用水泥喷涂，墙体由厚到薄，开以梯形大进深窗洞，镶以彩色玻璃，是对哥特式教堂的彩色玫瑰窗的活学活用。细长竖向高窗设计来源于哈德里安住宅，其垂直体量与室内水平向空间平衡（图2-3-13）。柯布西耶一向注重建筑的顶部造型。朗香教堂的屋顶被喻为“修女的帽子”“树端的云彩或房子”。而昌迪加尔市政厅的屋顶设计灵感则来自于印度公牛的牛角形状（图2-3-14）。

内在要素的转译

设计者从非建筑概念开始，分析其内容和要素，以之为基础形成建筑设计方案，这也不失为一种创造性工作方法。其结果也许像是类比，但也具有所有隐喻的特征和价值。

D-1 变形

变形原理允许设计者选择任何形式，根据特定的环境或功能需求进行变化。变形首先要求感受和理解原型的主要特征，对于一些次要特征可以进行澄清、加强和建构。任何形式都可以理解为另一个形的变形。

Transformation

The principle of transformation allows a designer to select any form and to change it through a series of discrete manipulations to respond to the specific conditions, context, functional requirements of the design task at hand. Transformation requires first that the property of the prior be perceived and understood so that, through a series of finite changes and permutations, the certain aspects of property can be clarified, strengthened and built upon. Any form can be understood to be transformations of the other forms that are generated by the manipulation of their dimensions by following series of operation.

图2-3-14 柯布西耶设计的昌迪加尔政府行政楼，1953—1961年

the idea was conceived and developed long before 1948 when the motif first appeared in a sketch. Rather than simply a manifesto of a personal vision, Le Corbusier also intended to make this a metaphor of what Chandigarh, "the temple of new India" stood for: "India may value the idea of placing the symbolic and evocative sign of the open hand among the palaces that will house the institutions and authority of the Capitol of Chandigarh at present under construction: open to receive the newly created prosperity, open to distribute it to its people and to others. The open hand will confirm that the second era of the machine age has begun: the era of harmony." [170]

The sculptural image of a metaphor transcends time and culture. As its meaning is symbolic, it creates forms and spaces which invite various interpretations, and which adds interests to the building. In the design of the Ronchamp Chapel, Le Corbusier's sensitivity to design starts from his shaping a sense of arrival to the building. Visitors have to climb up a shallow hill slope, much like a pilgrimage to a traditional holy place. Upon entering, the pilgrim discovers that the building lacks the usual nave and apse found in the Christian, especially Roman Catholic, tradition. Here, the random placement of colored windows puncturing a heavy, thick wall brings in natural light in an unexpected manner. The windows are laid out like constellations: in the south wall, one may relate Orion, Taurus, the Pleiades and Aries(Pic.2-3-11).[171] It plays magic; it renders the interior space and forms serene and spiritual, similar to a natural cave or a medieval monastery. He further expressed this space with curved and soaring walls. His inspiration for the roof was found in a crab shell on a Long Island, New York beach. "The shell is placed over the deliberately heavy walls in which reinforced concrete columns have been embedded. The shell will rest, here and there, on top of these columns, but it will not touch the walls."[172] The ceiling seemed to float on a halo of light with the small gap between roof and walls (Pic.2-3-12).He left no major surface on a simple plane. The interior floor followed the natural arched gradient of the hilltop. The southeast wall is warped, splayed, and angled to make deep truncated pyramids of luminous color stained glass, modern cousins to earlier Gothic examples. In the design of the tall, narrow slots of light, Le Corbusier adopted a similar device found in Hadrian's Villa to introduce a vertical counterpoint to the interior space(Pic.2-3-13). Le Corbusier also enjoyed placing dramatic roof forms in his buildings. The roof of Ronchamp Chapel, on the other hand, has been widely described as "a nun's hat" or "a cloud or a house in the treetops". On the other hand, the roof of Chandigarh resembled the shape of an Indian bull's horn (Pic.2-3-14).

Conveyance of Inner Content

In the case where a designer starts from a metaphor, analyzes its content and essentials, and then creates a project on the basis of the content of these two, we have another possible means of creativity. The result may not look like metaphorical analogue, but it has the attributes and virtues of metaphoric circumstances.

变形的形仍然可以保持其本质特征，如缩短或加长立方体的高度、宽度或厚度可以将其变形为各种长方体。
偶然和非理性的变形称为扭曲。扭曲有很多种，如改变高宽比，斜扭，环形扭曲等，将形状旋转、弯曲或扭动，可以得到各种扭曲的空间。

A form can be transformed by altering and still retain its family identity. A cube can be transformed into other rectangular prismatic forms by shortening or elongating its height, width, or depth.
Transformation can be come distortion if the change is accidental or irrational. There are many kind of distortions, such as changing the proportion of its height and width, diagonal distortion, circular distortion or any other distortions, in which shapes being rotated, bent or twisted and result in a great variety of spatial distortions.

图2-3-15 米兰大教堂

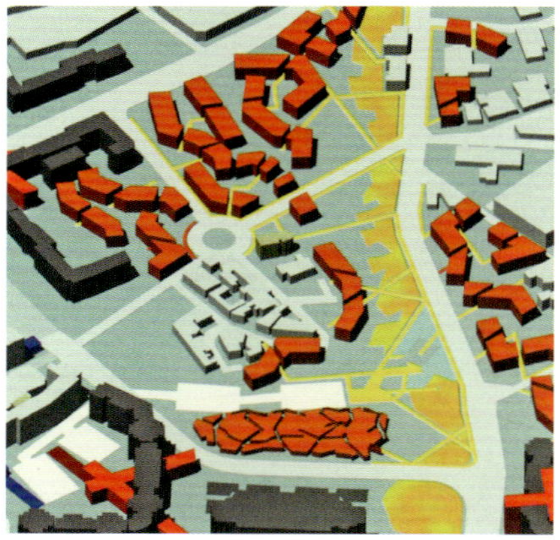

图2-3-16 戴维森和“实验室”事务所为布加勒斯特做的2000年总体规划（局部）

传统哥特式教堂完美体现了超离尘世的思想，高矗的主殿，夸张的飞扶壁和从玫瑰窗射入的彩色光线，让教堂传达了一种北欧松林特有的空间质量（图2-3-15）。

现在的规划设计专业常以“文本”一词来形容不断变化和扩展的城市环境。这里“文本”是比喻，用来理解城市的物质形态。一部文本是开放的结构，有不同的阅读方式。城市自如文本，可以重读，不停修改，或者重写，城市是一部展开的书卷。在建筑事务所“实验室”的作品中，城市充分体现了变化过程，没有一种将要形成的终极形态，像是敞开的书需要人阅读，题注或者改写（图2-3-16）。[173] 他们的设计尽可能保留城市现状，着眼于重新利用，因为包括新建建筑在内的所有一切都是城市历史生活中的组成部分，应该保留。而另一方面，这些设计主张改变现有建筑之间的关系，从几何形和轴线布局，转向模式和肌理的相似性重复，从而使新建筑和室外空间与现状结合成丰富而统一的整体。设计手法之一是以（建筑）形体之间的过渡形体替代传统规划设计中的建筑形体作为空间的主宰。

理性的变形是指形根据一个固定模型变化。通常用变形率和比例来控制形状和尺寸上的变形。
变形率：要素变形前后的比率，通常用a/b或a:b来表示。
比例：两个或两个以上的变形率的比较。两个相互比较的变形率中存在一个相同数值的，称为连续比例；不存在共同数值的，称为不连续比例。

The Gothic cathedral displays a graceful interpretation of transcendence.Through the verticality of its central nave, the expressive nature of flanking buttresses and diffuse quality of light through its rose windows, the Gothic cathedral portrays the spatial quality of a northern European coniferous forest.(Pic.2-3-15)

Currently, the word "text" is used in the design and planning professions to describe an urban environment under constant change and expansion. Here the "text" is itself the metaphor, with which the city is understood from a physical point of view. A multi-layered text is then understood as a text open in its structure suggesting a multiplicity of readings. As a result, a host of possibilities emerges for re-writing the city text, a text to be read and re-read; in other words, as a palimpsest in an expanding field. In the work of LAB, the transformation of the city is gradual, lacking a finished or determined image of what is to come; it is an open text to be read and rewritten(Pic.2-3-16). [173] Their scheme tried to retain and re-utilize as much of the existing city as possible, including recent construction, all of which continue to be part of the history and life of the city. On the other hand, they suggest a transformation of the relationships of existing buildings, from geometric and axial alliances to patterned and textured affiliations. As result, new buildings and landscapes coalesce with those already existing to form diverse and yet coherent fields. Dominance of form (the buildings) shifts to a mediation of form between forms.

Rational transformations are those changes of form following a defined model. Ratio and proportion are frequently used to control change of shape and size.
Ratio: A comparison of two equal quantities, and are expressed as fractions a/b or a:b.
Proportion:A comparison of two or more equal ratios. Continuous proportion compares equal ratios that have a common quantity between them. Discontinuous proportion compares equal ratios that do not have a common quantity between them.

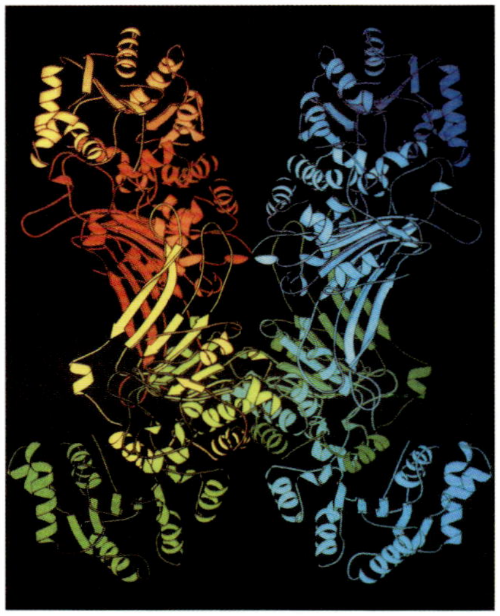

图2-4-1 广东人基因三维X光结构模拟图

图2-4-2 詹克斯的橱柜装饰

图2-4-3 詹克斯的大门设计，苏格兰，1994年

2.4 宇宙的隐喻和全球市场

建筑学已经被抽象化为人与他所处世界的关系的反映或者处理方式。这种哲学反映在中世纪哥特式教堂，其中上帝是人的主宰，也体现于后来文艺复兴时人代替了上帝成为思想的中心。思想的巨变带来一系列连锁反应：以个人为主体的新的神学观念导致人文主义思想产生，而人文主义思想又激发了现代科学的产生。随着20世纪“宇宙爆炸说”的创立，科学家又一次坚信他们已经找到认识宇宙起源和演化的关键。人与世界的关系在近年来又一次受到挑战。有些建筑师和理论家认为应将新的科学发现、科学思想和世界观引入形体设计，主张以最新科学发现为起点，积极开发建筑表现新形式。

詹克斯探寻的新形体、模式和隐喻，根据的是尚可称为新的科学“复杂性理论”。一个不断扩张的宇宙多样性始于一个球形体，从中螺旋式地展开一层层连续的宇宙，如层层海浪不断聚集力量冲向沿岸（图2-4-1）。[174] 他说：

> *复杂性是一种关于一个新生的组织如何将其中相互作用的元素（通过增强能量、事件和信息）推到远离平衡而达到秩序和混乱的临界线上的理论。这个重要的临界线正是一个体系突变分裂，或者以非线性的不可预料的方式创造性地相互作用的开始，也是一个新生组织通过反馈和持续的能量输入而得以延续的地方。在这个过程中一些质素同时出现，如自我组织性、意义、价值、开放性、碎片体、引力和不断增强的多样性（一种更大程度上的自由）等。*[175]

复杂性理论认为，处于纯秩序和混乱之间的现象具有更高层次的组织，比处于两极的组织“更好”。体现这种新观点的作品包括詹克斯自己的一些家具和环境设计，弗兰克·盖里设计的毕尔巴鄂市（西班牙）古根海姆美术馆，彼得·艾森曼的辛辛那提阿若诺夫中心，和丹尼尔·利比斯金设计的柏林犹太人纪念馆。这些“非线性”建筑一定程度上是用非线性的操作方式（包括计算机设计）形成的。每件作品都对建筑中传统的隐喻提出质疑，即如何选择和改变建筑的“语言”，并发现在转变过程中新的意义。詹克斯指出，“新科学 = 新语汇 = 新隐喻”。建筑学不仅应反映不同的思想矛盾，而且它本身应成为不断提倡新知识的学科。

詹克斯1992年设计的“兔柜”（图2-4-2），采用“S”形曲线装饰，装饰纹路按倍数递进，混乱不断加强，犹如母兔不断生出小兔，数量与混乱性同时增强，但有趣的是又一次次回到一种自我相似性秩序。几条抛物曲线强化了混乱背后的秩序。[176] 他还在其他的雕塑、园艺等艺术形体中试验对这种相互作用力体系的理解（图2-4-3，图2-4-4）。

D-2 表面的表现力

人们对于物体形状、规模、尺度、比例和视觉重量的感知与物体的外表面有很大关系。
可以通过表面与周围区域的色彩对比来加强形状的表现力。
可以通过控制表面色调来增加或减少平面的视觉重量。
平面的正面显示其真实的形状，而倾斜的视线使之变形。
平面内的已知尺度的要素可以帮人们感知平面的大小。
改变平面表面的质感会影响其视觉重量、比例和反光性。

图2-4-4 詹克斯设计的蛇形园林景观，1993年

2.4 Metaphors of the Universe and Global Market

Architecture has been theorized as a reflection or manifestation of man's place in relation to his world. This is obvious in the case of the Western medieval Gothic cathedral where God was placed on centre stage, and later in the Renaissance, when man displaced God to become the new centre. Such a radical change of thought was caused by a domino effect: individualistic theology in large part triggered the rise of humanism, which in large part triggered the rise of modern science. With the establishment of the 20th century "Big Bang Theory", scientists (once again) believe they have uncovered the key to understanding the origin and evolution of our universe. Man's relationship to his world has again been challenged, especially in recent years. Some architects and architectural theorists feel obliged to convey new scientific ideas, philosophies and worldviews in formal ways. One forerunner who is inspired by the new science of our day to develop new modes of architectural expression is Charles Jencks.

With the still-new scientific Complexity Theory, Jencks has sought new forms, models and metaphors. The dynamism of the unfolding universe is presented by a spherical model, a holistic globe spiralling out from a center, like a wave gathering momentum (Pic.2-4-1).[174] He explains the theory:

> *Complexity is the theory of how emergent organisation may be achieved by interacting components pushed far from equilibrium (by increasing energy, matter or information) to the threshold between order and chaos. This important border or threshold is where the system often jumps, bifurcates or creatively interacts in a new nonlinear, unpredictable way (the Eureka moment) and where the new organization may be sustained through feedback and the continuous input of energy. In this process quality emerges spontaneously as self-organization, meaning, value, openness, fractal patterns, attractor formations and (often) increasing complexity (a greater degree of freedom).* [175]

Complexity theory posits that phenomena between the extremes of pure order and pure chaos have higher levels of organization, and are "better" than those found at either extreme. The earliest representations of this new understanding include Jenck's own furniture and environmental designs, Frank Gehry's Guggenheim Museum in Bilbao, Peter Eisenman's Aronoff Centre in Cincinnati, and Daniel Libeskind's Jewish Museum in Berlin. These "non-linear" buildings were partly generated by non-linear methods including computer design and layout. Each one raises critical questions about the role of metaphor in architecture: that is, choosing and modifying a language of continuous variation and discovering new meanings inherent in its use. As Jencks suggests, "new Science = new language = new metaphors". Architecture not only reflects a different paradigm of thought but also itself becomes a discipline of unfolding knowledge.

Charles Jencks designed a Rabbit Cabinet in 1992 (Pic.2-4-2) which has an overall s-curve on its cabinet door surface, shows in its ornament the period-doubling route to increasing chaos. As the mother rabbit has more children, the population doubles towards increasing chaos, but then—amazingly—jumps back into self-similar order three times. Parabolic curves reveal further organization hidden in the randomness.[176] Jencks also experimented with sculpture, landscape and other art forms to reflect his understanding of this system of interacting forces (Pic.2-4-3, Pic.2-4-4).

Surface Articulation

Our perception of a object's shape, size, scale, proportion, and visual weight is affected by its surface properties.
A plane's shape can be articulated by contrasting the colors of its surface and the surrounding field.
The visual weight of a plane can be increased or decreased by manipulating the tonal value of its surface color.
A frontal view of the plane reveals its true shape, while oblique view distorts it.
Elements of know size within a plane's visual field can aid our perception of its size and scale.
Change of texture of a plane's surface will affect its visual weight, scale, and light-reflective qualities.

图2-4-5 维多利亚和阿尔伯特艺术馆扩建设计模型

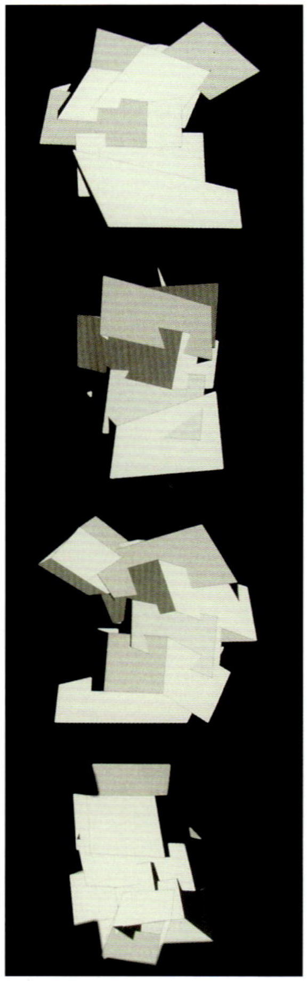

图2-4-6 分析图

丹尼尔·利比斯金的维多利亚和阿尔伯特艺术馆的扩建设计以三个抽象概念组织空间：艺术和历史的螺旋式运动；内外空间的叠合；扑朔迷离的过程（图2-4-5）。这三个概念都集中在“历史螺旋”这个隐喻中，以一个有机的功能紧凑的空间整体来表现。艺术史的螺旋运动反映在整体造型和内部流线两方面，外表连续的立面反衬由片片斜墙组成的形体，其内部空间围绕着垂直向上而角度多变的螺旋轴线（图2-4-6）。参观者在走过馆内不同功能空间时，不自觉地被卷入这个螺旋形的运动中。这种流线也将参观者引向馆内各个空间，以平衡现有建筑的横向张力。内外空间的联结通过体块的螺旋式叠加而形成，它让参观者通过对内外视线流通和历史元素的直接体验，感觉到历史和现在，城市和艺术之间的紧密关系。螺旋式演进的历史是混乱的，因为其中心位置不停变换，轨道在跳跃，留下的痕迹相互联结、相互叠加。

艺术馆的形体产生自一个十字形空间和一个上升的曲线连续而开放，无始无终。重复、变形、倾斜形体，叠加在十字线形的结构节点，结构本身就是型，独立存在，无须核心体或者圈梁，楼板薄如膜，结构无梁柱，室内平静安逸（图2-4-7）。混凝土清水墙平整无缝，与扭曲的结构结合，顶部螺旋体选用玻璃，引入自然光。[177]

利比斯金自己曾坦率地指出建筑的意义和其多样性的重要。他说，参观者获得的多重意义信息与建筑本身同样重要（图2-4-8）。埃及金字塔并不是为一个死人建造的，用几个世纪造一座金字塔来自许多人的信念，这也是建金字塔真正的目的，这种感觉对今天的参加者同样重要。“一方面，这是考古学上的一个建筑，一个保存下来的遗迹；另一方面，时代的发展和这些东西毫无关系。它的意义并不在于这个物体本身。”他说，展览馆应向参观者介绍展品，而参观者的理解应超过展品本身，如果他的心灵和想象力在走过这些展品时候能充分调动出来。而且一个好的展览馆应能向不同的观众讲述不同的故事（图2-4-9）。利比斯金用“无结局小说”来比喻他的设计，不同的人从博物馆里找到不同故事，而且有时相互矛盾，无法归纳到任何一个主题。对利比斯金来说最重要的是“建筑不应束缚于物理原则”。[178]

埃森曼致力于折叠式的断裂的立方体研究，而弗兰克·盖瑞则打开了由形体堆砌而形成的波动表层和形式语汇。盖瑞设计的毕尔巴鄂市古根海姆艺术馆，正如詹克斯形容的，“金属和石灰石做的光滑的形体流入中心，然后又像花瓣一样绽放开来”。这座建筑综合采用了大量新技术，与城市不断地扩张结合，它是另一种“大地型建筑”，兼容力强，接受城市现实而不是故步自封（图2-4-10）。它是新型模糊性建筑，比“玻璃盒”更开放，因为后者带有现代主义的透明狭隘定义。而这座建筑形体与环境交相映射，有如水晶结构般的自我相似性，玻璃面体与交界的处理表现出由层次丰富的碎片组成虚幻的形象。形体感由于反光墙面而虚化，反衬出坡道、屋顶平台

D-3　内部变形

Internal Change

将一个内部区域由实心变为空心，这时形及其视觉冲击力不变，内部细节可能改变。

To change the internal area from a solid plane to an empty space. The form of the object and its visual impact remains the same. The internal details might have already changed.

图2-4-7 剖面透视图

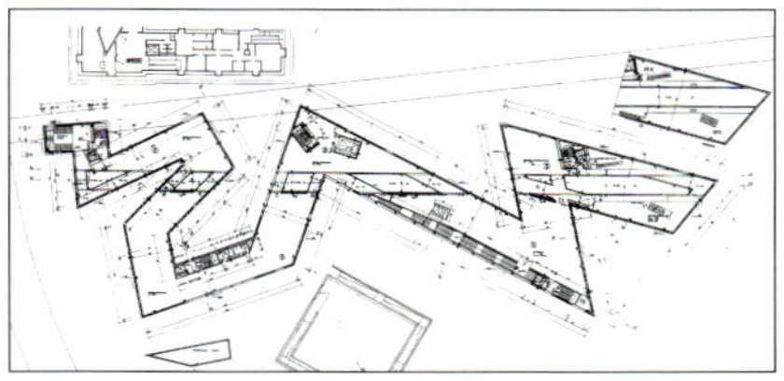

图2-4-8 a.柏林犹太人纪念馆平面图

图2-4-8 b.柏林犹太人纪念馆地下层室内

Daniel Libeskind's design of the Victoria & Albert Museum Extension is structured around three abstract dimensions: the spiral movement of art and history, the interlocking of inside and outside, and the labyrinth of discovery (Pic.2-4-5). These dimensions are evolved out of "the Spiral of History" and are translated into a coherent ensemble of functionally related spaces. The spiral movement of art and history manifests itself in the overall form of the extension building and its circulation system. The enclosure is created out of a continuous wall, which mirrors the perimeter walls of the entire block, spiralling around a virtual and ever shifting vertical axis (Pic.2-4-6). Visitors are implicated in a spiral movement as they circulate through the various functions of the museum. This movement distributes the public in a dynamic way to the rest of the museum through strategic connections; it acts as a counterpoint to the lateral, horizontal movement in the existing buildings. An interlock between interior and exterior is created by the winding and the unwinding spiral which brings the visitor into close relation with past history and the present, and with the city and the museum, through a direct experience of interpenetrating views and histories. The spiral of history is chaotic—its centre moves, the orbits jump. The resulting trace is one of interlock and overlap.

The form of the Museum was developed as an evolving trajectory, criss-crossing space, continuous and open ended, spiralling upwards. By tracing, translating and tilting the chaotic spiral form of V&A, the criss-crossing of overlapped lines becomes the structural bearing point. The structure, as it were, "builds" on itself, standing free; internal cores or extra braces are not needed. Floors act as diaphragms and columns do not penetrate the volumes, giving to the interior spaces a meditative and serene quality (Pic.2-4-7). The walls are of concrete, weaving seamlessness into the twisting structure; and at the top, to gain light, the spiral turns into glass. [177]

The description on Berlin Jewish Museum, in Libeskind's own words, make the use of metaphor even more clear: the multi-suggestive message obtained by the audience is as important as the building itself (Pic.2-4-8). For example, the Egyptian pyramids were not brought into existence for only one dead person. Many decades of effort were invested in constructing the pyramids because of the faith and belief of many people, not just one. That was what they were built for; and this feeling is very palpable to visitors today. "On the one hand, there is the archaeology of the structure—the remnants, the ruins—while on the other hand, there are developments that have very little to do with what one finds; reality comes from elsewhere—not from the physical structure itself." A museum may lead the audience to its exhibits; however, the audience should understand more about what is not being shown, or not able to be shown, if their minds and imaginations were sufficiently motivated as they walked about. A good museum should be able to tell different stories to different audience. Libeskind used the word "open narrative" as metaphor for his museum(Pic.2-4-9). "Open narrative" means that the various stories one can make about the museum are at odds with each other and also cannot be reconciled by any overall theme. What is essential for Libeskind is "one could not deal with architecture as being bound by physics." [178]

Whereas Eisenman pushes for the folded plates and staccato cubes, Frank Gehry advances in developing a vocabulary of undulating surfaces through formal juxtapositions. Gehry's Guggenheim Museum in Bilbao, as Jencks describes, have "smooth, continuous forms in steel and limestone (which) flow towards a centre point to erupt in a flower of petals". This building is also another landform building that ties into the large-scale technology and sprawl of the city(Pic.2-4-10). This is an inclusive work; urban realities are accepted, not denied. The result is a new kind of ambiguous architecture, more folded onto itself than the glass box which introduced orthodox Modernist notions

D-4 连接

Linking

两个独立的形可以通过突出物或者第三物体进行连接。

Two separate shapes can be linked with protrusions growing from these two objects and simply by a third party.

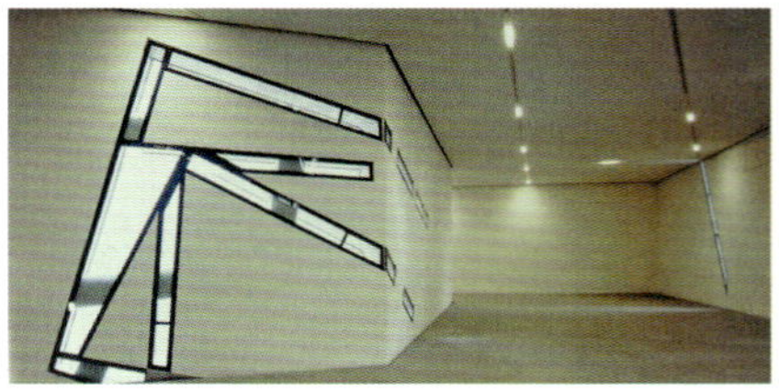

图2-4-9 a.纪念馆室内

图2-4-9 b.纪念馆外墙

等建筑中的公共空间，这些空间又与城市风景、河流结为一体。这一切使艺术馆成为城市明珠。最后，它隐喻着一朵怒放的鲜花，花瓣在风中狂舞（图2-4-11）。

错综复杂的形体，一般认为是“解构主义”语汇。而过去的10年里却出现一种与之相反的趋势：简单庞大的箱形建筑。两种形态都针对建筑中的不确定性，即以连续开放的空间适应不同使用者的需要。而以简洁庞大形体为特征的后一种趋势直接隐喻当今世界经济发展，即全球化市场的时代特征之一。它否认地域和文化的区别，主张通用方法，号称是真正面对“新的现实”（即全球化）。它与20世纪早期的现代主义有某种联系（图2-4-12）。这种建筑形体毫无特征：“它们没有意义，没有场地关系，没有文化形象或者个性”，代表全球市场化特点，[179] 克林曼把这种特点概括为：

1. 由全球化经济不断扩大而产生的“融化”；
2. 传统多元性的逐渐混合所导致的社会“同化”；
3. 对于转瞬即逝现象的重视而出现的“中和”效果。

由于经济重心由生产转向消费，建筑中的经济要求也随之转变。建筑本身是市场作用下的产品，为了提高生产效率，建筑不得不按照商品推销的方式运作。由于推销已成为经济竞争中的支柱，产量增加意味着优化建筑的效率。短期内最大的投资回报成为金科玉律。早期现代主义“功能”思想是在形和内容间建立明确对立关系，从而最大限度提高笛卡儿式机器效率，而市场因素通过宣扬不同个性，在一定程度上抗拒和重新包装“效率”观念。形式和内容在不断变化的市场策略和推销的压力下逐渐脱离。进而发展到建筑和电视机一样，外表单调，而节目内容和图像不停变化（图2-4-13）。

“（建筑的）普适化反对以相互区别为标志的多样化个性，而主张新的个性结合，这种结合在很大程度上是由于在全球化市场中出现的垄断需要。”[180] 放弃建筑个性和风格，建筑可以从既定的功能、文化和地域条件中解放出来（图2-4-14）。其无形之形正好适应全球经济的快速转变，强调文化的交流和混合。“普适”建筑没有地方性，正如全球经济中的一个产品，可以出现在任何一个文化圈，无论是欧洲、美洲还是亚洲（图2-4-15）。

法国建筑师多明尼克·皮劳尔设计的巨大盒子形建筑，室内完全开放灵活，外表直接反映环境光线的变化。立面表皮强化动态，和背后室内现实的模糊性对应（图2-4-16）。建筑的形体隐

D-5 碰撞

当两个形相互碰撞、相互穿插时，可能会产生以下三种情况：
· 破坏各自的独立性，产生新的构图。
· 其中一个成为主体。
· 两个形保留各自的独立性，出现第三个形作为连接部分。

Formal Collisions

When two forms collide and interpenetrate each other's boundaries and the following three situation may evolve:
· The two forms can subvert their individual identities and merge to create a new composite form.
· One of the two forms dominate the other.
· The two forms can retain their individual identities and the interlocking portions of become a third part.

图2-4-10 a.盖瑞的古根海姆艺术馆构思草图及模型 1991—1992年

图2-4-10 b.古根海姆的艺术馆及其环境，1999年

of transparency. Here are reflections of reflections and the self-similarity of crystals, the handling of glass facets and their intersections, which causes a virtual image to splinter into many-layered fragments. Views are partly veiled by walls of light that lead the eye up to the public ramps and roof terraces, which in turn give onto the urban landscape and river – making the museum a celebrant of the city. Finally we have the organic metaphor—the robust flower with its riotous petals blowing in the wind(Pic.2-4-11).

In contrast with the complexity of overlapping and folding forms known as the "deconstructionist" language, in the past decade another tendency towards simple, large, box-like buildings has emerged. Proponents of both tendencies claim they are reacting to uncertainty; in other words, the needs of continuous space, opened to multiple user interpretations. The latter tendency, that of extreme simplicity and huge scales, is rooted in recent world economic development, the so-called the global market. This tendency ignores regional and cultural differences, and appears to provide a general solution for all, claiming to deal with the New Reality, in reference (and deference) to the early Modernists of the 20th century(Pic.2-4-12) .These architectural forms are essentially featureless: "they are devoid of meaning, contextual ambitions, cultural image and identity."[179] In this connection, Klingman summarized three characteristics of the global market:

1.The increasing dimension of interiority brought about by a globalizing economy;
2.The social aspect of indifference inaugurated by a gradual blending of formerly pluralistic identities;
3.The implications of mediated effects through a heightened emphasis of instantaneous phenomena.

Since the economy shifted from production to consumption, the economic expectations that were placed on architecture changed with it. Architecture itself is a product of market forces. As a means to increase production efficiency, increasing pressure was placed on architecture to perform as a marketable commodity. Since the marketing of a commodity became a central feature of economic competition, maximizing production meant optimising building efficiency. Maximum return on investment in the shortest time is the governing credo here.Whereas in the early Modernist period function had established a clear relation to form and programme in order to maximize efficiency in the manner of a Cartesian machine, market forces actually unsubordinated and masked "efficiency" to a degree, under the promotion of diversified identities through advertising. Form and programme gradually drifted apart under the constant pressure of frequent changes of new marketing strategies and advertised images. Here, buildings are not much different from a TV set; both are monotonous in form but offer different and constantly changing programmes and images (Pic.2-4-13).

"Genericism (of architecture) increasingly disregards the notion of a pluralistic identity marked by difference, empathizing instead with a new cohesion of identities, brought about to a large extent by the merging monopolies of a globalizing market."[180] By giving up building identity, generic architecture with "no style", could be free itself from pre-determined functions, cultural and territorial constrains(Pic.2-4-14). Its formlessness assimilates the rapid shifts of a global economy, intensifying cultural exchanges and mixtures. In other words, generic architecture refers to the locally unattached, non-specific product of a global economy that can appear in any cultural context, whether in Europe, America or Asia (Pic.2-4-15).

D-6 覆盖

Superimposition

一个或一组形覆盖在另外一个或一组形上，可以通过渗透或叠加创造出新的构图，同时保留各自原有的属性。

One form or a group of forms are imposed on another form or forms by penetration, or overlapping to create a new composition without obliterating both original identity.

藏在表面上瞬间影像后面，它像一层穿不透的皮，只“反射”光、环境和观察者自己。设计的目标是营造一种无义务形象，即形象不表示任何特定的内容或者个性，而只表示它自己。无论形体复杂的“折叠”建筑，还是形体极为简练的“普适”建筑，都关注“信息时代”，这个21世纪的时代性。这令人回想起20世纪初现代主义大师将建筑和机器的类比。折叠建筑和“普适”建筑都带有一种现代性精神，即形出自新的社会和经济发展需要，体现新技术、新科学和新认知。它们为新时代服务，也是新时代的象征（图2-4-17）。

实际上，今日科学和技术前景对设计提出的新挑战，在陈年黄历中是找不到答案的，因为传统中没有新东西。正如约翰·塔卡拉指出，是由于信息技术的作用才产生了无形建筑（从而与早期现代主义脱轨），并传播和创造了复杂性、抽象、非线性这些使今日区别于以往的技术的特征。[181] 譬如，电是抽象的，人看不到但知其强大（图2-4-18）。与传统载体（如雕塑、印刷纸、绘画和相片）相比较而言，信息技术中的信息载体极为抽象。这里只有电脉冲，1和0，或者是光的脉冲。[182] 而且原作和复制品的区别也消失了，现在复制一张数码的照片，即使是专家也难分辨出与原作的区别。塔卡拉进而认为，信息时代中的设计可以看作数据处理过程（通过全球生产线上的信息系统或者遍布在各种传媒中的图像），以及对数据的有效利用。当硬件产品间的功能区别消失以后，这种数据处理过程更趋向于进行象征性产品区别——这种“硬”件和“软”件结合的设计方法在设计史上绝无先例可循，而“软”的方面也许可以理解为“无材料的形”。

图2-4-11 a.艺术馆西南面

图2-4-11 b.艺术馆南面

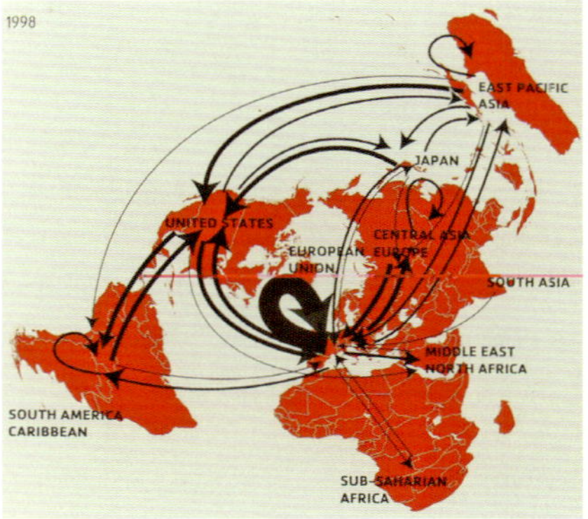

图2-4-12 1998年世界贸易分布示意图

图2-4-13 2002年香港地铁内的广告

图2-4-14 a.20世纪60年代作为香港支柱产业之一的塑料制品生产现已转移到内地农村，却仍远销世界

图2-4-14 b.休斯敦高层建筑

D-7 空间包被

大空间可以包含小空间，这时两个空间之间具有视觉和空间的连续性，但小空间在对外空间的联系上对大空间有依赖性。在这一类空间关系中，大的、外部的空间是其内部的小空间的空间范围。小空间可以与大空间同形或异形。

Space within a Space

A large space can envelop and contain within its volume, a smaller space. Visual and spatial continuity between the two spaces can be easily accommodated, but the smaller, “contained” space depends on the larger, enveloping space for its relationship to outdoor space. In this type of spatial relationship, the larger, enveloping space serves as a three-dimensional field for the space contained within it.

The contained space may share the form of the enveloping shape, or differ in form from the enveloping space.

图2-4-15 希宁设计的德国某分销中心，1999年

图2-4-16 法国建筑师皮劳尔设计的阿普里克斯工厂，1999年

图2-4-17 香港中环，2002年

The interiors of large box-like buildings, designed by French architect Dominique Perrault, afford complete flexibility;the exterior attracts attention through its changing effects, which can be instantly understood and assimilated (Pic.2-4-16). Their facade envelopes play on this notion of uncertainty and the hidden ambiguity of interior realities. The abstract form recedes behind the temporary perception of the surface. The object acts as a non-permeable surface, as a reflector of the observer, the light or the environment. In the end, the issue becomes the generation of a non-committal image, an image not signifying any particular program or identity but instead signifying appearance itself. Both folding architecture, characterized by complicated forms, and generic architecture, characterized by stark simplicity, share common interests in the Information Age, the new 21st century epoch. This thinking harks back to the Modernist 20th century association between architecture and the machine. Both folding and generic architecture share the spirit of modernity: forms generated by new social and economic developments, defined by new technologies and new science. They perform as the symbol as well as the service of the new epoch (Pic.2-4-17).

Actually some features of today's scientific and technical landscape do pose new challenges for design that will not be answered by archival research, where tradition has nothing new to offer. As John Thackara continues, it was the very functions of information technologies which create formlessness (neatly derailing the early Modernists) and which comprehend (and create) the complexity, abstraction, and non-linearity that distinguish today's technologies from those that preceded them. [181] For instance, electricity has an abstract character. One cannot see it but knows it is powerful(Pic.2-4-18). With information technology, the medium carrying the information becomes extremely abstract, when compared against traditional physical media of, sculpture, printed-paper, paintings and photography. There are merely electronic impulses, ones and zeroes – impulses of light. "The object no longer contains being, but only exists as contiguous electronic impulses." [182] The difference between original work and copies of the original has also disappeared. For it is now possible to digitize a photograph in such a way as to reproduce it so that even an expert cannot tell if it was the first instance or the second. Thackara argues that in relation to the information age, design may be seen as the process that takes data (such as that from information systems of global manufacturing or the images swirling around in the media) and does something useful with them. As the functional differences between hard products diminish, this process progressively involves symbolic product differentiation—a synthesis of "hard" and "soft" that has no precedent in the history of design. The "soft" part could be understood as "form-without-material".

图2-4-18 香港某商业中心的财经屏幕，2002年

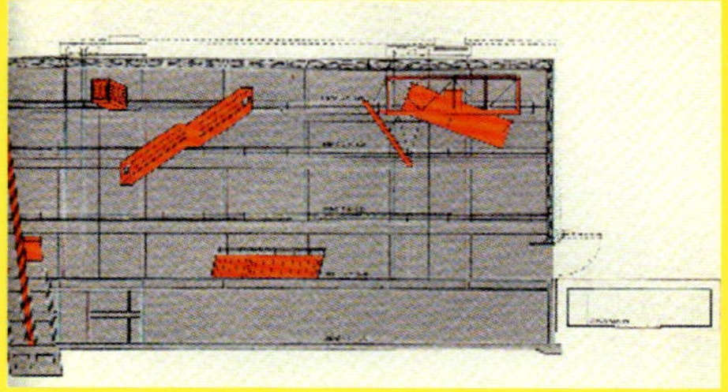

2.5 材料、造型和信息

材料是建筑的肉、骨和皮，建筑不能没有材料。恰当精心地使用建筑材料首先需要对它们的性能、生产和构造性能有充分的认识。尽管建筑材料无疑是人的身外之物，而20世纪60年代的艺术作品却开始让人“走进画面”，[183] 即人可以在充满材料的空间中走动，成为艺术材料的一部分，尤其重要的是光线和气味等无形材料也成为艺术要素。

物质形体和物质材料

材料是塑造视觉形体的物质媒介。对物质材料的加工需要智慧、理解和对材料素质的尊重。建筑实际上是让材料表现自己的过程。阿尔瓦·阿尔托曾说：“人即刻可以理解语言和书上的词汇，而人理解材料却很慢，这也许可解释为什么我们今天用的材料是那样古老。”[184] 材料在人类文明中用了很长时间才变得有效。所以阿尔托认为木是“活的材料”，其疤痕是生长中的纤维质，和人的肌肉一样。他的木制作品总是力求表现自然木材本性（图2-5-1）。而大理石在他看来则代表另一种个性。它的多孔质素可以体现在不同建筑和雕塑中。“一个人在处理这种古老材料时不可能对它没有一点感受。”[185] 建筑是材料与人和谐共处之所——阿尔托对材料的精心选择和处理正是出于这样的人文主义建筑思想（图2-5-2）。

图2-5-1 阿尔托设计的木雕

图2-5-2 a.迈里亚住宅门厅，1938—1941年

路易斯·康也非常关注和尊重材料的特性：

“假如你和一块砖头对话，问它要什么，它会说要建一座砖拱。你说，看，砖拱太贵，一根混凝土过梁就可以代替一座砖拱。而砖说，我知道会太贵，今天也许不再会建砖拱了，但如果你问我要什么，我还是要砖拱。”（图2-5-3，图2-5-4）[186]

柯布西耶喜欢表现混凝土的美，但不是那种完美，而是其斑驳、粗糙的质感（图2-5-5）。“裸露的混凝土上有很多洞眼，模板的连缝，木材的纤维纹和疤点……在男人和女人身上，你不也看到皱纹、胎记，以及鼻子上数不清的斑点吗？……缺陷是人性，是我们自己，是日常生活。为什么不能进一步，与之共处、强化，向更高的目标——崇高化！”“……我选择用对比来创造美，我要在处理野蛮和优雅，平淡和激情，精确和错误的对比中找到互补性，我要让人想一想，让人反思，这就是我用粗野喧闹、激情夸张的手法处理（混凝土）立面的原因。”[187]

图2-5-2 b.假日别墅中的“实验性砖墙”，1953年

走向非物质形体

建筑形体是为参观者、使用者和所有者的动态体验而建造的。随着交通技术的发展，人的运

D-8 叠加

Overlapping

一个平面形覆盖另一个平面形，从而或轻或重改变其属性。

Two flat forms may have a thin property or no appreciable thickness at all. When overlapping occurs, one of the two forms must have covered by the other one, and its property may changed, however slight the change may be.

图2-5-3 用铅笔、灰笔和水墨作的速写《公共大厅》，1928年

图2-5-4 印度管理学院，1962—1974年

图2-5-5 昌迪加尔某学院入口及墙面模度图案

2.5 Materials, Formation and Information

Materials are the flesh, bones and skin of architecture. Proper and sensible application of a building material demands a thorough understanding of its properties, availability, and buildability. While construction materials are unmistakably external to the human body, artwork starting from the 1960s literally allowed viewers to step "into the picture". [183] People could begin to move in spaces that were filled with materials and most important, noises, and lights, even smell.

Physical Form, Physical Materials

Material is more than simply a physical medium to create visible shapes or forms. In fact, working with physical material involves an intellectual process. Its nature must be understood and respected. Architecture should be a continual process allowing the materials to express themselves over time. As Alvar Aalto says, "The word, both spoken and written, has an immediate effect on a person, materials, on the other hand, 'speak' more slowly; perhaps this explains why the materials that we still use are so old."[184] It takes a long period of development before they become effective in human culture. Therefore, Aalto considers wood a "living material", of which the grains are the growing fibre, similar to human muscles. His wooden objects always try to follow the natural nature of wood(Pic.2-5-1). Marble, on the other hand, has different characteristic: its porosity would result in different architectural or sculptural forms. "One cannot work on these ancient materials without a feeling for the materials."[185] Aalto's careful choice and manipulation of materials is the basis of his humanistic architecture. To him, architecture is where the material world is in harmony with human life(Pic.2-5-2).

Louis Kahn was also always conscious of and respects the properties of the materials:

If you talk to a brick and ask it what it likes, it'll say it likes an arch. And you say to it, look arches are expensive and you can always use a concrete lintel to take the place of arch. And the bricks says, I know it's expensive and I'm afraid it probably cannot be built these days, but if you ask me what I like it's still an arch (Pic.2-5-3,Pic.2-5-4). [186]

Le Corbusier celebrated the beauty of concrete, not for its perfection, but rather for its defects and coarse texture (Pic.2-5-5). "Exposed concrete shows the least incidents of the shuttering, the joints of the planks, the fibres and knots of the wood, etc. ... In men and women do you not see the wrinkles and the birthmarks, the crooked noses, the innumerable peculiarities? ... Faults are human; they are ourselves, our daily lives. What matters is to go further, to live, to be intense, to aim high, and to be loyal!""...I have decided to make beauty by contrast. I will find its complement and establish a play between crudity and finesse, between the dull and the intense, between precision and accident. I will make people think and reflect, this is the reason for the violent, clamorous, triumphant polychrome of the (concrete) facades." [187]

Approaching Non-physical Form

Architectural forms are ideally built upon and built for the mobile experience of viewer, owners, users and visitors. When people move increasingly fast with the continued development of transportation technology, the

D-9 连锁

连锁即两个空间相互重叠形成一个共同区域，这时，各自都保留空间的特性，其相互连锁的部分可能：

· 共同拥有；

· 与其中一个空间连为一体，成为其体积的有机组成部分；

· 自成一体，作为联系两个空间的独立空间。

图2-5-6 佛罗伦萨圣·西玛修道院广场，1754年

图2-5-7 范·德·布耶克和巴克玛设计的鹿特丹林班中心，1951—1953年

图2-5-8 西欧航空线路图

动速度加快，作为建筑个体的形，视觉重要性逐渐减弱，甚至“消失”。中世纪意大利山城的尺度亲切的街道、广场和商铺是为行人服务的（图2-5-6）。20世纪城市中巨大简洁的建筑形体只有从飞驶的汽车、火车中欣赏才见其最佳效果（图2-5-7）。大量证据（包括勒·柯布西耶的速写）可以证明这种推论。今天越来越多的人经常乘飞机旅行。从空中看，建筑和城市地面交通更加模糊不清（图2-5-8）。（而有趣的是，不同地方人情风光更多地出现在飞行杂志上，而不是旅行者的实际体验。）现代城市火车和汽车常于地下行驶。越来越多的人依靠指示牌穿梭于地铁和地下通道（图2-5-9），地面上的标志性建筑越来越少为人所用。总之，随着人的运行速度增加，视觉上的非物质化现象越来越明显。而且，空间中交通网络发越增加，建筑的视觉形象越减弱。[188]以其运行要求建造的这些基础设施对城市空间的影响日益增强。建筑，特别是建筑的形变得相对次要，实际上在建筑史上，建筑的形还从来没有像今天这样无足轻重。在功能和技术问题解决之后，传统的建筑理论已无用武之地。在其他科学的参与下，如生态科学对建筑基地物种多样性的处理，我们传统的自然和城市景观知识正在失去其实用价值。

20世纪80年代中期乔舒亚·迈罗维奇著的一部畅销书《没道理的场所——电子传媒对社会行为的影响》受到广泛关注。书中分析了在美国这样的现代社会中，家庭、邻里等传统空间观念是如何因电视和计算机介入和影响社会生活而改变的。在传统社会，人的社会化成长过程直接与所处的物质空间相关。孩子们局限在家庭或者学校，与成人社会空间隔着一段距离。而今天的孩子们与世界保持着广泛的联系，因为电视已经跨越所有空间障碍（图2-5-10），它减弱了不同社会年龄和不同社会化过程中的人的区别。[189] 电视不仅揭开了不同地方的神秘面纱，而且提供了接触和打开所有地方的感知方式。“许多美国人不再关心‘他们所处的位置’，因为过去与地点相连的许多元素被电子传媒打散，无论在家里，还是在办公室或者在车里，人都可以接触甚至进入外部世界。”[190]

过去40年来的急剧变化都和电视的巨大影响力有关，因为它打破了“这里”和“那里”的分别，打破了对真实生活和对传播事件的体验的区别，同时将私密性和公共性混在一起。它将物质障碍和渠道变得毫无意义，公用信息模式的出现又进一步加剧了这种趋势（图2-5-11）。一项有趣的调查发现，美国大多数人支持乔治·布什攻打伊拉克，同时发现美国大多数人并不知道伊拉克在哪里。战争的地点变得不再重要，这在战争史上可能还是第一次。

迈罗维奇还发现，共用的信息环境，也同时改变了大家对这个环境的共识。生活在某个环境中的一群人，他们的社会行为等方面有更多的相似性。“现在我们到任何地方都会觉得似曾相

Interlocking

An interlocking spatial relationship consists of two spaces whose fields overlap to form a zoned or shared space. When two spaces interlock their volumes in this manner, each retains its identity and definition as a space. The interlocking portion of the two volumes can:

· Be shared equally by each space;
· Merge with one of the space and become an integral part of its volume;
· Develop its own integrity as a space that serves to link the two original spaces.

图2-5-9 建设中的香港尖沙咀地下步行系统，2002年

图2-5-10 香港公共汽车内景

individual forms of architecture start lose importance, and even become invisible. Italian towns with their human-scaled streets, plazas and shops, were clearly meant for pedestrians(Pic.2-5-6). Modern 20th century cities, with super blocks composed of simple forms, were meant to be appreciated from inside moving cars and trains (Pic.2-5-7). There is ample evidence (e.g. in many of Le Corbusier's sketches), which can justify this assumption. Today, people regularly travel in airplane (Pic.2-5-8), from which buildings and cities are even much less visible than ground surface transportation (curiously, different places more often appear in airplane journals than in the physical experience of the travellers themselves). In the modern city, trains and cars tend to disappear underground(Pic.2-5-9). More people travel underground with the guidance of text signage than those on the ground surface guided by landmark buildings. A connection between increasing speed and a tendency towards perceived dematerialization can be established. Moreover, the more traffic networks encroach upon physical space, the greater the loss of their visible form.[188] These infrastructures, dominated by their own discourse and (those of others), act so powerfully in current cities that architecture, especially architectural form, become a trivial matter; in fact they become the most trivial ever experienced in urban history. When all the functional and technical programmes are discussed, the usual arguments often fail to be effective. Confronting the participating disciplines, e.g., ecosystem science which deal with the biodiversity of a project site, our traditional comprehension of landscape or urbanscape increasingly loses its validity.

In the 1980s a popular book entitled *No Sense of Place—The Impact of Electronic Media on Social Behaviour* written by Joshua Meyrowitz received wide attention. It analyzed how, in a modern society as found in the United States, the traditional perception of space, such as home and neighbourhood, has changed since television and computer entered and influenced social life. Traditionally, each stage of socialization has been associated with its own physical location. Young children are separated from much of the adult world by being isolated in the home or classroom. Today however, children at home or school are no longer so isolated. Televisions bypass the isolation of place(Pic.2-5-10). And they thereby blur the differences between people at different stages of socialization and between those in different kinds socialization processes.[189] Television not only demystifies the places it reveals, but also promotes a new sense of access and openness to all places. "Many Americans may no longer seem to 'know their place' because the traditionally interlocking components of 'place' have been split apart by electronic media. Wherever one is now – at home, at work, or in a car—one may be in touch and tuned-in."[190]

The intensity of the changes in the last forty years has been related to the unique power of television to break down the distinctions between the "here" and "there", between live and mediated experience of events, and between private and public realms. It renders physical barriers and passageways relatively meaningless; this is further reinforced by patterns of access to shared information(Pic.2-5-11). A recent interesting survey found most of Americans support president George W. Bush in an as-yet unwaged war against Iraq, but more than half did not even know where Iraq is. For the first time in modern history, the world is relatively placeless, and a potentially senseless war is no longer constrained by territory.

Also of interest in Meyerowitz's findings is the discovery that a collectively shared information environment commonly biases our collective perception of that environment. When living together in the same environment, members are apparently more alike than when they live separately. "Places visited for the first time now look familiar if they (or places like them) have already been seen on television." And places that were once very different are now more similar because nearly every place has a television set, telephone, radio or Hi-Fi, and a computer workstation.

D-10 加法

一个形可由两个以上的形（要素）构成。通过增加要素可以改变形的体积。当简单增加要素时，形会变大；当要素完全相同时，形变得强壮；当要素各不相同时，形变得混乱。加法的过程可以保持或者改变形的属性。

Addition

A form can be composed of more than two smaller forms. The form can be transformed by the addition of elements to its volume. The form become bigger when smaller forms are added to it. It become stronger when smaller forms are identical. It becomes chaos when all smaller forms are different. The nature of the additive process will determine whether the identity of the initial form is retained or altered.

图2-5-11 a.城市街边广告

图2-5-11 b.香港地铁车厢内广告

识，因为在电视上看到过。”而原来很不同的地方也的确变得相似，因为到处都有电视、电话、收音机或者音像设备，而且还有一张计算机办公桌。“电子传媒使得孩子卧室、牧师家庭到监狱囚室等几乎所有地方都有明显的共同点。”电子传媒已经彻底改变了过去与某个特定的物质场所相关联的集体个性、社会化和社会阶层，并改变了和场所相关的特有经验。

计算机等新科技无疑进一步削弱了社会空间和物质空间的对应关系。任何个人电脑都可以进入任何一个“主系统”或者全球电话网络。计算机也将过去各自独立的技术，如电视、电话、音像设备、卫星和打印机连成一个大型信息网络。总之，今日社会从工作到娱乐都从物质性变得“信息化”，“这里”和“那里”的区别进一步消失，而我们的工作就是信息搜索和信息收集，我们是信息丛林中的猎人（图2-5-12）。

社会和物质环境相互同化的另一个影响，是我们把世界看作是模式而不是孤立的场所。这种观察方式的变化也是来自计算机的影响。计算机把各个方面的信息综合成统一的便于检索的信号。面对大量的信息，人们趋向于从中找到模式和关系，不在乎其出处。“这样出现了许多‘万金油’式的专家，他们对所有的事都不甚了解，却知道谁了解什么，谁有好的想法，怎样找到这些人，以及怎样把同样的问题联系到其他领域。这种什么都不懂的人，却为各类专家提供一种平台。这种观察方式也影响到建筑。建筑以单体区别划分已没有意义，因为内部的活动已相互结合在同一个体系和“场地”运行。

今天，人类从没有像今天这样面对大量图像（图2-5-13）。“计算机、电话、传真、电视、有线电视、录像、卫星和美国最著名的出口商品——迈克尔·杰克逊，整容手术，分子生物，各种人体形象改造技术、皮下技术齐头并进。对社会的影响直接而巨大，后果却又无法估计。高科技，后现代和全球化市场经济在20世纪90年代获得最终的胜利。”[191] 虚拟现实中的形象制造甚至可以不尊重任何的基本物理原则。“一张图内包含着另一张图，里面的图可以比外面的图更大。你可以随意设定尺度，你可以建造没有人见过的结构，如果你不喜欢，你只需抽出磁盘扔到垃圾桶里。”电子数码科技让人生脱离物质，以非物质的化学和生物过程给我们新的观念，无论是正确的还是错误的，即我们的外在现实，那些物质材料，并不是我们体验的全部。

这种趋势在许多方面动摇了建筑学的基础。首先，场所观念，以及和场所有关的地方特色出现了变化（图2-5-14）。场所重构为消费中心，一个进行货物比较、估价、买卖、使用和丢弃的地方（图2-5-15）。全世界的机场购物中心都是一样的，只卖几类商品。场所本身也是商品，一种视觉商品。“迪士尼乐园已向我们指出，科技可以超越自然向我们提供更现实的东西。”[192] 在今日世界

D-11　减法

Subtraction

形可以减去其中的一部分进行变形。减法的过程可以保持或完全改变原形的属性。

A form can be transformed by subtracting a portion of its volume. Depending on the extent of the subtractive process, the form can retain its initial identity, or be transformed into a form of another family.

图2-5-12 香港地铁车厢内电子新闻

"With electronic media, most places—from the child's room to the priest's home to the prisoner's cell – now have a strong common denominator." Those aspects of group identity, socialization, and hierarchy that were once dependent on particular physical locations and the special experiences available in them have been altered by electronic media.

The computer and other new technologies can certainly undermine the relationship between social place and physical place. Anyone's personal computer can now be hooked into any other "mainframe" or personal computer through massive global telephone networks. The computer is also stimulating the integration of various technologies-televisions, telephones, audio/video recorders, satellites, and printers—into one large information network. As work and play in our society is becoming increasingly "informational" than physical, there is a further decline in the difference between "here" and "there" and an enhancement of our roles as new-age hunters and gatherers (Pic.2-5-12).

Another impact of the generalization of our social and physical environment –enhanced by the computer – is that people see the world more as a pattern than as separated places. Computer signals give potentially equal access to data from all fields. With such an overwhelming amount of accessible data, people are tending more to see patterns and interrelationships among various types of data, regardless of their origin. "The resulting 'specialist in generalism' would be someone who does not 'know' everything about everything but who has a good idea of who knows what, where and how to find things and people, and how to link similar questions in diverse fields. This person who would know 'almost nothing about almost everything' could provide a balance for those specialists who, in our increasingly specialized world, know 'almost everything about almost nothing.'" This impact on architecture can be so strong that buildings are no longer seen as separated, but rather integrated and perform as one system and one field.

Today, people are more exposed to virtual images than at any other time in human history(Pic.2-5-13). "Computers, telephones, faxes, television, cable television, video, satellites, and America's most successful exports-Michael Jackson, cosmetic surgery, anabolic steroids. These are body-image, body-altering technologies, under the skin, subcutaneous technologies. These things are moving ahead on their own. They affect society drastically in unprecedentedly intimate ways. The high-tech, postmodern, globalized free market has won in the 1990s." [191] Imagery produced in a state of virtual reality is not subject even to the most elementary laws of physics. "You can have things inside things, where the inside is much bigger than the outside. You can change scale. You can build structures that are previously unknown, and if you don't like them, you can just pull the disk and throw it in the trash." The fact is that the dematerialization of human experience as a consequence of electronic digital technologies and the immateriality of chemical and biological processes all support the perception, rightly or wrongly, that our external reality, the material, is no longer the whole and complete world we experience.

This tendency challenges the foundations of architecture in many aspects. First the notions of place and local identity associated with place are transforming (Pic.2-5-14). Places are increasingly being restructured as centres for consumption, and as providing the context within which goods and services are compared, evaluated, purchased, used, and discarded(Pic.2-5-15). Airport retails shops are the same worldwide, but they clearly constrain the products they select and sell. Places themselves are in a sense consumed, particularly visually. "Disneyland tells us that technology can give us more reality than nature can."[192] In many places around the world today, local traditional architecture gains more capital support from the tourist industry than their respective cultural and heritage departments.

D-12 延伸

将形进行拉伸，超出其原有边界，或者创造出一个特定形状的框架作为背景，这两种变形手法称为延伸。这时形改变一个或几个方向的尺度，而仍然保持其本质属性。

Extension

A form can be extended beyond original border by stretching, or creating a frame of a certain shape, adding a shape to serve as background, can also be used as extensions. The form is transformed by altering one or more of its dimensions and still retain its family identity.

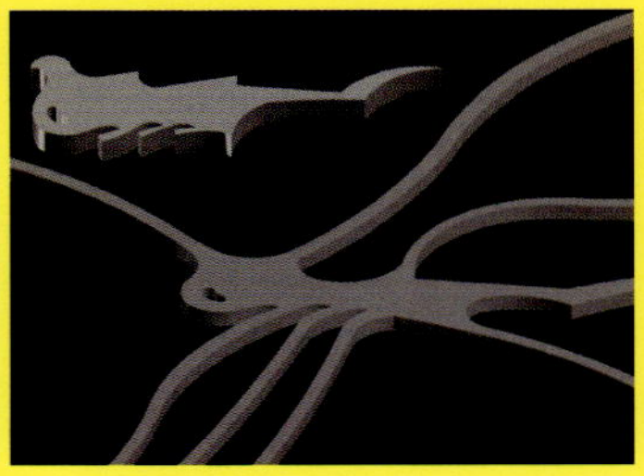

图2-5-13 香港某商业中心广告，2002年

图2-5-14 一位在地铁站月台上使用手机、观看电视屏幕的候车人

的许多地方，地方传统风格的建筑从旅游部门得到的资助比从文化遗产部门得到的还要多。

当空间分隔和建筑形象特征对人和社会生活中的影响力逐渐减弱以后（图2-5-16），建筑的其他内容，即前文所说的“软件”——活动、程序、人力资源、企业精神、过程性和环境因素相对而言更加重要。建筑没有风格或者明显形状的城市现象可以称为“单调城市的混乱”，或者“混乱城市的单调”。然而这正是今天的，也许是未来的城市形象。城市，在20世纪一度被现代主义和后现代主义形容为充满矛盾对比。在我们今天21世纪却被视为统一单调的机体。“在这样的城市中，差别的消逝和极端的对北同时存在，并化为一种模糊的空间延续的感觉。”[193] 失去了材料感，甚至重力感之后，城市体验犹如梦一场（图2-5-17）。正是这种心理空间或者建筑的软件，以其不确定的质量构筑了现代城市的结构基础。

建筑最后来到非物质阶段，形模糊了，或者相对于急速变化和交换的资本、人流、能量和垃圾，变得不再重要。而且，建造工业本身对非个性化建筑产生起了巨大的推动作用。建造工业的自动化趋势，像亚当·斯密的“无形的手”，无意识地控制着建筑和城市的形象运作方式。城市规划师，建筑设计者，无论怎样努力都没有真正理解所发生的一切。建造过程遵循自己的经济模式进行重复性生产、建造、改造、翻新，好像一切自动有效地进行着，人们对此越来越麻木。

图2-5-15 休斯敦

D-13　压缩

Compression

形受到外力挤压时会变小，但仍然保持其本质特征。

A form become smaller when squeezed by external force, however it still retain its family identity.

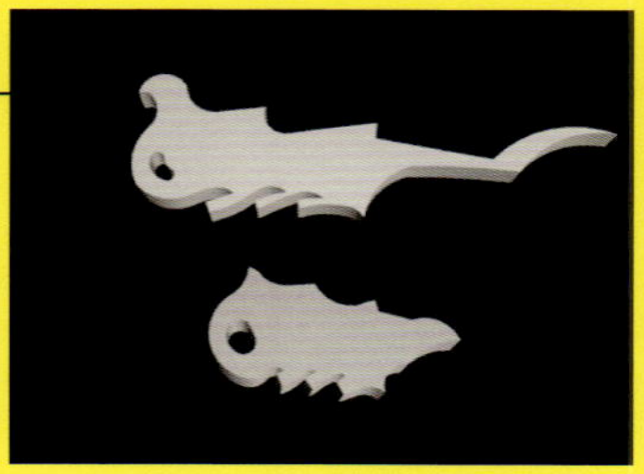

图2-5-16 跨国界城市化，美国和墨西哥边界情景

As spatial barriers and distinct architectural forms collapse (Pic.2-5-16), other issues of architecture, the previously mentioned "soft parts" of building—the programme, its workforce, the character of its entrepreneurialism, its history and its environment become important. Cities whose buildings lack articulated style or clearly defined forms can be rightly called either monotonous urban chaos or chaotic urban monotones. This is the city image of today and probably the future. The urban territory, once described as a heterogeneous entity by modernists and postmodernists of the 20th century, can thus be understood as a homogeneous field in our own 21st century. "In these cities, the elimination of differences as well as the stark contrast of extreme opposites—simultaneously experienced—brings about a sense of blurred spatial continuity."[193] The city is experienced in a state comparable to that of being submerged in a dream by losing all sense of materials and gravity (Pic.2-5-17). It is this psychological space, or the soft part of buildings, which in its indeterminate quality constitutes the fundamental datum of new city structures.

Architecture finally comes to the stage of de-materialization, in which form is either blurred or unimportant in comparison with the rapid change and exchange of capital, people, energy, and wastes. Paradoxically, the construction industry contributes probably the most powerful impact on the creation of de-materialized buildings. It guided by a kind of automatism, not unlike Adam Smith's "invisible hand", unconscious of what or how a city or a building should look or behave. Urban planners and building designers, despite their best efforts, cannot understand what is really going on. The construction process follows established economic models, reproduced again and again with little variation. Effectively, the buildings are produced, changed, and refurbished automatically, and with apparently increasing numbness.

图2-5-17 香港竖向城市景观，屋顶、街道、中庭式广场和地铁大厅

D–14 投射

投射可以将稳定和规则的空间和形置于一种不稳定和定向运动的状态之下，但仍然与原有形式存在亲密关系和视觉上的相似性。投射表现出一种强烈的动感。

Projection

The projective operation makes stable and regular space and forms occurs a situation of unstable and movement towards a defined direction. However, it has an affinity or visual likeness to the original figure. Projective operation gives a strong feeling of movement.

图2-6-1 曼彻斯特步行天桥

图2-6-2 古根海姆艺术馆的钛合金贴面

2.6 先进技术和灵活程序

新溶剂，新形状，新建筑材料和不断变化的观念以及建造方式，都在随着技术革新而不断进步。

随着计算机、科学和工程学的进步，经过不断实验，新材料和新结构成功地运用在建筑中，并对传统的建筑学提出挑战。在曼彻斯特建造的管状玻璃步行天桥（图2-6-1），采用了新的结构方式，外部钢网既是基本结构，也是幕墙的支撑体系。在这玻璃桥中并没有隐藏着的梁，其结构是由焊接在一起的九根笔直的钢管构成，围绕中轴线环形交叉布置，形成流线型双曲面，水平向运用这种结构在桥梁设计中还是第一次。

在西班牙毕尔巴鄂市的古根海姆艺术馆设计中，弗兰克·盖瑞为外部贴面材料费尽心思。“我们原想用铝化铜，由于其毒性而放弃了，不得不寻找其他和铝化铜一样反光的材料。这样花了很长时间，我们分析了不锈钢，试图改造并去掉它的冰冷的工业色彩……在我们最丧气的时候，发现了钛合金样片，观察它在光线中的效果，觉得这种温暖而有个性的金属有一定的潜力。”[194] 发现一种新的材料也可激发设计者重新思考一些问题。“石头的稳固性实际上是错觉，在城市污染的空气中，它们腐蚀得很快，而三分之一毫米的钛却可以保证一百年不褪色，我们不得不重新认识什么才代表稳固（图2-6-2）。”[195] 在资金限制下，运用这种材料还得借助于设计和建造过程中计算机技术的运用。盖瑞采用的CATIA计算机程序，可以计算雕塑形的结构，可以分析钢结构框架的有效性，找到理想的面材尺寸和形状，节省时间和资金，[196] 这个作品的成功应归功于新技术、新材料和新结构的完美结合。

弗兰姆普敦引用格雷戈里·特纳的研究发现，20世纪建筑技术进步“将设计的重点从混凝土砖结构形体，转向裙房、设备、体系和面层等结构件组件。”[197] 35年来这些组件的发展相互独立。研究还发现自19世纪末以来，电器设备在建筑总造价中的比重上升到了35%，而同时，建筑主体结构的造价比重则从80%下降到今天的20%。弗兰姆普敦由此认为20世纪末建筑的发展趋势是技术主导。设计内容也从砖体结构转向“反形体”的组合构件。新技术运用不仅改变了建筑的形，而且还改变了我们对建造环境的认知。传统的建筑形态受到挑战，传统的价值观，如人性尺度，比例，形和空间，装饰和隐喻，街道和广场等需要重新定义。而且由于新材料和技术的形成和发展沿着各自的专业轨道与建筑齐头并进，建筑的运行效果完全取决于相互间的结合是否成功。建筑学不可避免地从现有专业知识的局限迈向多学科的结合。[198]

D-15 透视

在透视图中，形体上的平行线汇聚在视平线上的灭点。形状相同，大小不同的物体暗示着强烈的消失感。巧妙地运用这种视觉效果可以加强或模糊空间的视觉稳定性。

Perspective

In a perspective operation, parallel lines on the figure converge at vanishing point on the visual horizon line. Objects with same shape but different dimension suggest strong visual sense of vanishing to the smaller one. Wisely use the visual effect can enhance or blurring space stability.

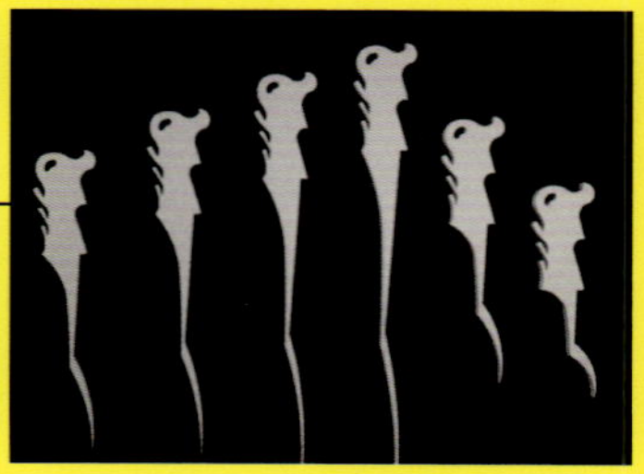

2.6 Advanced Technology and the Indeterminate Program

New solutions, new shapes, new building materials and steady changes in the concepts and methods of construction are continually created in the process of technological advancement.

With advances in computing, science and engineering, new properties of materials are experimented and successfully made available. New forms and applications of steel and glass are challenging traditional architectural discourse. For example, a tubular form of glass footbridge in Manchester (Pic.2-6-1) is an adventurous structural solution in that the outer steel lattice structure is both the primary spanning medium and the cladding support framework. There is no hidden main girder. This primary structure consists of a welded frame of nine perfectly straight tubes with the curved hyperbolic parabolic form being derived from the circular arrangement of these tubes around a central horizontal axis. The horizontal application of such a structure is believed to be the first in footbridge design.

For his Guggenheim Museum design in Bilbao, Spain, Frank Gehry went through a long search for an appropriate material to clad its exterior. "We originally planned to use lead copper but it was outlawed as a toxic material. We had to find another material that could play with the light like the lead copper did; it took a long time. We analysed stainless steel and we tried to take away the cold industrial look of the material ... It was during that frustration that we found some samples of titanium and looking at it in the light we realized that there was some potential for a metal that had warmth and character." [194] The discovery of a new material also triggered the designer to rethink other issues: "It's ironic that the stability given by stone is false, because stone deteriorates in the pollution of our cities whereas a third of a millimetre of titanium is a hundred-year guarantee against city pollution. We have to rethink what represents stability(Pic.2-6-2)."[195] It is also important to note that the application of such material and the delivery of the project within the construction budget had been possible only with the introduction of computer technology in the design and production process. The computer program employed, CATIA, allows sculptural shapes to be computed; a more time-saving and economic way of building to be devised; an appropriate structural steel frame to be analysed; and ideal cladding panel sizes and shapes to be devised and fabricated.[196] The combination of new technology and materials made this project successful.

R. Gregory Turner, cited by Frampton, demonstrated that building technology innovations in the 20th century "shifted the focus away from the homogeneous masonry mass towards the articulation of built-form into the categorical components of podium, services, framework and envelope."[197] During the past thirty-five years these sectors have grown independently. The cost of electromechanical services has risen, since the end of the 19th century, to some 35% of the total. In contrast, the proportion devoted to the basic structure has dropped from approximately 80 percent in the previous century to some 20 percent today. Frampton saw the new tendency in architecture, at end of the 20th century, was technological maximization. Buildings have shifted the focus away from load-bearing masonry towards"dematerialized"modes of assembly. New technological applications have continued to change the form of buildings, and consequently, our perceptions of the form of the built environment. Traditional building typologies are challenged and traditional architectural notions such as human scale, proportion, form and space, motifs and metaphors, streets and plaza are redefined. As these new materials and technologies emerge and develop in different specializations parallel to architecture, the final performance of the building ultimately depends on their successful integration. Architecture thus inevitably goes beyond the relatively constrained and static existing professional

D-16　级数

一套数量或数字，每个部分都通过一个统一规律与其他一个部分相关联。数学上有三种级数：等差级数、调和级数、等比级数。按级数变形后仍然保持形的本质特征。

Progression

This is a series of quantities or numbers in which each term is related to its predecessor by a uniform law. There are three kinds of progression in mathematics: arithmetic, harmonic and geometric.The identity of the form will still remains after the transformation.

图2-6-3 a.伊东丰雄设计的仙台传媒技术中心模型，2000年

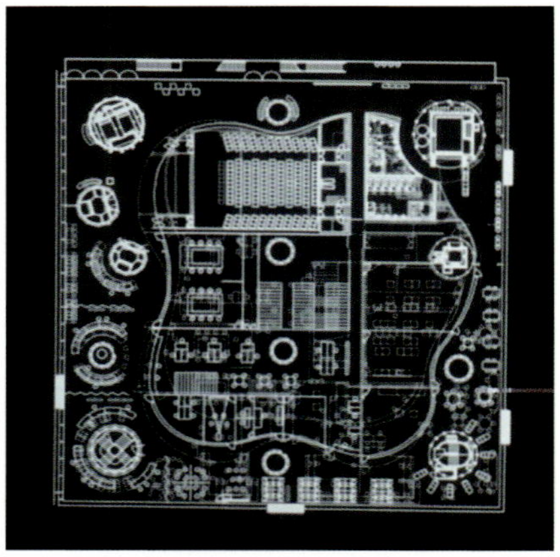

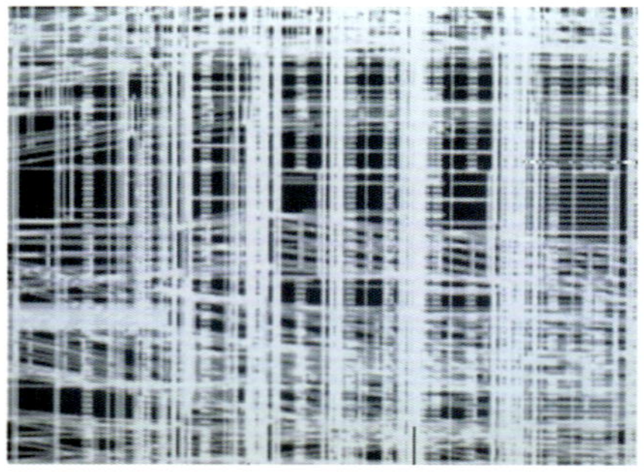

图2-6-3 b.平面和剖面的计算机模拟

毫无疑问，通信技术也改变了建筑的认知方式和视觉效果。传统建筑需要以纪念碑方式传达文化等信息。象征性建筑立面如雕塑一样重要。而在今天，文化和个性在急剧全球化的过程不断变化，用图像特别是因特网传递比用建筑立面更快、更有效，譬如一种形象可以在一秒钟时间内发送到几千个，甚至上百万个终端。同样，数码信息，无论是图像或是文字都无须出处或者物质场所。“对于建筑来说，这种视像也是建筑的形和空间秩序新的传达方式，逐渐替代传统的几何、材料和技术的传达方式，但是形和传播技术的结合也使形和形的组合方式发生改变（图2-6-3）。”[199]

当然，许多建筑师还在继续研究传统的材料，如石、砖和木材。但其他一些人却在探索新的通讯和建造技术的潜力。在世纪之交，总有对新技术既爱又怕的心理。而新的设计总是会关心今天这个时代的生活和本质的一些新课题。它们迎接新技术带来的挑战和问题，同时展示新的可能性。设计者“不应制造神话，应洗耳恭听新文化的含义，并在设计中解释这种含义”。[200] 这些新设计把我们的感觉扩大到世界范围。它们和传统不一样，不是先模仿自然，再以文化方式表达出来，而是用一种抽象、非物质、持续流动、不断变化的设计语言空间，表现“第二自然”。形虽不同，但都反对将建筑视为纪念碑，在这一点上它们可以说是对过去两千年的建筑史的反叛。更重要的是，正是这些设计第一次让建筑真正接近观众和使用者。

灵活内容

20世纪现代建筑的基础之一，形式和功能的紧密关系，在过去30年也受到挑战。如前文所述，社会空间不再依靠物质场所，而是“信息—体系”，社会空间的变化不需要改造建筑的墙或者走廊，不需要改变习俗或者法律。新的交流方式直接改革了社会形态，引入新社会运作方式，但建筑和城市形态并不随之而改变，社会空间的变化并不一定需要物质空间的变化。

另一方面，功能可以出现于不同形体中，甚至既可以在室内，也可以在室外。米罗维奇指出，电子传媒打破了某个场所和时间的特殊性。电视、收音机和电话把过去的私密空间变成公共空间。从某种意义上说，汽车音响、随身听和带微型显示屏的手提电话，则将公共空间私密化。“好像我们走到哪里，不同地方的事情就发生在哪里。”[201]

伯纳德·屈米认为建筑的本质不是形的构成，也不是功能，建筑本质是事件。[202] 他说自己的作品与概念艺术的动向有关，特别是电影，因为电影总是有行为和空间，事件同时是行动、活动或者运动。几十年来（如果不是几世纪以来），建筑设计的目的是找到空间根据，使其运作方式尽可能接近内容对它的要求。也就是说，设计是为了组织活动。与现代主义建筑相反，屈米主

D-17　畸形

畸形是指规则主导的设计中出现的不规则。一个原始的形可能部分加入一些异己，如打破、变形、重叠、消减或打碎等。畸形少量应用时会十分引人注意。如果畸形控制在限定范围内，可以创造出趣味中心。畸形带来运动和震动，因此将构图从单调中解放出来。当畸形规则应用到全部构图中时，原有的规则可能会完全改变，甚至在一个或多个区域变成无秩序。在这种情况下，畸形便威胁到设计的统一性。形的任何一种属性的改变都可能产生畸形，如形状、大小、颜色、质感、位置和方向等。

knowledge toward a multidisciplinary assembly. [198]

Communications technology has drastically changed the perception and visuality of architecture. Traditional architecture might often have functioned as monuments to impress viewers so that messages of culture or identity could be conveyed. Building facades were symbolically and visually important as sculptures. However, the message of culture and identity, which constantly changes in the rapid globalization process, can be better communicated by graphics, especially via the Internet. An identity can be sent out to thousands, perhaps millions, of destinations in one second. Likewise, electronic messages, whether graphic or textual, are received almost without recourse or physical location. "At stake for architecture is the degree to which this visuality and graphic cognition provides and alternative methodology and sensibility for producing architectural form and spatial order, outside the traditional implementations of geometry, history, or technological determinism—not as wholesale or full-scale replacements, but as transformative adjuncts which expand the vocabulary of form and technique (Pic.2-6-3)." [199]

While many architects remain in the traditional design realm of stone, brick, and wood, others are exploring new potentials offered by technology in realms of communication as well as of construction. There is also the counter-tendency, at the end of one millennium and the beginning of another, of profound ambivalence toward technology. New design normally suggests new stories, or new versions of old stories, about life and nature in our age. They often embody challenges and problems brought by new technology but certainly demonstrate new possibilities. The designers are "not creating myth but simply have an ear to the ground, picking up the sense of the culture and interpreting that sense in objects."[200] These designs expand the reach of our senses to global dimensions: seeing and hearing, or being seen or being heard, and from very far away. They do not simulate nature and present it as part of culture; rather the result is a design language that represents a "second nature", in an abstract, intangible, sense of continuously flowing and changing spaces. The forms may vary but they all oppose the assumption that building functions as if it were a monumental sculpture. In that case, they are unprecedented in more than two thousand years of architectural history. Another interesting aspect of these new designs is that buildings are moving closer to their audiences and users than ever before.

The Indeterminate Program

A close relationship between form and function, the foundations of Modernist 20th century architecture, has been challenged in the last 30 years. In fact, in "information-systems" rather than physical settings, a social space can be modified without building or removing walls or corridors, and perhaps more important, without changing customs and laws. The introduction and widespread use of this still-new medium of communication may restructure a broad range of situations and require new sets of social performances, but without changing any particular building or urban form. Social spaces can change without changing the physical container.

On the other hand a function can occur in different forms, or can be either interior or exterior in nature. As Meyrowitz pointed out, electronic media destroys the specialness of specific place and time. Television, radio, and telephone turn formerly private places into more public ones by making private paces more accessible to the outside world. Conversely, car stereos, the Sony "walkman", and mobile phones with built-in micro-TVs all make public spaces private. "Through such media, what is happening almost anywhere can be happening wherever we are." [201]

Bernard Tschumi regards the architectural essential is neither composition of form, nor function. Architecture is above all an event.[202] He claims that his work is related to what has happened in conceptual art and obviously, the

Anomaly

Anomaly is the presence of irregularity in a design in which regularity still prevails. An original shape may be made partially alien by disfiguration, transformation, and mutilation, cut up or broken up. When anomaly is used sparingly, it tends to stand out and attract immediate attention. Centre of interest can be created if anomaly happens only within a restricted area of design. Anomaly generates movement and vibration, and therefore relieve the composition from monotony. When anomaly principle is applied to whole design, the original regularity can be transformed into another. Or the regularity can be completely broken down into disorder in one or more areas. Anomaly seems to be more violent in this case threatening the unity of the design. Anomaly can happen in various properties of forms, such as shape, size, color, texture, position and direction.

图2-6-4 a.玻璃影像展廊外观

图2-6-4 b.内景

图2-6-5 展廊模型

张用灵活的内容代替僵化的功能。“建筑内容没有主次之分，建成的和在建的空间发生的，都同样重要。”建筑不仅是推进内容的物化，而且建筑自身应产生新的内容。他将这一认识又推进一步，直接声称他的作品是非物质建筑，这些非物质建筑通过事件——使用和内容的参与作用才变成真正的建筑。他设计的玻璃录像展览馆是透明的，白天几乎看不见（图2-6-4），里面用许多玻璃面反射无穷多电视屏幕画面。而建造起来的仅是一个背景、一个平台，要靠人的使用（打开电视机），真正的建筑才完成。所以“设计”的建筑最好应简单、平淡、被动——甚至以非物质形态出现——这样不仅能满足原有内容的需要，而且能超越这些内容进入新的活动场景（图2-6-5）。活动一旦进入建筑就应该成为产生新活动的动力。

“从20世纪初到90年代的建筑发展史可以视为从封闭到开放的过程。”[203] “开放空间”指建筑只有结构，没有目的，从而让结构自由服务于不同的目的（图2-6-6）。所以，建筑内应该没有封闭空间，空间只是交错重叠。来自威尼斯的蓝天合作事务所认为“19世纪那种建筑已经结束，我们必须用复杂性去处理全球社会的多样性”。“蓝天合作”的主将沃尔夫·普里克斯曾生动地描述他的设计方法，即空间营造不受某些特定功能的限制。

> *由于业主并不清楚自己想要什么，我们把大量时间用于交谈。但谈话的内容是关于情绪营造而不是功能或者需求。住宅不仅是房子，而且是一种感觉。形体和细部并不重要，重要的是光、高度、重量和视野。为了集中思想，我不用草图，而是闭上眼睛，用手势来表达袭来的感觉。我们画出来的甚至不应该叫作设计图，而应称为住宅精神图式（图2-6-7）。*[204]

艺术的本质是提出新问题。20世纪60年代的现代艺术活动针对历时性、瞬间性、事件性和务实性等问题做了许多探索。艺术评论家认为，现代艺术是对传统的学术权威的决裂。[205] 建筑学也是一种传统的学术，它的最大的问题是以自我为参照体系（即回到建筑本体等有关主张），总是在提出问题前就已经知道了自己的答案。

20世纪初，建筑的形态强调以严肃的和科学的准则为参照系。今天，这种参照系日益和灵活性、运行效果等概念连在一起。那种没有固定形态、内部灵活、可重组的大规模的结构似乎成为一种趋势。[206] 建筑形趋于集中、统一、内向，而且没有尺度，结构极简，内部空间灵活多变，立面一般不强调体块、材料和质感。

D-18　割裂

形状可以被部分割裂，或完全割裂成几个部分。割裂的边可能留作碎片，暗示一种外力的破坏。这种手法不常用。

Splitting

The shape may be split partially or completely into several fragments. The splitted edge might be left ragged to suggest a forced break. The operation is seemingly accidental.

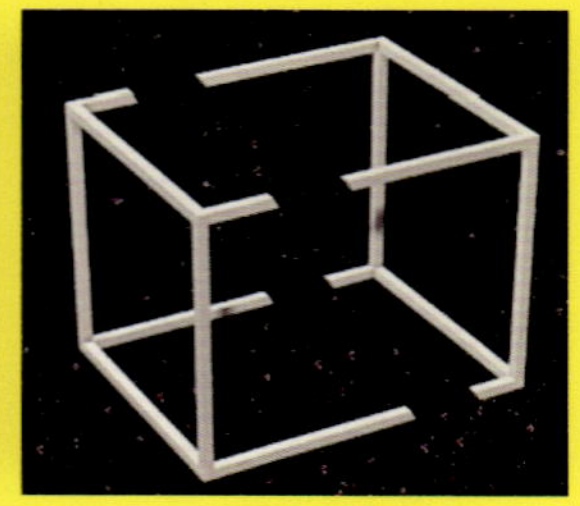

图2-6-6 奥地利建筑师沃恩德尔设计的“住宅概念”，1993年

图2-6-7 蓝天合作事务所设计的“开放住宅”，1990年

cinema, because movie relates to both space and action at the same time. Events are simultaneously actions, activities, and motion. To design architecture has been for decades (if not centuries) to find a means of spatial notation, which approaches as closely as possible to the definitions given by a program; in other words, the event organized. In contrast to Modernist architecture, here an indeterminate program replaces static function. “It is not possible to give priority to one aspect of architecture over another, to what is built or to what happens inside what is built”. Architecture is not only the materialization of the concepts embedded within the program, but should also generate new programs by itself. The architect can therefore push the concept even further. He can legitimately claim his work is to create an immaterial architecture that would be materialized either by an event, by its use, or by the program. The glass video museum is transparent and invisible except at night (Pic.2-6-4). It is like a hall of mirrors – the video screens are duplicated ad infinitum in every direction. It means what is built is only a background or platform for people to use, and made complete by virtue of that use. The “designed” architecture is therefore, preferably simple, plain, and passive – even immaterial – not only to meet the demands of the original program but now to extend the program into new territory (Pic.2-6-5). Once grounded within built structure, the ever-evolving program becomes a generator of new events.

“In fact, architectural history through the 20th century and into the 1990s can be interpreted as a path from a closed to an open space.” [203] Open space means architecture is built with structures without objectives, in order to release structures for free use(Pic.2-6-6). As result, there should be no enclosed spaces; they just interlace and open up. The Viennese firm Coop Himmelblau claimed that “architecture, as it was proposed in the 19th century, is over. We have to go for a complexity that mirrors the diversity of world society.” Coop Himmelblau principal Wolf Prix described his design method when specific functions could not be identified to dictate the space created:

> *We spent a lot of time talking to the client because he was not sure what he really wanted. But this discussion was for defining emotional, rather than functional, needs. The house existed not as a building but as a feeling. The form and the details were not important; what were important were the lighting, the height, the weight and even the view. In order not to be led astray, not even by the graphics, I closed my eyes and used my hands as a graph of the feelings that arose. We did not call it an architectural drawing, but rather a psychogram of the house (Pic.2-6-7).*[204]

Art by nature is meant to ask new questions. Modern art of the 1960s can be seen as a playing field where questions here asked about duration, the short-term quality, and the quality of being event-like and pragmatic. Art critics suggest that modern art is a way of breaking out of the authority of the established discourse. [205] Similarly, established architectural discourse has been a remains, to its great demerit – self-referential to the point that it always knows the answers to its own questions in advance.

In the early 20th century, architectural typologies emphasized the emergence of critical and scientific criteria and principles, neatly summarized as “form-follows-function”. Today, however, typology is not so much addressed as a creative method towards a new form, because the form is no longer seen as crucial. Building programmes today increasingly talk about concepts like flexibility and performance. They increasingly demand large-scale structures without fixed qualities of their own, and which can be flexibly programmed. [206] Their forms tend to favor neutrality, monotony, introversion and scalelessness. Facades are normally rendered immaterial by the tectonics of minimal surfaces and huge, simple spaces within.

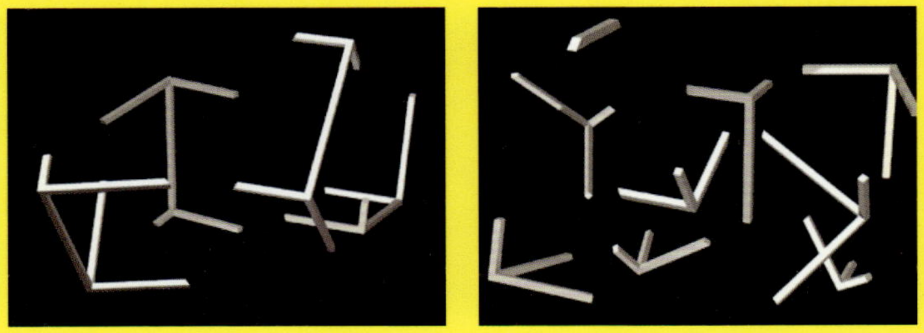

图2-7-1 a.毕加索《吉他构成》，1912年

图2-7-1 b.欧桑方《构成》，1925年

2.7 结语：关于创造性

建筑形的创作方法研究都会指向同一个结论，即建筑师的创造性来自与建筑本身无关的过程。有时这个过程可以通过培养训练而掌握，一定程度上结果在意料之中，有时它却是偶然的，出乎预料的。柯布西耶写道："创造性是一种耐心的探索。"他甚至直截了当地指出创造性心智的培养只有依靠艺术。

> *（现代人）需要理想的安全感，过去它来自宗教。现在由于对宗教和一切玄学的怀疑，人们把目光转向自己，这个真实世界的所在。但由此而来的痛苦空虚却无法弥补……除了用艺术……艺术以高级精神享受为使命，给人以精神满足，没有它，人们的心将无法平静。*[207]

艺术的创造性

想象——敢于梦想不可能的事物——是创造性的关键组成元素之一。想象超越既有的才智，是发展创造性活动的精神过程。

设计领域的创造性可以通过了解和从事其他创造性艺术活动调动起来，这些艺术包括文学、绘画、雕塑、摄影、舞蹈、音乐、舞美设计和戏剧等。20世纪初的包豪斯教学计划通过戏剧、印刷和绘画课程，向建筑系学生展示这些不同的艺术领域。当时的建筑师与前卫艺术家和画家关系密切，要么参与他们的讨论和组织，要么直接合作。柯布西耶早年曾经想做一名画家，后来，绘画却成了通向一个更大目标的方法。绘画是他的视觉试验室，他的未来建筑的试验地。"实际上我的艺术创作开始于1918年，作为画家而开始进行绘画创作，从此我没有一天间断过绘画。"[208]"通过绘画，我找到了建筑的形。"[209] 如果没有布拉克和毕加索在学术和生活两方面对柯布亚耶的巨大影响，他也许不可能形成自己的设计思想。如果他没有和阿姆丢·欧桑方合作并结友，他也不会成为理想立体主义艺术家（图2-7-1）。许多伟大的建筑师，无论古代还是现代的，都兴趣广泛，都想在不同的领域开发自己的潜质。如列奥纳多·达·芬奇（画家、科学家、发明家），米开朗琪罗（艺术家和雕塑家），路易斯·康（画家），柯布西耶（画家、雕塑家、规划师），阿尔瓦·阿尔托（艺术家、雕塑家），弗兰克·盖瑞（雕塑家），和丹尼尔·利比斯金（音乐家）等都是典型的例子。他们的速写也无不反映活跃的思想。他们的方案设计和建筑表现了不断演化的生动的形体和空间素质并且在作品中没有一个重复的设计，每个作品都有特殊的地位。他们在艺术领域的活动实际上强化了他们的设计技能，培养了他们的哲学思考，释放了他们的艺术天分，同时让他们在建筑的创造性工作中能随心所欲。阿尔瓦·阿尔托曾说：

D–19　切断和取消部分形状

Cutting and Removing Parts of Shape

形状的一部分或几部分可以切断和取消，改变其边界或创造出负形。

A portion, or portions of a shape can be cut and removed, altering its edge, or producing negative shapes.

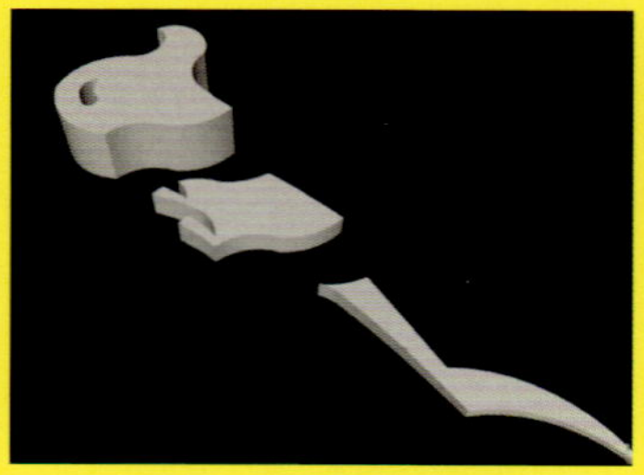

图2-7-1 c.勒·柯布西耶《竖放的吉他》，1921年

2.7 Concluding Remarks: Creativity

Studying numerous methodologies an architect may adopt in developing architectural forms reinforces the idea that creativity is a process triggered and sustained by disparate sources. One idea leads to and generates another one. Sometimes, this process may be cultivated, trained; to an extent, results may be reliably summoned at will. For others, it may simply happen spontaneously and unexpectedly. Le Corbusier wrote: "Creativity is a Patient Search". He believed that only by means of art could a creative mind can be cultivated:

> *(Modern man) has need of the ideal certainties which previously religion gave him; doubting it now and metaphysics also, he is driven in on himself where the true world goes on within; the anguishing emptiness which nothing can fill … except art … Art will have the mission of superior distraction and it will give this exalted contentment without which the calm of the soul is impossible.* [207]

Creativity in Art

Imagination— "daring to dream the impossible"—is one of the crucial elements in cultivating creativity. Imagination relates to more than inherent talent. Imagination is the mental process through which creative activity is developed.

Creativity in any design field can be greatly enriched and stimulated through continuous efforts to read and work in other creative arts, such as literature, painting, sculpture, photography, dancing, music, stage setting, and drama. The Bauhaus program in the early 20th century attempted to provide and expose its architecture students to this diverse field of arts through theatre, printing, and painting. Architects of that time also closely associated with the avant-garde artists and painters, either by joining their discussion or groups, or by directly collaborating with them. In his early years, Le Corbusier originally intended to become a painter. However, painting eventually became a means to a larger end. Painting was his visual laboratory, the field of experimentation for his future architecture. "In reality, the key to my artistic creativity is found in the work I began as a painter in 1918 and which I pursued regularly every day."[208] "It is through painting that I've found the forms for my architecture."[209] Le Corbusier might never have formulated his design ideas were it not for Braque and Picasso, who exerted enormous influence on the architect, both formally as well as in life style. Nor would he have gained an understanding of cubism were it not for his association and friendship with the painter Amadeus Ozenfant(Pic.2-7-1). Many great architects, ancient and contemporary, had diverse interests and the desire to explore their potentials in multiple disciplines. Leonardo da Vinci (painter, scientist, inventor), Michelangelo (painter, sculptor), Le Corbusier (painter, sculptor, city planner), Alvar Aalto (artist, sculptor), Louis Kahn (painter), Frank Gary (sculptor), and Daniel Libeskind (musician) are a few notable examples. Even their sketch paintings illustrate glimpses of their diverse thinking and ideas. Their projects and buildings demonstrate ever-evolving and dynamic formal and spatial qualities. Rarely would a project repeat itself in another context, but each is unique in its nature and claims its own right to exist. It is interesting to note that their activities in peripheral arts actually equip them with diverse skills, cultivate their philosophy, emancipate their artistic potential, and offer them a good deal of "relaxation" from their creative work in architecture. As Alvar Aalto noted:

D–20 错位

Dislocation

一个形强加到另一个场景中去，它所带来的矛盾成为吸引注意力的要素。

A form from family setting can be injected and impose to another setting, in which the conflicts maintained as attractions to the viewer.

图2-7-2 西拉《地板上的支撑柱》，1969年

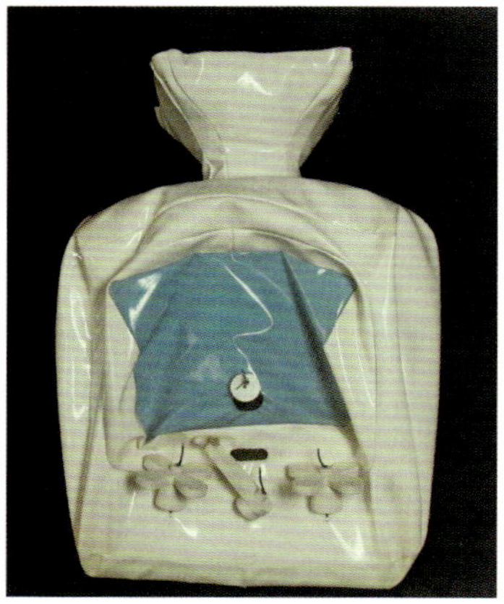

图2-7-3 奥登伯格《软性洗水池》，1965年

绘画和雕塑是我工作的一部分，它们和我的建筑关系密切，而且可以表达建筑以外的东西。许多建筑师将绘画作为一种独立的活动，在我却不同。也许有人会说我的雕塑和绘画并不属于真正专业的艺术。当然要证明这一点也很难，但对我来说，它们是一棵树上的分杈，而主干是建筑。[210]

弗兰克·盖里的创作灵感来自他长期与艺术家的协作、交流和合作。“路易斯住宅的形来自我在布拉格的ING办公楼（1995）。理查德·西拉看到了，因为在我的设计过程中，他常来我的工作室，他很感兴趣，并自己做了两个模型（图2-7-2）。我也常受奥登伯格的作品《膝盖》的影响（尽管我并没有意识到），但就在我的工作室，奥登伯格开始为高尔夫俱乐部做袋子（图2-7-3），开始和西拉一样对我的工作室的那些形状感兴趣……就是这样，我们的想象力相互补充，相互促进。”[211]

其他学科的影响

现代艺术的特点之一是它与不同学科结合交汇，是从艺术到建筑、设计、音乐、电影和时装设计等的一个创造过程。“如果你一直睁大眼睛关注他人的工作，你将会感受到他们的影响，创造性灵感不时地出现。”[212] 20世纪艺术评论家罗莎琳德·克劳斯分析了几位环境艺术家的作品，讨论他们叠加式的创作方法。[213] 如玛丽·米斯在纽约长岛场地的改建作品，看起来它是一块洼地，它给人的第一印象既是雕塑，又非雕塑（图2-7-4）。另一些“大地艺术”流派，包括场所标识，如，迈克尔·海哲尔在内华达州黑石沙漠中的作品，用一些木箱精心插入干涸的湖底（图2-7-5）。他的另一个大型的作品《双重负面》，是在摩门山边峭壁上的一道刻痕（图2-7-6），令人联想到地壳运动及其和土建工程的关系。这又是一种双重解读，在艺术和工程学间游移不定。它既是一种与景观的结合，但也是与景观的分离。克劳斯认为这类作品如山石碑刻，是通过改造环境传达某种概念。“这些作品的核心，作为雕塑的定义转换了。”“尽管这些作品与其介入的自然环境结合紧密，但也不是景观设计，同样，尽管在材料运用、建造技术等方面反映建筑特性，但也不是建筑。”这些雕塑艺术运作于雕塑和景观学科的分界面。

自从艺术进入建筑、城市规划和景观设计，安吉列尔就开始质疑建筑研究是否还有作茧自缚的必要。他主张用“建筑外化”的创作方式。“建筑的边界应从无，即非建筑，开始向外推进。”[214]

过去10年对建筑影响最大的学科之一也许是环境科学。可持续发展观

图2-7-4 米斯《标杆/亭子/陷阱》，1977—1978年

D–21　注入

向一个形里插入一个异形，则打破了它的稳定性和规则性。异形不断增多增大，使整个构图不断发生变化，直至形成一个新的规则形。

Injection

Inserting an alien form in to another and the stability and regularity of the latter is disturbed. The injected form usually seems grow in size or quantity. As a result the whole composition is in a continuously changing process, until a new regularity forms.

图2-7-5 海哲尔《内华达州的干湖，放荡2号》，1968年

图2-7-6 海哲尔《双重负面》，1969—1970年

The paintings and the sculptures area a part of my method of working, which is why I unwillingly see them as separated from my architecture, as if they could express something beyond it. Many architects have devoted themselves to painting as a separate activity. For me, the situation is different. One could say that I don't regard my sculptures and paintings as something that belongs to these professions. It is difficult to prove from case to case but they are for me branches of the same tree whose trunk is architecture. [210]

Frank Gehry's continuous association, interaction and collaboration with artists is an important source of his creativity. "For the Lewis house, I made shapes that derive from my ING office tower in Prague (1995). Richard Serra saw them, because he came here often while I was working on it; he was intrigued and made two models of his own (Pic.2-7-2). I was also looking back at Oldenburg's Knees (though I wasn't conscious of it), and then here in my studio, he started making bags for golf clubs (Pic.2-7-3). He had begun to look at the same shapes Serra was interested in...So there is a process of fertilizing one another's imagination. Nobody got in anybody's way." [211]

Association with Other Disciplines

Crossing borders of various disciplines, from fine art to architecture, to design, to music, film and fashion (among many others) is a creative process commonly witnessed in modern art history. "If you see other people's work constantly, if you keep your eyes open, and you're influenced by other people's work, (creative inspiration) will happen over time. "[212] The prominent 20th century art critic Rosalind Krauss analyzed several landscape artists and discussed their overlapping approaches.[213] For example, a site construction by Mary Miss on Long Island in New York could be considered simply as a pit in the earth (Pic.2-7-4). The first impression it gave was that it was both sculpture and nonsculpture. Other examples of the Land Art interventions genre include the marking of sites, such as Michael Heizer's incisions in the Black Rock Desert of Nevada, created by means of a series of wooden boxes carefully depressed within an existing dried lakebed(Pic.2-7-5). At a much larger scale, Michael Heizer's *Double Negative*, a cut within a cliff at the edge of the Mormon Mesa(Pic.2-7-6), recalls earth movements generally associated with civil engineering works. A similar double reading occurs here; one is left wondering whether it is art or engineering. This work is undoubtedly part of, and apart from, the landscape. Such structures, according to Krauss, are axiomatic in the sense that they belong to the transformation of a given condition based on the deployment of specific concepts. "At the core of these works, the very definition of sculpture seems to have been displaced". "As art works they are non-landscape, although inherently connected to the natural sites in which they are inserted. Similarly, they are non-architecture, although inherently tied to aspects of materiality, building technique, and production." Sculptural art operates on the outer limits of sculpture and landscape.

Since art has already penetrated into architecture, urban planning and landscape, Angelil questions the merit of architectural study limited to its own internal discourse. He suggests that approaches attempting what could be termed "externalization of architecture" need to be taken into consideration. "The limits of architecture need to be pushed from without, from that which it is not." [214]

D–22 弯曲

Curving or Bending

运用弯曲的原理，一个对称的矩形可以在改变朝向。

A symmetrical and rectangular form can change its orientation in the middle by using the principle of curving or bending.

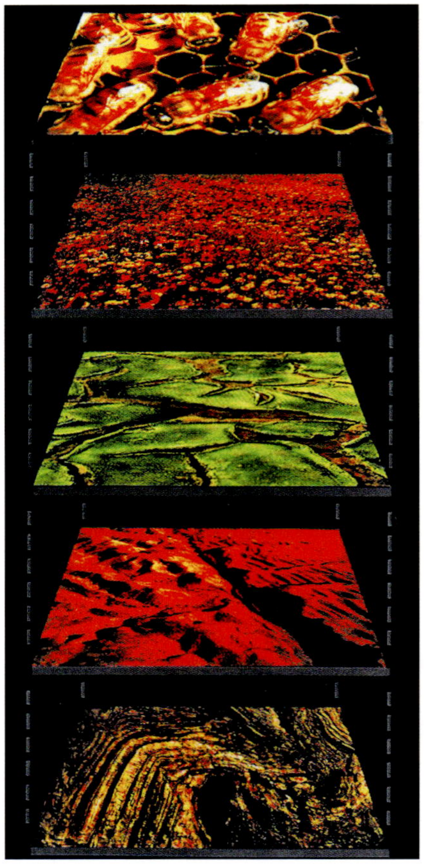

图2-7-7 基地地层分析图示

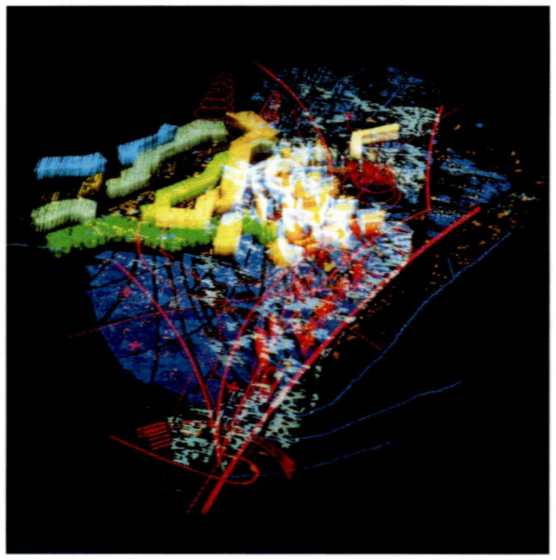

图2-7-8 “实验室”事务所设计的大学规划计算机模拟

念，即环境科学的社会口号，影响之广——从全世界政府的政策到日常购物袋都可以体现。环境科学也在建立新的目标。新美学，尤其是新的观念思想方面影响建筑和城市规划。例如新城开发现在必须考虑生态指标。总体规划中基地分析要结合环境工程学提供的生态基础数据。代表不同的水文和地貌因素的一系列层面使多维的数据分析成为可能。这些层面包括（图2-7-7）：

动物群：通过检测地区内生物的种类和分布，保护自然栖息物种的生态型组合。

植被：从视觉形象、机能状态等方面评价基地内生长的植物。

水文：水体和水系对总体规划的影响是多方面的。如调节性水面可以控制排灌，为夏季用水高峰期储存充足的水源。

地形：基础设施规划，居住/商业用地分布，以及景观设计都需要根据地形来确定。

地质和土壤：土壤的水渗性和地质条件对建筑的分布有决定性影响。良好的排水可以预防积水和水土流失。[215]

在澳大利亚一所大学的规划中，“试验室”设计事务所将生态知识作为规划和空间组织的内容依据。[216] 他们认为“生态系统”既非原始自然，也不是对自然的模仿和照搬，而是一种抽象的交织网络（图2-7-8）。它体现为大量不同的，动态性强的，相互关联的元素，这些元素以不同方式相互作用。所以生态系统不是设计出来的，而是在进化中自然形成的。大学规划的目标是建立进化最佳初始条件，提供促进这种进化的灵活而必要的措施。为了成功，要允许失败。他们规划的是一块连续的建造场地，是一组将教育、宿舍和管理结合为一体的高度灵活的网络（图2-7-9）。传统的大学教育结构、模式和特点在他们的设计中荡然无存。

安德利亚·布兰兹认为21世纪应始于一种“人造世界的生态学”，或者是他称之为建筑的第二次现代性，即以一种平衡的“生态”设计，一种介于技术和人文之间的媒介，作为宽松的管理工具。[217]

强调现实性

创造性来自敏锐的眼光，对日常现实的长期观察，从中抓住未来的迹象。有些建筑师认为，当今社会的基本现实是建立在竞争和经济之上的生产和消费文化。他们将其称为“新国际主义”，以示和20世纪早期的国际化相区别。他们认为20世纪70年代开始的对地方性和少数民族文化的研究和评价已经接近尾声。与过去的看法不同，传统的地方文化和少数民族文化，无法改变今日的现实。这些文化，即使不会完全消失，也会在全球化发展过程中逐渐沉寂。建筑学要生

D–23 卷曲

Curling

坚硬的平面通过卷曲，产生一种运动或有机性，这时可以看作一个柔软的平面。

A hard plan form can be treated as a soft plane that curls to reveal a movement or organic character.

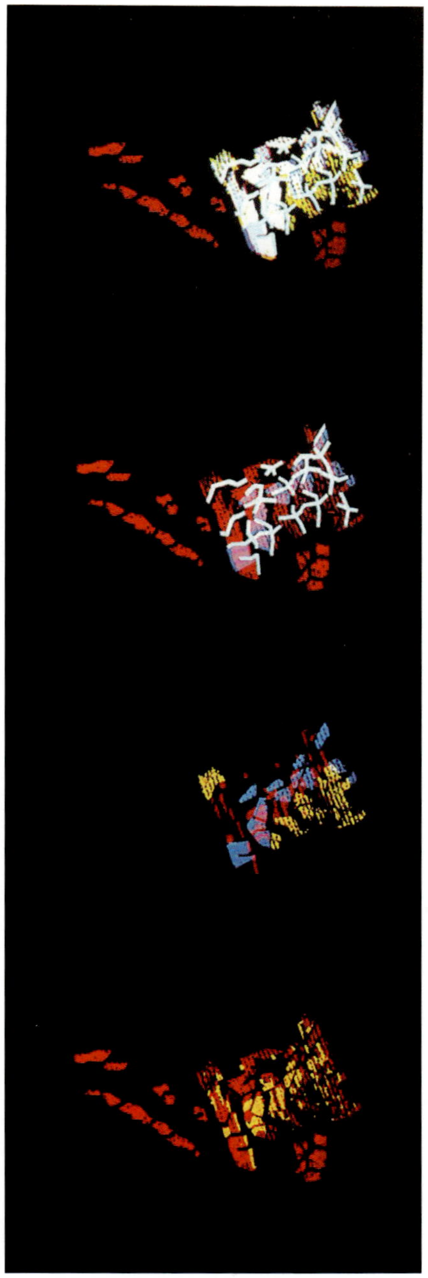

图2-7-9 a.科系、活动、设备、功能和景观的体量分析和组合

In last ten years among the most influential disciplines—if not the most influential – has been environmental science. The concept of sustainable development, the political flagship of environmental science, makes its presence felt in government policies worldwide as well as in the prosaic shopping bag. Environmental science influences architecture and urban planning in the forms of new objectives, new aesthetics, and most important, new conceptual programmes. For example, it has become necessary to include all ecological parameters underlying the development of a new town. An environmental engineering approach to master planning gives any site analysis an ecological basis. A matrix of analytical data can be created with a number of layers representing individual factors such as hydrology and topography. Layers to be considered include (Pic.2-7-7):

Fauna: By monitoring and recording the type and location of the wildlife of the region, the biotic composition of the natural habitat can be preserved.

Flora: The species growing on the site are assessed for their visual appearance, effect, and physical condition.

Hydrology: The water table and the natural watercourses across the site can have many implications for the form of the master plan. Balancing ponds, for example, can ensure a manageable degree of irrigation, as well as acting as a reservoir for summer water supply.

Topography: The topography of the land is instrumental when planning the infrastructure, and locating the residential/commercial areas and designing the landscape.

Geology and Soils: The permeability and geology of an area also have a determining role in positioning elements throughout the site. It is preferable to build in areas with good drainage and avoid those where water erosion or accumulation will occur. [215]

LAB design office took an ecological understanding as the programmatic basis for the planning and spatial organization for a university in Australia.[216] They saw an "ecosystem" neither as virginal nature nor as a representation or mapping of nature, but rather as an abstract, differentiated network (Pic.2-7-8). Characterized by large numbers of diverse, highly mobile and interlinked components that communicate through one or more modes, ecosystems simply cannot be "designed". Instead, they must self-organize through evolution. Therefore, the goal of master-planning the university (FGU) therefore becomes a best effort to structure the initial conditions and the dynamics necessary to stimulate such an evolution. In order to succeed, it must genuinely risk failure. The master plan actually consists of a continuous field of construction, which is in fact a highly dynamic network combining education, accommodation, and management (Pic.2-7-9). The traditional structures, models and character of university education have the potential for complete revision in LAB's design.

Andrea Branzi has proposed that the 21st century started with an "ecology of the artificial world", or as he calls it, the Second Modernity of architecture, which was based on a balanced, "ecological" notion of design as a benign management tool, a mediator between technocratic and humanistic cultures. [217]

Being Real

A creative mind is a sensitive mind which constantly observes everyday reality and capably grasps any indication of future change. Today some architects find that essential reality comes from a productive culture based on competition and economic priorities. They call it the New Internationalism with reference to the "old" version from

存，不仅应面对时代的问题，而且要发明社会交流新形体，因为旧东西已无关今日之痛痒。另一种正在出现的世界性现实是“新工业主义”，它代表新的功能主义和新的共同性战略。它来自全球工业文化，或者公共“消费文化”，它追从霸权垄断，排挤其他对手。它有自己的运作规律，对灵活性的质量重新定义。它尊重多样性，但这种多样性不能越出一条底线，即消费。今天的每个城市直接或间接为全球市场服务，扎根于后工业社会土壤。这也是为什么任何地方的设计都可以从周围的社会活动及其关系来分析研究。21世纪初的创造性思想认为，今日的全球化大趋势并不来自各自孤立的少数文化体系，而是来自相互间的融合，以及技术进步和全球后工业社会对新文化的需要。今天的国际化社会和全球市场是新的时代性，是这个时代的最基本的现实。所有以往的建筑理论都显得捉襟见肘，因为它们在形成过程中从未面对过这样的现实。今天的创造性心灵必须探索恰当的负责任的建筑答案。今日的世界有许多新名字，如信息时代、生态时代、全球市场、地球村、后工业社会等，我们无疑面对着许多新事物、新现象和新的需要，建筑无先例可循。

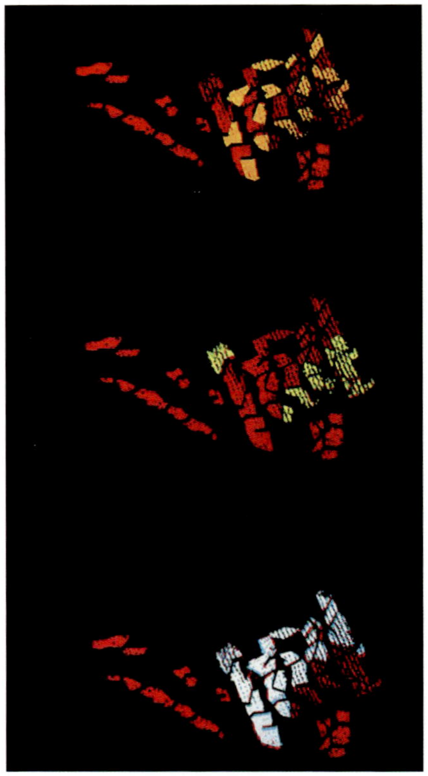

图2-7-9 b.科系、活动、设备、功能和景观的体量分析和组合

今天的建筑学存在的根本问题，还是如柯布西耶很久以前指出的，“有眼无珠，看不见时代的新美（图2-7-10）”。阳光下的一切事物都可以从美学的角度来评价，都可以成为品位和文化的中心。新建筑的形，无论是否已被解构，都需要建立在新的美学基础之上。不仅建筑师，所有的人如果长期面对异形世界都会有恐惧感。但无论如何，创造性心灵已决定跨越权威，走入未知世界。因为在未知世界发现新事物的渴望，是在已知世界中保持心理健康的必要条件。

今天，许多关于建筑形的问题还没有答案。

如果“建筑作为一个物体”矗立在地面上，对周围的新动向无动于衷，这种传统的建筑观是否真的结束了，建筑是否需要成为不断扩张的地域或者连续建造结构网络的一部分？

如果传统的“景观”观念是片面的，一块场地的空间是否还有必要由建筑来主导？

如果传统的基础设施和建筑分离在现代不断变化的城市中问题多多，那么一座与基础设施结为一体的，或者像基础设施一样运作的建筑应具有什么样的形象？

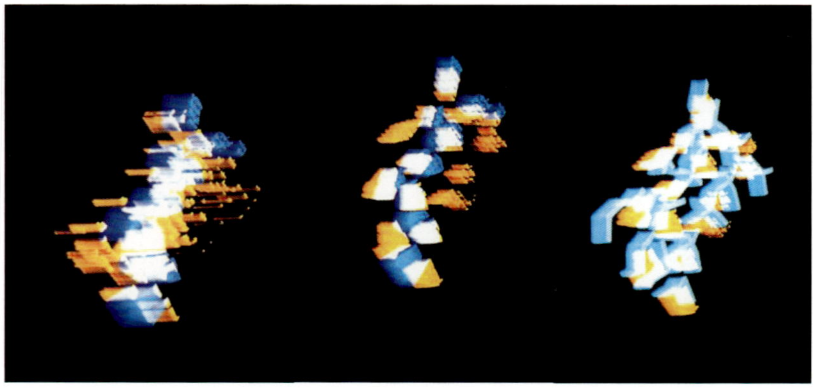

图2-7-9 c.科系、活动、设备、功能和景观的体量分析和组合

如果建筑技术的进步不断将建筑的立面变薄，变轻，更加透明，更加灵活地适应空间、光线和通风等的需求变化，那么如何利用仅有的稳

D-24　扭动

Twisting

一个形状可以通过绕一点或一个轴扭动，使其中部变窄，两端的方向改变。

A shape can be distorted by twisting it about a point or axis, narrowing its middle and changing orientation of the two ends.

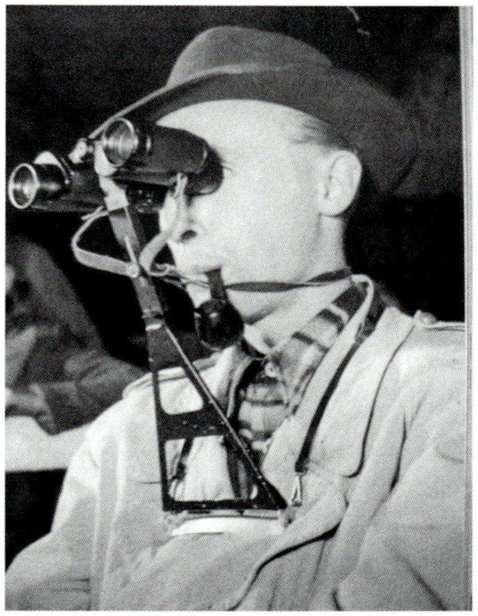

图2-7-10 1951年发明的望远镜免提支架

the early 20th century. They believe that the wave of research and evaluation into the world's local and minority cultures, which took off in the 1970s, is now declining. Traditional, local and minority cultures, contrary to previous consensus, do not provide viable alternatives to our current reality, and will eventually quietly retreat within the same global development model if not completely disappear. To survive, let alone address the problems of our time, one must invent new forms of social communication, because older ones are losing relevance. Another emerging world reality is New Industrialism, which means a new functionalism, and a new corporate strategy. This is the result of worldwide industrial culture, an explicit consumption culture that has removed all other alternatives in its quest for hegemony. It writes its own rules, and assumes new codes of flexibility and quality. It respects differences, provided such differences do not invalidate the bottom line, which again is consumption. Today, any city or building directly and indirectly serves the global market, and is embedded within a total post-industrial landscape. Thus it is possible to read any design in terms of surrounding social events and their mutual relationships. In our early 21st century, creative minds discover that emerging global trends do not originate from segregated development of minority cultures, but instead correspond, on the whole, to the technological and cultural needs of global post-industrial society. The present international society and the global market is the new Zeitgeist, the essential reality of our age and the new epoch. All previous established architectural discourse is handicapped because it was not invented to cope with this new reality. Today's creative minds have to find more suitable and responsive architectural answers. While there is no shortage of possible names for this era, such as the Information Age, the Ecological Age, the Global Market, the Earth Village, the Post-industrial Earth, etc., it is quite clear there are many events, phenomena and demands upon us now, which truly have no precedent.

The problem today remains one which Le Corbusier recognized long ago: "eyes which do not see the new beauty of the age (Pic.2-7-10). " Everything under the sun—in the universe—can be appreciated from an aesthetic point of view; and anything can act as a center around which taste and culture can form. New forms of architecture, de-formed or not, has to build upon a new aesthetics. Admittedly, many people, not only architects, will face negative side effects if they perpetually see the world as alien territory. By no means do creative minds need to constantly break beyond the established and enter the unknown. The promise of fresh discoveries in an unknown land is ideally balanced by a psychologically healthy anchorage in the known.

Today there are a great many questions about architectural form which remain Unanswered. A few are as follows:

If the conventional "architecture-as-object" is placed onto the land and nakedly exposed to newer approaches, can it still be considered a legitimate or welcome part of an ever-expanding field or network of built structure?

If the receiving site is perceived to suffer handicaps from a traditional viewpoint of what "landscape" ought to be, should the site in question be eligible for architectural consideration in the first place?

If the traditional segregation of infrastructure and architecture is no longer tenable in the constantly changing city, what does a building which functions as infrastructure look like?

If advances in building technology lead to building envelopes which are thinner, lighter, more transparent, and which more flexibly accommodate changes of space, light and ventilation, how shall the remaining minimal material be used to create a form, which is almost invisible?

D–25 波动

Weaving

两个以上的线性元素，或软或硬，可以一起扭动，创造出一个动态整体，同时保持元素的个性。

More than two liner elements, hard or soft, can be twisted together, to create a unit and dynamic whole while maintaining the individual character of the elements.

定材料构件去塑造建筑的几乎看不到的形？

如果建筑边界继续变得模糊，内外的关系会是怎样的？“室外”意味着什么？

如果建筑需要适应不断变化的内容（并不断产生新的活动），建筑是一种不断设计的过程，那么功能制定、取消、转换、缩短是否还是不变的设计策略？

如果一座建筑不再需要像纪念性雕塑一样传达信息——无论是以西方传统建筑的外在方式还是20世纪现代主义的内在方式——建筑设计是否应取消造型，或者形的构成？造型是否不再重要？如果不是这样，是否有鉴别形式游戏的新标准？

如果一座城市没有传统观念上的“建筑”——由于解型，非物质化，尺度模糊化，由非建筑学科交叉和专断的影响——人们将怎样在城市中生活，并仍旧能欣赏建筑的美？

D–26　皱褶

卷缩或揉皱一个形可以得到皱褶的效果，这里尖角连续出现在表面上。皱褶不会影响形的本质。

Creasing

Curling and rippling a shape can cause creases effect, in which a sharp angle appears in the formally continuos surface. Creasing can be effected only halfway down the shape.

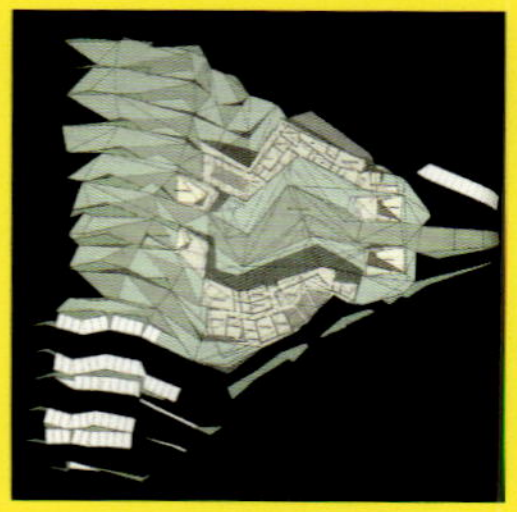

If the boundaries of a given building are now blurred, what is the new relation between inside and outside? And what is "outside" for?

If design is a life-long process where a building accommodates constantly changing programmes (which in turn generate new programmes), should programming, removal, displacement, and foreshortening therefore be considered legitimate design strategies?

If a building is no longer needed to communicate the messages of a monumental sculpture—either externally as in the Western Classical mode, or internally as 20th century Modernists might promote—should form, or composition of form, now be neglected in architectural design? Has form making been discounted and rendered irrelevant? If not, then what other rules can discrete architectural form play?

In a city without "architecture" as conventionally understood—due to deformation, dematerialization, scalar ambiguity, interventions or hegemonic influence by non-architectural disciplines—how shall people live, move about and appreciate the aesthetics of architecture?

D–27 理想化

Transfiguration

通过优化部分或全部形，可以将形理想化。

A form can be transfigured by changing a portion of the form or the entire form to something representational.

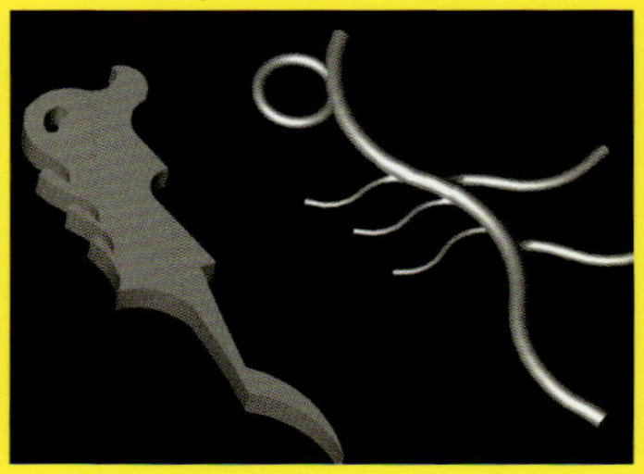

English Descriptions of Illustrations in the Main Text

（插图英文说明）

Pic.1-1-1	St. Andrea, Mantua by Alberti, around 1470
Pic.1-1-2	L. da Vince (1452—1519) , pencil
Pic.1-1-3	Plan and dome of St. Peter by Michelangelo, Rome 16th century
Pic.1-1-4	Illustration from Ten Books of Architecture by Alberti in 1651
Pic.1-1-5	Tower of Baoen Temple in Nanjing illustrated by Fischer von Erlach, 18th Century
Pic.1-1-6	Ink rendering,19th century
Pic.1-1-7	Drawing by Voillet suggest substitution of new materials for traditional material in late 19th century
Pic.1-1-8	Former Architectural Department of University of Pennsylvania (now library of art collage)
Pic.1-1-9	a. L. Kahn's student work published by the school in 1928. A Monumental Fountain
	b. Salk Institute California, 1959—1965
Pic.1-2-1	Street in poverty quarter London by Gustave Dorè, 1872
Pic.1-2-2	The Artists' Colony by J.M. Olbrich in Darmstadt, 1907
Pic.1-2-3	Hôtel Tassel by Victor Horta, 1893
Pic.1-2-4	Art School designed by van de Velde in Weimar
Pic.1-3-1	House by Le Corbusier Wiesenhofsiedlung Stuttgart, 1927
Pic.1-3-2	Facade of John D. van Allen & Son Store, Iowa by L. Sullivan, 1911—1914
Pic.1-3-3	Window from the Ca' Foscari, Venice, drawn by J. Ruskin
Pic.1-3-4	The opening characters of a page or chapter by w. Morris, 1896
Pic.1-3-5	"Gypsy Girl with Mandolin" by J B. Corot, 1874
Pic.1-3-6	"Seated Nude" by P. Picasso, 1909—1910
Pic.1-3-7	"Woman with a fan" by A. Archipenko, 1914
Pic.1-3-8	"Man with a Guitar" by J. Lipchitz, 1916
Pic.1-3-9	"Still like with Pile of Plates" by Le Corbusier, 1920
Pic.1-3-10	"Proun Room" by EI Lissitzky, 1923
Pic.1-3-11	"Complex Corner Relief" by V. Tatin, 1915
Pic.1-3-12	Process of abstraction by Theo van Doesburg, formed the "Sower" (1889—1890) by V. van Gogh to stained glad window, 1921—1922
Pic.1-3-13	Rietveld-Schoeder House, Utrecht, 1924
Pic.1-3-14	Row house by J.J.P. Oud in Wiesenhofsiedlung Stuttgart, 1927
Pic.1-3-15	"Counter-construction" by T.van Doesburg, 1923
Pic.1-3-16	Barcelona Pavilion by Mies van der Rohe (reconstructed), 1929
Pic.1-3-17	Broadway Boogie Woogie by P. Mondrian, 1942—1943
Pic.1-3-18	Master plan of Illinois Institute of Technology by Mies, 1955
Pic.1-3-19	Fagus Factory by W.Gropius &A. Meyer
Pic.1-4-1	Cover page of Bauhaus Manifesto
Pic.1-4-2	Gropius' Director's Office at the Bauhaus, Weimar, 1923
Pic.1-4-3	Front door of Summerfield house by J. Schmidt, 1921
Pic.1-4-4	Colored stained-glass window by J. Albers, 1922
Pic.1-4-5	Model of Villa Artists by T.van Doesburg, 1923
Pic.1-4-6	G. Muche in Itten's Bauhaus robe, 1921
Pic.1-4-7	"Mask (self-portrait)" by Moholy-Nagy, Photogram, 1922
Pic.1-4-8	"Light-Space Modulator" by Moholy-Nagy, 1922—1930
Pic.1-4-9	School near Berlin by H. Meyer in 1928
Pic.1-4-10	Mies' student work in 1931, virtually a copy of the Master. Major themes included the harmony between open space and limits

References
（参考文献）

Aalto, Alvar. 1980. Synopsis: Painting, Architecture, Sculpture. Basel, Switzerland: Birkhauser AG. 2nd Edition.

Abteilung fuer Architektur ETH Zurich. 1997. Jahrbuch 1997: Entwurf / Entwerfen und Konstruieren / Bilderisches Gestalten. Zurich: ETH Zurich Abteilung fuer Architektur.

Achilles, Rolf, Kevin Harrington and Charlotte Myhrum (ed.). 1986. Mies van der Rohe: Architect as Educator (Catalogue for the exhibition) Chicago: Illinois Institute of Technology.

Albers, Josef. 1963. Interaction of Color. New Haven: Yale University.

Andre, Carl. 1975. Carl Andre: Sculpture 1958—1974, Bern, Switzerland: Kunsthalle.

Angelil, Marc M. "Built environment is a multi-layered text, charged with traces, and written across the surface of the land." (Internet address http://a77.ethz.ch/Texte/Crossing.html) [accessed 1998]

Angèli, Mark M. 1996. Jahrbuch 1996. Zurich: Department und Abteilung Fuer Architectur, ETH.

Angélil, Mark M. "Sculpture in the Expanded Field" (Internet address http://a77.ethz.ch/Texte/Crossing.html) [accessed 1998]

Antliff, Mark and Patricia Leighten. 2001. Cubism and Culture. London/New York: Thames & Hudson World of Art.

Antoniades, Anthony C. 1992. Poetics of Architecture: Theory of Design. New York: John Wiley & Sons, Inc.

Ball, L. Susan. 1978. Ozenfant and Purism: The evolution of a style 1915—1930. Michigan: UMI Research Press.

Bax, Marty. 1991. Bauhaus Lecture Notes: 1930—1933. Amsterdam: Architecture & Natura Press.

Bechtler, Cristina (ed.). 1999. Art and Architecture in Discussion: Frank O. Gehry / Kurt W. Forster. Cantz Verlag, Ostfildern-Ruit. (723.673 G31 B3)

Bell, Jonathan and Sally Godwin. 2000. Architectural Design: The Transformable House. London: Wiley-academy.

Benevolo, Leonardo. 1991. Die Geschichte der Stadt. Frankfurt/New York.Campus Verlag.

Bideau, Andrè. 2000. "Territorium und Luftraum", Werk, Bauen+ Wohnen, February 200, No. 1+2.

Blotkamp, Carel. **1995.**	Mondrian: The Art of Destruction. New York: H.N. Abrams.
Boesiger, W. **1970.**	Le Corbusier: the last works, Volume 8. Zurich: Les Editions d'Architecture Artemis.
Boesiger, W. **1953.**	Le Corbusier: Volume 5 1946—1952, Zurich: Les Editions d'Architecture Artemis.
Boesiger, W. **1957.**	Le Corbusier: Volume 6 1952—1957, Zurich: Les Editions d'Architecture Artemis.
Boesiger et O.Stonorov (ed.). **1964.**	Le Corbusier (Et Pierre Jeanneret) Complete Works 1910—1929. Zurich: Les Èditions D'Architecture.
Borsi, Franco. **1973.**	Leon Battista Alberti: The Complete Work. New York: Electa/Rizzoli.
Broadbent, Geofrey. **1995.**	"Architectural Education", Education Architects, New York: Academy Editions.: 10—23.
Branzi, Andrea. **1993.**	"Design and the Second modernity: Theorems for an Ecology of the Artificial World", in The Edge of the Millennium: An International Critique of Architecture, Urban Planning, Product and Communication Design. New York: Whitney.: 125—127.
Brownlee, David B. and De Long, David G.. **1997.**	Louis I. Kahn. London: Thames and Hudson Ltd.: 9—10.
Basile, Giuseppe. **1993.**	Giotto: The Arena Chapel frescoes. London: Thames & Hudson.
Van Bruggen, Coosje. **1999.**	Frank O. Gehry: Guggenheim Museum Bilbao. New York: Guggenheim Museum Publications.
Busic-Snyder, Cynthia and Wallschlaeger, Charles. **1992.**	Basic Visual Concepts and Principles for Artists, Architects, and Designers. Dubuque, Iowa: Wm. C. Brown Publishers.
Caragonne, Alexander. **1995.**	The Texas Rangers: Notes from an Architectural Underground. Cambridge, Massachusetts: The Massachusetts Institute of Technology.
Ching, Francis D.K.. **1979.**	Architecture: Form, Space & Order. New York: Van Nostrand Reinhold Company.
Clark, Roger H., Pause, Michael. **1996.**	Precedents in Architecture. New York: Van Nostrand Reinhold. 2nd Edition.

Celant, Germano (1997)	Michael Heizer, Fondazione Prada, Milan, Italy.
Curtis, William (and others). 2001.	A&V: Louis I. Kahn. Span: Arquitectura Viva.
Le Corbusier. 1929 and 1987.	The City of Tomorrow and Its Planning. New York: Dover Publications, INC.
Le Corbusier. 1995.	Le Corbusier: Painter and Architect, Architectural Magazine, Denmark.
Le Corbusier. 1964.	Le Corbusier, 1946—1970. London: Hudson & Thompson,
Cottington, David. 1998.	Movements in Modern Art: Cubism. London: Cambridge University Press.
Droste, Magdalena. 1990.	Bauhaus: 1919—1933, Berlin: Bauhaus-Archiv Museum fur Gestaltung.
Editorial. March 2000	Werk, Bauen+ Wohen.
Editorial. Jan/Feb 2000.	Werk, Bauen+ Wohen: 9.
Eisenman, Peter. 1997.	"Presentness and the 'Being-only-once' of Architecture" New Architecture: Reaching for the Future (No.1).
ETH Zurich Abteilung fuer Architektur Entwerfen/ Konstruieren/Gestalten, 1994 and 1995.	Zurich: ETH Zurich Abteilung fuer Architektur.
External Relation Office. 2000.	Interflow. Hong Kong: The university of Hong Kong.
Fairbank, Wilma. 2000.	Liang and Lin: Patners in Exploring China's Architectural Past, 2000.
Fischer von Erlach, Johann Berhard. 1964.	Entwurff einer historischen Architectur, A reproduction of the 2nd German ed., Leipzig 1725. New Jersey: Gregg Press.
Foreign Office Architects Pusan, South Korea. 1997.	"Pusan High-Speed Railway Complex" Architectural Design – Architecture after Geometry. [ed. yy M. Toy]. UK: Academy Group Ltd.: 74—77.
Fleig, Karl (co-editor). 1963.	Alvar Aalto, Volume 1 1922-1962, Basel/Boston/Berlin, Switzerland: Birkhauser Verlag.

Frampton, Kenneth. 1997. "Technology, Place and Architecture", in Papadakis, Andreas (Ed). 1997. New Architecture: Reaching for the Future. Andreas Papadakis Publisher, Singapore: 13—17.

Friedman, Jonathan Block. 1989. Creation in Space: A Course in the Fundamentals of Architecture. Volume 1: Architectonics, Iowa: Kendall Hunt Publishing Co.

Futagawa, Yukio (ed.). 1986. GA Architect: Zaha M. Hadid, Tokyo: A.D.A. Edita.

Gadol, Joan. 1969. Leon Battista Alberti: Universal Man of the Early Renaissance. Chicago and London: The University of Chicago Press.

Galerie Renate Kammer. 1996. Zaha Hadid: Recent Projects 1990-1995. Hamburg: Architektur und Kunst. (723.642B H12 G)

Germany, Lisa. 2000. Harwell Hamilton Harris. Berkeley/Los Angeles/London: University of California Press.

Gomringer, Eugen. 1972. Josef Albers. Paris: Dessain et Tolra.

Guton, Jacques. 1981. The Ideas of Le Corbusier on Architecture and Urban Planning. New York: George Braziller.

Harkness, John C.. 1991. The Walter Gropius Archive: Volume 4 1945—1969 The Work of the Architects Collaborative. New York and London: Garland Publishing, INC.

Herdeg, Klaus. 1983. The Decorated Diagram. Cambridge, Massachusetts: The Massachusetts Institute of Technology.

Hertzberger, Herman. 1991. Lessons for Students in Architecture. Rotterdam: Uitgeverij 101 Publishers.

Hitchcock, Henry-Russell. 1948. Painting Toward Architecture. Meriden, Connecticut: The Miller Company.

http://www.architectureweek.com/2001/0103/design_1-1.html

http://www.zaha-hadid.com/

http://people.deas.harvard.edu/~jones/lab_arch/moneo/auditorio/auditorio.html

Itten, Johannes. 1963. Design and Form: The Basic Course at the Bauhaus. London: Thames and Hudson Ltd.

Itten, Johannes.
1970.
The Elements of Color. New York: Van Nostrand Reinhold.

Janssn, Jeurg, Hansueli Jeorg, Luca Maraini, Hanspeter Steockll.
1989.
Teaching Architecture:Bernhard Hoesli at the Department of Architecture at the ETH Zurich. Zurich: Eidgeneossische Technische Hochschule Zurich, Institut feur Geschichte und Theorie der Architektur (gta).

Jencks, Charles.
1997.
The Architecture of the Jumping Universe. London: Academy Editions. Revised Edition.

Jencks, Charles.
1987.
Le Corbusier and the Tragic View of Architecture. England: Penguin Books Ltd.

Jencks, Charles.
1995.
Architectural Design – Reaching for the skies IV (ed. by Maggie Toy) UK: Academy Group Ltd.: IV-V.

Jencks, Charles.
1973.
Le Corbusier and the Tragic View of Architecture. Cambridge: Harvard University Press.

Jenny, Peter.
1991.
The Sensual Fundamentals of Design. Zurich: Verlag der Fachvereine an den Schweizerischen Hochschulen und Techniken.

Jia, Beisi and Zhao Jun.
1999.
Da Shi Jian Zhu Hua, Nanjing, P.R. C.: Southeast University Press.

Jia, Beisi.
2002.
"Evaluation to an Architectural Studio with Problem-based Learning (PBL) Concept" in Proceedings to the Chinese Conference on Architectural Education. Wuhan, the People's Republic of China, October 24—26:96—102.

Jia, Beisi.
2000.
"Architectonics: a Basic Training on Principles of Forms"
"Master of Architecture Year 1 (First Semester)" and "Master of Architecture Year 1 (Second Semester): International Competition Projects" (co-author), World Architectural Review. Shenzhen, China.

Jia Beisi and He Weiling.
2000
"Technological Maximization and Training of Sensual Fundamentals in Architectural Basics Course" HKIA Journal, No.25/3rd Quarter 2000. Hong Kong: Hong Kong Institute of Architecture.: 54—61.

Jia Beisi.
2001.
"An implication of Urban Sustainable Development Study in Architecture Design Teaching", Architectural Journal (China) NO.390, February 2001, Beijing.: 31—33.

Jia Beisi.
2001
"Problem Based Learning in Crossing University Joint Studio of Architecture", Time & Architecture, Vol.60, August 2001, Shanghai.:54—55 and 39.

Joachimides, Christos M. and Norman Rosenthal.
1993.
American Art in the 20th Century, Germany: Prestel.

Johnson, Eugene J., Lewis, Michael J.. 1996. Drawn from the Source: The Travel Sketches of Louis I. Kahn. Cambridge Massachusetts: The MIT Press.

Kentgens-Craig, Margret (ed.). 1998. Bauhaus Dessau Foundation. The DessauBauhaus Building 1926—1999. Basel, Switzerland: Birkhauser.

Klingman, Anna. 2000. "Strategies of the Real", Werk, Bauen+ Wohen :9 March No.3, Switzerland.

Kostof, Spiro. 1999. The City Assembled: The Elements of Urban Form Through History. London: Thames & Hudson.

Koolhaas, Rem and Hardard (and others). 2000. Mutations. Barcelona; ACTAR.

Krustrup, Mogens. 1991. Porte email: Le Corbusier. Kobenhavn (Copenhagen): Arkitektens Forlag.

Latour, Alessandra (ed.). 1991. Louis I. Kahn: Writings, Lectures, Interviews. New York: Rizzoli.

Le Corbusier. 1961. The Modulor: A Harmonious Measure to the Human Scale Universally Applicable to Architecture and Mechanics. London: Faber and Faber Ltd. 2nd Edition.

Leyland, Nita. 1990. The Creative Artist: A Fine Artist's Guide to Expanding Your Creativity and Achieving Your Artistic Potential. Cincinnati, Ohio: North Light Books.

Libeskind, Daniel. 1994 . "An Architectural Design Interview" in Architecture Design: Deconstruction III (Ed. by Andreas C. Papadakis) London: Academy Groups:15—19.

Lobell, John. 1979. Between Silence and Light: Spirit in the Architecture of Louis I. Kahn. Colorado: Shambhala Publications, Inc.

Lynn, Greg. 1997. "An advanced form of movement." Architectural Design—Architecture After Geometry (Ed. by Maggie Toy). London: Academic Groups: 54—57.

Lynn, Greg. 1999. Animate Form. New York: Princeton Architectural Press.

Menges, Axel (ed.). 1998. Frank O. Gehry: Guggenheim Bilbao Museoa. Stuttgart / London: Edition Axel Menges.

McCoy, Michael. (1993) "Design and the New Mythology", in The Edge of the Millennium: An International Critique of Architecture, Urban Planning, Product and

Communication Design. New York: Whitney: 132—138.

Meyerowitz, Joshua. 1985. No Sense of Place—The Impact of Electronic Media on Social Behavior. New York: Oxford University Press.

Miss, Marry (and others). 1987. Mary Miss: Projects 1966—1987. London: Architectural Association.

Von Moos, Stanislaus. 1985. Le Corbusier: Elements of a Synthesis. Cambridge, Massachusetts: The MIT Press. 5th printing.

Moore, T., C.,F. (compilers). 2001. The Scholarship for Teaching and Learning Abstracts, Centre for the Advancement of University Teaching, The University of Hong Kong.

Naylor, Gillian. 1985. The Bauhaus Reassessed: Sources and Design Theory. London: The Herbert Press Ltd.

Nerdinger, Winfried (ed.) 1990. The Walter Gropius Archive: An Illustrated Catalogue of the Drawings, Prints, and Photographs in the Walter Gropius Archive at the Busch-Reisinger Museum, Harvard University, Volume 1. Massachusetts: Garland Publishing, Inc. and Harvard University Art Museums.

Neubauer, Hendrik. 1991. Curious Moments. Koeln: Koenemann.

Olsen Richard (ed.). 2000. Daniel Libeskind: The Space of Encounter. New York: Universe.

Papadakis, Andreas (ed). 1997. New Architecture: Reaching for the Future. Singapore: Andreas Papadakis Publisher.

Papadakis, Andreas (ed). 1990. Architectural Design: Deconstruction III. London: Academy Editions.

Passuth, Krisztina. 1985. Moholy-Nagy. London: Thames and Hudson.

Reima, Pietila. 1985. Intermediate Zones in Modern Architecture. Museum of Finnish Architecture and Alvar Aalto Museum. Helsinki: Martinpaino.

Pino, Musi. 1997. Mario Botta Architecture 1980—1995, Department of Architecture, The University of Hong Kong, Hong Kong.

Prix, Wolf. 1990. “On the Edge” (recent work of Coop Himmelblau) in Architecture Design: Deconstruction III. Edited by Andreas C. Papadakis. London: Academy Editions.

Powell, Helen and David eatherbarrow. Master Pieces of Architectural Drawing. London: Orbis Publishing.

1982. Natural in Design (in Chinese). Jiangsu, China: Conran Octopus.

Powers, Alan.
1999.

Quantrill, Malcolm.
1983. Alvar Aalto: A Critical Study. New York: Schocken Books.

Reed, Peter.
1998. Alvar Aalto : Between Humanism and Materialism. Museum of Modern Art, New York, U.S.A.

Rogers, R. Carl.
1969. Freedom to Learn. Macmillan College Publishing Company.

Rowe, Peter G..
1993. Modernity and Housing. London: The MIT Press.

Reed, Peter.
1998. Alvar Aalto: Between Humanism and Materialism. New York: Museum of Modern Art.

Rowe, Colin and Slutzky, Robert.
1997. Transparency. Basel: Birkhauser.

Ruby, Andreas.
2000. "Ein Umsteigebahnhof fuer globale Gueter", Werk, Bauen+Wohnen, March 2000, No.3, Switzerland.

Ruskin, John.
1880 and 1989. Seven Lamps of Architecture, New York: Dover Publications, INC.

Spies, Werner.
1970. Albers. New York: Harry N. Abrams, Inc.

Solà-Morales, Ignasi, Cirici, Cristian, and Ramos, Fernando.
1993. Mies van der Rohe : Barcelona Pavilion. Barcelona: G. Gili.

Schildt, Goran (ed.).
1979. "Conversation", in Alvar Aalto: Sketches. Cambridge, Massachusetts: The MIT Press.

Schneider, Ulrich and Marc Feustel.
1999. Toyo Ito: Blurring Architecture. Milan: Das Suermondt Ludwig Museum.

Solà-Morales, Ignasi, Cirici, Cristian, and Ramos, Fernando.
1993. Mies van der Rohe : Barcelona Pavilion. Barcelona: G. Gili.

Sterling, Bruce Sterling & Viemeister, Tucker.
1993. "Momentum" in The Edge of the Millennium: An International Critique of Architecture, Urban Planning, Product and Communication Design. New York: Whitney: 145—159.

Van Straaten, Evert.
1994.
Theo van Doesburg: Constructor of the new life. Otterlo: Kroeller-Mueller Museum.

Stungo, Naomi.
1999.
Frank Gehry. London: Carlton Books Ltd.

Selgmann, Werner.
1989.
"The Texas Years and the Beginning at the ETH Zurich 1956—61" in Jeurg Janssn, Hansueli Jeorg, Luca Maraini, Hanspeter Steockll (1989) Teaching Architecture: Bernhard Hoesli at the Department of Architecture at the ETH Zurich, Eidgeneossische Technische Hochschule Zurich, Institut feur Geschichte und Theorie der Architektur (gta): 7—16.

Steockli, Hanspeter.
1989.
"Teaching the basic course". In Jeurg Janssn, Hansueli Jeorg, Luca Maraini, Hanspeter Steockll. Teaching Architecture:Bernhard Hoesli at the Department of Architecture at the ETH Zurich, Eidgeneossische Technische Hochschule Zurich, Institut feur Geschichte und Theorie der Architektur (gta): 17—80.

Thackara, John.
1993.
"Consumption and Creativity in the Information Age", in The Edge of the Millennium: An International Critique of Architecture, Urban Planning, Product and Communication Design. New York: Whitney: 160—167.

The Bauhaus — Its Impact on the World of Design.
1976.
Illinois: Roland Films on Art. (Video recording)

Toy, Maggie (ed.).
1997.
"New Science = New Architecture", Architectural Design, vol. 67, No. 9/10. London: Academy Groups.

Toy, Maggie (ed.).
1997.
Architecture Design: Architecture After Geometry, London: Academy Editions.

Tschumi, Bernard.
1997.
"Architecture and Events" in Papadakis, Andreas (ed). 1997. New Architecture: Reaching for the Future. Singapore: Andreas Papadakis Publisher: 24—27.

Urry, John,
2000.
Werk, Bauen+ Wohen:16. June.

Ursprung, Philip.
2000.
Interieur, Atmosphaere und Ambiente in der neueren Kunst: Makro_ Privatheit und Mikro-Oeffentlichkeit, Werk, Bauen+ Wohen:77. June.

Van Bruggen, Coosje.
1999.
Frank O. Gehry: Guggenheim Museum Bilbao. New York: Guggenheim Museum Publications.

Venturi, Robert, Brown, Denise Scott, and Izenour, Steven.
1977.
Learning from Las Vegas: The Forgotten Symbolism of Architectural Form. Cambridge, Massachusetts: MIT Press.

Weston, Richard.
1995.

Alvar Aalto. London: Phaidon Press, London.

Wong, Wucius.
1993.

Principles of Form and Design. New York: Van Nostrand Reinhold Company.

Warncke, Carsten-Peter.
1994.

De Stijl 1917—1931, Taschen, Koeln.

Yelavich, Susan.
1993.

"Setting the stage for the Third Millennium" in The Edge of the Millennium: An International Critique of Architecture, Urban Planning, Product and Communication Design. New York: Whitney: 10—14.

Van Zanten, David, and Cervin Robinson (photographs).
2000.

Sullivan's City. New York and London: W.W. Norton & Company.

Illustration and Photo Sources
（插图来源）

Pic. 1-1-1 and 1-1-4: Gadol, Joan 1969, pp. 141 and 79 respectively.

Pic. 1-1-2, 1-1-6, 1-7-6 and 1-3-5: Jia Beisi and Zhao Jun 1999, pp. 67, 81, 97 and 98 respectively.

Pic. 1-1-3, 2-1-5, 1-4-3, 1-2-1 and 2-1-11: Benevolo, Leonardo 1991, pp. 619, 620, 905, 911, 793 and 944 respectively.

Pic. 1-1-5: Fischer von Erlach 1964, Plate XII of Volume 3.

Pic. 1-1-7: Powell, Helen and David Leatherbarrow 1982, p. 43

Pic. 1-1-8: Fairbank, Wilma 2000

Pic. 1-1-9a, 2-3-6b and 2-5-3: Johnson, Eugene J. 1996, pp.3, 30 and 41 respectively.

Pic. 1-1-9b and 2-5-4: Curtis, William (and others) 2001, pp.46 and 66 respectively.

Pic. 1-2-1, 1-2-4, 1-4-1, 1-7-1, 1-5-1, 1-3-4,1-5-9,1-4-6,1-4-4,1-4-3,1-6-3,1-6-4,1-4-9 and 1-4-10: Droste, Magdalena 1990, pp. 7, 18, 23, 25, 10, 32, 32, 47, 48, 61, 142, 142, 192 and 215 respectively.

Pic. 1-3-2: Van Zanten, David, and Cervin Robinson (photographs) 2000, p. 123

Pic.1-3-3: Ruskin, John (1880 and 1989), p. 97

Pic. 1-3-6,1-3-5,2-7-1a and 1-3-11: Cottington, David 1998, pp. 41, 41, 56, 58 and 74 respectively.

Pic. 1-3-7,1-3-8,1-3-20a,1-10-6, and 1-3-9: Antliff, Mark and Patricia Leighten 2001, pp. 99, 171, 209, and 212 respectively.

Pic. 1-3-12,2-2-3 and 1-3-10: Warncke, Carsten-Peter 1994, pp. 52-54, 116&117, and 159 respectively.

Pic. 1-3-19. Blotkamp, Carel 1995, p. 239.

Pic.1-4-5 and 1-3-17: Van Straaten, Evert 1994, pp. 32 and 44 respectively.

Pic. 2-2-9: Andre, Carl 1975, pp. 18 and 20 respectively.

Pic. 1-4-7,1-4-8 and 1-8-1: Passuth, Krisztina 1985, pp. 106, 177 and 217 respectively.

Pic. 1-5-2,1-5-5,1-5-6,1-5-8a,1-5-4,1-5-7,1-5-3: Itten, Johannes 1963, pp. 14, 20, 30, 33, 31, 36, 81 and 108 respectively.

Pic. 1-6-1,1-6-2,1-6-6,1-6-7,1-6-8and1-6-9: Gomringer, Eugen 1972, pp. 21, 31, 46, 132, 168 and 145 respectively.

Pic. 1-7-2,1-10-1, 1-10-2,1-10-3,1-10-4, 1-10-5,1-10-7, 1-10-8 and 1-11-2: Rowe, Colin and Robert Slutzky 1997, pp. 42, 60, 27, 30, 42—43, 26, 35, 61, 68 and 32 respectively.

Pic. 1-7-3,1-7-4 and 1-7-5: Kentgens-Craig, Margret(ed.) 1998, pp.25, 186 and 200 respectively.

Pic. 1-7-8,1-7-7 and 1-8-2: Harkness, John C. 1991, p.15, 29 and 31.

Pic. 1-8-7,1-4-11,1-6-5,1-8-5,1-8-6,1-8-3 and 1-8-4: Achilles, Rolf, Kevin Harrington and Charlotte Myhrum (ed.) 1986, pp. 58, 90, 92, 97, 99, 107 and 107 respectively.

Pic. 1-8-8 and 1-8-9: Germany Lisa 2000, pp.13 and pp.18 respectively.

Pic. 1-9-1,1-9-2,1-9-3,1-9-4,1-9-5,1-9-6,1-9-7,1-9-8,1-9-9 and 1-11-13: Caragonne, Alexander 1995, pp.126, 176, 180, 181, 184, 205, 377, 300, 197 and 380 respectively.

Pic. 1-11-1,1-11-7,1-11-6,1-11-5,1-11-9,1-11-10,1-11-11,1-11-12 and 1-12-1: Janssn, Jeurg, Hansueli Jeorg, Luca Maraini, Hanspeter Steockll 1989, pp. 21, 9, 10, 11, 52—53, 55, 56, 60—61 and 118—119 respectively.

Pic. 1-11-4 and 2-1-7: W.Boesiger 1953, pp. 50 and 179 respectively.

Pic. 1-11-8a and 2-3-6: Latour, Alessandra (ed.) 1991, pp. 69 and 96.

Pic. 1-11-8b: Borsi, Franco 1973, p. 173.

Pic. 1-12-2,1-12-3,1-12-6,1-12-8,1-12-10 and 1-12-11: Jenny, Peter 1991, pp. 27, 126, 132, 35, 61 and 187 respectively.

Pic. 1-12-7 and 1-12-15: Abteilung fuer Architektur ETH Zurich 1997, pp. 89 and 88 respectively.

Pic. 1-12-9: ETH Zurich Abteilung fuer Architektur 1994, p. 12.

Pic. 1-12-12: ETH Zurich Abteilung fuer Architektur 1995, p. 12.

Pic. 1-12-13,2-7-3,2-2-7,1-4-8 and 2-7-2: Joachimides, Christos M. and Norman Rosenthal 1993, plates 93, 172, 173, 206 and 219 respectively.

Pic. 2-0-1: Klingmann, Anna 2000, p. 29.

Pic. 2-1-1: Boesiger et O.Stonorov (ed.) 1964, p. 33.

Pic. 2-1-2: Musi Pino 1997, p30.

Pic. 2-1-3: Le Corbusier 1929 and 1987, p. 59

Pic. 2-1-4: Le Corbusier 1964, p. 48.

Pic. 2-1-6b: Guton, Jacques 1981, p.23.

Pic. 2-1-14: Lynn, Greg 1999, pp. 108, 109, 110 and 117.

Pic. 2-2-1: Hertzberger, Herman 1991, p. 133

Pic. 2-2-2 and 2-7-10: Neubauer, Hendrik 1991, pp. 179 and 127 respectively.

Pic. 2-2-4a&b: Solà-Morales, Ignasi (and others) 1993, p.197.

Pic. 2-2-5a: Aalto, Alvar 1980, p. 105.

Pic. 2-2-5b: Powers, Alan 1999, p. 110.

Pic. 2-2-6a and 2-2-6b: Karl Fleig (co-editor) 1963, pp. 49 and 51 respectively.

Pic. 2-2-8, 2-2-10,2-2-11 and 2-2-12: Bechtler, Cristina (ed.) 1999, pp. 68, 23, 98 and 22 respectively.

Pic. 2-2-13a and 2-2-13b: Futagawa, Yukio (ed.) 1986, pp. 91 and 111 respectively.

Pic. 2-2-15: http://www.zaha-hadid.com/

Pic. 2-2-16: http://people.deas.harvard.edu/~jones/lab_arch/moneo/auditorio/auditorio. html

Pic. 2-2-17 and 2-2-18: Ursprung, Philip 2000, pp. 37 and 35 respectively.

Pic. 2-3-1: Pietila 1985, pp. 54 and 56 respectively.

Pic. 2-3-2, 2-3-5 and 2-4-8: "New Science = New Architecture" 1997, pp. 17, 20 and 58 respectively.

Pic. 2-3-3 and 2-3-4: http://www.architectureweek.com/2001/0103/design_1-1.html

Pic. 2-3-8 and 2-7-1c: Le Corbusier 1995, pp. 132 and 31 respectively.

Pic. 2-3-9: Krustrup, Mogens 1991, p. 107.

Pic. 2-3-10 and 2-5-5: W.Boesiger 1970, pp. 67 and 108 respectively.

Pic. 2-3-12 and 2-3-13: W.Boesiger 1957, pp. 27 and 35 respectively.

Pic. 2-3-16,2-1-12,2-1-13,2-2-20,2-2-21,2-2-22a&b, 2-7-7,2-7-8 and 2-7-9a&b: Toy, Maggie (ed.) 1997, pp. 41, 42, 50, 77, 75, II, 32, 34—35 and 36 respectively.

Pic. 2-4-1: External Relation Office 2000, cover page.

Pic. 2-4-2,2-4-3 and 2-4-4: Jencks, Charles 1997, pp. 54, 51 and 54 respectively.

Pic. 2-4-6,2-2-14,2-4-5 and 2-4-7: Papadakis Andreas (ed.) 1997, pp. 82, 82, 78 and 81 respectively.

Pic. 2-4-9 a&b: Olsen Richard (ed.) 2000, pp.43 and 41 respectively.

Pic. 2-4-10a, 2-4-10b and 2-4-10c: Van Bruggen, Coosjec 1999, pp. 90, 94 and 105 respectively.

Pic. 2-4-11b, 2-6-2 and 2-4-11a: Menges, Axel (ed.) 1998, pp. 27, 33 and 37 respectively.

Pic. 2-4-12,2-5-11a&b,2-5-15, 2-4-14b and 2-5-16: Koolhaas, Rem and Hardard (and others) 2000, pp. 53, 229, 492, 493, 531 and 587 respectively.

Pic. 2-4-15,2-4-16a and 2-4-16b: Ruby, Andreas 2000, pp. 11, 18 and 19 respectively.

Pic. 2-5-1 and 2-5-2: Reed, Peter 1998, pp. 99 and 96.

Pic. 2-5-6 and 2-5-7: Kostof, Spiro 1999, pp.128 and 241 respectively.

Pic. 2-5-8: Bideau, Andrè 2000, p. 56.

Pic. 2-6-3a and 2-6-3b: Schneider, Ulrich and Marc Feustel 1999, pp. 152, 119 and 118 respectively.

Pic. 2-6-6: Bell, Jonathan and Sally Godwin 2000, p.86-89

Pic. 2-6-7,2-6-4a. 2-6-4b and 2-6-5: Papadakis, Andreas (ed.) 1990, pp. 71, 42-43, 40-41 and 38 respectively.

Pic. 2-7-1b: Ball, L. Susan 1978, p. 109.

Pic. 2-7-5 and 2-7-6: Celant, Germano 1997, pp. 97 and 230 respectively.

Pic. 2-7-4: Miss, Marry (and others) 1987, pp. 57 and 59 respectively.

Notes

（注释）

1 Broadbent, Geofrey (1995) "Architectural Education", Education Architects, Academy Editions, New York, p.12
2 Ibid., p.13—14
3 Powell & Leatherbarrow, Master Pieces of Architectural Drawing, 1982, p.42
4 Broadbent, p.16
5 Magdalena Droste, Bauhaus: 1919—1933. Berlin: Bauhaus-Archiv Museum fur Gestaltung, 1990. p.14
6 Ibid., p.15
7 Magdalena Droste, Bauhaus: 1919—1933. Berlin: Bauhaus-Archiv Museum fur Gestaltung, 1990. p.12
8 Naylor, p.17
9 Ibid., p.50
10 Row, Peter G., Modernity and Housing, The MIT Press, 1993 London, p.37
11 Henry-Russell Hitchcock. Painting Toward Architecture. Meriden, Connecticut: The Miller Company, 1948. p. 16—17
12 Ibid., p.13
13 Ibid., p.19
14 Ibid., p.22
15 Ibid., p.10
16 Ibid., p.23
17 Jenks Charles 1973. Le Corbusier and the Tragic View of Architecture. Cambridge: Harvard University Press, p.20, quoted from Le Corbusier, 1925. L'Art decoratif d'aujourd'hui, Paris: P.198
18 Naylor. p.93
19 Droste. p.54
20 Hitchcock. p.34
21 Rowe, p.40
22 Ibid., p.41
23 Jenks, p.70 quoted from Le Corbusier, The City of Tomorrow, p.38
24 Jenny, Peter. 1991. The Sensual Fundamentals of Design. Zurich: Verlag der Fachvereine an den Schweizerischen Hochschulen und Techniken, p.34
25 Gillian Naylor, The Bauhaus Reassessed: Sources and Design Theory. London: The Herbert Press Ltd., 1985. p. 9
26 "Bauhaus Manifesto" quoted by Naylor. p.54
27 Droste, p.34
28 Broadbent, p.17
29 Droste, p.56
30 Ibid., p.58
31 Jenks, p.29
32 Droste, p.58
33 Ibid., p.79
34 Ibid., p.161
35 Broadbent, p.18
36 Marty Bax, Bauhaus Lecture Notes 1930—1933. Amsterdam: Architectura & Natura Press. 1991. p.46
37 Ibid.
38 Naylor. p.167
39 Droste, p.193
40 Broadbent, p.18
41 Gillian Naylor. The Bauhaus Reassessed: Sources and Design Theory. London: The Herbert Press Ltd., 1985.
42 Ibid.
43 Johannes Itten. Design and Form: The Basic Course at the Bauhaus. London: Thames and Hudson Ltd. 1963. p.12
44 Ibid., p.7—8
45 Ibid., p.9

46 Ibid., p.9, 12
47 Naylor. p.77
48 Droste. p.56
49 Naylor. p.78
50 Itten. p.12
51 Droste. p.25
52 Ibid., p.25, 27
53 Itten. p.12
54 Droste. p.12
55 Naylor, p.
56 Werner Spies. Albers. New York: Harry N. Abrams, Inc., 1970. p. 9
57 Ibid., p.11
58 Ibid., p.12
59 Droste. p.140
60 Naylor. p.155—156
61 Ibid., p.155
62 Ibid.
63 Spies. p.26
64 Winfried Nerdinger (editor). The Walter Gropius Archive: An Illustrated Catalogue of the Drawings, Prints, and Photographs in the Walter Gropius Archive at the Busch-Reisinger Museum, Harvard University, volume 1. Massachusetts: Garland Publishing, Inc. and Harvard University Art Museums, 1990. p.XIX
65 Ibid., p.XX
66 Ibid., p.XXII
67 Ibid., p.129
68 Ibid., p.132
69 Gropius quoted by Row, p.45
70 Nerdinger, p.132
71 Ibid., p. XXIV
72 Quoted by Jenks, p.84, from Le Corbusier, 1925, La Peinture Moderne, p. 170—172
73 Ibid., p. XXV
74 Klaus Herdeg. The Decorated Diagram. Cambridge, Massachusetts: The Massachusetts Institute of Technology, 1983. p.80
75 Ibid., p.87
76 Ibid., p.87
77 Broadbent, p.11
78 Ibid., p.19—20
79 Alexander Caragonne, The Texas Rangers: Notes from an Architectural Underground. Cambridge, Massachusetts: The Massachusetts Institute of Technology, 1995. p. 144
80 Ibid., p.79
81 Selgmann, Werner 1989."The Texas Years and the Beginning at the ETH Zurich 1956—1961" in Jeurg Janssn,(and etc.) Teaching Architecture:Bernhard Hoesli Department of Architecture at the ETH Zurich, p.7
82 Caragonne, p. 30
83 Ibid., p.78
84 Ibid., p.80
85 Ibid., p.12
86 Ibid., p.154

87 Ibid., p.156
88 Ibid., p.33
89 Ibid., p.45
90 Ibid., p.115—116
91 Robert Maxwell, "Colin Rowe: 1920—1999", Architectural Research Quarterly. Volume 4, number 1, 2000. p. 9—14
92 Caragonne. p.8
93 Werner Spies. Albers. New York: Harry N. Abrams, Inc., 1970
94 Ibid., p.187
95 Ibid.
96 Ibid., p.174
97 Ibid., p.194
98 John Hejduk, Mask of Medusa.
99 Ibid., p.147
100 Colin Rowe. "Architectural education in the USA", Lotus International, No.27. New York: Rizzoli Publications, 1980. p.43
101 Ibid., p.164
102 Colin Rowe and Robert Slutzky. Transparency. Basel: Birkhauser, 1997. p. 8
103 Ibid., p.22—23
104 Ibid., p.23
105 Ibid., p.43
106 Ibid., p.41, 43
107 Ibid., p.54
108 Caragonne. p.73
109 Ibid., p.110
110 Ibid., p.109
111 Ibid., p.108
112 Ibid., p.110
113 Ibid., p.200
114 Selgmann, p.9
115 Hoesli, quoted by Steockli, Hanspeter 1989. "Teaching the basic course." In Jeurg Janssn &etc., Teaching Architecture: Bernhard Hoesli at the Department of Architecture at the ETH Zurich, p.23
116 Ibid.
117 Ibid., P.24
118 Ibid., P.25
119 Selgmann, p.13
120 Moore, T., C., F. (compilers) The Scholarship for Teaching and Learning Abstracts, Centre for the Advancement of University Teaching, The University of HK, p.3
121 Carl R. Rogers, Freedom to Learn. Macmillan College Publishing Company, 1994, p.333
122 Selgmann, p.12
123 Jenny, Peter. The Sensual Fundamentals of Design, ETH Zurich, 1991. p.8
124 Ibid.
125 Ibid., p.58—59
126 Ibid., p.36
127 Ibid., p.35
128 Ibid., p.37
129 Jenks, p.84, quoted from Corbusier, La Peinture Moderne, Paris, 1925
130 Jenny, p.58

131 Ibid., p.59

132 Ibid., p.7

133 Ibid., p.9

134 Ibid., p.36

135 Ibid., p.34

136 Ibid., p.14

137 Ibid., p.36

138 Ibid., p.31

139 Ibid., p.42—43

140 Ibid., p.45

141 Eisenman, Peter. 1997. "Presentness and the 'Being-only-once' of Architecture" New Architecture: Reaching for the Future (No.1)

142 Jenks, quoted from Le Corbusier, The City of Tomorrow: p.7

143 Ibid., p.70

144 Le Corbusier. The Modulor: A Harmonious Measure to the Human Scale Universally Applicable to Architecture and Mechanics. London: Faber and Faber Ltd.:p.216 2nd Edition

145 Ibid., p.130—131

146 Davidson, Peter and Bates, Ronald L. 1997. Architecture Design: Architecture After Geometry

147 Jahrbuch 1996, Department und Abteilung Feur Architectur, ETH Zurich: p.47

148 Kipnis, Jeff. 1997. "[Architecture] After Geometry: An Anthology of Mysteries Case Notes to the Mystery of the School of Fish" in Architectural Design: Architecture After Geometry

149 Friedman, Jonathan Block. 1989. Creation in Space: A Course in the Fundamentals of Architecture. Iowa: Kendall.Hunt Publishing Co.

150 Silvetti, p.43

151 Jencks, Charles:1973. Le Corbusier and the Tragic View of Architecture. Cambridge: Harvard University Press:79 quoted from L' Art Dècoratif d'aujourd'hui:p.76

152 Aalto Alvar. 1980. Synopsis: Painting, Architecture, Sculpture. Birkhauser AG, Basel, Switzerland. 2nd Edition: p.17.

153 Van Bruggen, Coosje. 1999. Frank O. Gehry: Guggenheim Museum Bilbao. New York: Guggenheim Museum Publications: p.15

154 Bechtler, Cristina (ed.). 1999. Art and Architecture in Discussion: Frank O. Gehry / Kurt W. Forster. Ostfildern-Ruit: Cantz Verlag: p.62—63

155 Ibid., p.25

156 Ibid., p.26

157 Galerie Renate Kammer, 1996. Zaha Hadid: Recent Projects 1990—1995. Hamburg: Architektur und Kunst, Hamburg

158 Klingmann, Anna. 2000. Werk, Bauen+ Wohen: 22 March

159 Ursprung, Philip. 2000. Werk, Bauen+ Wohen: 76, June

160 Lynn, Greg. 1997. "An Advanced Form of Movement" in Architectural Design — Architecture After Geometry: p.54

161 Foreign Office Architects. 1997. "Pusan, South Korea — Pusan High-Speed Railway Complex" in Architectural Design – Architecture after geometry: p.74—77

162 Antoniades, Anthony C. 1992. Poetics of Architecture: Theory of Design. New York: John Wiley & Sons, Inc.: p.247

163 Jencks, Charles. 1997. The Architecture of the Jumping Universe. Academy Editions, London. Revised Edition.

164 Eisenman, p.1997

165 Brownlee, David B. and De Long, David G. 1997. Louis I. Kahn. Thames and Hudson Ltd., London: P.9—10

166 Johnson, Eugene J. and Lewis, Michael J. 1996. Drawn from the Source: The Travel Sketches of Louis I. Kahn. Cambridge Massachusetts: The MIT Press:p.72

167 Ibid., p.70

168 von Moos, Stanislaus. 1985. Le Corbusier: Elements of a Synthesis. Cambridge Massachusetts: The MIT Press. Fifth Printing: p.291

169 Ibid.

170 Ibid., p.292

171 Le Corbusier: Painter and Architect. 1995. Denmark: Architectural Magazine: p.127

172 Guton, Jacques. 1981. The Ideas of Le Corbusier on Architecture and Urban Planning. New York: George Braziller. p.48

173 Davidson, Peter and Bates, Donald L Bates. 1997. "Bucuresti 2000 Master Plan" [by LAB], Architecture Design: Architecture after Geometry, op cit.

174 Jencks, Charles. 1997. The Architecture of the Jumping Universe. London: Academy Editions, Revised Edition:p.10

175 "New Science = New Architecture", 1997. Architectural Design, 67 [9/10]. London. September-October:p.22

176 Charles Jencks. 1997. The…Jumping Universe. op. cit. p.46

177 Balmond, Cecil 1997. "New Structure and The Informal", Architectural Design 67 [9/10], London. September-October:p.90

178 Daniel Liebskind, Daniel. 1990 "An Architectural design Interview" in Architecture Design; Deconstruction III. Edited by Andreas C. Papdakis.

179 Klingmann, Anna March 2000, op cit.: p.22

180 Ibid., p.23

181 Thackara, John "Consumption and Creativity in the Information Age" in The Edge of the Millennium: An International Critique of Architecture, Urban Planning, Product and Communication Design: p.163

182 Eisenman 1997

183 Ursprung, Philip 2000, Werk, Bauen+ Wohen: 77 June.

184 Aalto, Alvar. 1980 Synopsis: Painting, Architecture, Sculpture. Basel, Switzerland: Birkhauser AG, 2nd Edition: p.25

185 Ibid., p.26

186 Latour, Alessandra (Ed.), 1991. Louis I. Kahn, Writings, Lectures, Interviews. New York: Rizzoli, New York: p.296

187 Jenks 1973:p.142,144; quoted from Le Corbusier, Oeuvre Complete, Volume V. 1946—1952:p.191

188 Editorial, Jan/Feb 2000, Werk, Bauen+ Wohen:P.9

189 Meyrowitz, Joshua. 1985. No Sense of Place – The Impact of Electronic Media on Social Behavior. New York: Oxford University Press: p.181

190 Ibid., p.308

191 Sterling, Bruce & Viemeister, Tucker.1993. "Momentum" in The Edge of the Millennium: An International Critique of Architecture, Urban Planning, Product and Communication Design.

192 Urry, John. June 2000, Werk, Bauen+ Wohen:p.22, quoted from Eco, Umberto. 1986. Travels in Hyper-Reality, London: Picador.

193 Angèli, Mark. 1996. Jahrbuch 1996, Department und Abteilung Fuer Architectur, ETH Zurich. p. 49

194 Van Bruggen, Coosje. 1999. Frank O. Gehry: Guggenheim Museum Bilbao. New York: Guggenheim Museum Publications, p.141

195 Ibid.

196 Ibid., p.136

197 Frampton, K. 1997. "Technology, Place and Architecture", in Papdakis, Andreas (Ed.) 1997. New Architecture: Reaching for the Future. Andreas Papadakis, publisher. Singapore.

198 Jia, Beisi. 2002. "Evaluation to an Architectural Studio with Problem-based Learning (PBL) Concept" in Proceedings to the Chinese Conference on Architectural Education. Wuhan, People's Republic of China, 24—26 October, p.101

199 Davidson, Peter and Bates, Ronald L. 1997. Editorial page, in Architecture Design: Architecture After Geometry.

200 McCoy Michael. 1993 "Design and the New Mythology" in The Edge of the Millennium: An International Critique of Architecture, Urban Planning, Product and Communication Design

201 Meyrowitz, op.cit. p.125

202 Tschumi, Bernard. "Architecture and Events" in Papdakis, Andreas (ed.) 1997. New Architecture: Reaching for the Future. Andreas Papadakis, publisher. Singapore

203 Prix, Wolf. 1990 "On the Edge" (Coop Himmelblau) in Architecture Design: Deconstruction III. Edited by Andreas C. Papadakis

204 Prix, Wolf.1990. "On the Edge" (recent work of Coop Himmelblau) in Architecture Design: Deconstruction III.

205 Ursprung, Op cit.:P.77

206 Editorial, March 2000, Werk, Bauen+ Wohen:9

207 Jenks 1973:P.85, quoted from La Peinture Moderne, Paris, 1925:P.10

208 Le Corbusier: Painter and Architect. 1985. Denmark: Architectural Magazine, Denmark:P.17

209 Ibid.:P.13

210 Schildt, Goran (ed.). 1979 "Conversation", in Alvar Aalto: Sketches. Cambridge, Massachusetts: The MIT Press: P.171

211 Bechtler 1999:P.84

212 Ibid.:P.85

213 Angélil, Mark M. "Sculpture in the Expanded Field" http://a77.ethz.ch/Texte/Crossing.html

214 Ibid.

215 McCarthy, Battle. 1997. "Multi-Source Synthesis - Working with the Elements" Architecture Design: Architecture After Geometry

216 Davidson, Peter & Bates, Donald L. (LAB design) with Kipis, Jeff. 1997. "Future Generations University, Central Coast, NSW, Australia", Architecture Design: Architecture After Geometry

217 Branzi, Andrea. 1993 "The End of the Culture of Complexity" The Edge of the Millennium: An International Critique of Architecture, Urban Planning, Product and Communication Design:P.128

练习十五　向大师学习

目的：

建筑知识获取的途径多种多样，而分析大师作品也许是最直接的一种。学习不是简单模仿，它必须包括两个过程：分析和综合，或者叫“演绎”。

这个练习从训练分析大师作品开始，分析重点放在建筑形体构成上。然后重新演绎这些原理，在一个抽象环境中做一个雕塑。

方法：

1. 分析是将一个事物分成几个部分来观察的方法——部分可以是元素，也可以是元素组织方式。建筑构造形态的基本组合方式，如网格、韵律、围合、开敞、实体和空间、光和影等，都可以分析，并分别表现出来。

2. 用速写本记录发现的东西。

3. 在综合阶段，我们将运用分析得出的构成原理做一个雕塑。雕塑尺寸是18厘米×18厘米×18厘米的立方体，位于一块想象的30厘米×24厘米×18厘米的实体当中，也就是说雕塑是“挖掘”出来的。雕塑体和所处的“基地”应完美结合。

注意事项：

在练习六的“蒙德里安的方盒子”练习中，我们自己设计，或者是从蒙德里安作品中抽象出一种网格，并把其作为“结构网格”的构成方法运用在新的设计中。而在这一练习中，构成的原理出自分析过的建筑作品。

工具和材料：

白卡纸、棕色瓦楞纸，刀具、胶水等。

成果：

一件尺寸为30厘米×24厘米×18厘米的建筑构造形态雕塑。

Exercise 15.   LEARNING FROM MASTERS

Objective:

We can learn architecture from almost anything, but studying a masterpiece of architecture is probably among the easiest ways. Learning is not copying. It includes two processes: analysis and synthesis, or interpretation

In this exercise we will first practice the skills of analyzing masters' buildings with emphasis on the principles of form composition. Then we interpret and represent these principles with a new sculpture in an abstract setting.

Methods:

1.Analysis is a way to look at something in its separate pieces—not only the physical pieces or elements, but also the intangible principles applied to organize these elements. The architectonic quality of a building can be discerned, when essence of the composition, such as grid, rhythms, enclosure and openness, solid and void, light and shadow, etc., are represented respectively.

2.Use sketchbook to record what the student finds.

3.In the synthesis process we make a sculpture by applying the form composition principles learned from the analyzed building. The setting of the sculpture is a box (30cm×24cm×18cm), in which a smaller cubic volume (18cm×18cm×18cm) is assumed to be dug up or “excavated”. In the cubic space we make an architectonic sculpture which should be integrated into the whole setting of the larger box.

Notes:

1.We have already made a box in Exercise 6: A Mondrian Box. In that exercise we either made a grid by ourselves or borrowed a grid from one of Mondrian's paintings. We applied a composition principle called the structure grid. For the present exercise we use the composition principles found in our analysis of the master buildings.

Material:

Limit the material to white card paper, or yellow-gray corrugated box-paper, for the whole object.

Presentation:

An architectonic sculpture within a maximum volume of 30cm × 24cm × 18cm.

Chan Hau Man
So Hoi Yan
Hui Lung Nin
Lo Chung Man
Unkown

练习十六　程序和操作

目的：

这个练习让学生认识到目的性因素是如何影响建筑形体的。在当前这种抽象建筑（如建筑设计中借助隐喻、标志和风格）盛行的时候，我们也应关注现实的具体的因素如何影响建筑形体和结构（这些因素包括使用者的改变，程序和功能的变化，建筑体系化的运用和环境的变化等）。

从任何一件家庭用品分析开始，通过一系列创造性的转型过程，发展一个抽象的建筑构成。

在这个练习中，我们将以热情、真诚和专心的态度来研究一个平常的物件。这样的研究让我们有所发现，并改变我们旧的观念。我们可以从任何一个物件中学有所获。因为我们可以了解它们的工作原理。这个练习也要求对材料有充分的认识并运用精练的工作方法。

方法：

这个练习分为两步：分析和创造。

1. 我们可任选一件没有“设计效果”的日用品，然后对它进行研究分析，并把分析成果记录和表现出来。分析的目的是清晰地阐明物体的结构、组成和运作方式，从而深化我们对形体的内在逻辑的认识。

2. 在分析之前，我们应了解分析和研究的方法。这样研究的对象不仅是物件本身，而且也包括现象背后的多重关系，如结构、模数、围合、尺寸、比例、质感及使用效果等。

3. 在分析的基础上，练习的第二步是设计一件雕塑，这件雕塑应体现建筑形体和空间特征。

注意事项：

演绎的过程是操作的过程。这意味着我们无须根据已知的结果来塑造形体；相反，形的源泉是模糊的或者是仅有启发作用的东西。分析过程可以有不同的演绎方式和不同的演绎结果。

工具和材料：

1. 水彩纸；

2. 铅笔、水彩、彩色铅笔、粉笔、油画棒或者墨水笔；

3. 卡纸或者瓦楞纸。

成果：

1. 表现分析结果的图案设计（A2）。

2. 一件雕塑模型（大约18厘米×18厘米×18厘米），应体现形体创作、形体试验的建筑特征和形成建筑的潜力。

Exercise 16.　PROCESS AND OPERATION

Objective:

This exercise builds an awareness of the objective determinants that affect and produce architectural form. At a time when increasing emphasis is placed on the abstract qualities of architecture (i.e. metaphorical, iconic, and stylistic aspects of architectural design), it becomes increasingly important to balance this with an understanding of how practical issues can also change building form and structure (i.e., change of users, programs, functions, and implications of building systems, and change of context).

From a household object, students will develop an abstract architectonic object through an analytical and creative form-making process.

In this exercise we examine a simple object with zeal, doggedness, honesty and keen perception. This often leads to new discoveries and disposing of earlier presumptions and preconceptions. We can learn from any utilitarian object. They themselves can tell us, step by step, how it works. The exercise necessitates an understanding of materials and promotes an economy of means.

Methods:

The work process has two phases: analysis and creation.

1.We select, examine, analyze, record, and present observations of objects of our own choice that are not shaped for “design” effects. The aim of analysis is to restore clarity to the logic which make utilitarian objects work. By doing this we achieve a new understanding of the inner logic of form.

2.In order to begin the analysis, we first carefully consider the methodologies of analysis and research. By doing this we not only look at the object itself, but also the multiple aspects hidden behind the appearance: structure, modules, enclosure, dimension, proportion, texture, the result of the object’s performance, etc..

3.According to the findings, we move to the second phase, creating a sculpture. The sculpture should have the qualities of architectural form and space.

Notes:

Interpretation IS operation. This means that we do not define the form from a known result, but from a much more ambiguous source or stimulation. Different interpretations are allowed in analysis; different solutions are also possible.

Tools and Materials:

1.Watercolor paper;

2.Pencil, water color, color charcoals, chalk, oil paste or ink pen;

3.Cardboard or corrugated paper.

Presentation:

1.A graphic design (in A2-size), showing the results of analysis.

2.A model sculpture (about 18cm×18cm×18cm), which shows the possibilities and architectural features which can be created and, with which, experimented.

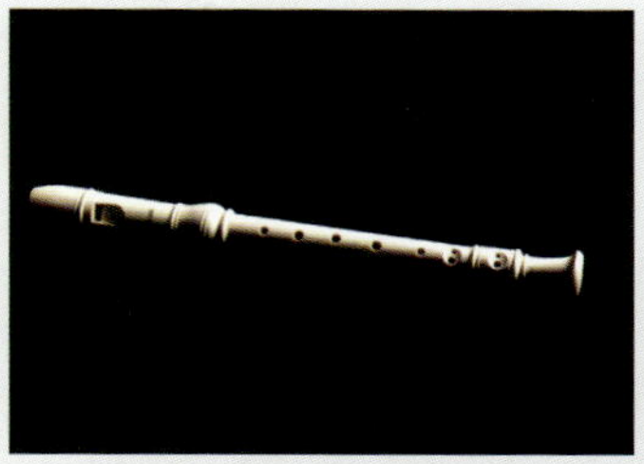

YLo Man Sze
Ang Bing Hung
Sze Chun Nga

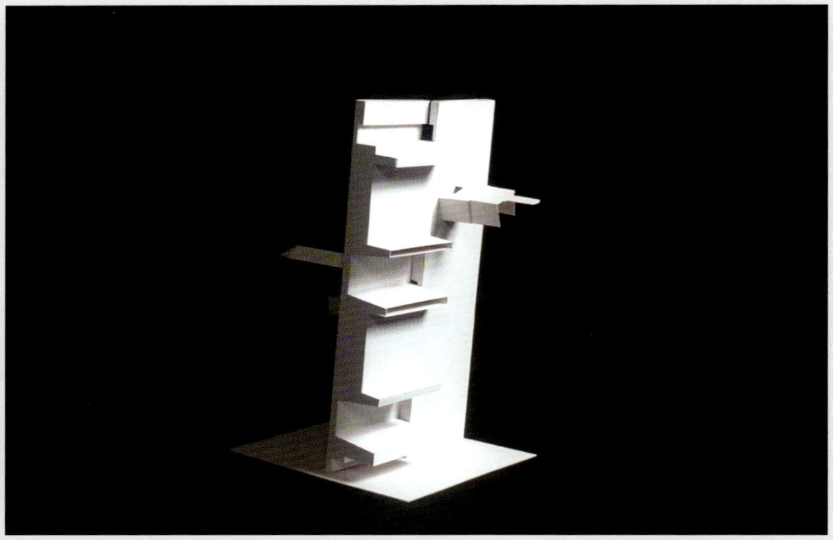
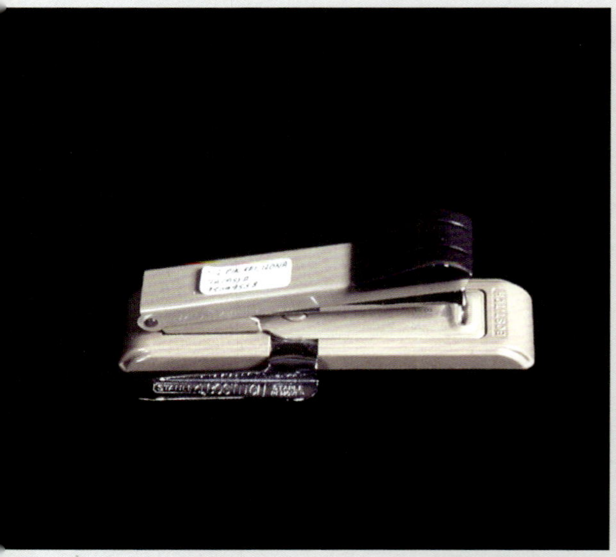

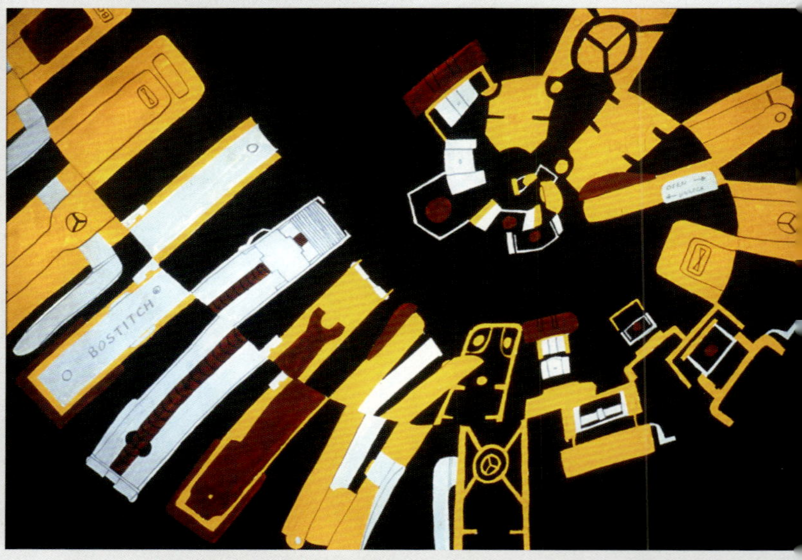

Yeung Mei Nai
Law Sin Hang
Tsang Boon Chi
Ng Pik Kei

Lee Sim Kui
Lau Pui Chuen
Woo Ching Hang
Chan Hau Man

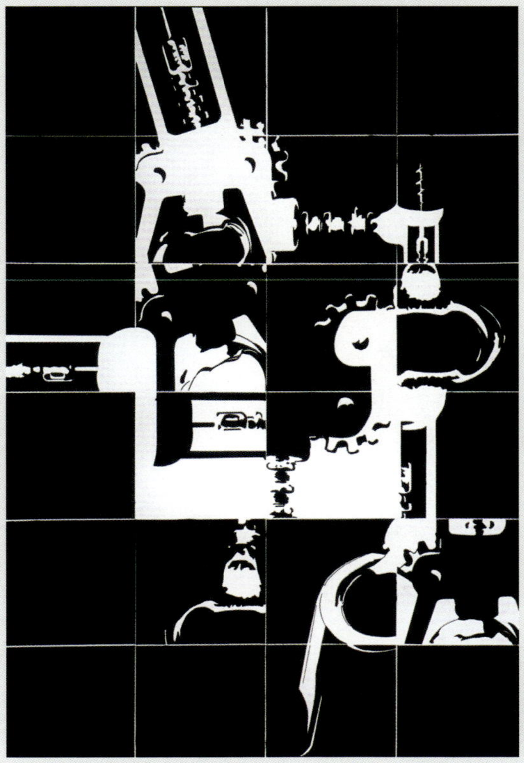

练习十七　结构和形体

目的：

这个练习综合了前面练习所用的知识和技能。我们将设计一系列的模型，来体现创作的过程。运用所有知识、条件和能力做一套抽象的结构，体现无始无终的演绎过程。

方法：

1. 我们首先拿到一个只有形状而毫无意义的东西，由此开始漫长的创作过程。

2. 我们端详着它，想知道它是什么东西，这时会发现我们在用自己的记忆去解释这件东西。但现在不要用记忆，而要用前面练习中我们分析过的建筑作品来解释这件东西。

3. 我们将它视为空间结构。这时需要注意两点：第一，这个空间形体不是一座建筑；第二，每次只用建筑中的某一方面去解释这个空间。做两次解释，做两个空间结构表现解释的结果。

4. 将这两个空间结构作为下一步创作的起点。方式和先前的一样，但需要另一种介入体。这次可以用“练习十六”中的日用品，将空间结构转变成一个空间形体。由此我们创作了另一个结构形体。

5. 只要有新的介入体，这种解释和转换型就可以继续下去。只要将功能介入，如“一座实验楼”，我们便进入了建筑设计。而这个过程可以不断重复下去。

注意事项：

1. 在这个练习中我们处理的是建筑构成语言，或者是形体词汇，并综合运用构成原理。

2. 模型要体现被分析物体的结构和空间规律，但我们也要考虑模型材料本身的技术条件是否能胜任这一工作。练习不仅要考虑技术结构，而且要考虑结构的概念和思想，并强化我们对精简的结构的理解。

3. 模型要体现建筑构成的要素，如空间、体量、围合、开敞、结构和空间连续等。形态具体而又抽象，体现对材料和经济性的认识。

工具和材料：

1. 模型木板；

2. 木条；

3. 胶水等。

成果：

三个表现设计过程不同阶段的模型。

Exercise 17. STRUCTURE AND FORM

Objective:

This exercise is a synthesis of previous exercises. We will design a series of models showing the stages of the creative process. Use all knowledge, possibilities, and capabilities to create a sequence of abstract structures, with an infinite process of interpretations and reinterpretations.

Methods:

1.We receive an object devoid of any meaning. It is nothing, except a form. This is a starting point of our long journey of creation.

2.We look at it and think what it might be. We then notice that we are trying to use memory to interpret it. However, we should not use memory. Instead, we take the master building, which we analyzed in the previous exercise, to interpret the object.

3.We interpret the object as a spatial form. There are two things to always consider. First, the spatial form of the object is not a building. Second, only one of the many aspects of the master building can be used for each interpretation. Choose two aspects to interpret two separate times, creating two spatial forms of the object.

4.We take the two spatial forms (models) as starting points again and continue our creation journey. The process is the same as before, but now what is needed is a new input for further interpretation. This time we take a utilitarian object, which we analyzed in Exercise 16, to give a structure to one of the spatial forms (models). As the consequence, we create another structural object.

5.We can repeat the interpretation again and again by introducing new inputs. When we assign a function to the structural object, such as “a research laboratory," we have finally entered building design. This process is iterative and as such could have no end. But our course of Architectonics must stop here. Real building design will continue in future courses.

Explanation:

1.We handle the thematic architectonic language – or the form vocabulary. Coherently think about the composition principles in this project.

2.Make models showing the structural and spatial logic of the new object. We also take into consideration whether model materials a/o technological constraints can accommodate the architectonic form or not. Not only the programmatic structure, but also the conceptual and poetic aspects of the structure should be considered, to further enhance our understanding of structural economics.

2.Models should include architectonic features: space, volumes, enclosures, openings, structures, and space connection elements. They should have a concrete and abstract form, and show an understanding of resources, materials, and economics.

Tools and Materials:

1.Soft wood panel;

2.Wood rods;

3.Glue.

Presentation:

Three models built with wood panels and/or wood rods.

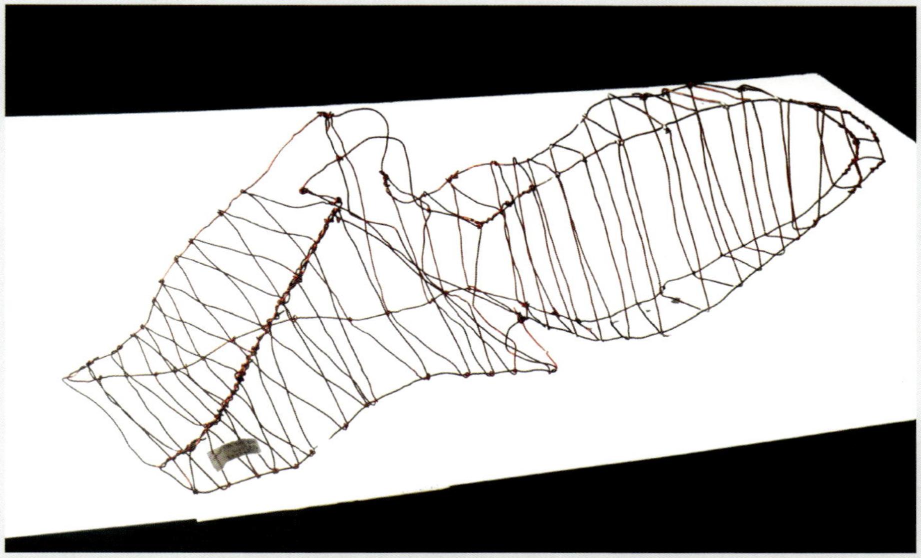

Ng Pik Kei
Yu Ka Wah

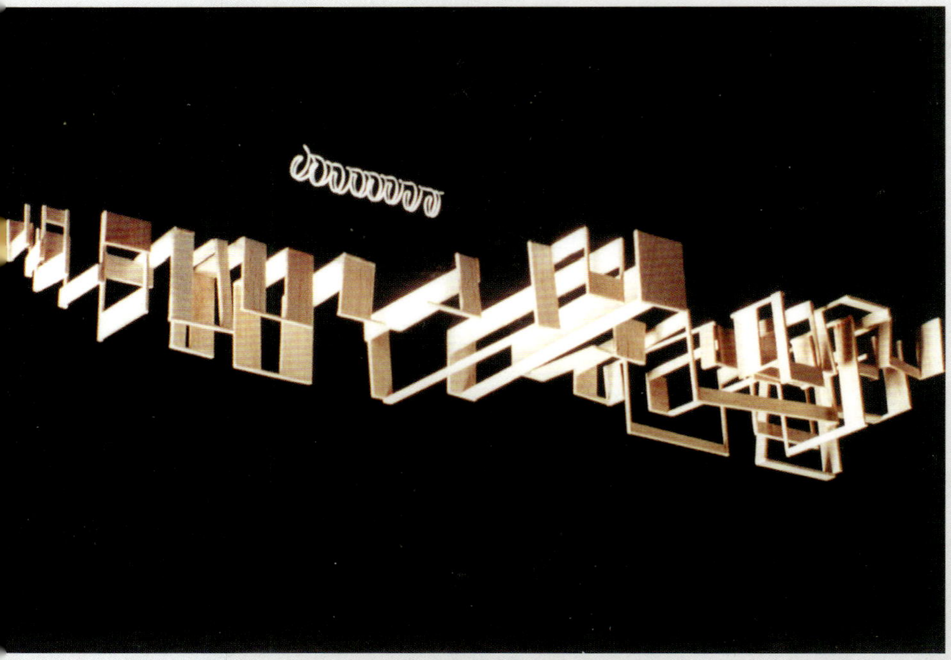

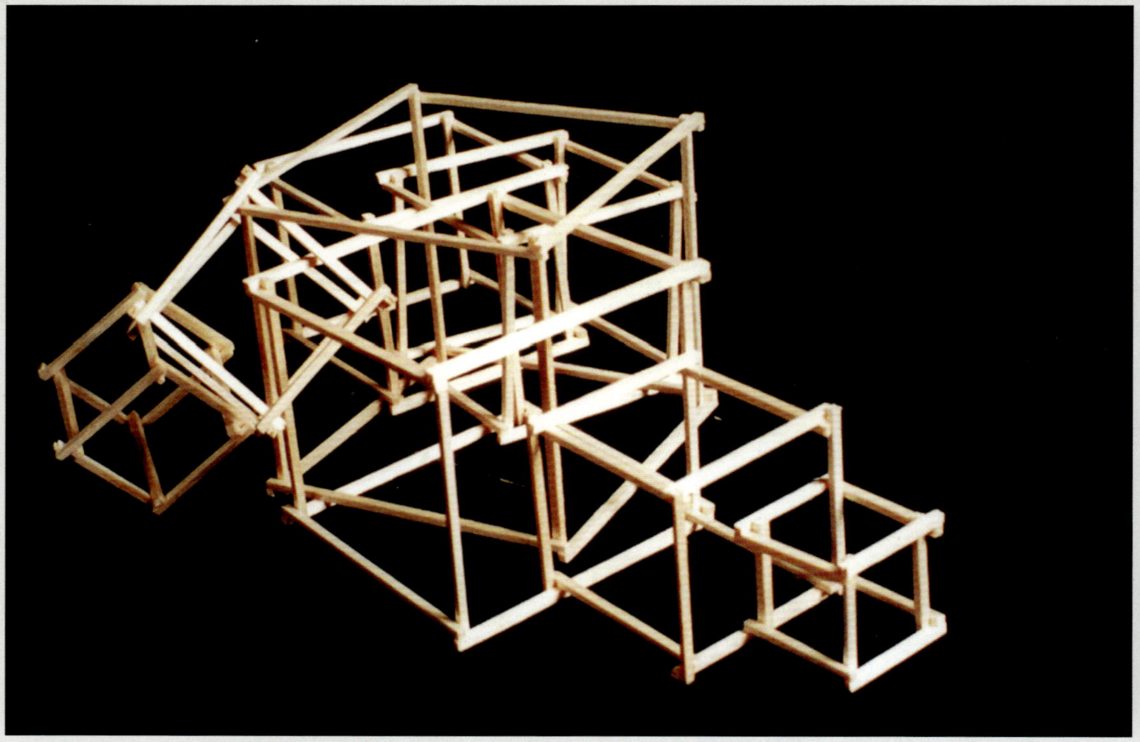

Tsang Boon Chi
Unknown

Mok Chung Shun
Hui Kei Yan
Unknown

图书在版编目（CIP）数据

名校名师系列. 香港大学. 贾倍思. 型和现代主义：汉英对照 / 贾倍思著.—西安：陕西人民美术出版社,2017.5
全国高等学校建筑美术教程
ISBN 978-7-5368-3287-9

Ⅰ.①名… Ⅱ.①贾… Ⅲ.①建筑画－绘画技术－高等学校－教材－汉、英 Ⅳ.①TU204.11

中国版本图书馆CIP数据核字(2017)第012859号

丛书策划　邱晓宇
责任编辑　邱晓宇
责任校对　熊　菁
封面设计　王立波

全国高等学校建筑美术教程·名校名师系列

香港大学·贾倍思——型和现代主义 汉英对照

作　　者　贾倍思
出 版 人　李晓明
出版发行　陕西新华出版传媒集团
　　　　　陕西人民美術出版社
经　　销　新华书店
地　　址　西安市北大街147号
邮　　编　710003
印　　刷　西安五星印刷有限公司
开　　本　889mm×1194mm　1/12
印　　张　17⅓
字　　数　450千字
版　　次　2017年5月第1版　2017年7月第1次印刷
印　　数　1–2000
书　　号　ISBN 978-7-5368-3287-9
定　　价　145.00元
发行电话　029–87262491　　传真：029–87265112